MADISON AREA TECHNICAL COLLEGE IRC
00010123838 4

D1451055

Renaissance Drama by Women: Texts and Documents

Gathered for the first time in this unique volume are plays and documents which show that, contrary to traditional thinking, women did participate in the theatrical culture of the Renaissance. Women were authors, translators, performers, spectators, and even part-owners of theatres.

Included in this meticulously edited volume are four full-length plays, a fragment of a translation from Seneca by Queen Elizabeth I, a masque written for performance by a ladies' school before Queen Anne and a collection of historical documents.

Renaissance Drama by Women: Texts and Documents is the first collection to offer such a wealth of literary and historical material. The editors assist the reader in understanding the richness of the texts by providing modernized spellings, full notes, annotations of unfamiliar words and phraseology, biographical essays and a bibliography. This volume will be invaluable to students and scholars of Renaissance studies, theatre history and women's studies.

S.P. Cerasano is Associate Professor of English at Colgate University. She is currently writing a biography of the Renaissance actor and theatre entrepreneur Edward Alleyn.

Marion Wynne-Davies is Senior Lecturer in English at the University of Dundee, and the editor of the Routledge English Text edition of Chaucer's *The Tales of the Clerk and the Wife of Bath* (Routledge 1992).

Renaissance Drama by Women: Texts and Documents

EDITED BY S.P. CERASANO

AND MARION WYNNE-DAVIES

LONDON AND NEW YORK

First published 1996
by Routledge
11 New Fetter Lane, London EC4P 4EE

Simultaneously published in the USA and Canada
by Routledge
29 West 35th Street, New York, NY 10001

Typeset in Galliard by Keystroke, Jacaranda Lodge, Wolverhampton

Printed and bound in Great Britain by
TJ Press (Padstow) Ltd, Padstow, Cornwall

British Library Cataloguing in Publication Data

A catalogue record for this book is available from the British Library.

Library of Congress Cataloging in Publication Data

Renaissance Drama by Women: Texts and Documents / edited by S.P. Cerasano
and Marion Wynne-Davies.
p. cm.
Includes bibliographical references and index.
1. English drama – Early modern and Elizabethan, 1500–1600.
2. English drama – Women authors. 3. English drama – 17th century.
4. Women in the theater – England – History – 17th century – Sources.
5. Women in the theater – England – History – 16th century – Sources.
6. Women and literature – England – History – Sources. 7. Renaissance –
England – Sources. I. Cerasano, S. P. II. Wynne-Davies, Marion.
PR1263.R46 1966
822'.3099287 – dc20 95–14783

ISBN 0–415–09806–8 (hbk)
ISBN 0–415–09807–6 (pbk)

For our sisters Ann and Lisa

Contents

Illustrations

Preface

Gathered together for the first time in this volume are plays and documents suggesting that, contrary to traditional thinking, women did participate in the theatrical culture of the English Renaissance – as authors, translators, performers, spectators and even as part-owners of public playhouses. Included are four full-length plays, a fragment of a translation from Seneca by Queen Elizabeth I, an occasional masque written for performance by the women of Ladies Hall before Queen Anne, and a collection of documents illustrating many ways in which women took part in a broad range of theatrical activity between the early 1590s and 1645.

In the course of teaching it quickly becomes all too clear that no existing collection of primary sources adequately suggests an overall picture of the role of women in the Renaissance theatre. Despite the current interest in interdisciplinary scholarship and teaching, seldom does a textbook offer literary, historical and cultural insights. Moreover, although a few plays, such as *The Tragedy of Mariam* and *The Tragedy of Antonie*, have appeared in scholarly, single-text editions, some of these are out of print, and most are inappropriate for classroom use, lacking the necessary notes and textual apparatus to render them accessible to undergraduate students.

The collection presented here offers one corrective to this problem. It takes as its model the Routledge Major Authors Series, following the general rules of editorial convention set forth therein. In addition, the reader will find a more detailed statement relating to the preparation of specific texts after each introductory note. In presenting all of the texts in this volume spelling has been modernized and punctuation has been rationalized, modern forms of elision (rather than Elizabethan conventions) have been adopted, and abbreviations and speech prefixes have been expanded. In editing plays, act and scene divisions, and the lineation in the original texts have generally been preserved, as have the original stage directions. (The exception to this is Lady Mary Wroth's *Love's Victory*, in which scene numbers have been added.) The transcribing and editing of historical material follows similar conservative conventions. In all cases – whether the original sources are printed editions or manuscripts – editorial additions and interventions are shown in square brackets.

In compiling both texts and annotations the needs of students have been the primary influence guiding our decisions; however, due to the richness of the material included in this collection it is hoped that the current volume will find its audience among students and scholars of all levels, and lay readers interested in the fields of Renaissance drama and theatre history, gender studies, women's history and cultural studies.

Acknowledgements

S.P. CERASANO wishes to acknowledge the invaluable assistance of the officers and staff of the Public Record Office, the British Library, the Department of Western Manuscripts of the Bodleian Library, the Wodehouse Library at Dulwich College, the Corporation of London Record Office, the Department of Manuscripts at the Guildhall Library, the Manuscripts Collection of Hatfield House (and the Marquess of Salisbury), the Royal Commission on Historical Manuscripts, the Institute for Historical Research, the Northamptonshire Record Office, the Folger Shakespeare Library, the Pierpont Morgan Library, the Huntington Library and the Colgate University Library. Two Deans of the Faculty at Colgate University (Bruce Selleck and Jane Pinchin), the Colgate University Research Council, and the Division of Humanities (directed first by Jane Pinchin and later by Christopher Vecsey) have all provided generous support throughout this project. An editing seminar run by Paul Werstine at the Folger Shakespeare Library in October 1993 generated much useful commentary and encouragement. This work was enriched by Charles R. Forker's sound experience in editorial matters. To this, J. Leeds Barroll added his own thorough guidance and wisdom. Generous thanks are also due to the Director of the London Goodenough Trust (David Emms), and the Trust's accommodation officers (Helen Burrows and Val Martin) for providing comfortable lodging during the preparation of this manuscript. Friends and family – too numerous to list here – have provided unwavering support and professional assistance. Deserving of special mention are Wil Albrecht, Martin Andrews, Andrea Berkowitz, Don and Wanda Berry, Margaret and T. Blackton, Helen Burrows, Johanna Cerasano, Martin Chandler, Andrea Duncan, Loreen Giese, Carol Gould, Constance Harsh, George Hudson, Debbie and Raul Huerta, Grace Ioppolo, Michael Jamieson, Kay Johnston, Margaret Maurer, JoAnn McLaughlin, Alan Nelson, Mary Rampolla, Warren and Molly Ramshaw, Sybil Spence, John Tanner and Margaret Tyndale. Tess Jones intervened heroically at moments of crisis in the preparation of this manuscript. Not least of all, Marion Wynne-Davies deserves much praise for her knowledge, friendship and steady co-operation.

MARION WYNNE-DAVIES would like to thank the staff of Keele University Library, the Sidney Jones Library at Liverpool University, the British Library, and the Bodleian Library for their assistance and kind co-operation. She is also indebted to the members of the Northern Renaissance Seminar for their comments about a paper given on *The Concealed Fancies* at the Autumn 1993 meeting and to individual members (Stephanie Wright in particular) for their comments upon her work. In the earlier stages of the preparation of this text, she received valuable advice and encouragement from her head of department, the late Professor John Goode, and she will sadly miss both his friendship and his sharp academic insights. But she owes more than she can say to her husband, Geoff Ward, who not only provided practical help in the editing and checking of the playtexts, but heroically looked after their baby, Richard, single-handed, while she completed the final corrections. Lastly, she wishes to thank her co-editor and friend, Susan, who has been understanding, erudite and inspiring; and she hopes that their writing partnership will continue for many years to come.

Not least of all, the editors wish to thank Talia Rodgers, our editor at Routledge, for her faith in our abilities, her patience with our enquiries, and for her careful work upon this book.

Abbreviations

Antiquities	Flavius Josephus, *The Antiquities of the Jews*
Dunstan	A. C. Dunstan (ed.), *The Tragedy of Mariam*
Ferguson and Weller	Margaret Ferguson and Barry Weller (eds), *The Tragedy of Mariam, The Fair Queen of Jewry*
Garnier	Robert Garnier, *Marc Antoine*
Hall	James O. Halliwell (ed.), *A Brief Description of the Ancient and Modern Manuscripts Preserved in the Public Library Plymouth*
Hunt	Huntington Library MS HM600
Pen	Penshurst MS of *Love's Victorie*
Plutarch	Antonius in *Lives*; there is one reference to *Caesar* (*The Tragedy of Mariam*, I.3)
Wroth's poems	all references are to *The Poems of Lady Mary Wroth*, ed. Josephine A. Roberts

PART 1
Texts

Introduction

In *A Room of One's Own* (1929) Virginia Woolf conjured up a Renaissance woman dramatist and called her Judith Shakespeare, William Shakespeare's sister. Woolf believed that she had to create Judith because there were no real women writing plays in England during the Elizabethan and Jacobean periods, and she lamented the fact that Renaissance women had been so occupied with their homes and families that they had not had the opportunity – the £500 a year and a room of their own – to write. Woolf was by no means alone in her assumption that there were no English women dramatists before Aphra Behn, and it was not until the last decade, the late twentieth century, that we began to rediscover these female playwrights, even though they were well known during their own lifetimes. This is a familiar story to anyone researching the introduction of women writers into the canons of national literatures: the process of assimilation is slow, but irreversible. Indeed, this edition of playtexts and contexts is part of that trend, and the four full plays, one fragment and one masque contained in the Texts section of the book are intended to introduce Renaissance theatre by women into the canon of English drama. Yet, if Woolf was wrong about the actuality of female writers, she was not wrong about the difficulties these women encountered when they wrote plays.

Renaissance women were assumed to be dutiful to their fathers and husbands, they were supposed to confine themselves to so-called 'feminine' activities such as child-rearing and needlework, and they were above all expected to restrain their use of language to verbal interchanges within their own homes. Women who chose to write were condoned only if that work was private and/or devotional, and any form of self-advertisement or publication revealed that the author had failed to live up to the Renaissance ideal of the chaste, silent and obedient woman. Indeed, it is often implied that a woman who was 'loose of tongue', that is outspoken and ready to exhibit her writerly skills, would also have 'loose morals', her independent speech being linked with a sexual freedom most Renaissance women never experienced. To write works, then, that specifically signified the necessity of performance was doubly condemned: playtexts not only allowed a woman's voice to be interpreted through the veiling medium of the printed page, but also, more scandalously, allowed her voice to be actually heard by many and various people, through the theatrical display suggested by the text's genre. Thus, Renaissance women dramatists directly challenged their society's demands that they remain within a private world of domesticity, by entering the very public world of drama. The virulent responses against women's participation – even as members of the audience, let alone as performers – in the production of plays is evidenced in the Documents section of this anthology. Yet, despite all the difficulties the women dramatists encountered in producing their works, even these textual rebellions were circumscribed, since none of the plays reproduced here was ever put on in a public theatre. The playwrights – Elizabeth I, Mary Sidney, Elizabeth Cary, Mary Wroth, Elizabeth Brackley and Jane Cavendish – chose a literary form which simultaneously liberated and policed their voices; they balanced their works precariously between their private and public roles, and between silence and self-expression.

The double-edged nature of these women's literary involvements can be seen partly in the decision by two of them to translate a work already published and written by a canonical male author, rather than to write their own original story. This choice was made by the two earliest women dramatists in this collection, Queen Elizabeth I and Mary Sidney, Countess of Pembroke. The queen translated a segment from Seneca's *Hercules Oetaeus*, mainly as an academic exercise, and it is highly unlikely that she ever intended the scene to be performed, even in private. Yet Mary Sidney, writing during Elizabeth's reign, produced a very broad translation of the full text of Robert Garnier's *Marc Antoine*, and it is likely that she intended her work to be read aloud – not acted – by members of her household, family and friends. Therefore, although she did not write an original play, Mary Sidney's translation is loose enough to affirm her own literary abilities, and this fact, together with her interest in, and use of, closet drama, suggest a pointer towards the greater independence of writers such as Cary and Wroth. However, before moving on to the writing of new and challenging dramas, we should recognize that the majority of women authors collected here had a further ancillary role in the production of playtexts. Apart from translating works written by men, they also supported male dramatists as their patrons. Each woman considered in this anthology was thanked at some time or another by a male writer for her generous and gracious patronage. But of all the works collected in the Texts section of this book, it is Robert White's masque, *Cupid's Banishment*, which best exemplifies this aspect of female involvement in Renaissance drama. The masque might have been written by a man, but its initiator and patron was Lucy Countess of Bedford, it was performed mainly by the girls of Ladies Hall school in Deptford, and it was staged before Queen Anne. Contemporary attitudes towards women as patrons of the theatre may be seen in the Documents section of the book.

The precedent of Mary Sidney's *The Tragedy of Antonie* seems to have liberated other women's voices, and we can see the influence of Sidney's Senecan tone in Elizabeth Cary's *The Tragedy of Mariam*, while the Countess of Pembroke's personal influence on her niece, Mary Wroth, clearly encouraged Wroth to write her own play, *Love's Victory*, in emulation of her learned aunt. These two plays are milestones in the history of English theatre, for they constitute the first original tragedy (*The Tragedy of Mariam*) and the first original comedy (*Love's Victory*) to be written by Englishwomen. Moreover, although of interest in terms of their female authorship, the plays also slot neatly into the dramatic conventions of their time, and, as such, one cannot help but wonder if they would have been 'lost' for four hundred years if they had been written by men. The final play in this anthology is a collaborative effort, *The Concealed Fancies*, having been written by the sisters Elizabeth Brackley and Jane Cavendish. It is a romantic comedy which was composed while the two women were imprisoned in Welbeck Abbey during the English Civil War. Its fast action, witty language and clear stage directions mark the play as a bridge between the Shakespearean style of comedy, such as that produced by Wroth, and Restoration comedy, which may be represented by Behn. Moreover, the play proves that, rather than being abandoned altogether, women's drama persisted through the Interregnum, and that Renaissance theatre by women was not an isolated spurt of activity, but an essential and innovative aspect of the overall development of the woman playwright in England.

The plays included in this anthology may thus be read as a form of history, uncovering the changes between the early translators and the later writers of comedy. However, there are also characteristics which make the group homogeneous and, perhaps, particularly Renaissance in character. One of the similarities has already been referred to – the understanding that the plays would not be performed on the public stage, but would be read, or acted, within the privacy of family houses. Sidney's *Antonie* and Wroth's *Love's Victory* were produced within the safe surroundings of the Sidney family homes, and they were respected, not as innovative women playwrights, but as inheritors of the Sidney tradition of literary brilliance. A similar protective coterie surrounded Elizabeth Brackley and Jane Cavendish, for despite the difficult circumstances they had to endure during the Parliamentarian occupation of their home, their father, brothers and husbands all encouraged their skills as writers. The Cavendish household, like the Sidney one before it, provided a safe haven for the woman author. Unfortunately, the same could not be said for Elizabeth Cary, who wrote in spite of all the efforts of her family to force her into a more conventional role. It was not until her daughter undertook a defence of her mother, in the biography *The Lady Falkland, Her Life*, that Cary received any familial recognition at all. Nevertheless, the fact that all the women referred to here rejected the public theatre as a venue for their plays underscores the closeted nature of women's lives during the Renaissance. Even though they were able to write plays, these women had no power to ensure the theatrical production of their work.

The literary restraints discussed above mirror the actual lives of Sidney, Cary, Wroth and the Cavendishes. Indeed, there are several autobiographical elements in the plays, some more clear than others. Wroth's *Love's Victory* is a drama replete with contemporary allegory in which she represents three decades in the lives and loves of the Sidney family. The Cavendish play, *The Concealed Fancies*, is more politically informed, although it too, as suggested by the title, is a thinly veiled presentation of Cavendish interests. Any autobiographical elements in Sidney's and Cary's plays are more carefully hidden, the authors focusing more upon the general themes of public responsibility and personal desire. But even if no firm identifications were made, each of the texts reproduced here is significantly more sympathetic to its female characters than is usual in plays of the time written by men. Elizabeth I chose to translate the one piece of *Hercules Oetaeus* where women are allowed to praise women (for their fidelity) and to attack men (for their inconstancy). Mary Sidney altered the character of Cleopatra, changing her from a devious seductress into a tragic heroine who truly loves Antony. Elizabeth Cary idealizes Mariam, making her into a Christ-like martyr, but, more significantly, she presents us with a Salome who is intelligent, articulate and strong, and who, moreover, argues convincingly that women should be allowed to divorce their husbands. Wroth's *Love's Victory* returns to the idea of how male and female versions of love differ, and she emphasizes the importance of female friendship at the end of the play. This differs from the more conventional move towards marriage, which bonds women to men and intimates that any former single-sex associations were lacking in maturity. The Cavendish play, *The Concealed Fancies*, follows the same pattern as Wroth's work; both are comedies with the required 'happy ending'. But Elizabeth and Jane also repeat Wroth's emphasis upon female friendship, and after the marriage ceremony the action returns to the two sisters, who ironically comment upon their husbands' behaviour since the wedding. Indeed, none of the authors collected here appears to have a very high regard for marriage – altogether they idealize an adulterous relationship, argue convincingly for a woman's right to divorce her husband, attack husbands for being unfaithful, and ridicule wedlock. Surely, this is not quite what Virginia Woolf would have expected from these supposedly chaste, silent and obedient women.

It might still be impossible to find an actual 'Judith Shakespeare', but the wealth of individual skill and imagination revealed by the plays reproduced in this edition, and in the characterizations of the women who wrote them (these are described in the individual introductory notes), will, we hope, both surprise and interest the present-day reader. The range of literary activity represented here – from the 1590s to the 1640s and from formal translation, through powerful tragedy to witty comedy – shows conclusively that Renaissance theatre by women must finally assume its rightful place in the canon of English literature.

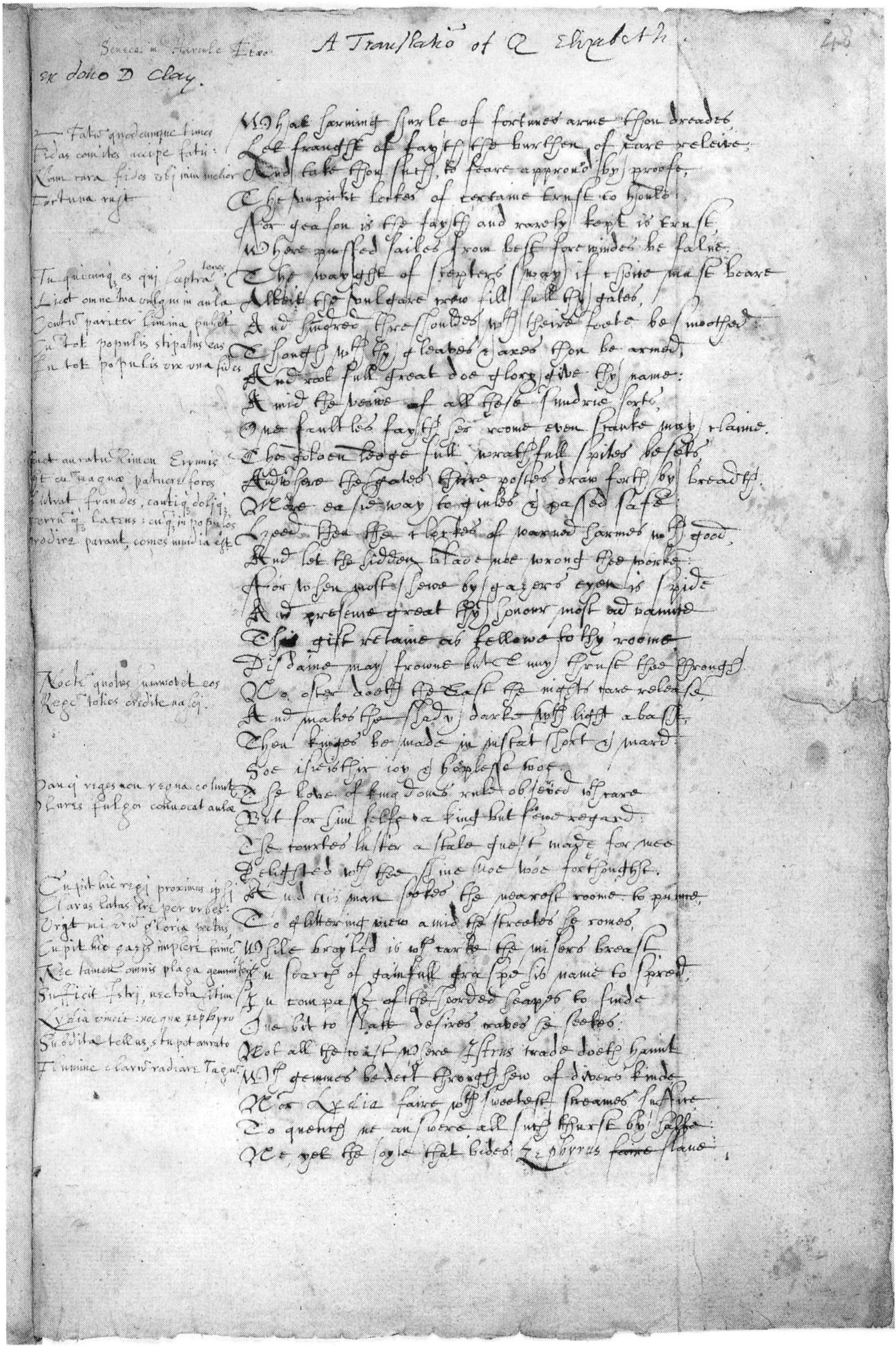

1 First page of *Hercules Oetaeus* by kind permission of the Bodleian Library Oxford

1 *Hercules Oetaeus*

QUEEN ELIZABETH I

INTRODUCTION

The following translation, 123 lines from Seneca's *Hercules Oetaeus*, appears in Bodleian MS e Museo 55, fols 48^r–49^r. Across the top of the first page of the manuscript is written 'A Translation of Q Elizabeth'. Although neither the handwriting of the translation, nor that of the attribution, is that of Elizabeth I, the translation has been identified with the queen by various scholars and for an assortment of reasons.

Translation was a lifelong avocation for Elizabeth I. How old she was when she began her language studies is unknown; however, she was certainly producing translations from the time she was very young. According to one account, when she was 12 years old she offended her father, Henry VIII, to such a degree that he banished her from court. Catherine Parr, then the king's wife, interceded on the girl's behalf. To show her gratitude Elizabeth translated 'out of French rhyme into English prose', a poem, binding it into a cover which she embroidered and presented the book as a gift to her stepmother.[1] Under the supervision of her kindly governess, Kat Ashley, she learned French, Italian, Spanish and Flemish, and she acquired some Welsh from another of her attendants, Blanche Parry. Richard Cox, headmaster of Eton and later Bishop of Ely, and William Grindal, a fellow of St John's College, Cambridge, supervised her education in Latin and Greek. Later, when Grindal died, Roger Ascham, one of the most influential English humanists and educational theorists of his day, asked to be appointed as the princess's tutor.

Ascham found Elizabeth a remarkable pupil. By the time she was 14 she spoke French fluently; she could also converse in Italian, Latin and Greek. With the daughters of Anthony Cooke, one of Ascham's Cambridge colleagues, Elizabeth read Cicero and Livy, Sophocles, Isocrates, the Greek New Testament, Cyprian and Melanchthon. Ascham referred to her as 'his brightest star', and privately he worried that, because she studied at such a fever pitch, she would advance too quickly beyond her peers.[2] Writing to Sir George Cheeke he confided, 'Yea, I believe, that beside her perfect readiness in Latin, Italian, French, and Spanish, she readeth here now at Windsor more Greek every day than some Prebendary of this Church doth read Latin in a whole week.'[3]

One of Elizabeth's earliest translations was a version of the Thirteenth Psalm, which was printed in 1548 as an end piece to her translation of Margaret of Navarre's *Godly Meditation of the Soul*.[4] She translated part of Petrarch's *Triumph of Eternity*, Plutarch's short treatise *De Curiositate* (*On Curiosity*), a play by Euripides, two orations of Isocrates, and the greater part of Horace's *De Arte Poetica* (*The Art of Poetry*). In the parlance of the time she also 'englished' a dialogue of Xenophon from the Greek, as well as several orations of Demosthenes, and the entirety of Boethius' *De Consolatione* (*The Consolation of Philosophy*). In 1598, at the age of 65, she translated Sallust's history *De Bello Jugurthino* (*The Jugurthine War*).[5]

From the accounts of Ascham and William Camden it would appear that Elizabeth worked at translation steadily throughout her life. Many of her efforts have been lost, but the entirety of her Boethius, Petrarch, Horace, Plutarch, and the Thirteenth Psalm of David have been preserved. (Of these, the translations of Boethius, Horace and Plutarch were gathered together into one manuscript now held by the Public Record Office.) Most of the Boethian 'meters' are written in her own hand, although the prose sections of the *Consolation* were either dictated to, or copied by, a clerk or secretary.[6] Perhaps because she was capable of working rapidly – one contemporary commentator estimated that she 'englished' a page of Boethius every half hour – Elizabeth's translations are frequently characterized by their 'literal' quality rather than for any poetic or artistic flair. (Pemberton characterized them as 'tolerably exact'.) Of the three, most readers find the *Consolation* to be the most poetical. But concurrently – probably due to her haste – Elizabeth occasionally mistook the meaning of the Latin text (a tendency that is more prevalent in her later pieces when she was ageing and loath to use glasses). Yet there is no sense that she meant her translations to be anything more than private exercises. It is worth noting that both Horace's *Ars Poetica* and Plutarch's *De Curiositate* were left in the rough, no fair copy being made of them. The extant versions were probably drafts, rather than polished pieces of work, and there is no indication that they were read by anyone except the queen and the secretaries who copied some of them.[7]

The excerpt from Seneca's *Hercules Oetaeus* reproduced below is consistent, in style and presentation, with others of Elizabeth's translations. In it the translator often followed the Latin word order and construction literally, creating an awkwardness that is typical of Elizabeth's work. For instance, a combination of literalness and an attempt to wrench the poetry into blank verse produced such constructions as: 'A pot of beechen tree full sure he keeps / With steady hand that fears no snatch from hold' (ll. 76–7). In addition, the translator showed a preference for outmoded words and expressions. To cite only a few examples, 'gleaves' (l. 10) was a rare, antiquated form of 'glaives' ('swords'), as was 'flee' (l. 117) for the more common 'fly'. 'Y-got' (l. 79) and 'y-tied' (l. 82) were used in place of the simpler 'got' and 'tied'. Moreover, the translator contrived the word 'newed' in the 'horned newed moon' (l. 63) simply to assist in the metre when a wholly different combination of words might have been more stylistically adept. Interestingly too, the mistaken translation of the Latin *Corus* ('the north-west wind') as the 'east wind' appeared both in *Hercules Oetaeus* and in Elizabeth's Boethius, one feature that argues for Elizabeth's authorship of *Hercules*.[8] But despite the fact that the translator made up whole lines and added them to the opening of the excerpt, the translation evidences no sustained attempt at stylistic felicity. Like Elizabeth's translations of Boethius and Horace the passage from *Hercules Oetaeus* seems to be a rough draft, a paraphrase, an attempt to set down, as quickly as possible, the meaning of the Latin verse. Like many other translations positively identified with Elizabeth I, it does not appear in the queen's hand but in the hand of a clerk, although this specific hand has not so far been identified.

Scholars have already noted that Elizabeth I seems frequently to have concentrated on authors whose work held some special significance for her. Reflecting upon that philosophy suitable 'for forming the minds of princes', Leicester Bradner noted that she 'chose to translate those things that were most central to her own thought'. These included themes such as 'praise of virtue, defiance of fortune, attack on slander and suspicion', many of which are mirrored in her original poems.[9] In the *Bellum Jugurthinum*, issues of statecraft are also central to the discussion; and it is probably significant that Elizabeth decided to translate this piece towards the end of her life as the future of the monarchy became increasingly an issue. Sallust's chief interest in the *Bellum Jugurthinum* concerned the incompetence of the nobility at handling the civil strife that erupted in Numidia over a question of succession. Consequently, the following excerpt from *Hercules Oetaeus*, taken from the first choral interlude, would seem especially compelling for Elizabeth because it explores the theme of the disloyalty of subjects to their leaders and the treachery of public office. Employing the familiar ship of state metaphor in its conclusion, the Latin original cautions against arrogance:'Let my frail boat keep close to shore . . . misfortune passes by tranquil ports and seeks ships sailing in the open seas whose topsails [through pride] touch the clouds' (ll. 692–9).[10]

The weight and variety of stylistic and thematic evidence has prompted many scholars, if only tentatively, to accept the passage as Elizabeth I's. In 1806 Horace Walpole transcribed the passage, identifying it as the work of Elizabeth I.[11] Like other commentators he found it 'a curious piece of pedantry' and concluded that

> if we could raise master [George] Puttenham and the other court critics of Elizabeth's age from their tombs, they would be driven to a nonplus to defend this euphuistic labor of their virgin queen from the charge of vying with the fustian of ancient Pistol.[12]

Almost a century later, Ewald Flügel transcribed the passage as part of a collection of the poetry of Queen Elizabeth.[13] More recently, Leicester Bradner included the piece as one of Elizabeth's verse translations in his collection, but – unlike Walpole or Flügel – he was circumspect about the controversy surrounding its authorship.

There were many editions of Seneca's plays

printed in the sixteenth century. One of the best known, J[ohn] S[tudley]'s English version of *Hercules Oetaeus*, was gathered together with translations of nine other plays by Thomas Newton and published in 1581. As in the excerpt printed below Studley adds lines and expands freely upon the Latin original; but it does not seem as if the translator of the excerpt below was copying Studley's translation, or another of the contemporary translations, in any obvious way. This version of Seneca's first choral interlude appears to have been wholly the author's own; and for the seventeenth-century clerk who identified it at the top of the manuscript, for Walpole and for Flügel, the passage reads as though it was Elizabeth's work.

The story of Hercules was popular on the public stage throughout the 1590s and into the early years of the seventeenth century. Philip Henslowe recorded a performance of the first part of an anonymous play entitled *Hercules* at the Rose Playhouse on 7 May 1595. Two weeks later the second part of *Hercules* was performed. The play was performed consistently for seven months until 6 January 1596. Two years later, an inventory list records all of the books in the company's ownership including the two parts of *Hercules*. Then, during the next week an inventory of theatrical props was compiled which included 'Hercolles lymes [i.e., armour]'. In May 1598, Henslowe noted that the Lord Admiral's Men paid £7 to purchase five plays, including another anonymous *Hercules* (probably a different play from the first), from actor Martin Slater (a member of the Admiral's Men, 1594–7, who left the company's service). Three months later, in mid-July, the company was apparently mounting another production of a Hercules play (perhaps that purchased from Slater) because Henslowe loaned actor Thomas Downton 40 shillings 'to buy a robe to play Hercules in'. Apparently the play continued to be popular, as an entry of 1601 would suggest: 'paid unto the little tailor 18 of December 1601 for diverse things for the play of Hercules the sum of . . . 5 shillings'.[14] Although there is no evidence that Elizabeth I actually saw any of these Hercules plays, her interest in theatrical matters was broad. It ranged from the plays performed before her by professional players at court, through the more private entertainments provided by her nobles at Kenilworth or Elvethan, to the well-choreographed displays of public, political ceremony such as that staged at her coronation.[15] Yet Elizabeth's translation of *Hercules Oetaeus* would seem to have been wholly a private exercise. In this she resembles other women dramatists of the period, such as Mary Sidney and Mary Wroth, none of whom wrote their plays for public performance.

Seneca's play opens at a time of victory when Hercules has conquered Eurytus (king of Oechalia). Hercules recounts his many toils on earth and prays to the gods that he might finally be given his proper place in heaven. He sends word to Deïanira, his wife, stating that he is on his way home. But just before the messenger's arrival, Deïanira sees Iole (the beautiful princess of the Oechalians) and learns of her husband's infatuation for the captive maiden. In a rage of jealousy Deïanira complains to her nurse and threatens vengeance on her faithless husband. Her nurse advises moderation, suggesting instead a recourse to magic in order to regain Hercules' love. Deïanira anoints a robe with the blood of Nessus, a dying centaur, which, he assures her, will act as a love charm. (Later, of course, we learn that the centaur has lied to Deïanira. The blood is, in fact, a poison.) She sends the robe to Hercules with Lichas, Hercules' herald. There follows a chorus spoken by the Aetolian women who have followed Deïanira since girlhood. In full sympathy with her plight, they recall their long history with her and pledge their undying fidelity. At the point that Elizabeth I's translation begins the women are describing the rarity of fidelity, especially in the courts of kings. Courtiers, they argue, are selfish and mercenary, the moral being that courtiers cannot be trusted. Moreover, people should not aspire to power and wealth, but instead should choose the *via media*, the middle road of life, which leads to happiness.

THE TEXT

The version of *Hercules Oetaeus* printed below is newly transcribed from Bodleian MS e Museo 55, a manuscript that consists of 155 leaves, primarily being copies of letters and papers concerning state affairs. The bits of marginalia, which duplicate the Latin original, have been left out.

HERCULES OETAEUS

(Hercules of Mount Oeta)

A translation from Seneca
attributed to

Queen Elizabeth I

[Hercules Oetaeus (Hercules of Mount Oeta)]

[A Translation from Seneca attributed to Queen Elizabeth I]

[CHORUS OF AETOLIAN WOMEN]

What harming hurl of fortune's arm thou dreadest,
Let fraught[1] of faith the burden of care relieve,
And take thou such, to fear approved by proof,
The unpicked locks of certain trust to hold;
For geason[2] is the faith, and rarely kept is trust,
Where puffed sails from best forewinds be fallen.
The weight of sceptre's sway if choice[3] must bear,
Albeit the vulgar crew fill full thy gates,
And hundred thresholds with their feet be smoothed:
Though with thy gleaves[4] and axes thou be armed,
And rout[5] full great do glory give thy name,
Amid the view of all these sundry sorts
One faultless faith her room even scant may claim.
The golden ledge[6] full wrathful spites besets,
And where the gates their posts draw forth by breadth
More easy way to guiles[7] and passed[8] safe.
Heed then the clocks of warned harms with good,
And let the hidden blade not wrong thy[9] work,
For when most show by gazers' eyes is spied,
And presence great thy honour most advance,
This gift[10] retain as fellow to thy room:
Disdain may frown, but envy thrust thee through.
No ofter[11] doth the east[12] the night's care release
And makes the shady dark with light abash[13]
Than kings be made in an instant short, and marred;
So icy[14] is their joy and hopeless woe.
The love of kingdom's rule observed with care,
But for himself a king but few regard.
The court's lustre a stale guest made for me,
Delighted with the shine no woe forethought.
And this man seeks the nearest room to prince,
To glittering view amid the streets he comes;
While broiled is with cark[15] the miser's breast
In search of gainful grasp his name to spread.
In compass of the hoarded heaps to find
One bit to slake[16] desire's wave he seeks.
Not all the coast where Istrus'[17] trade doth haunt,
With gems bedecked through hue of diverse kind,
Nor Lydia[18] fair with sweetest streams suffice
To quench nor answer all such thirst by half;
Nor yet the soil[19] that bides Zephirus'[20] slave,
Abashed at golden shining Tagus'[21] beams,
Nor Hebrus'[22] service may content at full,
Rich though Hydaspes'[23] hedge his fields throw out,
Though Ganges'[24] course his confines all do graze
With filled force to water all his lands.
To greedy grating wights[25] enough not all
That nature well doth please his lack not so.[26]
This man doth homage unto kingly force,
And harbour Rome adores where last he haunts,
Not meaning that this ploughshare should advance
Like crooked hind[27] his master's gain with clots[28]
By murdering the ground; no ease of toil
Though thousand leas[29] his husbandmen turn up.
Well pleased rests his hearth with goods even such
As pleasure may by gift another need.
A badder sort the prince's court regard
With foiled[30] foot that stumble gives at all
And each to lose with no avail to one.
That might may equal harm thy power achieve
Whose living's thread drawn out is of such length
Whom hap nor takes ere nature calls away.
The horned newed moon[31] them blessed calls
Whose wane them misers judges when day doth fall.
A man full rarely happy is and old.

More surer sleeps thee downy[32] turfs procure:
All Tyre,[33] where purple woven is and made,
Not so sound slumber doth his owner yield.
The gilded[34] roofs the quiet rest bereave,
And waking nights the purple draws from ease.
O that the breasts of rich men naked were,
The smoothed dreads[35] of lofty lucks[36] that hide;
The Brutian[37] stream more milder course doth hold
When eastern wind[38] him strikes with force's stroke.
In franched[39] mind from care the silly soul possessed,[40]
A pot[41] of beechen tree full sure he keeps
With steady hand that fears no snatch from hold.
No sudden fright affrays, no thief he dreads;
With ease y-got[42] and single show he feeds
And recks[43] not for the girded blades to thigh.[44]
The golden cup of bloody mixture keeps.
The wife that is y-tied[45] to man of mean estate
No carking[46] hath in order pain to set,
Nor shining gift of reddy[47] sea she wears
Her ears free from the pluck of gemmy weight;[48]
No stone of Eoas'[49] waves her cumber[50] makes.
Soft wool ingrained with Sidon's[51] purple fair
Drinks not the red for use that her befalls;
No Maeon[52] needle filleth she with skeins
By parted hues that give the shade with art.
The silky land that lies to sunny east
Needs not the fruit from eastern tree to pluck;
Every herb the colours' die may mix
That distaff[53] fills with yarn that skill not spun.
She nursed not the doubts of wedlock bed;
Of lewd suspect[54] of weary work she shuns.
The[55] wrathful lamp Erinis[56] lighteth up
The feastful day adorns[57] by pestering rout.[58]
The poor man deemeth not his happy state
Till wealthy folk by fall it show.
Who so, therefore, the middle way eschews
The wry[59] and crooked balk's[60] most sure to tread.
While Phaeton[61] boy one day of father got
To rule the reins and eke[62] his wain[63] to guide
In leaving wonted[64] walk and worned[65] ways
Which by slide, while the uncouth[66] skies he shares
Such place as heat of Phoebus'[67] flame knew not.
His ruin was the world his fellow plain.
Daedalus[68] yet more larger scope[69] and broader took,
Who never yet a sea by name did grace.
Though Icarus sought the true and living birds
By guile to pass and win the tryer's right,
His father's feathered wings despised with scorn,
To Phoebus near with swifty gait he hies,
And christened by this slip[70] the sea was sure.
Evil bought the great where ill exceeds the good.
Let one full happy be and highly flee.[71]
God shield that mighty me the vulgar call.
The lee[72] of shore my silly[73] boat shall loathe,[74]
Let no full wind to depth my bark bequeath.
From safest creeks doth fortune glide and shun,
With search in middest[75] sea for tallest ship
And takes its dearest prey the nearer to cloud.

2 *The Tragedy of Antonie*

MARY SIDNEY, COUNTESS OF PEMBROKE

INTRODUCTION

Mary Sidney (1561–1621) was a member of one of the most illustrious families of the English Renaissance.[1] It was not that the Sidneys were particularly wealthy or aristocratic in comparison with other Elizabethan and Jacobean nobles, but that in the field of culture and intellect they were recognized as pre-eminent. Mary's siblings included Sir Philip Sidney, who was idealized as the exemplary courtier, excelling in martial, diplomatic and literary skills, and Robert Sidney, who was a less well-known poet and the father of Lady Mary Wroth whose play, *Love's Victory*, is included in this collection. It is not surprising, therefore, that Mary Sidney herself was a renowned patron of the arts, and an accomplished editor, translator and author in her own right. She was educated with her brothers at Penshurst, the Sidney home, where she learned the French, Italian, Latin, Greek and Hebrew languages which were to provide a basis for the numerous translations she would undertake in adult life. As a Renaissance noblewoman, however, she was expected above all to make a successful marriage, and in 1575, a year after attending Elizabeth I's court, she became the bride of Henry Herbert, Earl of Pembroke. She was 15 years old; he was 50.

In terms of social alliance and wealth, the marriage was certainly a 'success', and there is no evidence that Mary resented the age difference or, indeed, behaved in any way other than as an exemplary wife and mother (the couple had four children between 1580 and 1584). The numerous dedications to her portray a chaste, pious, gracious and intelligent woman, the exact female counterpart of her famous brother: if Philip Sidney was depicted as the ideal Renaissance man, then Mary came to personify the ideal Renaissance woman.[2] Moreover, the Countess's writings bear out this tendency towards conventionality, in that her participation in literary activity was primarily of an auxiliary nature; she edited, translated and acted as a patron, rather than taking the more censured path of independent female authorship. Still, it would be inaccurate to pigeon-hole her as a submissive and conservative woman, subservient to her celebrated brother, incapable of autonomous authorship, and determined to defend traditional literary values. Rather, the key to understanding the complex nature of her work must be excavated from her close bonding with the Sidney family and the ideologies they espoused.

There are two important pieces of information about Mary Sidney which help to unravel this aporia of conventionality and subversion. First, after her marriage she chose to retain the Sidney coat of arms as a form of identification, thereby asserting her familial inheritance and suggesting that the link with them was more important to her sense of self than the alliance with her husband.[3] In other words, Mary Sidney presented herself to the court as a woman of culture, and *not* as a wife and mother. Second, the year 1586, in which her parents and her brother all died, proved a watershed for the Countess, and it is from this point that she seems to have taken on the Sidney mantle, transforming her home, Wilton House, into an academy for artists of all kinds, and reconstructing herself as a Sidneian scholar, fully capable of continuing the textual endeavours initiated by her brother. However, rather than interpreting, as many commentators have done, Mary's post-1596 literary activity as a refuge from grief, it is more perceptive to discern a brilliant woman who, having been nurtured within the safety of a cultured familial group and then suddenly finding herself that family's most potent representative, rose to the challenge with exemplary skill and an extraordinary sense of purpose.[4]

Under the guidance of Mary Sidney, Wilton House became for twenty-five years (1586–1601), in the words of John Aubrey, 'like a College, there were so many learned and ingenious persons'.[5] It

2 *Mary Sidney, Countess of Pembroke*, engraving by Simon Van der Passe, by courtesy of the National Portrait Gallery, London

is as well to remember, however, that this description was written over half a century after the Countess's death, and that, while her patronage was certainly generous and far-reaching, she would not have known all the writers who dedicated their work to her.[6] Nevertheless, it is clear that she had direct contact with, among others, Spenser, Nashe, Donne, Jonson, Daniel and, of course, her niece, Lady Mary Wroth. In addition to Wroth's *Love's Victory*, another play written by a Renaissance woman, Elizabeth Cary's *The Tragedy of Mariam* (also included in this collection), shows the influence of Sidney's own Senecan drama, *The Tragedy of Antonie*.[7] The Countess of Pembroke, therefore, was able to shift from the role of a muse inspiring other authors to that of exemplar, encouraging writers such as Daniel, Cary and Wroth to imitate her own creative achievements.

Yet, despite strong evidence of the importance of Mary Sidney's writings to her contemporaries, since the Renaissance the extent of her canon and originality has often been underrated. For example, the psalms she translated in conjunction with Philip (1586–99) are often neglected as 'mere translations' or simply as an appendage to his greater imaginative skill.[8] In fact, they both worked on only forty-three poems (Mary translated Psalms 44–150 on her own after her brother's death) and hers are the more complex stylistically; indeed, there is no collection of lyrics in English which uses such a wide range of metre.[9] Moreover, the notion of 'translation' has altered considerably since the sixteenth century. Whereas twentieth-century readers expect as near as possible to an objective and verbatim rendering of the original, a Renaissance readership would have accepted a considerable degree of licence in interpretation. Mary Sidney's ability to transform the biblical language of the psalms into a form both pleasurable and inspirational to her courtly contemporaries would have been acknowledged as evidence of her artistic expertise, and certainly not as a deficiency of autonomous authorship. Apart from the psalms, she translated Petrarch's *The Triumph of Death* (*c.* 1600); Philippe de Mornay's *A Discourse of Life and Death* (1592); and the play included in this collection, Robert Garnier's *Marc Antoine* (1592).[10] Perhaps her most famous contribution to literary studies, however, is her editorial work on her brother's *Arcadia* (1593), a text on which she made extensive additions and major revisions.[11] Unfortunately, however, those of Mary's completely original writings which remain extant are small in number; they include two elegies on Philip Sidney's death ('The Doleful Lay of Clorinda' (1588) and 'To the Angel Spirit of the Most Excellent Sir Philip Sidney' (1599)), a dedicatory poem to Elizabeth I ('Even Now That Care' (1599), a pastoral dialogue intended as an entertainment for the queen on a visit to Wilton ('A Dialogue Between Two Shepherds' (*c.* 1600)), and numerous letters to her family, friends and court officials.[12] This list, dominated as it is by Protestant politics, makes it immediately apparent that the Countess of Pembroke saw her textual productivity as, in one form or another, continuing Philip Sidney's work and championing those values, literary, religious and political, that he had held dear.

Mary Sidney's translation of Garnier's tragedy was no exception, although precisely which of her brother's ideals she used this version of the play to perpetuate has become a contentious issue.[13] The play belongs to the neo-Senecan tradition which had become popular in France: thematically it upholds the Stoic ideals of self-reliance and personal responsibility in the face of an unstable and unjust world, while formally it corresponds with classical models, emulating the dramatic unities, the long monologues, the formal debates, and characteristic rhetorical constructions such as stichomythia, anaphora and apostrophe.[14] In addition, *Antonie* is a 'closet drama', that is, a play meant for private performance to be read aloud in a noble household, rather than a popular drama to be performed on the public stage. Apart from the late sixteenth-century vogue for such restricted dramatic activities, it is also important to realize that as a female author/translator, not to mention a member of the nobility, Mary Sidney would have opened her reputation to considerable risk by involving herself in public theatre. The extent of a Renaissance noblewoman's participation would have been to act as a patron, and this the Countess did, sponsoring the small, and rather unsuccessful company, Pembroke's Men.[15] Thus, by rendering a male author's text into English (although her translation is a remarkably free one) and by involving herself in the private and protected environment of closet drama, Mary Sidney accomplished an extraordinary balancing act. Although she appeared to remain silent, merely repeating another's words, her voice must be articulated through the translation, and although the actual production of her play was confined within a domestic sphere, its textual production was distinctly public.

Still, critics have countered, even if the Countess may be credited with a certain independence from Garnier, she was still bound by the ideas of her dead brother. Until the last twenty years – a period which has seen the exposition of more thorough research on Mary Sidney's canon – it was generally assumed that *Antonie* was one of several plays written by the Countess of Pembroke's Wilton circle which rejected the innovative public theatre written by Shakespeare in favour of the classical tradition praised by Philip Sidney in his *Apologie For Poetry* (1595).[16] These works include Thomas Kyd's *Cornelia* (1594), Samuel Daniel's *The Tragedy of Cleopatra* (1594) and *Philotas* (1595), and Fulke Greville's *Mustapha* (*c.* 1599) and his lost play *Antony and Cleopatra*.[17] This so-called 'Wilton group' – together with Philip Sidney's call for a rejection of 'gross absurdities' and a return to the 'notable morality' and 'stately speeches' of neo-Senecan drama – has been interpreted as an overall Sidneian rejection of the public theatre, which had become increasingly popular towards the end of the sixteenth century.[18] The main evidence for this assumption about Mary Sidney's emulation of her brother comes from Samuel Daniel's preface to his own Senecan play, *Cleopatra*, which was written as a companion piece to *Antonie*. Daniel begins by referring to the Countess as 'Great sister of the Muses' glorious star' (i.e. Philip Sidney), while describing her home as the 'delicious *Wilton* . . . / That arbour of the Muses graced by thee'. He then continues by calling upon Mary to persist in her writing in order that the 'music of our well-tuned isle' will retain the reputation of excellence it achieved through her brother's work.[19] Daniel's linking of Philip's reputation with Mary's artistic endeavour is summarized in T.S. Eliot's well-known comment that:

> It was after Sidney's death, that his sister, the Countess of Pembroke, tried to assemble a body of wits to compose drama in the proper Senecan style, to make head against the popular melodrama of the time . . . the shy recluses of Lady Pembroke's circle were bound to fail.[20]

Eliot made three assumptions which have been questioned by more recent criticism. First, it is no longer accepted that the neo-Senecan plays of the late Elizabethan period were written by the Wilton 'body of wits'. As Michael Brennan points out, 'such an assemblage, in all probability, simply did not exist'.[21] Second, it is difficult to interpret *Antonie* as a failure when it went through five editions in fifteen years.[22] Third, Mary Sidney could hardly have been attacking the 'popular melodrama' of Shakespeare, since he had written very little by 1590. On the contrary, she should be acknowledged as one of the earliest contributors to politicized historical drama. As Hannay writes, 'Her work was thus near the outset of the dramatic movement to comment on contemporary affairs by means of Roman historic allusions, parallel to the use of the psalms as a privileged genre for political statement.'[23] Instead of reading *Antonie* as the unpopular work of a reclusive woman bound by tradition and obsessive loyalty to her dead brother, recent criticism suggests that we should interpret the play as an innovative and important contribution to a radical form of historical drama which employed the past as a veiling device for acute comment upon the contemporary political situation. Instead of closeting herself within a classical and Sidneian past, the Countess of Pembroke explored new forms of theatre which allowed her to offer covert criticism of the government of her own day.

One of the ways in which Mary Sidney's independent artistry exercised itself was in her rejection of the classical convention praised by her brother, as for example, when she rejected Garnier's original alexandrines in favour of the more contemporary and particularly English form of blank verse. This alteration allowed for more naturalistic dialogue and, consequently, permitted her to strengthen the characterization with powerful and moving speeches. Cleopatra, in particular, becomes a believable and sympathetic protagonist, rather than a stereotypical villainess. The only versification Mary Sidney retains from Garnier is the chorus's lyric stanzas. Nevertheless, these are transformed, by comparison with the fluid energy of the blank verse, from Garnier's authoritative statements on unchanging truths to banal repetitions of a simplistic fatalism. Contrast, for example, the chorus's trite comment upon human grief,

> Lament we our mishaps,
> Drown we with tears our woe,
> For lamentable haps
> Lamented easy grow;
> And much less torment bring
> Than when they first did spring,
>
> (II. 85–90)

with Antony's grim acceptance of his own culpability,

> I must a noble death,
> A glorious death, unto my succour call,
> (III.378–9)

and with Cleopatra's passionate desire to die with him,

> Live, if thee please, if life be loathsome, die.
> Dead and alive, Antonie, thou shalt see
> Thy princess follow thee, follow, and lament
> Thy wrack, no less her own than was thy weal.
> (II.310–13)

Stylistically, therefore, the Countess was clearly determined to undermine the traditional neo-Senecan language with the more contemporary blank verse. Again, what initially appears to be an obedient compliance with Philip Sidney's admiration for the form of classical drama shifts to allow Mary Sidney's own literary endeavours full articulation.

A parallel counterbalancing between her Sidneian inheritance and her personal commitments occurs in Mary's political and religious observations in *Antonie*. In political terms, for example, the play advocates the need for the individual to remain steady in spite of an unstable and corrupt state. Yet at the same time it warns of the dangers of civil war, stressing the need for rulers to fulfil their obligations to their subjects and not to allow passion to cloud their judgements. Although these convictions would certainly have been upheld by Philip Sidney, they were particularly apposite for the 1590s when the aged Elizabeth I's refusal to name an heir, together with her ill-advised dalliance with Essex, seemed to incite a threat of public rebellion and civil war.[24] Thus, Mary Sidney's *Antonie* should be read as much for its part in the social unease of the 1590s, which was ultimately to lead to the Essex rebellion of 1601, as for its continuation of Philip's 1580s Protestant politics.

In a final and significant departure from earlier Sidneian conventions the Countess foregrounded the female characters in her play and made them more sympathetic. Mary Sidney's Cleopatra is a major alteration of the traditional Renaissance view of that character. Instead of being presented as an unscrupulous, selfish and domineering seductress, Cleopatra is transformed into an example of stoic female heroism: constant in her love for Antony, she exhibits a wifely faithfulness, being prepared to die with and for him.[25] It has been suggested that this defence of adulterous love and the harsh portrayal of Antony's loveless union to Octavia were semi-autobiographical, revealing Mary Sidney's hidden discontent with her own marriage; but, it should be remembered that it is impossible to determine the veracity of this theory.[26] What we do know is that, when the Earl of Pembroke died in 1601, Mary Sidney chose not to remarry, taking on the role of virtuous widow. But even in this final piece of self-fashioning, the Countess continued to juggle orthodox and unconventional identities. For while she appeared to resign herself to a life of chaste mourning, in reality it seems that she took a lover, Sir Matthew Lister, a physician ten years her junior. While court correspondence testifies to the scandalous nature of this alliance, a much more sympathetic view is offered by Lady Mary Wroth in *Love's Victory*, in which she depicts her aunt as the virtuous Simeana, sister of the poet Philisses (Philip Sidney) and loved by his friend Lissius (Lister).[27] Conventionality triumphed in the end, however, for when the Countess died in 1621 she was buried in Salisbury Cathedral, positioned suitably beside her husband.

Throughout her life and work Mary Sidney appears to have been able to sustain a balance between what was customarily expected of a Renaissance noblewoman and what could have been considered shocking and subversive. There can be no question that the familial inheritance she chose to capitalize on enabled her to sustain this rather delicate equilibrium. However, it was certainly not exploited by Wroth, whose own Sidneian affiliations were to prove her downfall rather than her salvation.[28] Nevertheless, without the example of her aunt's circumscribed independence it is doubtful whether Wroth could have written so much original material. In this way, the Countess of Pembroke's own work should be viewed, not as a simple continuation of Philip's greater genius, but as a point of transition, signalling a shift from male to female creativity and heralding a new age for women playwrights in her own family and beyond.

THE TEXT

Mary Sidney had probably completed her translation of Garnier's play by 1590, and it was published first in 1592 under the title *Antonius: A Tragedie* together with her rendering of Mornay's *A Discourse of Life and Death*, by William Ponsonby. The play was published singly again by Ponsonby, with the amended title of *The Tragedie of Antonie*, in 1595. It is this version that we have used in the preparation of our own edition.[2] In preparing our text we have also consulted A.A. Luce's 1897 edition and Geoffrey Bullough's version of the text in *Dramatic Sources of Shakespeare* (1964). The latter provides a useful modern text but has no annotation. A critical edition of Mary Sidney's collected works is being prepared by Margaret P. Hannay and Noel Kinnamon; unfortunately, this was not available at the time of our going to press with the present edition.

The Tragedy of Antonie

[by ROBERT GARNIER]

Done into English by the COUNTESS OF PEMBROKE

[Mary Herbert (Sidney)] London, 1595

The Actors

Antonius
Cleopatra
Eras } *Cleopatra's women*
Charmion }
Philostratus, a philosopher
Lucilius
Diomede, secretary to Cleopatra
Octavius Caesar
Agrippa
Euphron, teacher of Cleopatra's children
Cleopatra's children
Dircetus, the messenger
Chorus of Egyptians
Chorus of Roman soldiers

The Argument

After the overthrow of Brutus and Cassius, the liberty of Rome being now utterly oppressed and the empire settled in the hands of Octavius Caesar[1] and Marcus Antonius[2] (who for knitting a straighter bond of amity between them had taken to wife Octavia, the sister of Caesar), Antonius undertook a journey against the Parthians,[3] with intent to regain on them the honour won by them from the Romans at the discomfiture and slaughter of Crassus.[4] But coming in his journey into Syria, the places renewed in his remembrance the long intermitted love of Cleopatra,[5] queen of Egypt, who before time had both in Cilicia[6] and at Alexandria[7] entertained him with all the exquisite delights and sumptuous pleasures which a great prince and a voluptuous lover could to the uttermost desire. Whereupon, omitting his enterprise he made his return to Alexandria, again falling to his former love without any regard of his virtuous wife Octavia, by whom nevertheless he had excellent children. This occasion Octavius took of taking arms against him, and preparing a mighty fleet encountered him at Actium,[8] who also had assembled to that place a great number of galleys of his own beside sixty which Cleopatra brought with her from Egypt. But at the very beginning of the battle Cleopatra with all her galleys betook her to flight, which Antonie seeing could not but follow, by his departure leaving to Octavius the greatest victory which in any sea battle hath been heard of.[9] Which he, not negligent to pursue, follows them the next spring and besiegeth them within Alexandria, where Antonie finding all that he trusted to fail him, beginneth to grow jealous, and to suspect Cleopatra. She thereupon enclosed herself with two of her women in a monument she had before caused to be built, thence sends him word she was dead, which he believing for truth, gave himself with his sword a deadly wound. But died not until a messenger came from Cleopatra to have him brought to her, to the tomb. Which she, not daring to open lest she should be made a prisoner to the Romans and carried in Caesar's triumph, cast down a cord from an high window, by the which (her women helping her) she trussed up Antonius half-dead, and so got him into the monument. The stage supposed Alexandria; the chorus, first Egyptians, and after Roman soldiers; the history to be read at large in Plutarch in the life of Antonius.[10]

Act I

[*Enter* CHORUS OF EGYPTIANS *who remain on stage throughout the first three acts. Afterwards, enter centre stage*] ANTONIUS [*alone*].

ANTONIUS

Since cruel heaven's against me obstinate;
Since all mishaps of the round engine[1] do
Conspire my harm; since men, since powers
divine,
Air, earth, and sea, are all injurious;
And that my queen herself, in whom I lived,
The idol of my heart, doth me pursue:
It's meet[2] I die. For her have I forgone
My country, Caesar unto war provoked
(For just revenge of sister's wrong, my wife,

THE
TRAGEDIE OF
Antonie.

Doone into English by the
Countesse of
Pembroke

Imprinted at London for *William*
Ponsonby 1595.

3 First page of *The Tragedy of Antonie*, by kind permission of the British Library

Who moved my queen – ah me! – to jealousy),
For love of her, in her allurements caught,
Abandoned life. I honour have despised,
Disdained my friends, and of the stately Rome
Despoiled the empire of her best attire,
Contemned that power that made me so much feared;
A slave become unto her feeble face.
O cruel traitress, woman most unkind,
Thou dost, forsworn, my love and life betray,
And giv'st me up to rageful enemy,
Which soon (o fool!) will plague thy perjury.
  Yielded Pelusium[3] on this country's shore,
Yielded thou hast my ships and men of war,
That nought remains (so destitute am I)
But these same arms which on my back I wear.
Thou should'st have had them too, and me unarmed
Yielded to Caesar naked of defence,
Which while I bear let Caesar never think
Triumph of me shall his proud chariot grace,
Nor think with me his glory to adorn,
On me alive to use his victory.
  Thou only Cleopatra triumph hast,
Thou only hast my freedom servile made,
Thou only hast me vanquished; not by force
(For forced I cannot be) but by sweet baits[4]
Of thy eyes' graces, which did gain so fast
Upon my liberty, that nought remained.
None else henceforth, but thou my dearest queen,
Shall glory in commanding Antonie.
  Have Caesar fortune, and the gods his friends
To him have love, and fatal sisters[5] given
The sceptre of the earth; he never shall
Subject my life to his obedience.
But when that death, my glad refuge, shall have
Bounded the course of my unsteadfast life,
And frozen corpse under a marble cold
Within tomb's bosom, widow of my soul;
Then at his will let him it subject make,
Then what he will let Caesar do with me,
Make me limb after limb be rent, make me,
My burial take in sides of Thracian wolf.[6]
  Poor Antonie! Alas what was the day,
The days of loss, that gained thee thy love
(Wretch Antonie), since Megaera[7] pale
With snaky hairs enchained thy misery?
The fire thee burnt was never Cupid's fire[8]
(For Cupid bears not such a mortal brand),
It was some Fury's torch, Orestes' torch[9],
Which sometimes burnt his mother-murdering soul
(When wandering mad, rage boiling in his blood,
He fled his fault which followed as he fled),
Kindled within his bones by shadow pale
Of mother slain returned from Stygian[10] lake.
  Antony, poor Antony! Since that day
Thy old good hap did far from thee retire,
Thy virtue dead, thy glory made alive
So oft by martial deeds is gone in smoke.
Since then the bays[11], so well thy forehead knew,
To Venus' myrtles[12] yielded have their place;
Trumpets to pipes; field tents to courtly bowers;
Lances and pikes to dances and to feasts.
Since then, o wretch, instead of bloody wars
Thou should'st have made upon the Parthian kings
For Roman honour filed[13] by Crassus' foil,[14]
Thou threw'st thy cuirass[15] off, and fearful helm,
With coward-courage unto Egypt's queen
In haste to run, about her neck to hang,
Languishing in her arms, thy idol make:
In sum, given up to Cleopatra's eyes.
Thou breakest at length from thence, as one encharmed
Breaks from th'enchanter that him strongly held.
For thy first reason (spoiling of their force,
The poisoned cups of thy fair sorceress)
Recured[16] thy spirit; and then, on every side
Thou mad'st again the earth with soldiers swarm!
All Asia hid; Euphrates'[17] banks do tremble
To see at once so many Romans there;
Breath horror, rage, and, with a threatening eye,
In mighty squadrons cross his swelling streams.
Nought seen but horse and fiery sparkling arms;
Nought heard but hideous noise of muttering troops.
The Parth,[18] the Mede,[19] abandoning their goods
Hide them for fear in hills of Hyrcanie:[20]
Redoubting thee. Then willing to besiege
The great Phraate,[21] head of Media,
Thou camped'st at her walls with vain assault,
Thy engines[22] fit (mishap!) not thither brought.
  So long thou stay'st, so long thou dost thee rest,
So long thy love, with such things nourished,
Reframes,[23] reforms itself, and stealingly
Retakes his force and rebecomes[24] more great.
For of thy queen, the looks, the grace, the words,
Sweetness, allurements, amorous delights,
Entered again thy soul; and day and night,
In watch, in sleep, her image followed thee;
Not dreaming but of her, repenting still

That thou for war had'st such a goddess left.
Thou car'st no more for Parth, nor Parthian bow,
Sallies, assaults, encounters, shocks, alarms,
For ditches, ramparts, wards, entrenched grounds:
Thy only care is sight of Nilus' streams,[25]
Sight of that face whose guileful semblant doth
(Wandering in thee) infect thy tainted heart.
Her absence thee besots; each hour, each hour
Of stay, to thee impatient seems an age.
Enough of conquest, praise thou deem'st enough,
If soon enough the bristled[26] fields thou see
Of fruitful Egypt and the stranger flood,
Thy queen's fair eyes', another Pharos',[27] lights.
Returned low, dishonoured, despised;
In wanton love a woman thee misleads,
Sunk in foul sink. Meanwhile respecting nought
Thy wife Octavia and her tender babes,
Of whom, the long contempt against thee whets
The sword of Caesar, now thy lord become.
Lost thy great empire, all those goodly towns
Reverenced thy name, as rebels now thee leave,
Rise against thee, and to the ensigns flock
Of conquering Caesar, who enwalls thee round,
Caged in thy hold, scarce master of thyself;
Late master of so many nations.
Yet, yet, which is of grief extremest grief?
Which is yet of mischief highest mischief?
It's Cleopatra alas! Alas, it's she;
It's she augments the torment of thy pain,
Betrays thy love, thy life alas betrays,
Caesar to please, whose grace she seeks to gain;[28]
With thought her crown to save and fortune make,
Only thy foe, which common ought have been.
If I her always loved, and the first flame
Of her heart-killing love shall burn me last,
Justly complain I she disloyal is;
Not constant is, even as I constant am;
To comfort my mishap, despising me
No more than when the heavens favoured me.
But ah, by nature women wavering are;[29]
Each moment changing and rechanging minds;
Unwise who, blind in them, thinks loyalty
Ever to find in beauty's company. [*Exit.*]

CHORUS[30]

The boiling tempest still
Makes not sea-waters foam,
Nor still the northern blast
Disquiets quiet streams.
Nor, who his chest to fill
Sails to the morning beams
On waves wind-tosseth fast,
Still keeps his ship from home.
Nor Jove[31] still down doth cast,
Inflamed with bloody ire
On man, on tree, on hill,
His darts of thundering fire.
Nor still the heat doth last
On face of parched plain,
Nor wrinkled cold doth still
On frozen furrows rain.
But, still as long as we
In this low world remain,
Mishaps, our daily mates,
Our lives do entertain;
And woes which bear no dates,
Still perch upon our heads;
None go, but straight will be
Some greater in their steads.
Nature made us not free
When first she made us live;
When we began to be,
To be began our woe;
Which growing evermore,
As dying life doth grow,
Do more and more us grieve,
And tire us more and more.
No stay in fading states;
For more to height they reach,
Their fellow miseries
The more to height do stretch.
They cling even to the crown,
And threatening furious wise
From tyrannizing pates[32]
Do often pull it down.
In vain on waves untried
To shun them go we should,
To Scythes[33] and Massagetes[34]
Who near the pole reside,
In vain to boiling sands
Which Phoebus' battery beats;[35]
For with us still they would
Cut seas, and compass lands.
The darkness no more sure
To join with heavy night;
The light which gilds the days
To follow Titan[36] pure;
No more the shadow light
The body to ensue,[37]
Than wretchedness always
Us wretches to pursue.
O blest[38] who never breathed,
Or whom, with pity moved,
Death from his cradle reaved
And swaddled in his grave;
And blessed also he
(As curse may blessing have),
Who low and living free

No prince's charge hath proved.
By stealing sacred fire
Prometheus[39] then unwise,
Provoking gods to ire,
The heap of ills did stir;
And sickness pale and cold,
Our end which onward spur
To plague our hands too bold
To filch the wealth of skies.
In heaven's hate since then,
Of ill with ill enchained,
We race of mortal men
Full fraught our breasts have borne;
And thousand, thousand woes
Our heavenly souls now thorn,[40]
Which free before from those,
No earthly passion pained.
War and war's bitter cheer
Now long time with us stay,
And fear of hated foe
Still, still encreaseth sore;
Our harms worse daily grow,
Less yesterday they were
Than now, and will be more
Tomorrow than today.

Act II

[*Enter*] PHILOSTRATUS.

PHILOSTRATUS

What horrible fury, what cruel rage,
O Egypt, so extremely thee torments?
Hast thou the gods so angered by thy fault?
Hast thou against them some such crime conceived,
That their engrained hand lift up in threats,
They should desire in thy heart-blood to bathe?
And that their burning wrath, which nought can quench,
Should pitiless on us still 'lighten down?[1]
We are not hewn out of the monstrous mass
Of giants,[2] those which heaven's wrack[3] conspired;
Ixion's[4] race, false prater of his loves;
Nor yet of him who feigned lightnings found;[5]
Nor cruel Tantalus,[6] nor bloody Atreus,[7]
Whose cursed banquet for Thyestes' plague
Made the beholding sun for horror turn
His back and backward from his course return,
And hastening, his wing-footed horses[8] race,
Plunge him in sea for shame to hide his face,
While sullen night upon the wondering world,
For mid-day's light, her starry mantle cast.
But what we be, what ever wickedness
By us is done, alas, with what more plagues,
More eager torments, could the gods declare
To heaven and earth that us they hateful hold?
With soldiers, strangers, horrible in arms,
Our land is hid, our people drowned in tears.
But terror here, and horror, nought is seen,
And present, death prizing[9] our life each hour.
Hard at our ports and at our porches waits
Our conquering foe; hearts fail us, hopes are dead,
Our queen laments, and this great emperor,
Sometime (would now they did) whom worlds did fear,
Abandoned, betrayed, now minds no more
But from his evils by hastened death to pass.
Come, you poor people tired with ceaseless plaints
With tears and sighs, make mournful sacrifice
On Isis'[10] altars; not ourselves to save,
But soften Caesar and him piteous make
To us, his prey, that so his lenity[11]
May change our death into captivity.
Strange are the evils the fates on us have brought;
O, but alas! How far more strange the cause!
Love, Love (alas, who ever would have thought?)
Hath lost this realm, inflamed with his fire.
Love, playing Love, which men say kindles not
But in soft hearts, hath ashes made our towns.
And his sweet shafts, with whose shot none are killed
Which ulcer[12] not, with deaths our lands have filled.
Such was the bloody, murdering, hellish love
Possessed thy heart, fair, false guest, Priam's son,[13]
Firing a brand which after made to burn
The Trojan towers by Grecians ruinate.
By this love, Priam, Hector, Troilus,
Memnon, Deiphobus, Glaucus, thousands mo[14]
Whom red Scamander's armour-clogged streams
Rolled into seas, before their dates, are dead.[15]
So plaguy[16] he, so many tempests raiseth;
So murdering he, so many cities razeth;
When insolent, blind, lawless, orderless,
With mad delights our sense he entertains.
All-knowing gods our wracks did us foretell
By signs in earth, by signs in starry spheres,
Which should have moved us, had not destiny
With too-strong hand warped[17] our misery.
The comets flaming though the scattered clouds
With fiery beams, most like unbraided hairs;
The fearful dragon whistling at the banks;
And holy Apis[18] ceaseless bellowing
(As never erst)[19] and shedding endless tears;

Blood raining down from heaven in unknown
    showers;
Our gods' dark faces overcast with woe;
And dead men's ghosts appearing in the night.
Yea, even this night – while all the city stood
Oppressed with terror, horror, servile fear,
Deep silence over all – the sounds were heard
Of diverse songs and diverse instruments
Within the void of air, and howling noise
Such as mad Bacchus'[20] priests in Bacchus' feasts
On Nysa[21] make, and (seemed) the company,
Our city lost, went to the enemy.
  So, we forsaken both of gods and men,
So are we in the mercy of our foes;
And we henceforth obedient must become
To laws of them who have us overcome. [*Exit*]

CHORUS

Lament we our mishaps,[22]
  Drown we with tears our woe,
  For lamentable haps
  Lamented easy grow;
  And much less torment bring
  Than when they first did spring.
We want that woeful song,
  Wherewith wood-music's queen[23]
  Doth ease her woes among
  Fresh springtime's bushes green,
  On pleasant branch alone
  Renewing ancient moan.
We want that moanful sound,
  That prattling Procne[24] makes
  On fields of Thracian ground
  Or streams of Thracian lakes,
  To empt'[25] her breast of pain,
  For Itys by her slain.
Though halcyons do still,
  Bewailing Ceyx's[26] lot,
  The seas with plainings fill,
  Which his dead limbs have got,
  Not ever other grave
  Than tomb of waves to have.
And though the bird in death,[27]
  That most Meander loves,
  So sweetly sighs his breath
  When death his fury proves,
  As almost softs his heart
  And almost blunts his dart.
Yet all the plaints of those,
  Nor all their tearful 'larms,[28]
  Cannot content our woes,
  Nor serve to wail the harms
  In soul which we, poor we,
  To feel enforced be.
Nor they of Phoebus bred[29]
  In tears can do so well,
  They for their brother shed
  Who into Padus fell,
  Rash guide of chariot clear,
  Surveyor of the year.
Nor she[30] whom heavenly powers
  To weeping rock did turn,
  Whose tears distil in showers,
  And show she yet doth mourn,
  Wherewith his top to skies
  Mount Sipylus doth rise.
Nor weeping drops which flow
  From bark of wounded tree,
  That Myrrha's[31] shame doth show,
  With ours compared may be,
  To quench her loving fire
  Who durst embrace her sire.
Nor all the howlings made
  On Cybel's[32] sacred hill
  By eunuchs of her trade,
  Who Attis, Attis still,
  With doubled cries resound,
  Which Echo[33] makes rebound.
Our plaints no limits stay,
  Nor more than do our woes;
  Both infinitely stray
  And neither measure knows.
  In measure let them plain,
  Who measured griefs sustain.[34]

[*Enter*] CLEOPATRA, ERAS, CHARMION [*and*] DIOMEDE.

CLEOPATRA

That I have thee betrayed, dear Antonie,
My life, my soul, my sun? I, had such thought?
That I have thee betrayed my lord, my king?
That I would break my vowed-faith to thee?
Leave thee? Deceive thee? Yield thee to the rage
Of mighty foe? I ever had that heart?
Rather sharp lightning 'lighten[35] on my head;
Rather may I to deepest mischief fall;
Rather the opened earth devour me;
Rather fierce tigers feed them on my flesh;
Rather, o rather let our Nilus[36] send,
To swallow me quick, some weeping crocodile.
  And did'st thou then suppose my royal heart
Had hatched, thee to ensnare, a faithless love?
And changing mind, as Fortune changed cheer,
I would weak thee, to win the stronger, lose?
O wretch! O caitiff! O too cruel hap![37]
And did not I sufficient loss sustain
Losing my realm, losing my liberty,
My tender offspring, and the joyful light
Of beamy sun, and yet, yet losing more;
Thee Antony, my care, if I lose not,
What yet remained? Thy love, alas! Thy love,
More dear than sceptre, children, freedom, light.

So ready I to row in Charon's barge[38]
Shall lose the joy of dying in thy love;
So the sole comfort of my misery,
To have one tomb with thee, is me bereft.
So I in shady plains shall 'plain[39] alone,
Not (as I hoped) companion of thy moan;
O height of grief!

ERAS

Why with continual cries
Your grieful harms do you exasperate?
Torment yourself with murdering complaints?
Strain your weak breast so oft, so vehemently?
Water with tears this fair alabaster?
With sorrows sting, so many beauty's wound?
Come of so many kings, want you the heart,
Bravely, stoutly, this tempest to resist?

CLEOPATRA

My evils are wholly unsupportable,
No human force can them withstand, but death.

ERAS

To him that strives, nought is impossible

CLEOPATRA

In striving lies no hope of my mishaps.

ERAS

All things do yield to force of lovely face.

CLEOPATRA

My face too lovely caused my wretched case.
My face hath so entrapped, to cast us down,
That for his conquest Caesar may it thank,
Causing that Antonie one army lost,
The other wholly did to Caesar yield;
For not enduring (so his amorous sprite[40]
Was with my beauty fired) my shameful flight;
Soon as he saw from rank wherein he stood
In hottest fight, my galleys making sail,
Forgetful of his charge (as if his soul
Unto his lady's soul had been enchained)
He left his men, who so courageously
Did leave their lives to gain him victory,
And careless both of fame and army's loss,
My oared galleys followed with his ships,
Companion of my flight; by this base part
Blasting his former flourishing renown.

ERAS

Are you therefore cause of his overthrow?

CLEOPATRA

I am sole cause. I did it, only I.

ERAS

Fear of a woman troubled so his sprite?

CLEOPATRA

Fire of his love was by my fear inflamed.

ERAS

And should he then to war have led a queen?

CLEOPATRA

Alas! This was not his offence, but mine.
Antonie (ah me! who else so brave a chief!)
Would not I should have taken seas with him,
But would have left me, fearful woman, far
From common hazard of the doubtful war.
O that I had believed! Now, now of Rome
All the great empire, at our beck should bend.
All should obey; the vagabonding Scythes,[41]
The feared Germans, back-shooting Parthians,[42]
Wandering Numidians,[43] Britons far removed,
And tawny nations scorched with the sun.
But I cared not; so was my soul possessed
(To my great harm) with burning jealousy,
Fearing lest in my absence Antonie
Should, leaving me, retake Octavia.

CHARMION

Such was the rigour of your destiny.[44]

CLEOPATRA

Such was my error and obstinacy.

CHARMION

But since gods would not, could you do withal?

CLEOPATRA

Always from gods good haps, not harms, do fall.

CHARMION

And have they not all power on men's affairs?

CLEOPATRA

They never bow so low as worldly cares,
But leave to mortal men to be disposed,
Freely on earth, whatever mortal is.
If we therein sometimes some faults commit,
We may them not to their high majesties,
But to ourselves impute, whose passions
Plunge us each day in all afflictions.
Wherewith, when we our souls do thorned feel,
Flattering ourselves, we say they destinies are –
That gods would have it so, and that our care
Could not impeach but that it must be so.

CHARMION

Things here below are in the heavens begot
Before they be in this our world born,
And never can our weakness turn awry
The sailess course of powerful destiny.
Nought here – force, reason, human providence,
Holy devotion, noble blood – prevails;
And Jove himself whose hand doth heavens rule,
Who both to gods and men as king commands,
Who earth (our firm support) with plenty stores,
Moves air and sea with twinkling of his eye,
Who all can do, yet, never can undo
What once hath been by their hard laws decreed.
When Trojan walls, great Neptune's workmanship,[45]
Environed were with Greeks, and Fortune's wheel

Doubtful ten years, now to the camp did turn,
And now again towards the town returned,
How many times did force and fury swell
In Hector's[46] veins, egging[47] him to the spoil
Of conquered foes, which at his blows did fly
As fearful sheep at feared wolves' approach,
To save (in vain. For why? It would not be)
Poor walls of Troy from adversary's rage,
Who dyed them in blood and cast to ground,
Heaped them with bloody burning carcases.
  No Madam, think, that if the ancient crown
Of your progenitors that Nilus ruled,
Force take from you, the gods have willed it so,
To whom oft-times princes are odious.
They have to everything an end ordained;
All worldly greatness by them bounded is;
Some sooner, later some, as they think best;
None their decree is able to infringe.
But, which is more to us disastered[48] men
Which subject are in all things to their will,
Their will is hid; nor while we live, we know
How, or how long we must in life remain.
Yet, must we not for that feed on despair
And make us wretched ere we wretched be;
But always hope the best, even to the last,
That from ourselves the mischief may not grow.
  Then, madam, help yourself, leave off in time
Antonie's wrack,[49] lest it your wrack procure;
Retire you from him; save from wrathful rage
Of angry Caesar both your realm and you.
You see him lost, so as your amity[50]
Unto his evils can yield no more relief;
You see him ruined, so as your support
No more henceforth can him with comfort raise;
Withdraw you from the storm, persist not still
To lose yourself; this royal diadem
Regain of Caesar.

CLEOPATRA

Sooner shining light
Shall leave the day and darkness leave the night,
Sooner moist currents of tempestuous seas
Shall wave in heaven and the nightly troops
Of stars shall shine within the foaming waves,
Than I, thee Antonie, leave in deep distress.
I am with thee: be it thy worthy soul
Lodge in thy breast, or from that lodging part
Crossing the joyless lake[51] to take her place
In place prepared for men demi-gods.
  Live, if thee please, if life be loathsome, die.
Dead and alive, Antonie, thou shalt see
Thy princess follow thee, follow, and lament
Thy wrack, no less her own than was thy weal.[52]

CHARMION

What helps his wrack this ever-lasting love?[53]

CLEOPATRA

Help, or help not, such must, such ought I prove.

CHARMION

Ill done to lose yourself, and to no end.

CLEOPATRA

How ill think you to follow such a friend?

CHARMION

But this your love nought mitigates his pain.

CLEOPATRA

Without this love I should be inhumane.[54]

CHARMION

Inhumane he, who his own death pursues.

CLEOPATRA

Not inhumane who miseries eschews.[55]

CHARMION

Live for your sons.

CLEOPATRA

Nay, for their father die.

CHARMION

Hardhearted mother!

CLEOPATRA

Wife, kindhearted, I.

CHARMION

Then will you them deprive of royal right?

CLEOPATRA

Do I deprive them? No, it's destiny's might.

CHARMION

Do you not them deprive of heritage,
That give them up to adversary's hands;
A man forsaken fearing to forsake,
Whom such huge numbers hold environed;
T'abandon one 'gainst whom the frowning world,
Banded with Caesar, makes conspiring war?

CLEOPATRA

The less ought I to leave him, least of all;
A friend in most distress should most assist.
If that, when Antonie great and glorious
His legions led to drink Euphrates'[56] streams,
So many kings in train redoubting[57] him,
In triumph raised as high as highest heaven,
Lord-like disposing as him pleased best
The wealth of Greece, the wealth of Asia,
In that fair fortune, had I him exchanged
For Caesar, then, men would have counted me
Faithless, inconstant, light; but now the storm
And blustering tempest driving on his face,
Ready to drown – alas, what would they say?
What would himself in Pluto's mansion[58] say,
If I, whom always more than life he loved,
If I, who am his heart, who was his hope,
Leave him, forsake him (and perhaps in vain)
Weakly to please who him hath overthrown?
Not light, inconstant, faithless should I be,
But vile, forsworn, of treacherous cruelty.

CHARMION
Cruelty to shun, you self-cruel are.
CLEOPATRA
Self-cruel, him from cruelty to spare.
CHARMION
Our first affection to ourself is due.
CLEOPATRA
He is my self.
CHARMION
Next it extends unto
Our children, friends, and to our country soil.
And you, for some respect of wifely love
(Albee[59] scarce wifely), lose your native land,
Your children, friends, and (which is more) your life.
With so strong charms doth love bewitch our wits,
So fast in us this fire once kindled flames.
Yet if his harm, by yours, redress might have –
CLEOPATRA
– With mine it may be closed in darksome grave.
CHARMION
And that, as Alcest[60] to herself unkind,
You might exempt him from the laws of death.
But he is sure to die; and now his sword
Already moisted[61] is in his warm blood,
Helpless for any succour you can bring
Against death's sting, which he must shortly feel.
Then let your love be like the love of old,
Which Carian queen[62] did nourish in her heart
Of her Mausolus. Build for him a tomb
Whose stateliness a wonder new may make;
Let him, let him have sumptuous funerals;
Let grave[63] thereon the horror of his fights;
Let earth be buried with unburied heaps;
Frame[64] the Pharsaly,[65] and discoloured streams
Of deep Enipeus;[66] frame the grassy plain
Which lodged his camp at siege of Mutina;[67]
Make all his combats and courageous acts;
And yearly plays to his praise institute;
Honour his memory; with doubled care
Breed and bring up the children of you both
In Caesar's grace, who as a noble prince
Will leave them lords of this most glorious realm.
CLEOPATRA
What shame were that! Ah gods! What infamy!
With Antonie in his good haps to share,
And overlive[68] him dead, deeming enough
To shed some tears upon a widow tomb!
The after-livers justly might report
That I him only for his empire loved
And high estate, and that in hard estate
I for another did him lewdly leave;
Like to those birds wafted[69] with wandering wings
From foreign lands in spring-time here arrive,
And live with us so long as summer's heat
And their food lasts, then seek another soil;
And as we see with ceaseless fluttering
Flocking of seely[70] flies a brownish cloud
To vintage wine yet working[71] in the tun,[72]
Nor parting thence while they sweet liquor taste,
After, as smoke, all vanish in the air
And of the swarm not one so much appear.
ERAS
By this sharp death what profit can you win?
CLEOPATRA
I neither gain nor profit seek therein.
ERAS
What praise shall you of after-ages[73] get?
CLEOPATRA
Nor praise, nor glory in my cares are set.
ERAS
What other end ought you respect, than this?
CLEOPATRA
My only end, my only duty is.
ERAS
Your duty must upon some good be founded!
CLEOPATRA
On virtue it, the only good, is grounded.
ERAS
What is that virtue?
CLEOPATRA
That which us beseems.[74]
ERAS
Outrage ourselves? Who that beseeming deems?
CLEOPATRA
Finish I will my sorrows, dying thus.
ERAS
'Minish[75] you will your glories doing thus.
CLEOPATRA
Good friends, I pray you seek not to revoke
My fixed intent of following Antonie.
I will die. I will die. Must not his life,
His life and death, by mine be followed?
Meanwhile, dear sisters, live; and while you live,
Do often honour to our loved tombs.
Strew them with flowers, and sometimes happily
The tender thought of Antonie your lord
And me poor soul to tears shall you invite,
And our true loves your doleful voice commend.
CHARMION
And think you madam, we from you will part?
Think you alone to feel death's ugly dart?
Think you to leave us, and that the same sun
Shall see at once you dead, and us alive?
We'll die with you, and Clotho,[76] pitiless,
Shall us with you in hellish boat embark.

CLEOPATRA
Ah live, I pray you. This disastered woe
Which racks my heart, alone to me belongs;
My lot 'longs[77] not to you; servants to be,
No shame, no harm to you, as is to me.
Live, sisters! Live, and seeing his suspect
Hath causeless[78] me in sea of sorrows drowned,
And that I cannot live, if so I would,
Nor yet would leave this life, if so I could,
Without his love, procure me, Diomede,
That 'gainst poor me he be no more incensed.
Wrest out of his conceit[79] that harmful doubt,
That since his wrack he hath of me conceived
(Though wrong conceived: witness you reverent gods,
Barking Anubis[80], Apis bellowing),[81]
Tell him, my soul burning, impatient,
Forlorn with love of him, for certain seal[82]
Of her true loyalty my corpse hath left,
T'increase of dead the number numberless.
Go then, and if as yet he me bewail,
If yet for me his heart one sigh forth breathe,
Blest shall I be, and far with more content[83]
Depart this world, where so I me torment.
Mean season, us let this sad tomb enclose,
Attending here till death conclude our woes.

DIOMEDE
I will obey your will.

CLEOPATRA
So the desert,[84]
The gods repay of thy true faithful heart.
[*Exeunt all but*] DIOMEDE.

DIOMEDE
And is't not pity, gods, ah gods of heaven,
To see from love such hateful fruits to spring?
And is't not pity that this firebrand so
Lays waste the trophies of Philippi[85] fields?
Where are those sweet allurements, those sweet looks,
Which gods themselves right heart-sick would have made?
What doth that beauty, rarest gift of heaven,
Wonder of earth? Alas, what do those eyes,
And that sweet voice all Asia understood,
And sunburnt Africke wide in deserts spread?
Is their force dead? Have they no further power?
Can not by them Octavius be surprised?
Alas! If Jove[86] in midst of all his ire,
With thunderbolt in hand some land to plague,
Had cast his eyes on my queen, out of hand
His plaguing bolt had fallen out of his hand;
Fire, out of his wrath, into vain smoke should turn,
And other fire within his breast should burn.
Nought lives so fair. Nature by such a work
Herself, should seem, in workmanship hath passed.
She is all heavenly; never any man
But seeing her was ravished with her sight.
The alabaster[87] covering of her face,
The coral colour her two lips engrains,[88]
Her beamy eyes two suns of this our world,
Of her fair hair the fine and flaming gold,
Her brave straight stature, and her winning parts –
Are nothing else but fires, fetters, darts.
Yet this is nothing to th'enchanting skills
Of her celestial spirit, her training speech,
Her grace, her majesty, and forcing voice,
Whether she it with fingers' speech consort,
Or hearing sceptred kings' ambassadors
Answer to each in his own language make.
Yet now, at need, it aids her not at all:
With all these beauties, so her sorrow stings.
Darkened with woe, her only study is
To weep, to sigh, to seek for loneliness.
Careless of all, her hair disordered hangs;
Her charming eyes whence murdering looks did fly,
Now rivers grown whose wellspring anguish is,
Do trickling wash the marble of her face;
Her fair discovered breast with sobbing swollen
Self-cruel she still martyreth with blows.
Alas! It's our ill hap, for if her tears
She would convert into her loving charms,
To make a conquest of the conqueror
(As well she might, would she her force employ),
She should us safety from these ills procure,
Her crown to her, and to her race assure.
Unhappy he, in whom self-succour lies,
Yet self-forsaken wanting succour dies. [*Exit.*]

CHORUS
O sweet fertile land, wherein
Phoebus[89] did with breath inspire
Man who men did first begin,
Formed first of Nilus' mire,[90]
Whence of arts the eldest kinds,
Earth's most heavenly ornament
Were as from their fountain sent
To enlight our misty minds,
Whose gross sprite from endless time
As in darkened prison pent,
Never did to knowledge climb.
Where the Nile, our father good,
Father-like doth never miss
Yearly us to bring such food
As to life required is;
Visiting each year this plain,
And with fat slime covering it,
Which his seven mouths do spit,[91]

As the season comes again,
Making thereby greatest grow
Busy reapers, joyful pain,
When his floods do highest flow.
Wandering prince of rivers thou,
Honour of the Ethiope's land,
Of a lord and master now,
Thou a slave in awe must stand;
Now of Tiber[92] which is spread
Less in force and less in fame,
Reverence thou must the name,
Whom all other rivers dread,
For his children swollen in pride,
Who by conquest seek to tread
Round this earth on every side.
Now thou must begin to send
Tribute of thy watery store,
As sea paths thy steps shall bend,
Yearly presents more and more;
Thy fat scum,[93] our fruitful corn,
Pulled from hence with thievish hands,
All unclothed shall leave our lands
Into foreign country born,
Which, puffed up with such a prey,
Shall thereby the praise adorn
Of that sceptre Rome doth sway.
Nought thee helps thy horns to hide
Far from hence in unknown grounds,
That thy waters wander wide,
Yearly breaking banks, and bounds;
And that thy sky-coloured brooks
Through a hundred peoples pass,
Drawing plots for trees and grass
With a thousand turns and crooks,
Whom all weary of their way,
Thy throats, which in wideness pass,
Pour into their mother sea.
Nought so happy hapless life,
In this world as freedom finds,
Nought wherein more sparks are rife
To inflame courageous minds;
But if force must us enforce,
Needs a yoke to undergo,
Under foreign yoke to go,
Still it proves a bondage worse,
And doubled subjection
See we shall, and feel, and know,
Subject to a stranger grown.
From hence forward for a king,
Whose first being from this place
Should his breast by nature bring
Care of country to embrace;
We at surly face must quake
Of some Roman madly bent,
Who our terror to augment
His proconsul's axe[94] will shake,
Driving with our kings from hence
Our established government,
Justice sword, and law's defence.
Nothing worldly of such might,
But more mighty destiny,
By swift Time's unbridled flight,
Makes in end his end to see;
Everything Time overthrows,
Nought to end doth steadfast stay;
His great scythe mows all away
As the stalk of tender rose;
Only immortality
Of the heavens doth it oppose
'Gainst his powerful deity.
One day there will come a day
Which shall quail thy fortune's flower
And thee ruined low shall lie
In some barbarous prince's power;
When the pity-wanting fire
Shall, o Rome, thy beauties burn,
And to humble ashes turn
Thy proud wealth and rich attire,
Those gilt roofs which turret-wise,
Justly making envy mourn,
Threaten now to pierce[95] skies.
As thy forces fill each land,
Harvests making here and there,
Reaping all with ravening hand,
They find growing anywhere;
From each land, so to thy fall,
Multitude's repair shall make,
From the common spoil to take
What to each man's share may fall;
Fingered[96] all thou shalt behold
No iota left for token's sake,
That thou wert so great of old.
Like unto the ancient Troy,
Whence derived thy founders be,
Conquering foe shall thee enjoy,
And a burning prey in thee;
For within this turning ball
This we see, and see each day:
All things' fixed-ends do stay;[97]
Ends to first beginnings fall;
And that nought, how strong or strange,
Changeless doth endure alway,
But endureth fatal change.

Act III

[*Enter*] M[ARCUS] ANTONIUS [*and*] LUCILIUS.

ANTONIUS

Lucil, sole comfort of my bitter case,
The only trust, the only hope I have

In last despair: ah, is not this the day
That death should me of life and love bereave?
What wait I for, that have no refuge left,
But am sole remnant of my fortune left?
All leave me, fly me; none, no not of them
Which of my greatness greatest good received,
Stands with my fall; they seem as now ashamed
That heretofore they did me ought regard;
They draw them back, showing they followed me,
Not to partake my harms, but cozen me.

LUCILIUS
In this our world nothing is steadfast found,
In vain he hopes, who here his hopes doth ground.

ANTONIUS
Yet nought afflicts me, nothing kills me so,
As that I so my Cleopatra see
Practise with Caesar, and to him transport
My flame, her love, more dear than life to me.

LUCILIUS
Believe it not. Too high a heart she bears,
Too princely thoughts.

ANTONIUS
Too wise a head she wears,
Too much inflamed with greatness, evermore
Gaping for our great empire's government.

LUCILIUS
So long time you her constant love have tried.[1]

ANTONIUS
But still with me good fortune did abide.

LUCILIUS
Her changed love what token makes you know?

ANTONIUS
Pelusium[2] lost and Actium overthrown,
Both by her fraud; my well-appointed fleet
And trusty soldiers in my quarrel armed,
Whom she, false she, instead of my defence,
Came to persuade to yield them to my foe;
Such honour Thyre[3] done, such welcome given,
Their long close talks I neither knew, nor would;
And treacherous wrong Alexas[4] hath me done –
Witness too well her perjured love to me.
But you, o gods (if any faith regard),
With sharp revenge her faithless change reward.

LUCILIUS
The dole she made upon our overthrow,
Her realm given up for refuge to our men,
Her poor attire when she devoutly kept
The solemn day of her nativity,
Against the cost and prodigal expense
Showed when she did your birthday celebrate,
Do plain enough her heart unfeigned prove;
Equally touched – you loving, as you love.

ANTONIUS
Well, be her love to me, or false, or true,
Once in my soul, a cureless wound I feel.
I love, may burn in fire of her love;
Each day, each night her image haunts my mind,
Herself my dreams; and still I tired am,
And still I am with burning pincers nipped.
Extreme my harm; yet sweeter to my sense
Than boiling torch of jealous torments' fire,
This grief, nay rage, in me such stir doth keep,
And thorns[5] me still both when I wake and sleep.
Take Caesar, conquest, take my goods, take he
Th'honour to be lord of the earth alone,
My sons', my life, bent headlong to mishaps,
No force – so not my Cleopatra take.
So foolish I, I cannot her forget,
Though better were I banished her my thought.
Like to the sick whose throat the fever's fire
Hath vehemently with thirsty drought inflamed,
Drinks still, albe[6] the drink he still desires
Be nothing else but fuel to his flame;
He cannot rule himself, his health's respect
Yieldeth to his distempered stomach's heat.

LUCILIUS
Leave of this love, that thus renews your woe.

ANTONIUS
I do my best, but ah, cannot do so.

LUCILIUS
Think how you have so brave a captain been,
And now are by this vain affection fallen.

ANTONIUS
The ceaseless thought of my felicity
Plunges me more in this adversity.
For nothing so a man in ill torments,
As who to him his good state represents.
This makes my wrack,[7] my anguish, and my woe
Equal unto the hellish passions grow,
When I to mind my happy puissance call,
Which erst I had by warlike conquest won,
And that good fortune which me never left,
Which hard disaster now hath me bereft.
With terror, tremble all the world I made
At my sole word, as rushes in the streams
At water's will; I conquered Italy;
I conquered Rome, that nation's so redoubt
I bore (meanwhile besieging Mutina)[8]
Two consuls'[9] armies for my ruin brought,
Bathed in their blood, by their deaths' witnessing,
My force and skill in matters martial.
To wreak[10] thy uncle, unkind Caesar,[11] I
With blood of enemies the banks embrued

Of stained Enipeus,[12] hindering his course
Stopped with heaps of piled carcases;
When Cassius and Brutus,[13] ill betide,
Marched against us, by us twice put to flight,
But by my sole conduct; for all the time
Caesar, heart-sick with fear and fever lay.
Who knows it not? And how by everyone,
Fame of the fact was given to me alone.
There sprang the love, the never-changing love,[14]
Wherein my heart hath since to yours been bound.
There was it, my Lucill, you Brutus saved,
And for your Brutus, Antonie you found.[15]
Better my hap in gaining such a friend,
Than in subduing such an enemy.
Now former virtue, dead, doth me forsake;
Fortune[16] engulfs me in extreme distress;
She turns from me her smiling countenance,
Casting on me mishap upon mishap.
Left and betrayed of thousand thousand[17] friends
Once of my suit, but you Lucill are left,
Remaining to me steadfast as a tower,
In holy love, in spite of Fortune's blasts.
But if of any god my voice be heard,
And be not vainly scattered in the heavens,
Such goodness shall not gloryless be lost,
But coming ages, still, thereof shall boast.

LUCILIUS

Men in their friendship ever should be one,
And never ought with fickle Fortune shake;[18]
Which still removes,[19] nor will, nor knows the way,
Her rolling bowl[20] in one sure state[21] to stay.
Wherefore we ought as borrowed things receive
The goods' light she lends us, to pay again;
Not hold them sure, nor on them build our hopes
As on such goods as cannot fail and fall.
But think again, nothing is durable,
Virtue except, our never-failing host:
So, bearing sail when favouring winds do blow,
As frowning tempests may us least dismay
When they on us do fall; not over-glad
With good estate, nor over-grieved with bad,
Resist mishap.

ANTONIUS

Alas! it is too strong.
Mishaps oft times are by some comfort born,
But these, ah me, whose weights oppress my heart,
Too heavy lie, no hope can them relieve.
There rests no more, but that with cruel blade
For lingering death a hasty way be made.

LUCILIUS

Caesar, as heir unto his father's state,[22]
So will his father's goodness imitate,
To you-ward,[23] whom he knows allied in blood,
Allied in marriage, ruling equally
Th'empire with him, and with him making war
Have purged the earth of Caesar's murderers.
You into portions parted have the world
Even like co-heirs their heritages part;
And now with one accord so many years
In quiet peace both have your charges ruled.

ANTONIUS

Blood and alliance nothing do prevail
To cool the thirst of hot ambitious breasts;
The son his father hardly can endure,
Brother his brother, in one common realm.
So fervent this desire to command,
Such jealousy it kindleth in our hearts,
Sooner will men permit another should
Love her they love, than wear the crown they wear.
All laws it breaks, turns all things upside down:
Amity, kindred, nought so holy is
But it defiles. A monarchy to gain
None cares which way, so he may it obtain.

LUCILIUS

Suppose he monarch be and that this world
No more acknowledge sundry emperors,
That Rome him only fear, and that he join
The east with west and both at once do rule;
Why should he not permit you, peaceably
Discharged of charge and empire's dignity,
Private to live reading philosophy
In learned Greece, Spain, Asia, any land?[24]

ANTONIUS

Never will he his empire think assured
While in this world Mark Antonie shall live.
Sleepless suspicion, pale distrust, cold fear,
Always to princes' company do bear,
Bred of reports, reports which night and day
Perpetual guests from court go not away.

LUCILIUS

He hath not slain your brother Lucius,[25]
Nor shortened hath the age of Lepidus,[26]
Albeit both into his hands were fallen,
And he with wrath against them both inflamed.
Yet one, as lord in quiet rest doth bear
The greatest sway in great Iberia;[27]
The other, with his gentle prince, retains
Of highest priest the sacred dignity.

ANTONIUS

He fears not them; their feeble force he knows.

LUCILIUS
He fears no vanquished overfilled with woes.
ANTONIUS
Fortune may change again.
LUCILIUS
A downcast foe
Can hardly rise, which once is brought so low.
ANTONIUS
All that I can is done; for last assay
(When all means failed) I to entreaty fell
(Ah coward creature!), whence again repulsed,
Of combat I unto him proffer made,
Though he in prime, and I by feeble age
Mightily weakened both in force and skill.
Yet could not he his coward heart advance,
Basely afraid to try so praiseful chance.
This makes me plain,[28] makes me myself accuse;
Fortune in this her spiteful force doth use,
'Gainst my gray hairs; in this, unhappy, I
Repine[29] at heavens in my haps[30] pitiless.
A man, a woman both in might and mind,
In Mars[31] his school who never lesson learned,
Should me repulse, chase, overthrow, destroy,
Me of such fame, bring to so low an ebb?
Alcides'[32] blood, who from my infancy
With happy prowess crowned have my praise.
Witness thou, Gaul unused to servile yoke,
Thou valiant Spain, you fields of Thessaly,
With millions of mourning cries bewailed,
Twice watered now with blood of Italy.[33]
LUCILIUS
Witness may Afrique, and of conquered world
All four quarters witnesses may be.
For in what part of earth inhabited,
Hungry of praise have you not ensigns spread?
ANTONIUS
Thou know'st, rich Egypt (Egypt of my deeds
Fair and foul subject). Egypt ah, thou know'st
How I behaved me fighting for thy king,
When I regained him his rebellious realm,
Against his foes in battle showing force,
And after fight in victory remorse.
Yet if to bring my glory to the ground,
Fortune had made me overthrown by one
Of greater force, or better skill than I –
One of those captains feared so of old,[34]
Camill, Marcellus, worthy Scipio,
This late great Caesar, honour of our state,
Or that great Pompey aged grown in arms,
That after harvest of a world of men
Made in a hundred battles, fights, assaults,
My body through-pierced with push of pike,
Had vomited my blood, in blood my life,
In midst of millions, fellows in my fall –
The less her wrong, the less should be my woe;
Nor she should pain,[35] nor I complain me so.
No, no, whereas I should have died in arms,
And vanquished oft new armies, should have armed,
New battles given; and rather, lost with me
All this whole world submitted unto me,
A man who never saw enlaced[36] pikes[37]
With bristled points against his stomach bent,
Who fears the field, and hides him cowardly
Dead at the very noise the soldiers make.
His virtue: fraud, deceit, malicious guile.
His arms: the arts that false Ulysses[38] used,
Known at Modena,[39] where the consuls both
Death-wounded were, and wounded by his men
To get their army, war with it to make
Against his faith, against his country soil.
Of Lepidus,[40] which to his succour came,
To honour whom he was by duty bound,
The empire he usurped, corrupting first
With baits and bribes the most part of his men.
Yet me hath overcome and made his prey,
And state of Rome with me hath overcome.
Strange! One disordered act at Actium
The earth subdued, my glory hath obscured.
For since, as one whom heaven's wrath attaints,
With fury caught, and more than furious,
Vexed with my evils, I never more had care
My armies lost, or lost name to repair –
I did no more resist.
LUCILIUS
All war's affairs,
But battles most, daily have their success:
Now good, now ill; and though that Fortune have
Great force and power in every worldly thing,
Rule all, do all, have all things fast enchained
Unto the circle of her turning wheel,[41]
Yet seems it more than any practice else
She doth frequent Bellona's[42] bloody trade;
And that her favour, wavering as the wind,
Her greatest power therein doth oftenest show
Whence grows; we daily see, who in their youth
Get honour there, do lose it in their age,
Vanquished by some less warlike than themselves,
Whom yet a meaner man shall overthrow.
Her use is not to lend us still her hand,
But sometimes headlong back again to throw,
When by her favour she hath us extolled,
Unto the top of highest happiness.
ANTONIUS
Well ought I curse within my grieved soul,

Lamenting day and night, this senseless love,
Whereby my fair enticing foe entrapped
My heedless reason, could no more escape.
It was not Fortune's ever-changing face,
It was not destiny's changeless violence,
Forged my mishap. Alas! Who doth not know
They make, nor mar, nor anything can do?
Fortune, which men so fear, adore, detest,
Is but a chance whose cause unknown doth rest,
Although oft-times the cause is well perceived,
But not th'effect the same that was conceived.
Pleasure, nought else, the plague of this our life,
Our life which still a thousand plagues pursue,
Alone hath me this strange disaster spun,
Fallen from a soldier to a chamberer,[43]
Careless[44] of virtue, careless of all praise.
Nay, as the fatted swine in filthy mire
With glutted heart I wallowed in delights,
All thought of honour trodden under foot.
So I me lost; for finding this sweet cup
Pleasing my taste, unwise I drunk my fill,
And through the sweetness of that poison's power
By steps I drove my former wits astray.
I made my friends, offended, me forsake;
I helped my foes against myself to rise;
I robbed my subjects; and for followers
I saw myself beset with flatterers;
Mine idle arms fair wrought with spider's work;
My scattered men without their ensigns strayed.
Caesar meanwhile, who never would have dared
To cope with me, me suddenly despised,
Took heart to fight, and hoped for victory
On one so gone, who glory had forgone.

LUCILIUS

Enchanting pleasure, Venus'[45] sweet delights,
Weaken our bodies, over-cloud our sprights,[46]
Trouble our reason, from our hearts out chase
All holy virtues, lodging in their place;
Like as the cunning fisher takes the fish
By traitor[47] bait whereby the hook is hid,
So pleasure serves to vice instead of food
To bait our souls thereon too lickerish.[48]
This poison deadly is alike to all,
But on great kings doth greatest outrage work,
Taking the royal sceptres from their hands,
Thence forward to be by some stranger borne;
While that their people, charged with heavy loads,
Their flatterers pill[49] and suck their mary[50] dry,
Not ruled, but left to great men as a prey;
While this fond[51] prince himself in pleasures drowns,
Who hears nought, sees nought, doth nought of a king,
Seeming himself against himself conspired.
Then equal Justice wand'reth banished
And in her seat sits greedy Tyranny;
Confused disorder troubleth all estates;
Crimes without fear and outrages are done.
Then mutinous Rebellion shows her face,
Now hid with this, and now with that pretence,
Provoking enemies, which on each side
Enter at ease, and make them lords of all.
The hurtful works of pleasure here behold.

ANTONIUS

The wolf is not so hurtful to the fold,
Frost to the grapes, to ripened fruits the rain,
As pleasure is to princes full of pain.

LUCILIUS

There needs no proof, but by th'Assyrian king,[52]
On whom that monster woeful wrack did bring.

ANTONIUS

There needs no proof, but by unhappy I,
Who lost my empire, honour, life, thereby.

LUCILIUS

Yet hath this ill so much the greater force,
As scarcely any do against it stand –
No, not the demi-gods the old world knew,
Who all subdued, could pleasure's power subdue.
  Great Hercules:[53] Hercules once that was
Wonder of earth and heaven, matchless in might,
Who Antaeus, Lycus, Geryon overcame,
Who drew from hell the triple-headed dog,
Who Hydra killed, vanquished Achelous,
Who heaven's weight on his strong shoulders bore;
Did he not under pleasure's burden bow?
Did he not captive to this passion yield,
When by his captive, so he was inflamed,
As now yourself in Cleopatra burn?
Slept in her lap, her bosom kissed and kissed,
With base unseemly service bought her love,
Spinning at distaff,[54] and with sinewy hand
Winding on spindles thread, in maid's attire?
His conquering club at rest on wall did hang;
His bow unstrung he bent not as he used;
Upon his shafts the weaving spiders spun;
And his hard cloak the fretting[55] moths did pierce.
The monsters, free and fearless all the time,
Throughout the world the people did torment,
And more and more increasing day by day
Scorned his weak heart, become a mistress' play.[56]

ANTONIUS

In only this like Hercules am I,

In this I prove me of his lineage right,
In this himself, his deeds I show in this,
In this, nought else, my ancestor he is.
  But go we. Die I must, and with brave end
Conclusion make of all foregoing harms.
Die, die I must. I must a noble death,
A glorious death, unto my succour call.
I must deface the shame, of time abused,
I must adorn the wanton loves I used,
With some courageous act; that my last day
By mine own hand my spots may wash away.
  Come dear Lucill. Alas! Why weep you thus?
This mortal lot is common to us all.
We must all die, each doth in homage owe
Unto that god, that shared the realms below.
Ah sigh no more. Alas! Appease your woes,
For by your grief my grief more eager grows.
    [*Exeunt.*]

CHORUS[57]

Alas, with what tormenting fire
Us martyreth this blind desire
  To stay our life from flying?[58]
How ceaselessly our minds doth rack,
How heavy lies upon our back
  This dastard[59] fear of dying?
Death, rather, healthful succour gives,
Death, rather, all mishaps relieves,
  That life upon us throweth;
And ever to us doth unclose
The door whereby from cureless woes
  Our weary soul out goeth.
What goddess else more mild than she
To bury all our pain can be,
  What remedy more pleasing?
Our pained hearts when dolour stings,
And nothing rest, or respite brings,
  What help have we more easing?
Hope which to us doth comfort give,
And doth our fainting hearts revive,
  Hath not such force in anguish;
For promising a vain[60] relief,
She oft us fails in midst of grief,
  And helpless lets us languish.
But Death, who call on her at need,
Doth never with vain semblant[61] feed,
  But when them sorrow paineth –
So rids their souls of all distress,
Whose heavy weight did them oppress,
  That not one grief remaineth.
Who fearless and with courage bold
Can Acheron's[62] black face behold,
  Which muddy water beareth;
And crossing over in the way,
Is not amazed at peruke[63] grey,
  Old rusty Charon[64] weareth?
Who void of dread can look upon
The dreadful shades[65] that roam alone,
  On banks where sound no voices;
Whom with her fire-brands and her snakes
No whit afraid Alecto[66] makes,
  Nor triple-barking noises.[67]
Who freely can himself dispose
Of that last hour which all must close,
  And leave this life at pleasure;
This noble freedom more esteems,
And in his heart more precious deems,
  Than crown and kingly treasure.
The waves which Boreas'[68] blasts turmoil,
And cause with foaming fury boil,
  Make not his heart to tremble;
Nor brutish[69] broil[70], when with strong head
A rebel people madly led
  Against their lords assemble;
Nor fearful face of tyrant wood,[71]
Who breathes but threats, and drinks but
    blood,
  No, nor the hand which thunder –
The hand of Jove, which thunder bears,[72]
And ribs of rocks in sunder tears,
  Tears mountains' sides in sunder;
Nor bloody Mars' butchering bands,
Whose lightnings desert lay the lands,
  Whom dusty clouds do cover,
From off whose armour sun-beams fly,
And under them make quaking lie
  The plains whereon they hover;
Nor yet the cruel murdering blade
Warm in the moisty[73] bowels made
  Of people pell-mell[74] dying
In some great city put to sack,
By savage tyrant brought to wrack,
  At his cold mercy lying.
How abject him, how base think I,
Who wanting courage cannot die,
  When need him thereto calleth.
From whom the dagger drawn to kill
The cureless griefs that vex him still,
  For fear and faintness falleth?
O Antonie, with thy dear mate
Both in misfortunes fortunate,
  Whose thoughts to death aspiring,
Shall you protect from victor's rage,
Who on each side doth you encage,
  To triumph much desiring.
That Caesar may you not offend,
Nought else but death can you defend,
  Which his weak force derideth.
And all in this round earth contained,
Powerless on them whom once enchained,
  Avernus' prison hideth;[75]

Where great Psammetique's[76] ghost doth rest,
Not with infernal pain possest,
But in sweet fields detained;
And old Amasis'[77] soul likewise,
And all our famous Ptolemies,[78]
That whilom[79] on us reigned. [*Exeunt.*]

Act IV

[*Enter* CHORUS *of Roman soldiers; afterwards enter*] CAESAR [*and*] AGRIPPA.

CAESAR

You ever-living gods which all things hold
Within the power of your celestial hands;
By whom heat, cold, the thunder, and the wind,
The properties of interchanging months,
Their course and being have; which do set down
Of empires, by your destined decree,
The force, age, time; and, subject to no change,
Change all, reserving nothing in one state.
You have advanced, as high as thundering heaven,
The Roman's greatness by Bellona's[1] might,
Mastering the world with fearful violence,
Making the world widow of liberty.
Yet at this day the proud exalted Rome,
Despoiled, captived, at one man's will doth bend:
Her empire mine, her life is in my hand,
As monarch I both world and Rome command.
Do all, can all; forth my commandment cast
Like thundering fire from one to other pole,
Equal to Jove, bestowing by my word
Haps and mishaps[2], as fortune's king and lord.[3]
No town there is, but up my image sets,[4]
But sacrifice to me doth daily make;
Whether, where Phoebus[5] join his morning steeds,
Or where the night them weary entertains,
Or where the heat the Garamante[6] doth scorch,
Or where the cold from Boreas'[7] breath is blown,
All Caesar do, both awe and honour bear,
And crowned kings his very name doth fear.
Antonie knows it well, for whom not one
Of all the princes all this earth do rule
Arms against me, for all redoubt the power
Which heavenly powers on earth have made me bear.
Antonie, he poor man with fire inflamed,
A woman's beauties kindled in his heart,
Rose against me, who longer could not bear
My sister's wrong he did so ill entreat;
Seeing her left while that his lewd delights
Her husband with his Cleopatra took
In Alexandria, where both nights and days
Their time they passed in nought but loves and plays.
All Asia's forces into one he drew,
And forth he set upon the azured[8] waves
A thousand and a thousand ships, which filled
With soldiers, pikes, with targets,[9] arrows, darts,[10]
Made Neptune quake, and all the watery troops
Of Glauces[11] and Tritons[12] lodged at Actium.[13]
But mighty gods, who still the force withstand
Of him who causeless doth another wrong,
In less than moment's space reduced to nought
All that proud power by sea or land he brought.

AGRIPPA

Presumptuous pride of high and haughty spirit,
Voluptuous care of fond and foolish love,
Have justly wrought his wrack;[14] who thought he held
(By overweening) fortune in his hand.
Of us he made no count, but as to play
So fearless came our forces to assay.
So sometimes fell to sons of mother earth,[15]
Which crawled to heaven, war on the gods to make,
Olymp on Pelion, Ossa on Olymp,
Pindus on Ossa, loading by degrees,
That at hand-strokes with mighty clubs they might
On mossy rocks the gods make tumble down.
When mighty Jove with burning anger chafed,
Disbrained with him Gyges and Briareus,[16]
Blunting his darts upon their bruised bones.
For no one thing the gods can less abide
In deeds of men, than arrogance and pride.
And still the proud, which too much takes in hand,
Shall foulest fall, where best he thinks to stand.

CAESAR

Right as some palace, or some stately tower,
Which overlooks the neighbour buildings round
In scorning wise, and to the stars up grows,
Which in short time his own weight overthrows.
What monstrous pride, nay what impiety
Incensed him onward to the gods' disgrace?
When his two children, Cleopatra's brats,
To Phoebe and her brother[17] he compared,
Latona's race, causing them to be called
The sun and moon? Is not this folly right,
And is not this the gods to make his foes?
And is not this himself to work his woes?

AGRIPPA

In like proud sort he caused his head to lose

The Jewish king Antigonus,[18] to have
His realm for balm, that Cleopatra loved,
As though on him he had some treason proved.

CAESAR

Lydia[19] to her, and Syria he gave,
Cyprus of gold, Arabia rich of smells;
And to his children more – Cilicia,
Parths, Medes, Armenia, Phoenicia[20] –
The king of kings proclaiming them to be,
By his own word, as by a sound degree.

AGRIPPA

What? Robbing his own country of her due?
Triumphed he not in Alexandria,
Of Artabazus[21] the Armenian king,
Who yielded on his perjured word to him?

CAESAR

Nay, never Rome more injuries received,
Since thou, O Romulus,[22] by flight of birds
With happy hand the Roman walls didst build,
Than Antonie's fond loves to it hath done.
Nor ever war more holy, nor more just,
Nor undertaken with more hard constraint,
Than is this war; which were it not, our state
Within small time all dignity should lose.
Though I lament (thou sun my witness art,
And thou great Jove) that it so deadly proves,
That Roman blood should in such plenty flow,
Watering the fields and pastures where we go.
What Carthage[23] in old hatred obstinate,
What Gaul[24] still barking at our rising state,
What rebel Samnite,[25] what fierce Pyrrhus'[26] power,
What cruel Mithridate,[27] what Parth[28] hath wrought,
Such woe to Rome? Whose commonwealth[29] he had,
Had he been victor, into Egypt brought.

AGRIPPA

Surely the gods – which have this city built
Steadfast to stand as long as time endures,
Which keep the Capitol,[30] of us take care,
And care will take of those shall after come –
Have made you victor, that you might redress
Their honour, grown by past mischiefs less.

CAESAR

The seely[31] man, when all the Greekish sea
His fleet had hid in hope me sure to drown,
Me battle gave; where fortune in my stead,
Repulsing him his forces disarrayed.
Himself took flight, soon as his love he saw
All wan[32] through fear with full sails fly away.
His men, though lost, whom none did now direct,
With courage fought, fast grappled ship with ship,
Charging, resisting, as their oars would serve,
With darts,[33] with swords, with pikes, with fiery flames.
So that the darkened night her starry veil
Upon the bloody sea had over-spread,
Whilst yet they held; and hardly, hardly then,
They fell to flying on the wavy plain,
All full of soldiers overwhelmed with waves.
The air throughout with cries and groans did sound;
The sea did blush with blood; the neighbour shores
Groaned, so they with shipwrecks pestered were;
And floating bodies left for pleasing food
To birds, and beasts, and fishes of the sea.
You know it well Agrippa.[34]

AGRIPPA

Meet it was.
The Roman empire so should ruled be,
As heaven is ruled; which turning over us,
All under-things by his example turns.
Now as of heaven, one only lord we know,
One only lord should rule this earth below.
When one self-power is common made to two,
Their duties they nor suffer will, nor do;
In quarrel still, in doubt, in hate, in fear:
Meanwhile the people all the smart do bear.

CAESAR

Then to the end none, while my days endure,
Seeking to raise himself may succours find;
We must with blood mark this our victory,
For just example to all memory.
Murder we must, until not one we leave,
Which may hereafter us of rest bereave.

AGRIPPA

Mark it with murders? Who of that can like?

CAESAR

Murders must use, who doth assurance seek.

AGRIPPA

Assurance, call you enemies to make?

CAESAR

I make no such, but such away I take.

AGRIPPA

Nothing so much as rigour doth displease.

CAESAR

Nothing so much doth make me live at ease.

AGRIPPA

What ease to him that feared is of all?

CAESAR

Feared to be, and see, his foes to fall.

AGRIPPA

Commonly fear doth breed and nourish hate.

CAESAR

Hate without power comes commonly too late.

AGRIPPA
A feared prince hath oft his death desired.
CAESAR
A prince not feared hath oft his wrong conspired.
AGRIPPA
No guard so sure, no fort so strong doth prove,
No such defence, as is the people's love.
CAESAR
Nought more unsure, more weak, more like the wind,
Than people's favour still to change inclined.
AGRIPPA
Good gods! What love to gracious prince men bear!
CAESAR
What honour to the prince that is severe!
AGRIPPA
Nought more divine then is benignity.
CAESAR
Nought likes the gods as doth severity.
AGRIPPA
Gods all forgive.
CAESAR
On faults they pains do lay.
AGRIPPA
And give their goods.
CAESAR
Oft times they take away.
AGRIPPA
They wreak them not, o Caesar, at each time
That by our sins they are to wrath provoked.
Neither must you, believe, I humbly pray,
Your victory with cruelty defile.
The gods it gave, it must not be abused,
But to the good of all men mildly used;
And they be thanked that having given you grace
To reign alone and rule this earthly mass,
They may hence-forward hold it still in rest,
All scattered power united in one breast.
CAESAR
But what is he that breathless comes so fast,
Approaching us, and going in such haste?
AGRIPPA
He seems afraid, and under his arm I
(But much I err) a bloody sword espy.
CAESAR
I long to understand what it may be.
AGRIPPA
He hither comes; it's best we stay and see.
[*Enter* DIRCETUS *the messenger.*]
DIRCETUS
What good god now my voice will reenforce,
That tell I may to rocks, and hills, and woods,
To waves of sea which dash upon the shore,
To earth, to heaven, the woeful news I bring?
AGRIPPA
What sudden chance thee towards us hath brought?
DIRCETUS
A lamentable chance. O wrath of heavens!
O gods too pitiless!
CAESAR
What monstrous hap
Wilt thou recount?
DIRCETUS
Alas, too hard mishap!
When I but dream of what mine eyes beheld,
My heart doth freeze, my limbs do quivering quake,
I senseless stand, my breast with tempest tossed,
Kills in my throat my words, ere fully born.
Dead! Dead he is! Be sure of what I say;
This murdering sword hath made the man away.
CAESAR
Alas, my heart doth cleave, pity me racks,
My breast doth pant to hear this doleful tale.
Is Antonie then dead? To death, alas!
I am the cause despair him so compelled.
But soldier, of his death the manner show,
And how he did this living light forgo.
DIRCETUS
When Antonie no hope remaining saw
How war he might, or how agreement make;
Saw him betrayed by all his men of war
In every fight as well by sea, as land;
That not content to yield them to their foes
They also came against himself to fight;
Alone in court he 'gan himself torment,
Accuse the queen, himself of her lament,
Called her untrue and traitress, as who sought
To yield him up she could no more defend;
That in the harms, which for her sake he bare,
As in his blissful state, she might not share.
But she again, who much his fury feared,
Got to the tomb's dark-horror's dwelling place,
Made lock the doors, and pull the hearses[35] down.
Then fell she wretched, with herself to fight:
A thousand plaints, a thousand sobs she cast,
From her weak breast which to the bones was torn.
Of women, her, the most unhappy called,
Who by her love, her woeful love, had lost
Her realm, her life, and more – the love of him
Who while he was, was all her woe's support.
But that she faultless was, she did invoke
For witness heaven and air and earth and sea.
Then sent him word: she was no more alive,
But lay enclosed, dead within her tomb.

This he believed, and fell to sigh and groan,
And crossed his arms, then thus began to moan.

CAESAR

Poor hopeless man!

DIRCETUS

What does thou more attend!
'Ah Antonie! Why dost thou death defer,
Since Fortune thy professed enemy,
Hath made to die, who only made thee live?'
Soon as with sighs he had these words up closed,
His armour he unlaced and cast it off,
Then all disarmed, he thus again did say:
'My queen, my heart, the grief that now I feel
Is not that I, your eyes, my sun, do lose,
For soon again one tomb shall us conjoin;
I grieve, whom men so valorous did deem
Should now than you of lesser valour seem.'
So said, forthwith he Eros to him called,
Eros his man, summoned him on his faith
To kill him at his need. He took the sword
And at that instant stabbed therewith his breast,
And ending life fell dead before his feet.
'O Eros, thanks' quoth Antony, 'for this
Most noble act, who powerless me to kill,
On thee hast done, what I on me should do.'
Of speaking thus he scarce had made an end
And taken up the bloody sword from ground,
But he his body pierced; and of red blood
A gushing fountain all the chamber filled.
He staggered at the blow, his face grew pale,
And on a couch all feeble down he fell,
Swooning with anguish; deadly cold him took,
As if his soul had then his lodging left.
But he revived, and marking all our eyes
Bathed in tears, and how our breasts we beat
For pity, anguish, and for bitter grief,
To see him plunged in extreme wretchedness,
He prayed us all to haste his lingering death –
But no man willing, each himself withdrew.
Then fell he new to cry and vex himself,
Until a man from Cleopatra came,
Who said from her he had commandment
To bring him to her, to the monument.
The poor soul at these words, even rapt with joy
Knowing she lived, prayed us him to convey
Unto his lady. Then upon our arms
We bore him to the tomb, but entered not.
For she who feared captive to be made,
And that she should to Rome in triumph go,
Kept close the gate. But from a window high
Cast down a cord, wherein he was impacked.[36]
Then by her women's help the corpse[37] she raised,
And by strong arms into her window drew.
So pitiful a sight was never seen:
Little and little Antonie was pulled,
Now breathing death; his beard was all unkempt,
His face and breast all bathed in his blood.
So hideous yet, and dying as he was,
His eyes half-closed upon the queen he cast,
Held up his hands, and help himself to raise;
But still with weakness back his body fell.
The miserable lady with moist eyes,
With hair which careless on her forehead hung,
With breast which blows had bloodily benumbed,
With stooping head, and body downward bent,
Enlaced her in the cord, and with all force
This life-dead man courageously upraised.
The blood with pain into her face did flow,
Her sinews stiff, her self did breathless grow.
The people which beneath in flocks beheld,
Assisted her with gesture, speech, desire,
Cried and encouraged her, and in their souls
Did sweat, and labour, no whit less then she,
Who never tired in labour, held so long
Helped by her women, and her constant heart –
That Antony was drawn into the tomb,
And there (I think) of dead augments the sum.
The city all to tears and sighs is turned,
To plaints and outcries horrible to hear;
Men, women, children, hoary-headed age,
Do all pell-mell[38] in house and street lament;
Scratching their faces, tearing of their hair,
Wringing their hands, and martyring their breasts;
Extreme their dole, and greater misery
In sacked towns can hardly ever be.
Not if the fire had scalded the highest towers;
That all things were of force and murder full;
That in the streets the blood in rivers streamed;
The son his sire saw in his bosom slain;
The sire his son; the husband reft of breath
In his wife's arms, who furious runs to death.
Now my breast wounded with their piteous plaints
I left their town, and took with me this sword,
Which I took up at what time Antonie
Was from his chamber carried to the tomb,
And brought it you, to make his death more plain,
And that thereby my words may credit gain.

CAESAR

Ah gods, what cruel hap! Poor Antonie!
Alas, hast thou this sword so long-time borne
Against thy foe, that in the end it should
Of thee his lord the cursed murderer be?

O death, how I bewail thee! We (alas!)
So many wars have ended, brothers, friends,
Companions, cousins, equals in estate;
And must it now to kill thee be my fate?

AGRIPPA

Why trouble you yourself with bootless grief?
For Antonie why spend you tears in vain?
Why darken you with dole your victory?
Meseems[39] yourself your glory do envy.
Enter the town, give thanks unto the gods.

CAESAR

I cannot but his tearful chance lament,
Although not I, but his own pride the cause,
And unchaste love of this Egyptian.

AGRIPPA

But best we sought into the tomb to get,
Lest she consume in this amazed case
So much rich treasure, with which happily
Despair in death may make her feed the fire;
Suffering the flames her jewels to deface,
You to defraud, her funeral to grace.
Send then to her, and let some mean be used
With some device, so hold her still alive,
Some fair large promise; and let them mark
Whether they may by some fine cunning slight
Enter the tombs.

CAESAR

Let Proculeius[40] go,
And feed with hope her soul disconsolate.
Assure her so, that we may wholly get
Into our hands her treasure and herself.
For this of all things most I do desire
To keep her safe until our going hence,
That by her presence beautified may be
The glorious triumph Rome prepares for me.
[*Exeunt.*]

CHORUS OF ROMAN SOLDIERS

Shall ever civil bate[41]
Gnaw and devour our state?
Shall never we this blade,
Our blood hath bloody made,
Lay down? These arms down lay
As robes we wear alway?
But as from age to age
So pass from rage to rage?
Our hands shall we not rest
To bathe[42] in our own breast?
And shall thick in each land
Our wretched trophies stand,
To tell posterity,
What mad impiety
Our stony[43] stomachs led
Against the place us bred?
Then still must heaven view
The plagues that us pursue,
And everywhere descry,
Heaps of us scattered lie,
Making the stranger plains
Fat with our bleeding rains,
Proud that on them their grave
So many legions have.
And with our fleshes still
Neptune[44] his fishes fill,
And drunk with blood, from blue,
The sea take blushing hue;
As juice of Tyrian[45] shell,
When clarified well
To wool of finest fields
A purple gloss it yields.
But since the rule of Rome,
To one man's hand is come,
Who governs without mate
Her now united state;
Late jointly ruled by three,
Envying mutuality,
Whose triple yoke much woe
On Latins' necks did throw.
I hope the cause of jar,[46]
And of this bloody war,
And deadly discord, gone
By what we last have done;
Our banks shall cherish now
The branchy pale-hued bough
Of olive, Pallas'[47] praise,
Instead of barren bays.
And that his temple door,
Which bloody Mars[48] before
Held open, now at last
Old Janus[49] shall make fast;
And rust the sword consume,
And, spoiled of waving plume,
The useless morion[50] shall
On crook[51] hang by the wall.
At least if war return,
It shall not here sojourn,
To kill us with those arms
Were forged for others' harms;
But have their points addressed,
Against the German's[52] breast,
The Parthian's feigned flight,[53]
The Biscaine's[54] martial might.
Old memory doth there,
Painted on forehead wear
Our father's praise, thence torn
Our triumph's bays have worn;
Thereby our matchless Rome
Whilome of shepherds come,
Raised to this greatness stands,
The queen of foreign lands.
Which now even seems to face

The heavens, her glory's place;
Nought resting under skies
That dares affront her eyes.
So that she needs but fear
The weapons Jove doth bear,
Who angry at one blow
May her quite overthrow. [*Exeunt.*]

Act V

[*Enter*] CLEOPATRA, EUPHRON, CHILDREN OF CLEOPATRA, CHARMION [*and*] ERAS.

CLEOPATRA

O cruel fortune! O accursed lot!
O plaguey[1] love! O most detested brand![2]
O wretched joys! O beauties miserable!
O deadly state! O deadly royalty!
O hateful life! O queen most lamentable!
O Antonie by my fault buriable![3]
O hellish work of heaven! Alas, the wrath
Of all the gods at once on us is fallen.
Unhappy queen! O would I in this world
The wandering light of day had never seen!
Alas, of mine the plague and poison, I
The crown have lost my ancestors me left,
This realm I have to strangers subject made,
And robbed my children of their heritage.
Yet this is nought (alas!) unto the price
Of you dear husband, whom my snares entrapped;
Of you, whom I have plagued, whom I have made
With bloody hand a guest of mouldy tomb;
Of you, whom I destroyed; of you, dear lord,
Whom I of empire, honour, life, have spoiled.
O hurtful woman! And can I yet live,
Yet longer live in this ghost-haunted tomb?
Can I yet breathe? Can yet in such annoy,
Yet can my soul within this body dwell?
O sisters, you that spin the threads of death![4]
O Styx![5] O Plegethon![6] You brooks of hell!
O imps of night!

EUPHRON

Live for your children's sake;
Let not your death of kingdom them deprive.
Alas what shall they do? Who will have care?
Who will preserve this royal race of yours?
Who pity take? Even now meseems[7] I see
These little souls to servile bondage fallen,
And borne in triumph.

CLEOPATRA

Ah most miserable!

EUPHRON

Their tender arms with cursed cord fast bound
At their weak backs.

CLEOPATRA

Ah gods what pity more!

EUPHRON

Their seely[8] necks to ground with weakness bend.

CLEOPATRA

Never on us, good gods, such mischief send.

EUPHRON

And pointed at with fingers as they go.

CLEOPATRA

Rather a thousand deaths!

EUPHRON

Lastly, his knife
Some cruel caitiff in their blood imbrue.

CLEOPATRA

Ah my heart breaks! By shady banks of hell,
By fields[9] whereon the lonely ghosts do tread,
By my soul, and the soul of Antonie,
I you beseech, Euphron, of them have care.
Be their good father, let your wisdom let
That they fall not into this tyrant's hands.
Rather, conduct them where their freezed[10] locks[11]
Black Ethiopes to neighbour sun do show;
On wavy ocean, at the water's will;
On barren cliffs of snowy Caucasus;[12]
To tigers swift, to lions, and to bears;
And rather, rather unto every coast,
To every land and sea – for nought I fear
As rage of him, whose thirst no blood can quench.
Adieu dear children, children dear adieu;
Good Isis[13] you to place of safety guide,
Far from our foes, where you your lives may lead
In free estate devoid of servile dread.
Remember not, my children, you were born
Of such a princely race; remember not
So many brave kings, which have Egypt ruled,
In right descent your ancestors have been;
That this great Antonie your father was,
Hercules'[14] blood, and more than he in praise.
For your high courage such remembrance will,
Seeing your fall, with burning rages fill.
Who knows if that your hands, false destiny,
The sceptres promised of imperious Rome
Instead of them shall crooked sheephooks bear,
Needles or forks, or guide the cart, or plough?
Ah learn t'endure; your birth and high estate,
Forget, my babes, and bend to force of fate.
Farewell, my babes, farewell, my heart is closed
With pity and pain, myself with death enclosed.
My breath doth fail. Farewell for evermore;
Your sire and me you shall see never more.
Farewell, sweet care, farewell.

CHILDREN
Madam, adieu.

CLEOPATRA
Ah this voice kills me. Ah, good gods, I swoon!
I can no more, I die!

ERAS
Madam, alas!
And will you yield to woe? Ah, speak to us!

EUPHRON
Come, children.

CHILDREN
We come.

EUPHRON
Follow we our chance.
The gods shall guide us.
[*Exit* EUPHRON *and* THE CHILDREN.]

CHARMION
O too cruel lot!
O too hard chance! Sister, what shall we do,
What shall we do, alas, if murdering dart
Of death arrive while that in slumbering swoon
Half dead she lie with anguish overgone?

ERAS
Her face is frozen.

CHARMION
Madam, for god's love
Leave us not thus; bid us yet first farewell.
Alas, weep over Antonie; let not
His body be without due rites entombed.

CLEOPATRA
Ah, ah!

CHARMION
Madam.

CLEOPATRA
Ah, me!

CHARMION
How faint she is!

CLEOPATRA
My sisters, hold me up. How wretched I,
How cursed, am; and was there ever one
By fortune's hate into more dolours thrown?
Ah, weeping Niobe,[15] although thy heart
Beholds itself enwrapped in causeful woe
For thy dead children, that a senseless rock
With grief become, on Sipylus thou stand'st
In endless tears – yet didst thou never feel
The weights of grief that on my heart do lie.
Thy children thou, mine I, poor soul, have lost –
And lost their father; more than them I wail:
Lost this fair realm. Yet me the heaven's wrath
Into a stone not yet transformed hath.
Phaeton's sisters,[16] daughters of the sun,
Which wail your brother fallen into the streams
Of stately Po, the gods, upon the banks
Your bodies to bank-loving alders turned.
For me, I sigh, I ceaseless weep, and wail,
And heaven, pitiless, laughs at my woe;
Revives, renews it still, and in the end
(Oh cruelty!) doth death for comfort lend.
Die Cleopatra then! No longer stay
From Antonie, who thee at Styx attends:
Go join thy ghost with his and sob no more,
Without his love, within these tombs enclosed.

ERAS
Alas, yet let us weep, lest sudden death
From him our tears and those last duties take,
Unto his tomb we owe.

CHARMION
Ah, let us weep
While moisture lasts, then die before his feet.

CLEOPATRA
Who furnish will mine eyes with streaming tears,
My boiling anguish worthily to wail?
Wail thee Antonie, Antonie my heart?
Alas, how much I weeping liquor want!
Yet have mine eyes quite drawn their conduits dry
By long beweeping my disastered[17] harms.
Now reason is that from my side they suck
First vital moisture, then the vital blood.
Then let the blood from my sad eyes outflow,
And smoking yet with thine in mixture grow.
Moist it, and heat it new, and never stop;
All watering thee, while yet remains one drop.

CHARMION
Antonie take our tears; this is the last
Of all the duties we to thee can yield
before we die.

ERAS
These sacred obsequies,
Take Antonie, and take them in good part.

CLEOPATRA
O Goddess, thou whom Cyprus doth adore,
Venus of Paphos,[18] bent to work us harm
For old Iulus' brood, if thou take care
Of Caesar, why of us tak'st thou no care?
Antonie did descend, as well as he,
From thine own son by long enchained line;[19]
And might have ruled, by one and self same fate
True Trojan blood, the stately Roman state.
Antonie, poor Antonie, my dear soul,
Now but a block,[20] the booty of a tomb,
Thy life, thy heat is lost, thy colour gone,
And hideous paleness on thy face hath seized.
Thy eyes, two suns, the lodging place of love,
Which yet for tents to warlike Mars did serve,

Locked up in lids (as fair day's cheerful light,
Which darkness flies) do winking hide in night.
Antonie by our true loves I thee beseech –
And by our hearts' sweet sparks have set on fire
Our holy marriage, and the tender ruth[21]
Of our dear babes, knot of our amity[22] –
My doleful voice thy ear let entertain,
And take me with thee to the hellish plain,
Thy wife, thy friend. Hear Antonie, o hear
My sobbing sighs, if here thou be, or there.
Lived thus long, the winged race of years
Ended I have as destiny decreed,
Flourished and reigned, and taken just revenge
Of him who me both hated and despised.[23]
Happy, alas too happy – if of[24] Rome
Only the fleet had hither never come.
And now of me an image great shall go
Under the earth to bury there my woe.
What say I? Where am I? O Cleopatra,
Poor Cleopatra, grief thy reason reaves.
No, no, most happy in this hapless case,
To die with thee, and dying thee embrace;
My body joined with thine, my mouth with thine,
My mouth, whose moisture-burning sighs have dried
To be in one self tomb, and one self chest,
And wrapped with thee in one self sheet to rest.
The sharpest torment in my heart I feel,
Is that I stay from thee, my heart, this while;
Die will I straight now, now straight will I die,
And straight with thee a wandering shade will be,
Under the cypress trees thou haunt'st alone,
Where brooks of hell do falling seem to moan.[25]
But yet I stay, and yet thee overlive,
That ere I die due rites I may thee give.
A thousand sobs I from my breast will tear,
With thousand plaints[26] thy funerals adorn;
My hair shall serve for thy oblations;
My boiling tears for thy effusions;
Mine eyes thy fire, for out of them the flame
(Which burnt thy heart on me enamoured) came.
Weep my companions, weep, and from your eyes
Rain down on him of tears a brinish[27] stream.
Mine can no more, consumed by the coals
Which from my breast, as from a furnace, rise.
Martyr your breasts with multiplied blows,
With violent hands tear off your hanging hair,
Outrage your face. Alas, why should we seek
(Since now we die) our beauties more to keep?
I spent in tears, not able more to spend,
But kiss him now, what rests me more to do?
Then let me kiss you, you fair eyes, my light,
Front seat of honour, face most fierce, most fair!
O neck, O arms, O hands, O breast where death
(O mischief) comes to choke up vital breath.
A thousand kisses, thousand, thousand more
Let you my mouth for honour's farewell give,
That in this office weak my limbs may grow,
Fainting on you, and forth my soul may flow.
[*She dies.*]

3 *The Tragedy of Mariam*

ELIZABETH CARY, VISCOUNTESS FALKLAND

INTRODUCTION

Elizabeth Cary (1585-1639) – her name is sometimes spelt Carew or Carey – was the only daughter of Sir Laurence and Lady Elizabeth Tanfield of Burford Priory, Oxford. She had a strict upbringing and was a somewhat isolated child who immersed herself in her studies. Her abilities as a linguist were prodigious and she was able to read fluently in, and later to translate for publication, French, Spanish, Latin and Hebrew. Her marriage to Sir Henry Cary, which was contracted in 1602, was arranged by her parents and appears to have been a very impersonal business, providing the Cary family with an heiress and the Tanfields with an aristocratic connection. Elizabeth was allowed to remain at home for the first year of married life, while her husband was fighting in the Netherlands, but in 1603, her mother-in-law, Lady Katherine, insisted that she join the Cary household. Lady Katherine proved even more strict than Elizabeth's mother, for while the latter had denied her daughter candles to provide light for reading, the former forbade her to read at all. Ironically, it was because of this prohibition that Elizabeth sought intellectual stimulation from writing her own works, so that when her husband came back, 'from this time she writ many things for her private recreation, on several subjects and occasions, all in verse'.[1] In 1606, Henry Cary returned to England from Spain, where he had been held prisoner since being captured in Ostend in 1605, and began a successful career at court which culminated in his appointment as Lord Deputy of Ireland in 1622. During this first period of their marriage the couple seem to have accepted one another, and had eleven children, born between 1609 and 1624. Signs of strain, however, were already beginning to show, as Elizabeth experienced long bouts of depression, and became increasingly aware of the conflict in religious belief between herself and her husband.

Elizabeth Cary had shown an interest in Catholicism from around 1605, but initially she had limited her spiritual leanings in order to conform with her husband's strict Protestantism. However, the harshness of his rule in Ireland and his persecution of the Irish Catholics appear to have precipitated the complete breakdown of their marriage, and, in 1625, he sent her back to England. Having returned to the English court, Elizabeth attempted to aid her husband's fortunes, although he does not appear to have appreciated her efforts; for example, he wrote to Sir Edward Conway, the Secretary of State, that,

> For her abilities in agency of affairs, as I was never taken with opinion of them, so I was never desirous to employ them if she had them, for I conceive women to be no fit solicitors of state affairs . . . for my part I should take much more comfort to hear that she were quietly retired to her Mother's into the country.[2]

The subtext of this comment was, however, Cary's desire to remove his wife from the influence of a small coterie of Catholic sympathizers and recusants who had gathered around Queen Henrietta Maria. It is probable that by 1626 Elizabeth had planned a covert profession of Catholicism, which would have been acceptable to the court and her husband, even if they had privately condemned her actions, but Lady Denby and her brother, the powerful Duke of Buckingham, informed the king of her conversion and the whole affair was forced into the open.[3] Cary was confined to her rooms for six weeks, and her husband immediately stopped her allowance, took away her children, and left her in abject poverty. A series of appeals from both parties ensued, resulting finally, in 1627, with a Privy Council decision in Elizabeth's favour which directed her husband to provide maintenance for her and to pay the debts she had already accrued. Relations appear to have remained pressured, however, until 1631 when Henrietta Maria arranged a partial reconciliation between the couple, and in 1633 Elizabeth helped nurse her husband at his death. The next six years saw little material or

4 *Portrait of Lady Falkland*, Sutherland, by kind permission of the Ashmolean Musuem, Oxford

economic improvement in Elizabeth's life, and she died in October 1639 in impoverished circumstances.

The details of Elizabeth Cary's biography derive mainly from *The Lady Falkland, Her Life*, written *c.* 1655 by one of her daughters (possibly Anne, later Dame Clementia), who had become a Benedictine nun. The manuscript is in the Imperial Archives at Lille, and an edition was published in 1861.[4] Written as a quasi-hagiography, it is difficult to distinguish how far events are made to correspond with a formulaic pattern; for example, Elizabeth's rebellion against authority is depicted as that of a spiritual martyr rejecting the demands of the material world (embodied in her husband) in favour of the true Catholic faith. Yet, from Cary's own writing it is possible to see that independent thought and freedom of speech are depicted as equally important. While clearly emphasizing her spiritual self, Cary was also intent upon creating an identity intimately linked to literary activity. Moreover, during her lifetime, even when exiled from the court and rejected by her husband, Elizabeth's writing was repeatedly praised by, among others, Michael Drayton, John Marston and Richard More.[5] However, probably the most interesting evocation of her as a writer occurs in the dedication of John Davies of Hereford's *The Muses Sacrifice or Divine Meditations* (1612), where he writes:

> CARY (of whom Minerva stands in feare,
> lest she, from her, should get ARTS Regencie)
> Of ART so moves the great-all-moving Spheare,
> that ev'ry Orbe of Science moves thereby.
>
> Thou mak'st Melpomen proud, and my Heart great
> of such a Pupill, who, in Buskin fine,
> With Feet of State, dost make thy Muse to mete
> the Scenes of Syracuse and Palastine.
>
> Art, Language; yea, abstruse and holy Tones,
> thy Wit and Grace acquir'd thy Fame to raise;
> And still to fill thine owne, and others Songs;
> thine, with thy Parts, and others, with thy praise.
>
> Such nervy Limbes of Art, and Straines of Wit
> times past ne'er knew the weaker Sexe to have;
> And Times to come, will hardly credit it,
> if thus thou give thy Workes both Birth and Grave.[6]

Davies praises Cary's own writing as well as her role as a patron, perhaps implying a certain pride in her work since he claims her as his 'Pupill', and in the dedication as a whole he ranks her alongside Mary Sidney and Lucy, Countess of Bedford (both of whom are included as authors in this anthology). Davies also implies that Cary should publish her work, rather than leave it in manuscript form – 'if thus thou give thy Workes both Birth and Grave' – and this injunction might well have influenced her decision to print *Mariam* shortly after (1613). Indeed, although this play remains extant, the other work alluded to by Davies, 'Scenes of Syracuse' ('Palestine' is the setting for *Mariam*), which probably went unpublished, has been lost.

Unfortunately, much of Cary's writing has suffered the same fate as the Syracusan text and, although her canon was extensive, only a few works now remain.[7] Yet, as a creative writer Elizabeth Cary's accomplishment remains outstanding. She was the first Englishwoman to write a tragedy, *The Tragedy of Mariam* (1602-4; published 1613) and the first Englishwoman to write a history play even though the text is a curious mixture of drama and prose, *The History of the Life, Reign, and Death of Edward II* (*c.* 1627-8). In verse she composed a 'Life of Tamurlane', hymns to the Virgin Mary, and poems on Mary Magdalene, Saint Agnes and Saint Elizabeth of Portugal. Her translations include: Abraham Ortelius' *Mirroir du Monde*, done before she was 17; several of Seneca's epistles; the complete works of Cardinal Perron; as well as works by other French and Flemish religious writers. Finally, she wrote prose tracts for her children advising them on moral behaviour and advocating the Catholic faith. Moreover, unlike most other women of her period, Cary was aware of her own talent. In the dedicatory letter to her translation of *The Reply of the Most Illustrious Cardinall of Perron* (1630), she comments without false modesty that 'I will confesse, I thinke it well done, and so had I confest Sufficientlie in printing it'.[8]

It is particularly fortunate that *The Tragedy of Mariam* was not consigned to the 'Grave', for it contributes a crucial element to our understanding of Renaissance drama.[9] Not only does it offer, almost uniquely, a female perspective upon the role of authority within the state and marriage, but it also illuminates the way in which Senecan tragedy was being adapted to the confines of closet theatre. The play's immediate antecedent was Mary Sidney's *The Tragedy of Antonie* (1595), which was also written in Senecan mode, was similarly composed as a play to be read aloud and not acted, and also evoked more sympathy for, and understanding of, the female characters.[10] Nevertheless,

Sidney's work remains a translation, however loose, of Garnier's original. It is Elizabeth Cary who has provided us with the first original drama written in English by an Englishwoman.

For *Mariam* Cary's source text was Josephus' *Antiquities of the Jews*, which had been translated in 1602 by Thomas Lodge.[11] She follows the pattern of events quite closely, but makes alterations in accordance with her own thematic interests and the different generic demands of the dramatic form. For example, Cary emphasizes the Christian overtones of the play's last act by adding a description of how the Butler has hanged himself – making him a Judas-like figure. She elaborates on the personal feelings of her characters, especially Mariam, and alters Josephus' depiction of the queen as a coquettish shrew, in order to accentuate the protagonist's virtue. Finally, the protracted historical narrative is reduced to a single day and place (Jerusalem) in order to conform with the classical ideal of the dramatic unities. The play, therefore, simultaneously foregrounds Cary's particular interests – Christianity and the role of women – as well as situating her work within a broader dramatic discourse.

It is generally acknowledged that Cary's play is the first account of the Herod and Mariam tale to shift the focus from the evil king to the wronged queen.[12] In Act I Mariam is given the opening soliloquy, which allows the audience or reader to appreciate her inner conflict and her desires to be both a virtuous wife – that is obedient to her husband – and an opposer of tyranny. The play turns on Mariam's decision to confront Herod with the fact that he has murdered her brother and grandfather, and to adopt a passive resistance to his unjust rule. Although the play initially conforms to its classical forerunners, presenting Mariam's tragic flaw as her haughty inability to conceal her true feelings, it gradually shifts towards a Christian tradition, recalling Herod's function in medieval drama as the Christian oppressor, and conferring the role of Christian martyr onto Mariam herself.[13] In this way, what might initially appear to be a condemnation of female independence – after all, Mariam is executed at the end of the play – is transformed into an allegorical affirmation of individual virtue in the face of tyrannical oppression. There can be no doubt as to where our sympathies lie at the end of the play, and that we, like Herod, accept that Mariam's only flaw was in being too perfect, too virtuous: 'Her excellencies wrought her timeless fall' (V. 229).

Considering the prominence given to a virtuous woman's inner conflicts, it is reasonable to suggest that *Mariam* is, to a certain extent, based on Cary's own experiences. However, not only does the play explore marital discord through the characters of Mariam and Herod, it also underlines this subject by depicting the stormy relations between Salome and Constabarus. Even though Salome is condemned for her adulterous and shrewish behaviour, she is one of the liveliest characters in the play, and is given a convincing and impassioned plea for the right of women to divorce their husbands:

> Why should such privilege to man be given,
> Or given to them, why barred from women then?
> Are men, than we, in greater grace in heaven,
> Or cannot women hate as well as men?
> I'll be the custom-breaker, and begin
> To show my sex the way to freedom's door.
> (I. 305-10)[14]

In contrast, the meek Graphina dwindles into insignificance, despite the fact that she represents the Renaissance ideals of feminine behaviour – chaste, silent and obedient.[15] Rather than identifying Elizabeth Cary closely with Mariam, perhaps it is more accurate to read the author's concerns as emerging through several of the play's female characters. In one sadly prescient moment, however, Cary refers to Alexandra's denunciation of her daughter Mariam:

> She [Alexandra] said, she shamed to have a part in blood
> Of her [Mariam] that did the princely Herod wrong.
> (V. 43-4)

When Cary herself was disowned by her husband more than twenty years later, Lady Tanfield, her mother, adopted a similarly accusatory tone: 'I perceive by your last letters . . . that I shall never have hope to have any comfort from you. . . . My desire was . . . to have you to live with your husband, and to live in that religion wherein you were bred.'[16]

The autobiographical material which may be uncovered reveals a fascinating interplay between the real lives of Renaissance women and their representation in contemporary drama, but it must be considered alongside the play's dramatic inheritance and *Mariam*'s position in the history of Renaissance tragedy.

As has already been noted, *Mariam* is a Senecan drama, although it was not intended for performance in the public theatre and hence, like its classical source, it eschews on-stage violence. The play has more in common with the neo-Senecan closet dramas popular in Mary Sidney's circle, which included her own *The Tragedy of Antonie* (1592), Samuel Daniel's *Cleopatra* (1594 and 1607) and *Philotas* (1605), and Fulke Greville's *Mustapha* (1609-10).[17] Thematically, these plays explore the relationship of private desire to public life, and the destructive nature of authority when applied with arbitrary tyranny. Stylistically Cary also follows the Senecan mode, emphasizing the unities of time, place and theme, as well as employing quatrains with alternate rhymes.[18] In addition, there are similarities between the character of Queen Margaret in Shakespeare's *Henry VI, Part I* (1591–2) and *Richard III* (1593) and *Mariam*'s repudiated queen, Doris, as well as between the Moor's jealousy in *Othello* and the Hebrew's unfounded suspicions in Cary's drama.[19] *The Tragedy of Mariam*, therefore, needs to be read, not only as addressing concerns particular to women and to Cary herself, but as part of the overall development of Renaissance tragedy.

THE TEXT

This edition of *The Tragedy of Mariam* is based on the 1613 edition printed in London by Thomas Creede; we have used one of the three copies available at the British Library, although we have also drawn on the Harvard and Huntington copies which contain the dedicatory sonnet and character list not found in the British book. The play was written between 1602 and 1604, although not published until 1613, when *The Life* claims that the manuscript was stolen and published without Cary's permission.[20] The primary available edition has been A.C. Dunstan's scholarly one prepared for the Malone Society (1914), which was reissued in 1992 with a new introduction; references to this edition are made in the annotation. However, just before going to press we obtained a copy of Margaret Ferguson and Barry Weller's edition, *The Tragedy of Mariam, The Fair Queen of Jewry With The Lady Falkland: Her Life* (1994); we have used this edition where possible. It is important to note, in addition, that there are several other individual scholarly editions of *The Tragedy of Mariam* being prepared; they include ones by R. Valerie Lucas (publisher unknown), Dianne Purkiss for Pickering Women's Classics, and Stephanie Wright for Keele University Press. As with the other plays in this collection, we have modernized spelling and punctuation throughout. In addition, we have moved individual scene numbers to the left-hand margin of the text. This has been done to signify that Cary's breaks-of-scene do not require the usual changes of character or place, but often simply denote a new speaker, as is common in closet drama.

THE
TRAGEDIE
OF MARIAM,
THE FAIRE
Queene of Iewry.

VVritten by that learned,
vertuous, and truly noble Ladie,
E. C.

LONDON.
Printed by Thomas Creede, for Richard
Hawkins, and are to be solde at his shoppe
in Chancery Lane, neere vnto
Sargeants Inne.
1613.

5 First page of *The Tragedy of Mariam*, by kind permission of the British Library

The Tragedy of Mariam, The Fair Queen of Jewry

Written by that learned, virtuous, and truly noble lady
E[lizabeth] C[ary] [London, 1613]

To Diana's Earthly Deputress, and my worthy sister, Mistress Elizabeth Cary[1]

When cheerful Phoebus[2] his full course hath run,
His sister's fainter beams our hearts doth cheer;
So your fair brother is to me the sun,
And you his sister as my moon appear.
You are my next beloved, my second friend,
For when my Phoebus' absence makes it night,
Whilst to th'Antipodes[3] his beams do bend,
From you my Phoebe,[4] shines my second light.
He like to Sol,[5] clear-sighted, constant, free,
You Luna-like,[6] unspotted, chaste, divine;
He shone on Sicily,[7] you destined be
T'illumine[8] the now obscured Palestine.
My first was consecrated to Apollo,[9]
My second to Diana[10] now shall follow.
E[lizabeth] C[ary]

The Names of the Speakers

Herod, king of Judea
Doris, his first wife
Mariam, his second wife
Salome, Herod's sister
Antipater, his son by Doris[11]
Alexandra, Mariam's mother
Silleus, prince of Arabia
Constabarus, husband to Salome
Pheroras, Herod's brother
Graphina, his love
Babus' First Son
Babus' Second Son
Annanell, the high priest
Sohemus, a counsellor to Herod
Nuntio, a messenger
Butler, another messenger
Soldiers, Herod's guard[12]
Chorus, a company of Jews

The Argument

Herod, the son of Antipater (an Idumean),[13] having crept by the favour of the Romans into the Jewish monarchy, married Mariam, the daughter of Hyrcanus,[14] the rightful king and priest; and for her (besides her high blood, being of singular beauty) he repudiated Doris, his former wife by whom he had children.

This Mariam had a brother called Aristobolus, and next him and Hyrcanus his grandfather, Herod in his wife's right had the best title. Therefore to remove them, he charged the first with treason and put him to death, and drowned the second under colour of sport.[15] Alexandra, daughter to the one and mother to the other, accused him for their deaths before Anthony.[16]

So when he was forced to go answer this accusation at Rome, he left the custody of his wife to Josephus, his uncle, that had married his sister Salome. And out of a violent affection (unwilling any should enjoy her after him) he gave strict and private commandment that if he were slain, she should be put to death. But he returned with much honour, yet found his wife extremely discontented, to whom, Josephus had (meaning it for the best, to prove Herod loved her) revealed his charge.

So by Salome's accusation he put Josephus to death, but was reconciled to Mariam, who still bore the death of her friends exceedingly hard.

In the meantime Herod was again necessarily to revisit Rome, for Caesar[17] having overthrown Anthony, his great friend, was likely to make an alteration of his fortune.

In his absence news came to Jerusalem that Caesar had put him to death; their willingness that it should be so, together with the likelihood, gave this rumour so good credit, as Sohemus, that had succeeded Josephus' charge, succeeded him likewise in revealing it. So at Herod's return, which was speedy and unexpected, he found Mariam so far from joy that she showed apparent signs of sorrow. He, still desiring to win her to a better humour, she being very unable to conceal her passion, fell to upbraiding him with her brother's death. As they were thus debating, came in a fellow with a cup of wine, who hired by Salome said, first it was a love potion which Mariam desired to deliver to the king, but afterwards he affirmed that it was poison and that Sohemus had told her somewhat which procured the vehement hate in her.

The king hearing this, more moved with jealousy of Sohemus than with this intent of poison, sent her away, and presently, by the instigation of Salome, she was beheaded. Which rashness was afterward punished in him with an intolerable and almost frantic passion for her death.

Act I

[*Enter* CHORUS *who remain on stage throughout the play. Afterwards, enter centre stage*] MARIAM *alone.*

MARIAM

How oft have I with public voice run on,
To censure Rome's last hero for deceit
Because he[1] wept when Pompey's life was gone?
Yet, when he lived, he thought his name too great.
But now I do recant and Roman lord
Excuse, too rash a judgement in a woman,
My sex pleads pardon: pardon then afford,
Mistaking is with us, but too too common.
Now do I find, by self-experience taught,
One object yields both grief and joy.[2]
You wept indeed when on his worth you thought,
But joyed that slaughter did your foe destroy.
So at his death your eyes true drops did rain,
Whom dead, you did not wish alive again.
When Herod lived, that now is done to death,
Oft have I wished that I from him were free;
Oft have I wished that he might lose his breath;
Oft have I wished his carcass dead to see.
Then rage and scorn had put my love to flight,
That love which once on him was firmly set;
Hate hid his true affection from my sight
And kept my heart from paying him his debt.
And blame me not, for Herod's jealousy
Had power even constancy itself to change;
For he, by barring me from liberty,
To shun[3] my ranging,[4] taught me first to range.
But yet too chaste a scholar was my heart,
To learn to love another than my lord,
To leave his love, my lesson's former part,
I quickly learned; the other, I abhorred.
But now his death to memory doth call
The tender love that he to Mariam bare,[5]
And mine to him. This makes those rivers[6] fall,
Which by another thought unmoistened are,
For Aristobolus, the lowliest[7] youth
That ever did in angel's shape appear,
The cruel Herod was not moved to ruth.[8]
Then why grieve Mariam, Herod's death to hear?
Why joy I not? The tongue no more shall speak
that yielded forth my brother's latest doom.
Both youth and beauty might thy fury break,
And both in him did ill befit a tomb.
And, worthy grandsire ill did he requite,
His high assent alone by thee procured;
Except he murdered thee to free the sprite[9]
Which still he thought on earth too long immured.[10]
How happy was it that Sohemus' mind[11]
Was moved to pity my distressed estate.
Might Herod's life a trusty servant find,
My death to his had been unseparate.[12]
These thoughts have power his death to make me bear,
Nay more, to wish the news may firmly hold.
Yet cannot this repulse some falling tear
That will against my will some grief unfold?
And more I owe him for his love to me,
The deepest love that ever yet was seen.
Yet had I rather much a milkmaid be,
Than be the monarch of Judea's queen.
It was for nought but love, he wished his end
Might to my death but the vaunt-currier[13] prove.
But I had rather still be foe then friend
To him that saves for hate and kills for love.
Hard-hearted Mariam, at thy discontent
What floods of tears have drenched his manly face?
How canst thou then so faintly now lament
Thy truest lover's death, a death's disgrace?
Ay, now mine eyes you do begin to right
The wrongs of your admirer and my Lord,
Long since you should have put your smiles to flight,
Ill doth a widowed eye with joy accord.
Why now methinks the love I bore him then,
When virgin freedom left me unrestrained,
Doth to my heart begin to creep again;
My passion now is far from being feigned.
But, tears, fly back and hide you in your banks,
You must not be to Alexandra seen;
For if my moan be spied,[14] but little thanks
Shall Mariam have, from that incensed queen.

[*Enter*] ALEXANDRA.

ALEXANDRA

What means these tears? My Mariam doth mistake
The news we heard did tell the tyrant's end.
What weep'st thou for thy brother's murthrer's[15] sake?
Will ever wight[16] a tear for Herod spend?
My curse pursue his breathless trunk and spirit,

Base Edomite[17] the damned Esau's heir!
Must he, ere Jacob's child,[18] the crown inherit?
Must he, vile wretch, be set in David's chair?[19]
No, David's soul within the bosom placed
Of our forefather Abraham was ashamed
To see his seat with such a toad disgraced,
That seat that hath by Juda's race[20] been
famed.[21]
Thou fatal enemy to royal blood,
Did not the murder of my boy suffice
To stop thy cruel mouth that gaping stood?
But must thou dim the mild Hyrcanus'[22] eyes,
My gracious father, whose too ready hand
Did lift this Idumean from the dust,
And he, ungrateful caitiff,[23] did withstand
The man that did in him most friendly trust?
What kingdom's right could cruel Herod claim,
Was he not Esau's issue, heir of hell?
Then what succession can he have but shame?
Did not his ancestor his birthright sell?
O yes, he doth from Edom's name[24] derive
His cruel nature which with blood is fed;
That made him me of sire and son deprive.
He ever thirsts for blood, and blood is red.
Weepst thou because his love to thee was bent?[25]
And read'st thou love in crimson characters?
Slew he thy friends to work thy heart's content?
No, Hate may justly call that action hers.
He gave the sacred priesthood for thy sake
To Aristobolus, yet doomed him dead
Before his back the ephod[26] warm could make
And ere the mitre settled on his head.
Oh, had he given my boy no less than right,
The double oil should to his forehead bring
A double honour, shining doubly bright –
His birth anointed him both priest and king.
And, say my father and my son he slew
To royalize by right your prince-born breath.
Was love the cause – can Mariam deem it true –
That Mariam[27] gave commandment for her
death?
I know by fits[28] he showed some signs of love,
And yet not love, but raging lunacy;
And this his hate to thee may justly prove –
That sure he hates Hyrcanus' family.
Who knows if he, unconstant wavering lord,
His love to Doris had renewed again,
And that he might his bed to her afford?
Perchance[29] he wished that Mariam might be
slain.

MARIAM[30]

Doris, alas her time of love was passed,
Those coals were raked in embers long ago:
If Mariam's love, and she, was now disgraced,
Nor did I glory in her overthrow.
He not a whit[31] his first-born son esteemed,
Because as well as his, he was not mine;
My children only for his own he deemed.
These boys that did descend from royal line,
These did he style his heirs to David's throne;
My Alexander, if he live, shall sit
In the majestic seat of Solomon;[32]
To will it so did Herod think it fit.

ALEXANDRA

Why? Who can claim from Alexander's[33] brood
That gold-adorned lion-guarded chair?
Was Alexander not of David's blood,
And was not Mariam Alexander's heir?
What more than right could Herod then bestow,
And who will think, except for more than right,
He did not raise them for they were not low,
But born to wear the crown in his despite.[34]
Then send those tears away that are not sent
To thee by reason. But by passion's power
Thine eyes to cheer, thy cheeks to smiles be
bent,
And entertain with joy this happy hour!
Felicity,[35] if when she comes, she finds
A mourning habit[36] and a cheerless look,
Will think she is not welcome to thy mind,
And so perchance her lodging will not brook.[37]
Oh, keep her whilst thou hast her; if she go
She will not easily return again.
Full many a year have I endured in woe,
Yet still have sued her presence to obtain;
And did not I to her, as presents, send
A table,[38] that best art did beautify,
Of two[39] to whom heaven did best feature lend,
To woo her love by winning Anthony?
For when a prince's favour we do crave,
We first their minions'[40] loves do seek to win;
So I, that sought Felicity to have,
Did with her minion Anthony begin.
With double slight I sought to captivate
The warlike lover – but I did not right,
For, if my gift had borne[41] but half the rate,
The Roman had been overtaken quite.
But now he fared like a hungry guest,
That to some plenteous[42] festival is gone:
Now this, now that, he deems[43] to eat were best;
Such choice doth make him let them all alone.
The boy's large forehead first did fairest seem,
Then glanced his eye upon my Mariam's
cheek
And that without comparison did deem;
What was in either but he most did like.[44]
And thus distracted, either's beauty's might
Within the other's excellence was drowned:
Too much delight did bear him from delight,
For either's love, the other's did confound.

Where, if thy portraiture had only gone,[45]
His life from Herod, Anthony had taken;
He would have loved thee, and thee alone,
And left the brown Egyptian clean forsaken.
And Cleopatra[46] then to seek had been
So firm a lover of her waned[47] face;
Then great Anthonius' fall we had not seen,
By her that fled to have him hold the chase.
Then Mariam in a Roman's chariot set,
In place of Cleopatra might have shown
A mart[48] of beauties in her visage met,
And part[49] in this, that they were all her own.

MARIAM
Not to be empress of aspiring Rome
Would Mariam like to Cleopatra live.
With purest body will I press my tomb,
And with no favours Anthony could give.

ALEXANDRA
Let us retire us,[50] that we may resolve
How now to deal in this reversed state.
Great are the affairs which we now must revolve,
And great affairs must not be taken late.

[*Enter*] SALOME.

SALOME
More plotting yet? Why, now you have the thing
For which so oft you spent your suppliant
breath.
And Mariam hopes to have another king,
Her eyes do sparkle joy for Herod's death.

ALEXANDRA
If she desired another king to have,
She might, before she came in Herod's bed,
Have had her wish. More kings than one did
crave
For leave to set a crown upon her head.
I think with more than reason she laments,
That she is freed from such a sad annoy –
Who is't[51] will weep to part from discontents?[52]–
And, if she joy, she did not causeless joy.

SALOME
You durst not thus have given your tongue the
rein
If noble Herod still remained in life.
Your daughter's betters far, I dare maintain,
Might have rejoiced to be my brother's wife.

MARIAM
My betters far! Base woman, 'tis untrue,
You scarce have ever my superiors seen,
For Mariam's servants were as good as you
Before she came to be Judea's queen.

SALOME
Now stirs the tongue that is so quickly moved;
But more than once your choler[53] I have born,
Your fumish[54] words are sooner said than proved,
And Salome's reply is only scorn.

MARIAM
Scorn those that are for thy companions held!
Though I thy brother's face had never seen,
My birth thy baser birth so far excelled
I had to both of you the princess been.
Thou parti-Jew and parti-Edomite,[55]
Thou mongrel, issued from rejected race!
Thy ancestors against the heavens did fight,
And thou, like them, will heavenly birth
disgrace.

SALOME
Still twit[56] you me with nothing but my birth,
What odds betwixt your ancestors and mine?
Both born of Adam,[57] both were made of earth,
And both did come from holy Abraham's line.

MARIAM
I favour thee when nothing else I say.
With thy black acts I'll not pollute my breath,
Else, to thy charge I might full justly lay
A shameful life, besides a husband's death.

SALOME
'Tis true indeed, I did the plots reveal
That passed betwixt your favourites and you;
I meant not, I, a traitor to conceal.
Thus Salome, your minion Joseph, slew.

MARIAM
Heaven, dost thou mean this infamy to smother?
Let slandered Mariam ope[58] thy closed ear:
Self-guilt hath ever been Suspicion's[59] mother,
And therefore I this speech with patience bear.
No, had not Salome's unsteadfast heart
In Joseph's[60] stead her Constabarus placed
To free herself, she had not used the art
To slander hapless Mariam for unchaste.

ALEXANDRA
Come, Mariam, let us go. It is no boot[61]
To let the head contend against the foot.

[*Exeunt* MARIAM *and* ALEXANDRA.]

SALOME
Lives Salome to get so base a style
As foot to the proud Mariam? Herod's spirit
In happy time for her endured exile,
For did he live, she should not miss her merit.
But he is dead, and though he were my brother,
His death such store of cinders cannot cast
My coals of love to quench; for though they
smother
The flames awhile, yet will they out at last.
Oh blest Arabia, in best climate placed,
I by the fruit will censure[62] of the tree;[63]
'Tis not in vain thy happy name thou hast
If all Arabians like Silleus be;
Had not my fate been too, too contrary
When I on Constabarus first did gaze,
Silleus had been object to mine eye,

Whose looks and personage must all eyes[64]
amaze.
But now ill-fated Salome, thy tongue
To Constabarus by itself is tied;
And now, except I do the Hebrew wrong,
I cannot be the fair Arabian bride.
What childish lets[65] are these? What stand I now
On honourable points?[66] 'Tis long ago
Since shame was written on my tainted brow,[67]
And certain 'tis, that shame is honour's foe.
Had I upon my reputation stood,
Had I affected an unspotted life,
Joseph's veins had still been stuffed with blood
And I to him had lived a sober wife.
Then had I never cast an eye of love
On Constabarus' now detested face;
Then had I kept my thoughts without remove,
And blushed at motion of the least disgrace.
But shame is gone and honour wiped away,
And Impudency on my forehead sits;
She bids me work my will without delay,
And for my will, I will employ my wits.
He loves, I love: what then can be the cause
Keeps me for being the Arabian's wife?
Is it the principles of Moses' laws?
For Constabarus still remains in life.
If he to me did bear as earnest hate,
As I to him, for him there were an ease:
A separating bill[68] might free his fate
From such a yoke that did so much displease.
Why should such privilege to man be given,
Or given to them, why barred from women
then?
Are men, than we, in greater grace in heaven,
Or cannot women hate as well as men?
I'll be the custom-breaker, and begin
To show my sex the way to freedom's
door;[69]
And with an offering will I purge my sin;
The law was made for none but who are poor.
If Herod had lived, I might to him accuse
My present lord, but for the future's sake,
Then would I tell the king he did refuse
The sons of Baba[70] in his power to take.[71]
But now I must divorce him from my bed,
That my Silleus may possess his room.[72]
Had I not begged his life he had been dead;[73]
I curse my tongue, the hinderer of his doom!
But then my wand'ring heart to him was fast,[74]
Nor did I dream of change. Silleus said
He would be here, and see he comes at last.
Had I not named him, longer had he stayed.
[*Enter*] SILLEUS.

SILLEUS

Well found fair Salome, Judea's pride.
Hath thy innated[75] wisdom found the way
To make Silleus deem him deified
By gaining thee, a more than precious, prey?

SALOME

I have devised the best I can devise;
A more imperfect means was never found.
But what cares Salome, it does suffice
If our endeavours with their end be crowned.
In this our land we have an ancient use
Permitted first by our law-giver's[76] head:
Who hates his wife, though for no just abuse,
May with a bill divorce her from his bed.
But in this custom women are not free.
Yet, I for once will wrest it – blame not thou
The ill I do, since what I do's[77] for thee,
Though others blame, Silleus should allow.

SILLEUS[78]

Thinks Salome, Silleus hath a tongue
To censure her fair actions? Let my blood
Bedash[79] my proper brow, for such a wrong,
The being yours, can make even vices good.
Arabia, joy! Prepare thy earth with green,
Thou never happy were indeed till now,
Now shall thy ground be trod by beauty's
queen;
Her foot is destined to depress thy brow.
Thou shall, fair Salome, command as much
As if the royal ornament[80] were thine:
The weakness of Arabia's king is such,
The kingdom is not his so much as mine.
My mouth is our Oboda's oracle,[81]
Who thinks not aught but what Silleus will.
And thou rare creature, Asia's miracle,
Shalt be to me as it, Oboda's still.[82]

SALOME

'Tis not for glory I thy love accept,
Judea yields me honour's worthy store;
Had not affection in my bosom crept
My native country should my life deplore.
Were not Silleus he with whom[83] I go,
I would not change my Palestine for Rome,
Much less would I a glorious state to show,
Go far to purchase an Arabian tomb.

SILLEUS

Far be it from Silleus so to think.
I know it is thy gratitude requites
The love that is in me, and shall not shrink
Till death do sever me from earth's delights.

SALOME

But whist,[84] methinks the wolf is in our talk![85]
Be gone Silleus. Who doth here arrive?
'Tis Constabarus that doth hither walk;
I'll find a quarrel, him from me to drive.

SILLEUS

Farewell, but were it not for thy command,

In his despite, Silleus here would stand.
[*Exit* SILLEUS *and enter*] CONSTABARUS.

CONSTABARUS

Oh Salome, how much you wrong your name,
Your race, your country, and your husband most!
A stranger's private conference is shame;
I blush for you, that have your blushing lost.
Oft have I found, and found you to my grief,
Consorted with this base Arabian here;
Heaven knows that you have been my comfort chief,
Then do not now my greater plague appear.
Now, by the stately carved edifice
That on Mount Sion[86] makes so fair a show
And by the altar fit for sacrifice,
I love thee more than thou thy self dost know.
Oft with a silent sorrow have I heard
How ill Judea's mouth doth censure thee,
And did I not thine honour much regard,
Thou shouldst not be exhorted thus for me.
Didst thou but know the worth of honest fame,
How much a virtuous woman is esteemed,
Thou wouldst like hell eschew deserved shame,
And seek to be both chaste and chastely deemed.
Our wisest prince did say, and true he said:
A virtuous woman crowns her husband's head.[87]

SALOME

Did I for this uprear thy low estate!
Did I for this requital beg thy life,
That thou hadst forfeited?[88] Hapless fate,
To be to such a thankless wretch the wife!
This hand of mine hath lifted up thy head,
Which many a day ago had fallen full low
Because the sons of Baba[89] are not dead –
To me thou dost both life and fortune owe.

CONSTABARUS

You have my patience often exercised;
Use make my choler keep within the banks.[90]
Yet boast no more, but be by me advised:
A benefit upbraided forfeits thanks.
I prithee Salome, dismiss this mood,
Thou dost not know how ill it fits thy place.
My words were all intended for thy good,
To raise thine honour and to stop disgrace.

SALOME

To stop disgrace? Take thou no care for me!
Nay, do thy worst; thy worst I set not by.[91]
No shame of mine is like to light on thee,
Thy love and admonitions I defy.
Thou shalt no hour longer call me wife,
Thy jealousy procures my hate so deep,
That I from thee do mean to free my life
By a divorcing bill before I sleep.

CONSTABARUS

Are Hebrew women now transformed to men?[92]
Why do you not as well our battles fight
And wear our armour? Suffer this, and then
Let all the world be topsy-turveyed[93] quite!
Let fishes graze, beasts swim,[94] and birds descend;
Let fire burn downwards while the earth aspires;[95]
Let winter's heat and summer's cold offend;
Let thistles grow on vines, and grapes on briars;
Set us to spin or sew, or, at the best,
Make us wood-hewers, water-bearing wights,[96]
For sacred service let us take no rest,
Use us as Joshua did the Gibeonites![97]

SALOME

Hold on your talk till it be time to end.
For me, I am resolved it shall be so,
Though I be first that to this course do bend,
I shall not be the last, full well I know.

CONSTABARUS

Why then, be witness heaven, the judge of sins;
Be witness spirits that eschew the dark;
Be witness angels; witness cherubins,
Whose semblance sits upon the holy ark;[98]
Be witness earth; be witness Palestine;
Be witness David's city – if my heart
Did ever merit such an act of thine,
Or if the fault be mine that makes us part.
Since mildest Moses, friend unto the Lord,
Did work his wonders in the land of Ham[99]
And slew the first-born babes without a sword
In sign whereof we eat the holy lamb,[100]
Till now, that fourteen hundred years are passed
Since first the Law[101] with us hath been in force:
You are the first and will, I hope, be last
That ever sought her husband to divorce.

SALOME

I mean not to be led by precedent;
My will shall be to me instead of law.

CONSTABARUS

I fear me much, you will too late repent
That you have ever lived so void of awe.
This is Silleus' love that makes you thus
Reserve all order – you must next be his.
But if my thoughts aright the cause discuss,
In winning you he gains no lasting bliss.
I was Silleus, and not long ago,
Josephus then was Constabarus now.
When you became my friend you proved his foe,
As now for him you break to me your vow.[102]

SALOME

If once I loved you, greater is your debt,
For certain 'tis that you deserved it not.
And undeserved love we soon forget,

And therefore that, to me, can be no blot.
But now fare ill[103] my once-beloved lord;
Yet never more beloved, than now abhorred.
[*Exit.*]

CONSTABARUS

Yet Constabarus biddeth thee farewell.
Farewell, light creature. Heaven forgive thy sin.
My prophesying spirit doth foretell
Thy wavering thoughts do yet but new begin.
Yet I have better 'scaped then Josephus did;
But if our Herod's death had been delayed,
The valiant youths that I so long have hid
Had been by her, and I for them, betrayed.
Therefore, in happy hour did Caesar give
The fatal blow to wanton Anthony;
For had he lived, our Herod then should live,
But great Anthonius' death made Herod die.
Had he enjoyed his breath, not I alone
Had been in danger of a deadly fall;
But Mariam had the way of peril gone,
Though by the tyrant most beloved of all.
The sweet-faced Mariam, as free from guilt
As heaven from spots; yet had her lord come back
Her purest blood had been unjustly spilt.
And Salome it was would work her wrack.[104]
Though all Judea yield her innocent,
She often hath been near to punishment. [*Exit.*]

CHORUS

Those minds that wholly dote upon delight,
Except they only joy in inward good;
Still hope at last to hop upon[105] the right,
And so from sand they leap in loathsome mud.
Fond[106] wretches seeking what they cannot find,
For no content[107] attends a wavering mind.

If wealth they do desire, and wealth attain,
Then wondrous, fain[108] would they to honour lep;[109]
If[110] mean degree they do in honour gain,
They would but with a little higher step.
Thus step to step, and wealth to wealth they add,
Yet cannot all their plenty make them glad.

Yet oft we see that some in humble state,
Are cheerful, pleasant, happy and content;
When those indeed that are of higher state,
With vain additions do their thoughts torment.
Th'one would to his mind his fortune bind,
Th'other to his fortune frames his mind.

To wish variety is sign of grief,
For if you like your state as now it is,
Why should an alteration bring relief?
Nay, change would then be feared as loss of bliss.
That man is only happy in his fate,
That is delighted in a settled state.

Still, Mariam wished she from her lord were free,
For expectation of variety;
Yet, now she sees her wishes prosperous be,
She grieves, because her lord so soon did die.
Who can those vast imaginations feed,
Where in a property, contempt doth breed.

Were Herod now perchance to live again,
She would again as much be grieved at that;
All that she may, she ever doth disdain,
Her wishes guide her to she knows not what.
And sad must be their looks, their honour sour,
That care for nothing being in their power.

Act II

[*Enter*] PHERORAS *and* GRAPHINA.[1]

PHERORAS

'Tis true, Graphina, now the time draws nigh
Wherein the holy priest with hallowed rite
The happy, long-desired, knot shall tie,
Pheroras and Graphina to unite;
How oft have I with lifted hands implored
This blessed hour, till now implored in vain,
Which hath my wished liberty restored
And made my subject self my own again.
Thy love fair maid upon mine eye doth sit,
Whose nature hot doth dry the moisture all,[2]
Which were in nature and in reason fit
For my monarchal brother's death to fall.
Had Herod lived he would have plucked my hand
From fair Graphina's palm perforce,[3] and tied
The same in hateful and despised band –
For I had had a baby to my bride;[4]
Scarce can her infant tongue with easy voice
Her name distinguish to another's ear.
Yet had he lived, his power and not my choice,
Had made me solemnly the contract swear.
Have I not cause in such a change to joy?
What? Though she be my niece, a princess born,
Near blood's without respect, high birth a toy,
Since love can teach us[5] blood and kindred's scorn.
What booted[6] it that he did raise my head,
To be his realm's co-partner, kingdom's mate,
Withal[7] he kept Graphina from my bed,

More wished by me than thrice Judea's state.
Oh, could not he be skilful judge in love,
That doted so upon his Mariam's face?
He, for his passion, Doris did remove.
I need not a lawful wife displace.
It could not be but he had power to judge,
But, he that never grudged[8] a kingdom's share,
This well-known happiness to me did grudge,
And meant to be therein without compare;
Else had I been his equal in Love's host.[9]
For though the diadem on Mariam's head
Corrupt the vulgar judgements, I will boast
Graphina's brow as white, her cheeks as red.
Why speak thou not fair creature? Move thy tongue,
For silence is a sign of discontent;
It were to both our loves too great a wrong
If now this hour do find thee sadly bent.[10]

GRAPHINA

Mistake me not, my lord, too oft have I
Desired this time to come with winged feet,
To be enwrapped with grief when 'tis too nigh;
You know my wishes ever yours did meet.
If I be silent, 'tis no more but fear
That I should say too little when I speak;
But since you will my imperfections bear,
In spite of doubt I will my silence break.
Yet, might amazement tie my moving tongue,
But that I know before Pheroras' mind;
I have admired[11] your affection long
And cannot yet therein a reason find.
Your hand hath lifted me from lowest state
To highest eminency, wondrous grace;
And me, your handmaid, have you made your mate,
Though all but you alone do count me base.
You have preserved me pure at my request,
Though you so weak a vassal[12] might constrain
To yield to your high will. Then last, not best,
In my respect a princess you disdain.
Then need not all these favours study crave,[13]
To be requited[14] by a simple maid?
And study[15] still you know must silence have;
Then be my cause for silence justly weighed.
But study cannot boot, nor I requite,
Except your lowly handmaid's steadfast love
And fast[16] obedience may your mind delight;
I will not promise more then I can prove.

PHERORAS

That study needs not. Let Graphina smile,
And I desire no greater recompense.
I cannot vaunt[17] me in a glorious style,
Nor show my love in far-fetched eloquence;
But this believe me – never Herod's heart
Hath held his prince-born, beauty-famed wife
In nearer place, than thou fair virgin art
To him that holds the glory of his life.
Should Herod's body leave the sepulchre
And entertain[18] the severed ghost again,
He should not be my nuptial hinderer,
Except he hindered it with dying pain.
Come, fair Graphina, let us go in state
This wish-endeared time to celebrate. [*Exeunt.*]

[*Enter*] CONSTABARUS *and* BABUS' SONS.

BABUS' FIRST SON

Now, valiant friend, you have our lives redeemed,
Which lives, as saved by you, to you are due;
Command and you shall see yourself esteemed,
Our lives and liberties belong to you.
This twice six years, with hazard of your life,
You have concealed us from the tyrant's sword;
Though cruel Herod's sister were your wife,
You durst[19] in scorn of fear this grace afford.
In recompense we know not what to say,
A poor reward were thanks for such a merit,
Our truest friendship at your feet we lay –
The best requital to a noble spirit.

CONSTABARUS

Oh how you wrong our friendship, valiant youth,
With friends there is not such a word as debt;
Where amity is tied with bond of truth
All benefits are there in common set.
Then is the Golden Age[20] with them renewed,
All names of properties are banished quite,
Division and distinction are eschewed,
Each hath to what belongs to others right.
And 'tis not sure so full a benefit,
Freely to give, as freely[21] to require.
A bounteous act hath glory following it;
They cause the glory that the act desire.
All friendship should the pattern imitate
Of Jesse's son and valiant Jonathan,[22]
For neither sovereign's, nor father's hate,
A friendship fixed on virtue sever can.
Too much of this; 'tis written in the heart
And need no amplifying with the tongue.
Now may you from your living tomb depart,
Where Herod's life hath kept you over long.
Too great an injury to a noble mind
To be quick buried.[23] You had purchased[24] fame
Some years ago, but that you were confined,
While thousand meaner did advance their name.
Your best of life, the prime of all your years,
Your time of action, is from you bereft.
Twelve winters have you overpassed in fears;
Yet, if you use it well, enough is left,

And who can doubt but you will use it well?
The sons of Babus have it by descent
In all their thoughts each action to excell,
Boldly to act and wisely to invent.

BABUS' SECOND SON

Had it not like the hateful cuckoo been,
Whose riper age his infant nurse doth kill,[25]
So long we had not kept ourselves unseen,
But Constabarus safely[26] crossed our will.
For had the tyrant fixed his cruel eye
On our concealed faces, wrath had swayed
His justice so, that he had forced us die.
And dearer price than life we should have paid,
For you, our truest friend, had fallen with us;
And we, much like a house on pillars set,
Had clean depressed our prop; and therefore, thus
Our ready will with our concealment met.
But now that you, fair lord, are dangerless,
The sons of Baba[27] shall their rigour show
And prove it was not baseness did oppress
Our hearts so long, but honour kept them low.

BABUS' FIRST SON

Yet do I fear this tale of Herod's death
At last will prove a very tale indeed;
It gives me strongly in my mind,[28] his breath
Will be preserved to make a number bleed.
I wish not, therefore, to be set at large;[29]
Yet peril to myself I do not fear.[30]
Let us for some days longer be your charge
Till we of Herod's state the truth do hear.

CONSTABARUS

What, art thou turned a coward, noble youth,
That thou beginst to doubt, undoubted truth?

BABUS' FIRST SON

Were it my brother's tongue that cast this doubt,
I from his heart would have the question out
With this keen falchion![31] But 'tis you, my lord,
Against whose head I must not lift a sword,
I am so tied in gratitude.

CONSTABARUS

Believe
You have no cause to take it ill.[32]
If any word of mine your heart did grieve,
The word dissented from the speaker's will.
I know it was not fear the doubt begun,[33]
But rather valour, and your care of me;
A coward could not be your father's son.
Yet know I doubts unnecessary be;
For who can think that in Anthonius' fall,
Herod, his bosom friend, should 'scape unbruised?
Then, Caesar, we might thee an idiot call,
If thou by him should'st be so far abused.

BABUS' SECOND SON

Lord Constabarus, let me tell you this:
Upon submission Caesar will forgive,
And therefore, though the tyrant did amiss,
It may fall out that he will let him live.
Not many years ago it is since I
Directed thither by my father's care,
In famous Rome for twice twelve months did lie,[34]
My life from Hebrew's cruelty to spare.
There, though I were but yet of boyish age,
I bent mine eye to mark, mine ears to hear.
Where I did see Octavius,[35] then a page,
When first he did to Julian's[36] sight appear;
Methought I saw such mildness in his face
And such a sweetness in his looks did grow,
Withall commixed with so majestic grace,
His physiognomy,[37] his fortune did foreshow.
For this I am indebted to mine eye,
But then mine ear received more evidence,
By that I knew his love to clemency,
How he with hottest choler[38] could dispense.

CONSTABARUS

But we have more than barely heard the news;
It hath been twice confirmed. And though some tongue
Might be so false, with false report t'abuse,
A false report hath never lasted long.
But be it so that Herod have his life,
Concealment would not then a whit avail;
For certain 'tis, that she that was my wife,
Would not so let[39] her accusation fail.
And therefore, now, as good the venture give
And free ourselves from blot of cowardice;
As show a pitiful desire to live,
For, who can pity, but they must despise?

BABUS' FIRST SON

I yield. But to necessity I yield.
I dare upon this doubt engage my arm
That Herod shall again this kingdom wield
And prove his death to be a false alarm.

BABUS' SECOND SON

I doubt it too, God grant it be an error;
'Tis best without a cause to be in terror,
And rather had I, though my soul be mine,
My soul should lie, than prove a true divine.[40]

CONSTABARUS

Come, come, let fear go seek a dastard's[41] nest,
Undaunted courage lies in a noble breast![42]

[*Exeunt.*]

[*Enter*] DORIS *and* ANTIPATER.

DORIS

You[43] royal buildings bow your lofty side
And scope[44] to her that is by right your queen,
Let your humility upbraid the pride

Of those in whom no due respect is seen.
Nine times have we with trumpets' haughty sound
And banishing sour leaven from our taste,
Observed the feast[45] that takes the fruit from ground,
Since I, fair city, did behold thee last.
So long it is since Mariam's purer cheek
Did rob from mine the glory. And so long
Since I returned my native town to seek;
And with me nothing but the sense of wrong.
And thee my boy, whose birth though great it were
Yet have thy after-fortunes proved but poor,
When thou wert born, how little did I fear
Thou should'st be thrust from forth thy father's door.
Art thou not Herod's right begotten son?
Was not the hapless Doris, Herod's wife?
Yes, ere[46] he had the Hebrew kingdom won,
I was companion to his private life.
Was I not fair enough to be a queen?
Why, ere thou were to me, false monarch, tied,
My lake of beauty might as well be seen
As after I had lived five years thy bride.
Yet then thine oaths[47] came pouring like the rain,
Which all affirmed my face without compare;
And that if thou might'st Doris' love obtain,
For all the world besides thou didst not care.
Then was I young, and rich, and nobly born,
And therefore worthy to be Herod's mate.
Yet thou ungrateful cast me off with scorn,
When heaven's purpose raised your meaner fate.
Oft have I begged for vengeance for this fact,
And with dejected knees,[48] aspiring hands,
Have prayed the highest power to enact
The fall of her that on my trophy stands.
Revenge I have according to my will,
Yet where I wished, this vengeance did not light.
I wished it should high-hearted Mariam kill,
But it against my whilom[49] lord did fight.
With thee, sweet boy, I came, and came to try
If thou before his bastards might be placed
In Herod's royal seat and dignity.
But Mariam's infants here are only graced,
And now for us there doth no hope remain.
Yet we will not return till Herod's end
Be more confirmed; perchance he is not slain.
So glorious fortunes may my boy attend;
For if he live, he'll think it doth suffice
That he to Doris shows such cruelty.
For as he did my wretched life despise,
So do I know I shall despised die.
Let him but prove as natural to thee,
As cruel to thy miserable mother,
His cruelty shall not upbraided be;
But in thy fortunes I his faults will smother.

ANTIPATER

Each mouth within the city loudly cries
That Herod's death is certain: therefore we
Had best some subtle hidden plot devise,
That Mariam's children might subverted be,
By poison's drink, or else by murderous knife,
So we may be advanced, it skills not how;[50]
They are but bastards, you were Herod's wife,
And foul adultery blotteth Mariam's brow.

DORIS

They are too strong to be by us removed,
Or else revenge's foulest spotted face
By our detested wrongs might be approved;
But weakness must to greater power give place.
But let us now retire to grieve alone,
For solitariness best fitteth moan. [*Exeunt.*]

[*Enter*] SILLEUS *and* CONSTABARUS.

SILLEUS

Well met Judean Lord, the only wight
Silleus wished to see. I am to call
Thy tongue to strict account.

CONSTABARUS

For what despite?
I ready am to hear, and answer all.
But if directly at the cause I guess,
That breeds this challenge, you must pardon me,
And now some other ground of fight profess,
For I have vowed, vows must unbroken be.

SILLEUS

What may be your exception?[51] Let me know.

CONSTABARUS

Why, aught[52] concerning Salome.[53] My sword
Shall not be wielded for a cause so low;
A blow for her my arm will scorn t'afford.

SILLEUS

It is for slandering her unspotted name!
And I will make thee in thy vows' despite
Suck up the breath that did my mistress blame,
And swallow it again to do her right.

CONSTABARUS

I prithee give some other quarrel ground
To find beginning: rail against my name,
Or strike me first, or let some scarlet wound
Inflame my courage, give me words of shame,
Do thou our Moses' sacred laws disgrace,
Deprave our nation, do me some despite –
I'm apt[54] enough to fight in any case.
But yet, for Salome I will not fight.

SILLEUS

Nor I for ought but Salome. My sword

That owes his service to her sacred name
Will not an edge for other cause afford;
In other fight I am not sure of fame.

CONSTABARUS
For her, I pity thee enough already.
For her, I therefore will not mangle[55] thee.
A woman with a heart so most unsteady,[56]
Will of her self sufficient torture be.
I cannot envy[57] for so light a gain;
Her mind with such inconstancy doth run,
As with a word thou didst her love obtain;
So with a word, she will from thee be won.
So light, as her possessions for most day,
Is her affections lost: to me 'tis known.
As good go hold the wind as make her stay;[58]
She never loves, but till she call her own.
She merely is a painted sepulchre,[59]
That is both fair and vilely foul at once:
Though on her outside graces garnish her,
Her mind is filled[60] with worse than rotten bones.[61]
And ever ready lifted is her hand
To aim destruction at a husband's throat.
For proofs, Josephus and myself do stand,
Though once on both of us she seemed to dote.
Her mouth, though serpent-like it never hisses,
Yet like a serpent poisons where it kisses.

SILLEUS
Well, Hebrew, well; thou bark'st but will not bite.

CONSTABARUS
I tell thee still, for her I will not fight.

SILLEUS
Why then I call thee coward!

CONSTABARUS
From my heart
I give thee thanks. A coward's hateful name
Cannot to valiant minds a blot impart,
And therefore I with joy receive the same.
Thou know'st I am no coward; thou wert by
At the Arabian battle th'other day
And saw'st my sword with daring valiancy,
Amongst the faint Arabians cut my way.
The blood of foes no more could let it shine,
As 'twas enamelled with some of thine.
But now, have at thee! Not for Salome
I fight, but to discharge a coward's style:[62]
Here 'gins[63] the fight that shall not parted be
Before a soul or two endure exile.
[*They fight.*]

SILLEUS
Thy sword hath made some windows for my blood
To show a horrid crimson physnomy.[64]
To breath, for both of us, methinks 'twere good;
The day will give us time enough to die.

CONSTABARUS
With all my heart take breath. Thou shalt have time
And, if thou list,[65] a twelve month. Let us end.
Into thy cheeks there doth a paleness climb,
Thou canst not from my sword thy self defend.
What needest thou for Salome to fight?
Thou hast her, and may'st keep her. None strives for her;[66]
I willingly to thee resign my right,
For in my very soul I do abhor her.
Thou seest that I am fresh, unwounded yet;
Then not for fear, I do this offer make.
Thou art with loss of blood, to fight unfit,
For here is one, and there another take.

SILLEUS
I will not leave, as long as breath remains
Within my wounded body. Spare your words.
My heart, in blood's stead, courage entertains;
Salome's love no place for fear affords.

CONSTABARUS
Oh, could thy soul but prophesy like mine,
I would not wonder thou should'st long to die:
For Salome, if I aright divine,[67]
Will be, than death, a greater misery.

SILLEUS
Then list:[68] I'll breath[69] no longer.

CONSTABARUS
Do thy will:
I hateless fight, and charitably kill.
They fight [*and* CONSTABARUS *continues to dominate*].[70]
Pity thyself Silleus, let not death
Intrude before his time into thy heart.
Alas, it is too late to fear; his breath
Is from his body now about to part.
How far'st thou brave Arabian?

SILLEUS
Very well.
My leg is hurt, I can no longer fight;
It only grieves me, that so soon I fell,
Before fair Salom's wrongs I came to right.

CONSTABARUS
Thy wounds are less than mortal. Never fear,
Thou shalt a safe and quick recovery find.
Come, I will thee unto my lodging bear;
I hate thy body, but I love thy mind.

SILLEUS
Thanks noble Jew, I see a courteous foe;
Stern enmity to friendship can no art.[71]
Had not my heart and tongue engaged me so,
I would from thee no foe, but friend, depart.
My heart to Salome is tied so[72] fast
To leave her love for friendship, yet my skill

Shall be employed to make your favour last,
And I will honour Constabarus still.

CONSTABARUS

I ope[73] my bosom to thee, and will take
Thee in, as friend, and grieve for thy complaint.
But if we do not expedition[74] make,
Thy loss of blood I fear will make thee faint.
[*Exeunt.*]

CHORUS

To hear a tale with ears prejudicate,[75]
It spoils the judgement, and corrupts the sense;[76]
That human error given to every state,
Is greater enemy to innocence.
It makes us foolish, heady, rash, unjust,
It makes us never try before we trust.

It will confound the meaning, change the words,
For it our sense of hearing much deceives;
Besides, no time to judgement it affords,
To weigh the circumstance our ear receives.
The ground of accidents it never tries,
But makes us take for truth ten thousand lies.

Our ears and hearts are apt to hold for good,
That we ourselves do most desire to be;
And then we drown objections in the flood
Of partiality, 'tis that we see,
That makes false rumours long with credit past,
Though they like rumours must conclude at last.

The greatest part of us prejudicate,
With wishing Herod's death, do hold it true;
The being once deluded doth not bate,[77]
The credit to a better likelihood due.
Those few that wish it not, the multitude,
Do carry headlong, so they doubts conclude.

They not object[78] the weak uncertain ground,
Whereon they built this tale of Herod's end;
Whereof the author scarcely can be found,
And all because their wishes that way bend.
They think not of the peril that ensueth,
If this should prove the contrary to truth.

On this same doubt, on this so light a breath,
They pawn their lives and fortunes. For they all
Behave them as the news of Herod's death,
They did of most undoubted credit call.
But if their actions now do rightly hit,[79]
Let them commend their fortune, not their wit.

Act III

[*Enter*] PHERORAS [*and*] SALOME.

PHERORAS

Urge me no more Graphina to forsake;
Not twelve hours since I married her for love,
And do you think a sister's power can make
A resolute decree so soon remove?

SALOME

Poor minds they are that honour not affects.[1]

PHERORAS

Who hunts for honour, happiness neglects.

SALOME

You might have been both of felicity,
And honour too, in equal measure seized.

PHERORAS

It is not you can tell so well as I
What 'tis can make me happy, or displeased.

SALOME

To match for neither beauty nor respects
One mean of birth, but yet of meaner mind,
A woman full of natural defects,
I wonder what your eye in her could find!

PHERORAS

Mine eye found loveliness, mine ear found wit,
To please the one, and to enchant the other;
Grace on her eye, mirth on her tongue doth fit,
In looks a child, in wisdom's house a mother.

SALOME

But say you thought her fair, as none thinks else;
Knows not Pheroras, beauty is a blast,
Much like this flower, which today excels
But longer than a day it will not last.

PHERORAS

Her wit exceeds her beauty.

SALOME

Wit may show
The way to ill, as good you know.

PHERORAS

But wisdom is the porter of her head,
And bars all wicked words from issuing thence.

SALOME

But of a porter, better were you sped,
If she against their entrance made defence.

PHERORAS

But wherefore comes the sacred Ananell,
That hitherward his hasty steps doth bend?
[*Enter* Ananell.]
Great sacrificer y'are[2] arrived well;
Ill news from holy mouth I not attend.[3]

ANANELL

My lips, my son, with peaceful tidings blessed
Shall utter honey to your listening ear:
A word of death comes not from priestly breast,

I speak of life – in life there is no fear!
And for the news I did the heavens salute
And filled the temple with my thankful voice!
For though that mourning may not me pollute,
At pleasing accidents I may rejoice.

PHERORAS
Is Herod then revived from certain death?

SALOME
What? Can your news restore my brother's breath?

ANANELL
Both so, and so: the King is safe and sound,
And did such grace in royal Caesar meet,
That he with larger style than ever crowned,
Within this hour Jerusalem will greet!
I did but come to tell you, and must back
To make preparatives[4] for sacrifice.
I knew his death your hearts, like mine, did rack,[5]
Though to conceal it, proved you wise.[6]
Exit.

SALOME
How can my joy sufficiently appear?

PHERORAS
A heavier tale did never pierce mine ear.

SALOME
Now Salome of happiness may boast.

PHERORAS
But now Pheroras is in danger most.

SALOME
I shall enjoy the comfort of my life.

PHERORAS
And I shall lose it, losing of[7] my wife.

SALOME
Joy heart, for Constabarus shall be slain.

PHERORAS
Grieve soul, Graphina shall from me be ta'en.[8]

SALOME
Smile cheeks, the fair Silleus shall be mine.

PHERORAS
Weep eyes, for I must with a child combine.[9]

SALOME
Well brother, cease your moans, on one condition
I'll undertake to win the King's consent:
Graphina still shall be in your tuition,[10]
And her[11] with you, be near, the less content.

PHERORAS
What's the condition? Let me quickly know,
That I as quickly your command may act;
Were it to see what herbs in Ophir[12] grow,
Or that the lofty Tyrus[13] might be sacked.

SALOME
'Tis not so hard a task: it is no more,
But tell the King that Constabarus hid
The sons of Baba, done[14] to death before –
And 'tis no more than Constabarus did
And tell him more, that he[15] for Herod's sake,
Not able to endure his[16] brother's foe,
Did with a bill our separation make,
Though loath from Constabarus else to go.

PHERORAS
Believe this tale foretold. I'll go from hence
In Herod's ear the Hebrew to deface;
And I that never studied eloquence,
Do mean with eloquence this tale to grace.
Exit.

SALOME
This will be Constabarus' quick dispatch,
Which from my mouth would lesser credit find.
Yet shall he not decease without a match,
For Mariam shall not linger long behind.
First, jealousy; if that avail not, fear
Shall be my minister to work her end.
A common error moves not Herod's ear,
Which doth so firmly to his Mariam bend.
She shall be charged with so horrid crime,
As Herod's fear shall turn his love to hate!
I'll make some swear that she desires to climb
And seeks to poison him for his estate.
I scorn that she should live my birth t'upbraid,
To call me base and hungry Edomite![17]
With patient show her choler I betrayed,
And watched the time to be revenged by slight.
Now tongue of mine with scandal load her name,
Turn hers to fountains, Herod's eyes to flame!
Yet, first I will begin Pheroras' suit,
That he my earnest business may effect;
And I of Mariam will keep me mute,
Till first some other doth her name detect.
[*Enter* SILLEUS' MAN.]
Who's there, Silleus' man? How fares your lord,
That your aspects[18] do bear the badge of sorrow?

SILLEUS' MAN
He hath the marks of Constabarus' sword,
And for a while desires your sight to borrow.

SALOME
My heavy curse the hateful sword pursue,
My heavier curse on the more hateful arm
That wounded my Silleus! But renew
Your tale again. Hath he no mortal harm?

SILLEUS' MAN
No sign of danger doth in him appear,
Nor are his wounds in place of peril seen;
He bids you be assured you need not fear –
He hopes to make you yet Arabia's queen.

SALOME
Commend my heart to be Silleus' charge;
Tell him, my brother's sudden coming now

Will give my foot no room to walk at large,
But I will see him yet ere night I vow. [*Exeunt.*]

[*Enter*] MARIAM *and* SOHEMUS.

MARIAM
Sohemus, tell me what the news may be
That makes your eyes so full, your cheeks so blue?[19]

SOHEMUS
I know not how to call them. Ill for me
'Tis sure they are, not so I hope for you.
Herod –

MARIAM
Oh, what of Herod?

SOHEMUS
Herod lives.

MARIAM[20]
How! Lives? What, in some cave or forest hid?

SOHEMUS
Nay, back returned with honour. Caesar gives
Him greater grace than ere Anthonius did.

MARIAM
Foretell the ruin of my family;
Tell me that I shall see our city burned;
Tell me I shall a death disgraceful die;
But tell me not that Herod is returned!

SOHEMUS
Be not impatient madam, be but mild;
His love to you again will soon be bred.

MARIAM
I will not to his love be reconciled,
With solemn vows I have forsworn his bed.

SOHEMUS
But you must break those vows.

MARIAM
I'll rather break
The heart of Mariam! Cursed is my fate.
But speak no more to me – in vain ye speak –
To live with him I so profoundly hate.

SOHEMUS
Great queen, you must to me your pardon give,
Sohemus cannot now your will obey:
If your command should me to silence drive,
It were not to obey, but to betray.
Reject and slight my speeches, mock my faith,
Scorn my observance, call my counsel nought:
Though you regard not what Sohemus saith,[21]
Yet will I ever freely speak my thought.
I fear ere long I shall fair Mariam see
In woeful state, and by herself undone.
Yet for your issues' sake more temperate be,
The heart by affability is won.

MARIAM
And must I to my prison turn again?
Oh, now I see I was an hypocrite:
I did this morning for his death complain,
And yet do mourn, because he lives ere night.
When I his death believed, compassion wrought
And was the stickler[22] 'twixt my heart and him.
But now that curtain's drawn from off[23] my thought,
Hate doth appear again with visage grim,
And paints the face of Herod in my heart
In horrid colours with detested look.
Then Fear would come, but Scorn doth play her part,
And saith[24] that Scorn with Fear can never brook.
I know I could enchain him with a smile
And lead him captive with a gentle word.
I scorn my look should ever man beguile
Of other speech, than meaning to afford.
Else Salome in vain might spend her wind,
In vain might Herod's mother whet her tongue,
In vain had they complotted and combined;[25]
For I could overthrow them all ere long.
Oh what a shelter is mine innocence,
To shield me from the pangs of inward grief,
'Gainst all mishaps it is my fair defence,
And to my sorrows yields a large relief.
To be commandress of the triple earth[26]
And sit in safety from a fall secure,
To have all nations celebrate my birth,
I would not that my spirit were impure.
Let my distressed state unpitied be,
Mine innocence is hope enough for me.
Exit.

SOHEMUS
Poor guiltless queen. Oh, that my wish might place
A little temper[27] now about thy heart;
Unbridled speech is Mariam's worst disgrace
And will endanger her without desart.[28]
I am in greater hazard. O'er my head,
The fatal axe doth hang unsteadily;[29]
My disobedience once discovered
Will shake it down – Sohemus so shall die.
For when the king shall find, we thought his death
Had been as certain as we see his life,
And marks withal I slighted so his breath[30]
As to preserve alive his matchless wife;
Nay more, to give to Alexandra's[31] hand
The regal dignity, the sovereign power;
How I had yielded up at her command
The strength of all the city, David's tower,[32]
What more than common death may I expect,
Since I too well do know his cruelty.
'Twere death, a word of Herod's to neglect;

What then to do directly contrary?
Yet, life I quit thee with a willing spirit
And think thou could'st not better be employed;
I forfeit thee for her that more doth merit,
Ten such were better dead than she destroyed!
But fare thee well chaste queen. Well may I see
The darkness palpable, and rivers part,[33]
The sun stand still,[34] nay, more retorted[35] be,
But never woman with so pure a heart.
Thine eyes' grave majesty keeps all in awe
And cuts the wings[36] of every loose desire;
Thy brow is table to the modest law,[37]
Yet though we dare not love, we may admire.
And if I die, it shall my soul content,
My breath in Mariam's service shall be spent.
[*Exit.*]

CHORUS
'Tis not enough for one that is a wife
To keep her spotless from an act of ill;[38]
But from suspicion she should free her life,
And bare herself of power as well as will.
'Tis not so glorious for her to be free,
As by her proper self restrained to be.

When she hath spacious ground to walk upon,
Why on the ridge should she desire to go?
It is no glory to forbear[39] alone,[40]
Those things that may her honour overthrow.
But 'tis thank-worthy, if she will not take
All lawful liberties for honour's sake.

That wife her hand against her fame doth rear
That more than to her lord alone will give
A private word to any second ear;
And though she may with reputation live,
Yet though most chaste, she doth her glory blot,
And wounds her honour, though she kills it not.

When to their husbands they themselves do bind,
Do they not wholly give themselves away?
Or give they but their body not their mind,
Reserving that, though best, for others, pray?
No sure, their thoughts no more can be their own,
And therefore should to none but one be known.

Then she usurps upon another's right,
That seeks to be by public language graced;
And though her thoughts reflect with purest light,
Her mind if not peculiar[41] is not chaste.
For in a wife it is no worse to find,
A common body, than a common mind.

And every mind though free from thought of ill,
That out of glory seeks a worth to show;
When any's ears but one therewith they fill,
Doth in a sort her pureness overthrow.
Now Mariam had (but that to this she bent)[42]
Been free from fear, as well as innocent.

Act IV

Enter HEROD *and his attendants.*

HEROD
Hail happy city, happy in thy store,
And happy that thy buildings such we see,
More happy in the temple where we adore,
But most of all that Mariam lives in thee.
Art thou returned? How fares my Mariam?[1]
Enter NUNTIO.

NUNTIO
She's well my lord, and will anon[2] be here
As you commanded.

HEROD
Muffle[3] up thy brow
Thou day's dark taper.[4] Mariam will appear,
And where she shines we need not thy dim light.
Oh haste thy steps rare creature, speed thy pace,
And let thy presence make the day more bright,
And cheer the heart of Herod with thy face.
It is an age since I from Mariam went,
Methinks our parting was in David's days
The hours are so increased by discontent.
Deep sorrow, Joshua-like,[5] the season stays,
But when I am with Mariam time runs on;
Her sight can make months, minutes, days of weeks.
An hour is then no sooner come than gone,
When in her face mine eye for wonders seeks!
You, world-commanding city, Europe's grace[6] –
Twice hath my curious eye your streets surveyed,
And I have seen the statue-filled place,
That once, if not for grief, had been betrayed,
I all your Roman beauties have beheld,
And seen the shows your Aediles[7] did prepare,
I saw the sum of what in you excelled:
Yet saw no miracle like Mariam rare.
The faire and famous Livia,[8] Caesar's love,
The world's commanding mistress, did I see,
Whose beauties both the world and Rome approve:
Yet Mariam, Livia is not like to thee.
Be patient but a little while, mine eyes,[9]

Within your compassed limits be contained;
That object straight shall your desires suffice
From which you were so long a while restrained.
How wisely Mariam doth the time delay,
Lest sudden joy my sense should suffocate.
I am prepared, thou need'st no longer stay!
Who's there? My Mariam? More than happy fate!
Oh no, it is Pheroras. Welcome brother.
Now, for a while, I must my passion smother.
[*Enter*] PHERORAS.

PHERORAS
All health and safety wait upon my lord,
And may you long in prosperous fortunes live
With Rome commanding Caesar at accord,
And have all honours that the world can give.

HEROD
Oh brother, now thou speak'st not from thy heart.
No, thou hast struck a blow at Herod's love
That cannot quickly from my memory part,
Though Salome did me to pardon move.
Valiant Phasaelus,[10] now to thee farewell,
Thou wert my kind and honourable brother;
Oh hapless hour, when you self-stricken fell,
Thou father's image, glory of thy mother.
Had I desired a greater suit of thee
Than to withhold thee from a harlot's bed,
Thou would'st have granted it; but now I see
All are not like[11] that in a womb are bred.
Thou would'st not, hadst thou heard of Herod's death,
Have made his burial time thy bridal hour.
Thou would'st with clamours, not with joyful breath,
Have showed the news to be not sweet, but sour.

PHERORAS
Phasaelus' great worth I know did stain
Pheroras' petty valour; but they lie
(Excepting you yourself) that dare maintain
That he did honour Herod more than I!
For what I showed, love's power constrained me show,
And pardon loving faults for Mariam's sake.

HEROD
Mariam, where is she?

PHERORAS
Nay, I do not know,
But absent use of her fair name I make.
You have forgiven greater faults than this,
For Constabarus, that against your[12] will
Preserved the sons of Baba,[13] lives in bliss,
Though you commanded him the youths to kill.

HEROD
Go, take a present order for his death,
And let those traitors feel the worst of fears.
Now Salome will whine to beg his breath,
But I'll be deaf to prayers and blind to tears.

PHERORAS
He is, my lord, from Salome[14] divorced,
Though her affection did to leave him grieve;
Yet, was she by her love to you enforced
To leave the man that would your foes relieve.

HEROD
Then haste them to their death. I will requite
Thee gentle Mariam. Salome, I mean.
The thought of Mariam doth so steal my sprite,[15]
My mouth from speech of her I cannot wean.
Exit [PHERORAS *and others. Enter*] MARIAM.

HEROD
And here she comes indeed. Happily met
My best and dearest half! What ails my dear?
Thou dost the difference certainly forget
'Twixt dusky habits[16] and a time so clear.[17]

MARIAM
My lord, I suit my garment to my mind,
And there no cheerful colours can I find.

HEROD
Is this my welcome? Have I longed so much
To see my dearest Mariam discontent?
What is it that is the cause thy heart to touch?
Oh speak, that I thy sorrow may prevent!
Art thou not Jewry's queen, and Herod's too?
Be my commandress, be my sovereign guide,
To be by thee directed I will woo,
For in thy pleasure lies my highest pride.
Or, if thou think Judea's narrow bound
Too strict a limit for thy great command,
Thou shalt be Empress of Arabia crowned,
For thou shalt rule, and I will win the land.
I'll rob the holy David's sepulchre[18]
To give thee wealth, if thou for wealth do care;
Thou shalt have all they did with him inter,
And I for thee will make the temple bare.

MARIAM
I neither have of power, nor riches want;
I have enough, nor do I wish for more.
Your offers to my heart no ease can grant,
Except they could my brother's life restore.
No, had you wished the wretched Mariam glad,
Or had your love to her been truly tied,
Nay, had you not desired to make her sad,
My brother nor my grandsire had not died!

HEROD
Wilt thou believe no oaths to clear thy lord?
How oft have I with execration sworn,
Thou art by me beloved, by me adored;

Yet are my protestations heard with scorn.
Hyrcanus plotted to deprive my head
Of this long-settled honour that I wear,
And therefore I did justly doom him dead,
To rid the realm from peril, me from fear.
Yet I for Mariam's sake do so repent
The death of one, whose blood she did inherit,
I wish I had a kingdom's treasure spent,
So I had ne'er[19] expelled Hyrcanus' spirit.[20]
As I affected[21] that same noble youth,[22]
In lasting infamy my name enroll,
If I not mourned his death with hearty truth.[23]
Did I not show to him my earnest love
When I to him the priesthood did restore.
And did for him a living priest remove,
Which never had been done but once before?

MARIAM

I know that moved by importunity,
You made him priest, and shortly after, die.

HEROD

I will not speak, unless to be believed!
This froward[24] humour will not do you good;
It hath too much already Herod grieved,
To think that you on terms of hate have stood.
Yet smile, my dearest Mariam, do but smile,
And I will all unkind conceits[25] exile.

MARIAM

I cannot frame disguise, nor never taught
My face a look dissenting from my thought.

HEROD

By heaven you vex me. Build[26] not on my love.

MARIAM

I will not build on so unstable ground.

HEROD

Nought is so fixed, but peevishness may move.

MARIAM

'Tis better slightest cause than none were found.

HEROD

Be judge your self, if ever Herod sought,
Or would be moved a cause of change to find.
Yet, let your look declare a milder thought
My heart again you shall to Mariam bind.
How oft did I for you my mother chide,
Revile my sister, and my brother rate,[27]
And tell them all my Mariam they belied;
Distrust me still, if these be signs of hate.
[*Enter*] BUTLER.

HEROD

What hast thou here?

BUTLER

A drink procuring love.
The queen desired me to deliver it.

MARIAM [*Aside*]

Did I? Some hateful practice[28] this will prove.
Yet can it be no worse than heavens permit.

HEROD

Confess the truth thou wicked instrument
To her outrageous will: 'tis poison[29] sure.
Tell true, and thou shalt 'scape the punishment
Which if thou do conceal thou shalt endure.

BUTLER

I know not. But I doubt it be no less;
Long since the hate of you her heart did seize.

HEROD

Know'st thou the cause thereof?

BUTLER

My Lord, I guess
Sohemus told the tale that did displease.

HEROD

O heaven! Sohemus false! Go let him die,
Stay not to suffer him to speak a word!
Oh damned villain, did he falsify
The oath he swore even of his own accord? [*Exit* Butler.]
Now do I know thy falsehood painted devil,
Thou white enchantress.[30] Oh thou art so foul,
That hyssop[31] cannot cleanse thee, worst of evil!
A beauteous body hides a loathsome soul!
Your love, Sohemus, moved by his affection,
Though he have ever heretofore been true,
Did blab[32] forsooth, that I did give direction,
If we were put to death, to slaughter you.
And you in black revenge attended[33] now
To add a murder to your breach of vow.

MARIAM

Is this a dream?

HEROD

Oh Heaven, that 'twere no more –
I'll give my realm to who can prove it so.
I would I were like any beggar poor,
So I for false my Mariam did not know.
Foul pith[34] contained in the fairest rind
That ever graced a cedar.[35] Oh, thine eye
Is pure as heaven, but impure thy mind,
And for impurity shall Mariam die.
Why did'st thou love Sohemus?

MARIAM

They can tell
That say I loved him; Mariam says not so.

HEROD

Oh, cannot impudence the coals expel,
That for thy love in Herod's bosom glow;
It is as plain as water, and denial
Makes of thy falsehood but a greater trial.
Hast thou beheld thyself? And couldst thou stain
So rare perfection? Even for love of thee
I do profoundly hate thee! Wert thou plain,
Thou shouldst the wonder of Judea be.

But oh, thou art not. Hell itself lies hid
Beneath thy heavenly show! Yet[36] wert thou chaste
Thou might'st exalt, pull down, command, forbid,
And be above the wheel of fortune[37] placed.
Had'st thou complotted Herod's massacre
That so thy son a monarch might be styled,
Not half so grievous such an action were,
As once to think, that Mariam is defiled,
Bright workmanship of nature sullied o'er
With pitched darkness.[38] Now thine end shall be,
Thou shalt not live fair fiend to cozen[39] more
With heavenly[40] semblance, as thou cozenest me.
Yet must I love thee in despite[41] of death,
And thou shalt die in the despite of love;
For neither shall my love prolong thy breath,
Nor shall thy loss of breath my love remove.
I might have seen thy falsehood in thy face:
Where couldst thou get thy stars that served for eyes
Except by theft, and theft is foul disgrace.
This had appeared before were Herod wise,
But I'm a sot! A very sot, no better!
My wisdom long ago a-wandering fell;
Thy face encountering it, my wit did fetter,
And made me for delight my freedom sell.
Give me my heart false creature. 'Tis a wrong
My guiltless heart should now with thine be slain;
Thou hadst no right to lock[42] it up so long.
And with usurper's name I Mariam stain.

Enter BUTLER.

HEROD

Have you designed[43] Sohemus to his end?

BUTLER

I have my lord.

HEROD

Then call our royal guard
To do as much for Mariam. They offend,
Leave[44] ill unblamed, or good without reward.

[*Enter* SOLDIERS.]

Here, take her to her death. Come back, come back!
What meant I to deprive the world of light,
To muffle Jewry in the foulest black,
That ever was an opposite to white?
Why, whither would you carry her?

SOLDIERS

You bad[45]
We should conduct her to her death my lord.

HEROD

Why, sure I did not. Herod was not mad.
Why should she feel the fury of the sword?
Oh, now the grief returns into my heart
And pulls me piecemeal. Love and Hate do fight,
And now hath Love[46] acquired the greater part,
Yet now hath Hate affection conquered quite.
And therefore bear her hence! And, Hebrew, why
Seize you with lion's paws the fairest lamb
Of all the flock?[47] She must not, shall not, die!
Without her I most miserable am.
And, with her, more than most. Away, away!
But, bear her but to prison, not to death.
And, is she gone indeed? Stay, villains, stay!
Her looks alone preserved your sovereign's breath.
Well, let her go. But yet, she shall not die.
I cannot think she meant to poison me,
But certain 'tis, she lived too wantonly,
And therefore shall she never more be free.

[*Exeunt all but the* BUTLER.]

BUTLER

Foul villain, can thy pitchy-coloured[48] soul
Permit thine ear to hear her causeless[49] doom,
And not enforce thy tongue that tale control,
That must unjustly bring her to her tomb?
Oh, Salome thou hast thyself repaid
For all the benefits that thou hast done;
Thou art the cause I have the queen betrayed,
Thou hast my heart to darkest falsehood won.
I am condemned. Heaven gave me not my tongue
To slander innocents, to lie, deceive,
To be the hateful instrument to wrong,
The earth of greatest glory to bereave.
My sin ascends, and doth to heaven cry:[50]
It is the blackest deed that ever was.
And there doth sit an angel notary,
That doth record it down in leaves[51] of brass;[52]
Oh how my heart doth quake. Achitophel,[53]
Thou foundst a means thyself from shame to free,
And sure my soul approves. Thou didest[54] well;
All follow some, and I will follow thee. [*Exit.*]

[*Enter*] CONSTABARUS, BABUS' SONS *and their guards.*

CONSTABARUS

Now here we step our last, the way to death;
We must not tread this way a second time.
Yet, let us resolutely yield our breath,
Death is the only ladder heaven to climb.

BABUS' FIRST SON

With willing mind I could myself resign,
But yet it grieves me with a grief untold
Our death should be accompanied with thine;
Our friendship we to thee have dearly sold.

CONSTABARUS
Still wilt thou wrong the sacred name of friend?
Then shouldst thou never style it friendship more,
But base mechanic traffic[55] that doth lend,
Yet will be sure they shall the debt restore.
I could with needless compliment return:
This[56] for thy ceremony, I could say,
'Tis I that made the fire your house to burn,
For, but for me, she would not you betray.
Had not the damned woman sought mine end,
You had not been the subject of her hate;
You never did her hateful mind offend,
Nor could your deaths have freed her[57] nuptial fate.
Therefore, fair friends, though you were still unborn,
Some other subtlety devised should be,
Whereby[58] my life, though guiltless, should be torn;
Thus have I proved, 'tis you that die for me.
And therefore should I weakly now lament
You have but done your duties: friends should die
Alone, their friends' disaster to prevent,
Though not compelled by strong necessity.[59]
But now, farewell fair city, never more
Shall I behold your beauty shining bright,
Farewell, of Jewish men the worthy store;
But no farewell to any female wight.[60]
You wavering crew – my curse to you I leave.
You had but one to give you any grace,
And you yourselves will Mariam's life bereave.
Your commonwealth[61] doth innocency chase;[62]
You creatures made to be the human curse;
You tigers, lionesses, hungry bears,
Tear massacring hyenas – nay, far worse,
For they for prey do shed their feigned tears.[63]
But you will weep – you creatures, cross[64] to good –
For your unquenched thirst of human blood;
You were the angels cast from heaven for pride,
And still do keep your angels' outward show –
But none of you are inly[65] beautified,
For still your heaven-depriving pride doth grow.
Did not the sins of man[66] require a scourge,
Your place on earth had been by this withstood;
But since a flood no more the world must purge,[67]
You stayed in office of a second flood.
You giddy[68] creatures, sowers of debate,
You'll love today and for no other cause,
But for you yesterday did deeply hate.
You are the wreck of order, breach of laws;
Your[69] best, are foolish, froward,[70] wanton, vain;
Your worst, adulterous, murderous, cunning, proud;
And Salome attends the latter train,
Or rather, she[71] their leader is allowed.
I do the sottishness[72] of men bewail,
That do with following you enhance your pride;
'Twere better that the human race should fail,
Than be by such a mischief multiplied.
Cham's servile curse to all your sex was given
Because in paradise you did offend;[73]
Then, do we not resist the will of heaven
When on your wills like servants we attend?
You are to nothing constant, but to ill;
You are with nought but wickedness endued;[74]
Your loves are set on nothing but your will.
And thus my censure I of you conclude:
You are the least of goods, the worst of evils;
Your best are worse than men, your worst, than devils.

BABUS' SECOND SON
Come let us to our death. Are we not blessed?
Our death will freedom from these creatures give,
Those trouble quiet,[75] sowers of unrest;
And this I vow: that had I leave to live,
I would forever lead a single life
And never venture on a devilish wife. [*Exeunt.*]

[*Enter*] HEROD *and* SALOME.

HEROD
Nay, she shall die. Die, quoth you, that she shall.
But for the means. The means! Methinks 'tis hard
To find a means to murder her withal[76] –
Therefore, I am resolved she shall be spared.

SALOME
Why? Let her be beheaded.

HEROD
That were well.
Think you that swords are miracles like you?
Her skin will every curtlax[77] edge refel[78] –
And then your enterprise you well may rue.[79]
What if the fierce Arabian notice take
Of this, your wretched weaponless estate?
They answer, when we bid resistance make,
That Mariam's skin their falchions[80] did rebate.[81]
Beware of this, you make a goodly hand
If you of weapons do deprive our land.

SALOME
Why, drown her then!

HEROD
Indeed a sweet device.

Why, would not every river turn her course,
Rather than do her beauty prejudice,
And be reverted to the proper source?
So not a drop of water should be found
In all Judea's quondam[82] fertile ground.

SALOME
Then let the fire devour her!

HEROD
'Twill not be.
Flame is from her derived into my heart;
Thou nursest flame, flame will not murder thee,
My fairest Mariam, fullest of desert.

SALOME
Then let her live for me.

HEROD
Nay, she shall die!
But can you live without her?

SALOME
Doubt you that?

HEROD
I'm sure I cannot. I beseech you try.
I have experience, but I know not what.

SALOME
How should I try?

HEROD
Why let my love be slain.
But if we cannot live without her sight,
You'll find the means to make her breath again,
Or else you will bereave my comfort quite.

SALOME
Oh ay, I warrant you. [*Exit.*]

HEROD
What, is she gone?
And gone to bid the world be overthrown.
What, is her heart's composure hardest
stone?
To what a pass[83] are cruel women grown? –
[*Enter* SALOME.]
She is returned already. Have you done?
Is't possible you can command so soon
A creature's heart to quench the flaming sun,
Or from the sky to wipe away the moon?

SALOME
If Mariam be the sun and moon, it is;
For I already have commanded this.

HEROD
But have you seen her cheek?

SALOME
A thousand times.

HEROD
But did you mark it too?

SALOME
Ay, very well.

HEROD
What is't?

SALOME
A crimson bush, that ever limes[84]
The soul whose foresight doth not much excel.

HEROD
Send word she shall not die. Her cheek a bush?
Nay, then I see indeed you marked it not!

SALOME
'Tis very fair, but yet will never blush,
Though foul dishonours do her forehead blot.[85]

HEROD
Then let her die. 'Tis very true indeed,
And for this fault alone shall Mariam bleed.

SALOME
What fault my lord?

HEROD
What fault is it, you that ask?
If you be ignorant, I know of none!
To call her back from death shall be your
task,
I'm glad that she for innocent is known.
For on the brow of Mariam hangs a fleece[86]
Whose slenderest twine is strong enough to bind
The hearts of kings; the pride and shame of
Greece,
Troy's[87] flaming Helen,[88] not so fairly shined!

SALOME
'Tis true indeed; she lays them out for nets
To catch the hearts that do not shun a bait.
'Tis time to speak, for Herod sure forgets
That Mariam's very tresses hide deceit.

HEROD
Oh do they so? Nay, then you do but well.
In sooth, I thought it had been hair;[89]
Nets you call them? Lord, how they do excel,
I never saw a net that showed so fair.
But have you heard her speak?

SALOME
You know I have.

HEROD
And were you not amazed?

SALOME
No, not a whit.

HEROD
Then 'twas not her you heard! Her life I'll
save,
For Mariam hath a world-amazing wit.

SALOME
She speaks a beauteous language, but within,
Her heart is false as powder,[90] and her tongue
Doth but allure the auditors to sin,
And is the instrument to do you wrong.

HEROD
It may be so. Nay, 'tis so. She's unchaste;
Her mouth will open to every stranger's ear.[91]
Then let the executioner make haste,

Lest she enchant him, if her words he hear.
Let him be deaf, lest she do him surprise,
That shall to free her spirit be assigned.
Yet what boots[92] deafness if he have his eyes?
Her murderer must be both deaf and blind,
For if he see, he needs must see the stars
That shine on either side of Mariam's face,
Whose sweet aspect will terminate the wars
Wherewith he should a soul so precious chase.
Her eyes can speak, and in their speaking move;
Oft did my heart with reverence receive
The world's mandates. Pretty tales of love
They utter, which can human bondage weave.
But shall I let this Heaven's model die,
Which for a small self-portraiture she drew;
Her eyes like stars, her forehead like the sky?
She is like Heaven, and must be heavenly true.

SALOME
Your thoughts do rave with doting on the queen!
Her eyes are ebon-hued,[93] and you'll confess,
A stable star[94] hath been but seldom seen.
Then speak of reason more, of Mariam less.

HEROD
Yourself are held a goodly creature here,
Yet so unlike my Mariam in your shape,
That when to her you have approached near,
Myself hath often ta'en you for an ape!
And yet you prate[95] of beauty: go your ways,
You are to her a sunburnt blackamoor.[96]
Your paintings[97] cannot equal Mariam's praise;
Her nature is so rich, you are so poor.
Let her be stayed from death, for if she die,
We do, we know not what, to stop her breath.
A world cannot another Mariam buy.
Why stay you lingering? Countermand her death!

SALOME
Then you'll no more remember what hath passed –
Sohemus' love, and hers, shall be forgot?
'Tis well in truth. That fault may be her last,
And she may mend, though yet, she love you not.

HEROD
Oh God, 'tis true – Sohemus. Earth and heaven,
Why did you both conspire to make me cursed,
In coz'ning[98] me with shows and proofs uneven?[99]
She showed the best, and yet did prove the worst.
Her show was such as, had our singing king
The holy David Mariam's beauty seen,
The Hittites had then felt no deadly sting,
Nor Bathsheba had never been a queen.[100]
Or had his son,[101] the wisest man of men
Whose fond delight did most consist in change,
Beheld her face, he had been stayed again;
No creature having her, can wish to range.
Had Ahasuerus seen my Mariam's brow,
The humble Jew, she might have walked alone,
Her beauteous virtue should have stayed below
While Mariam's mounted to the Persian throne.[102]
But what avails it all? For in the weight[103]
She is deceitful, light as vanity;
Oh, she was made for nothing but a bait
To train[104] some hapless[105] man to misery.
I am the hapless man that have been trained
To endless bondage. I will see her yet.
Methinks I should discern her if she feigned;
Can human eyes be dazed by woman's wit?
Once more these eyes of mine with hers shall meet
Before the headsman do her life bereave.
Shall I forever part from thee my sweet,
Without the taking of my latest leave?

SALOME
You had as good resolve to save her now!
I'll stay her death, 'tis well determined,
For sure she never more will break her vow;
Sohemus and Josephus both are dead.

HEROD
She shall not live. Nor will I see her face.
A long-healed wound, a second time doth bleed:
With Joseph I remember her disgrace,
A shameful end ensues[106] a shameful deed.
Oh, that I had not called to mind anew
The discontent of Mariam's wavering heart!
'Twas you, you foul-mouthed Ate,[107] none but you,
That did the thought hereof to me impart.
Hence from my sight, my black tormenter hence,
For hadst not thou made Herod insecure,
I had not doubted Mariam's innocence;
But still had held her in my heart for pure.

SALOME
I'll leave you to your passion. 'Tis no time
To purge me now, though of a guiltless crime.
Exit.

HEROD
Destruction take thee! Thou hast made my heart
As heavy as revenge. I am so dull
Methinks I am not sensible of smart,
Though hideous horrors at my bosom pull;
My head weighs downwards. Therefore will I go
To try if I can sleep away my woe.[108] [*Exit.*]

[*Enter*] MARIAM.

MARIAM
Am I the Mariam that presumed so much,

And deemed my face must needs preserve my breath?
Ay, I it was that thought my beauty such,
As[109] it alone could countermand my death.
Now Death will teach me; he can pale, as well
A cheek of roses, as a cheek less bright,
And dim an eye whose shine doth most excel,
As soon as one that casts a meaner light.
Had not myself against myself conspired,
No plot, no adversary from without,
Could Herod's love from Mariam have retired,
Or from his heart have thrust my semblance out.
The wanton queen that never loved for love,
False Cleopatra,[110] wholly set on gain
With all her slights did prove,[111] yet vainly prove,
For her the love of Herod to obtain.
Yet her allurements, all her courtly guile,
Her smiles, her favours, and her smooth deceit,
Could not my face from Herod's mind exile,
But were with him of less than little weight.
That face[112] and person that in Asia late
For beauty's goddess, Paphos' queen,[113] was ta'en;[114]
That face that did captive great Julius' fate;
That very face that was Anthonius' bane;[115]
That face that to be Egypt's pride was born;
That face that all the world esteemed so rare;
Did Herod hate, despise, neglect, and scorn,
When with the same he, Mariam's, did compare.
This made that I improvidently[116] wrought,
And on the wager even my life did pawn;
Because I thought, and yet but truly thought,
That Herod's love could not from me be drawn.
But now, though out of time, I plainly see
It could be drawn; though never drawn from me
Had I but with humility been graced,
As well as fair, I might have proved me wise.
But I did think because I knew me chaste,
One virtue for a woman might suffice.
That mind, for glory of our sex might stand,
Wherein humility and chastity
Doth march with equal paces hand in hand.
But one, if single seen, who setteth by?[117]
And I had singly one; but 'tis my joy
That I was ever innocent, though sour,
And therefore can they but my life destroy,
My soul is free from adversary's power.
Enter DORIS [*and* ANTIPATER].
You princes great in power and high in birth –
Be great and high, I envy not your hap;[118]
Your birth must be from dust, your power on earth;
In heaven shall Mariam sit in Sara's lap.[119]

DORIS
Ay, heaven! Your beauty cannot bring you thither,
Your soul is black and spotted, full of sin;
You in adultery lived nine year together,
And heaven will never let adultery in.

MARIAM
What art thou that dost poor Mariam pursue?
Some spirit sent to drive me to despair,
Who sees for truth that Mariam is untrue?
If fair she be, she is as chaste as fair.

DORIS
I am that Doris that was once beloved,
Beloved by Herod – Herod's lawful wife.
'Twas you that Doris from his side removed,
And robbed from me the glory of my life.

MARIAM
Was that adultery? Did not Moses say,
That he that being matched, did deadly hate,
Might by permission put his wife away
And take a more beloved to be his mate?

DORIS
What did he hate me for? For simple truth?
For bringing[120] beauteous babes? For love to him?
For riches, noble birth, or tender youth?
Or, for no stain? Did Doris' honour dim?
Oh, tell me Mariam, tell me if you know,
Which fault of these made Herod Doris' foe?
These thrice three years have I, with hands held up
And bowed knees fast nailed to the ground,
Besought for thee the dregs of that same cup,
That cup of wrath, that is for sinners found.[121]
And now thou art to drink it! Doris' curse,
Upon thy self did all this while attend,
But now it shall pursue thy children worse!

MARIAM
Oh Doris, now to thee my knees I bend.
That heart, that never bowed, to thee doth bow;
Curse not mine infants, let it thee suffice
That heaven doth punishment to me allow.
Thy curse is cause that guiltless Mariam dies.

DORIS
Had I ten thousand tongues, and every tongue
Inflamed with poison's power and steeped in gall,
My curses would not answer for my wrong,
Though I, in cursing thee, employed them all.
Hear thou, that didst Mount Gerazim[122] command
To be a place whereon with cause to curse,
Stretch thy revenging arm, thrust forth thy hand,
And plague the mother much – the children worse.

Throw flaming fire upon the baseborn heads
That were begotten in unlawful beds,
But let them live till they have sense to know
What 'tis to be in miserable state.
Then, be their nearest friends their
overthrow,
Attended be they by suspicious hate.
And Mariam, I do hope this boy of mine
Shall one day come to be the death of thine.
Exeunt [DORIS *and* ANTIPATER].

MARIAM
Oh! Heaven forbid! I hope the world shall see
This curse of thine shall be returned on thee!
Now earth, farewell! Though I be yet but young,
Yet I, methinks, have known thee too too long.
Exit.

CHORUS
The fairest action of our human life
Is scorning to revenge an injury;
For who forgives without a further strife,
His adversary's heart to him doth tie.
And 'tis a firmer conquest, truly said,
To win the heart, than overthrow the head.

If we a worthy enemy do find,
To yield to worth, it must be nobly done;
But if of baser metal be his mind,
In base revenge there is no honour won.
Who would a worthy courage overthrow,
And who would wrestle with a worthless foe?

We say our hearts are great and cannot
yield –
Because they cannot yield it proves them poor;
Great hearts are tasked[123] beyond their power,
but seld[124]
The weakest lion will the loudest roar.
Truth's school for certain doth this same allow,
High heartedness doth sometimes teach to
bow.

A noble heart doth teach a virtuous scorn:
To scorn to owe a duty over-long,
To scorn to be for benefits forborn,[125]
To scorn to lie, to scorn to do a wrong,
To scorn to bear an injury in mind,
To scorn a free-born heart slave-like to bind.

But if for wrongs we needs revenge must have,
Then be our vengeance of the noblest kind;
Do we his body from our fury save,
And let our hate prevail against our mind?
What can 'gainst him a greater vengeance be,
Than make his foe more worthy far than he?

Had Mariam scorned to leave a due unpaid,[126]
She would to Herod then have paid her love,
And not have been by sullen passion
swayed.
To fix her thoughts all injury above
Is[127] virtuous pride. Had Mariam thus been
proved,
Long famous life to her had been allowed.

Act 5

[*Enter*] NUNTIO.

NUNTIO
When, sweetest friend, did I so far offend
Your heavenly self, that you, my fault to quit,
Have made me now relater of your end?
The end of beauty, chastity and wit?
Was none so hapless in the fatal place
But I, most wretched, for the queen to choose?
'Tis certain I have some ill-boding face
That made me culled[1] to tell this luckless news.
And yet, no news to Herod. Were it new
To him, unhappy 't had[2] not been at all.
Yet do I long to come within his view,
That he may know his wife did guiltless fall.
And here he comes. Your Mariam greets you
well.
Enter HEROD.

HEROD
What? Lives my Mariam? Joy, exceeding joy!
She shall not die!

NUNTIO
Heaven doth your will repel.

HEROD
Oh do not with thy words my life destroy.
I prithee tell no dying-tale; thine eye
Without thy tongue doth tell but too too much.
Yet, let thy tongue's addition make me die;
Death welcome comes to him whose grief is
such.

NUNTIO
I went amongst the curious gazing troop,
To see the last of her that was the best;
To see if death had heart to make her stoop;
To see the sun admiring phoenix nest.[3]
When there I came, upon the way I saw
The stately Mariam not debased by fear;
Her look did seem to keep the world in awe,
Yet mildly did her face this fortune bear.

HEROD
Thou dost usurp my right! My tongue was
framed
To be the instrument of Mariam's praise!
Yet speak, she cannot be too often famed,
All tongues suffice not her sweet name to raise.

NUNTIO
But as she came, she Alexandra met,
Who did her death – sweet queen – no whit bewail,
But as if nature she did quite forget,
She did upon her daughter loudly rail.
HEROD
Why stopped you not her mouth? Where had she words
To darken[4] that, that heaven made so bright?
Our sacred tongue no epithet affords
To call her other than the world's delight.
NUNTIO
She told her, that her death was too too good,
And that already she had lived too long.
She said, she shamed to have a part in blood
Of her that did the princely Herod wrong.
HEROD
Base pick-thank![5] Devil! Shame! 'Twas all her glory
That she to noble Mariam was the mother.
But never shall it live in any story,
Her name, except to infamy, I'll smother.
What answer did her princely daughter make?
NUNTIO
She made no answer, but she looked the while,
As if thereof she scarce did notice take.
Yet smiled, a dutiful, though scornful smile.
HEROD
Sweet creature, I that look to mind do call;
Full oft hath Herod been amazed withal.
Go on.[6]
NUNTIO
She came unmoved, with pleasant grace
As if to triumph her arrival were,
In stately habit and with cheerful face;
Yet every eye was moist, but Mariam's, there.
When justly[7] opposite to me she came,
She picked me out from all the crew,[8]
She beckoned to me, called me by my name,
For she my name, my birth, and fortune knew.
HEROD
What, did she name thee? Happy, happy man!
Wilt thou not ever love that name the better?
But what sweet tune did this fair dying swan
Afford thine ear?[9] Tell all, omit no letter.
NUNTIO
'Tell thou my lord,' said she.
HEROD
Me, meant she me?
Is't true, the more my shame; I was her lord;
Were I not mad,[10] her lord I still should be;
But now her name must be, by me, adored.
Oh say, what said she more? Each word she said
Shall be the food whereon my heart is fed.
NUNTIO
'Tell thou my lord, thou saw'st me lose my breath.'
HEROD
Oh, that I could that sentence[11] now control.
NUNTIO
'If guiltily, eternal be my death.'
HEROD
I hold her chaste, even in my inmost soul.
NUNTIO
'By three days hence,[12] if wishes could revive,
I know himself would make me oft alive.'
HEROD
Three days, three hours, three minutes, not so much –
A minute in a thousand parts divide;[13]
My penitency for her death is such,
As in the first I wished she had not died.
But forward in thy tale.
NUNTIO
Why, on she went;
And after she some silent prayer had said,
She did as if to die she were content,
And thus to heaven her heavenly soul is fled.
HEROD
But art thou sure there doth no life remain?
Is't[14] possible my Mariam should be dead?
Is there no trick to make her breathe again?
NUNTIO
Her body is divided from her head.
HEROD
Why yet methinks there might be found by art
Strange ways of cure, 'tis sure rare things are done
By an inventive head and willing heart.
NUNTIO
Let not, my lord, your fancies idly run.
It is as possible, it should be seen,
That we should make the holy Abraham live,
Though he entombed two thousand years had been,
As breath again to slaughtered Mariam give.
But now for more assaults prepare your ears.
HEROD
There cannot be a further cause of moan,
This accident shall shelter me from fears.
What can I fear? Already Mariam's gone.
Yet, tell even what you will.
NUNTIO
As I came by
From Mariam's death, I saw upon a tree
A man that to his neck a cord did tie,
Which cord he had designed his end to be.[15]

When me he once discerned, he downwards bowed,
And thus with fearful voice he[16] cried aloud:
'Go tell the king he trusted ere he tried;
I am the cause that Mariam, causeless, died!'

HEROD

Damnation take him, for it was the slave
That said she meant with poison's deadly force
To end my life that she the crown might have;
Which tale did Mariam from herself divorce.
Oh, pardon me thou pure unspotted ghost.
My punishment must needs sufficient be
In missing that content I valued most,
Which was thy admirable face to see.
I had but one inestimable jewel,[17]
Yet one I had, no monarch had the like;
And therefore may I curse myself as cruel,
'Twas broken by a blow myself did strike.
I gazed thereon and never thought me blessed
But when on it my dazzled eye might rest,
A precious mirror made by wondrous art,
I prized it ten times dearer then my crown,
And laid it up, fast-folded in my heart.
Yet I, in sudden choler, cast it down,
And pasht[18] it all to pieces; 'twas no foe
That robbed me of it, no Arabian host,
Nor no Armenian guide hath used me so –
But Herod's wretched self hath Herod crossed!
She was my graceful moiety;[19] me accurst
To slay my better half and save my worst.
But sure she is not dead. You did but jest
To put me in perplexity a while.
'Twere well indeed if I could so be dressed;[20]
I see she is alive. Methinks you smile.

NUNTIO

If sainted Abel[21] yet deceased be,
'Tis certain Mariam is as dead as he.

HEROD

Why then, go call her to me. Bid her now
Put on fair habit, stately ornament;
And let no frown o'ershade her smoothest brow –
In her doth Herod place his whole content.

NUNTIO

She'll come in stately weeds[22] to please your sense
If now she come attired in robe of heaven.
Remember, you yourself did send her hence,
And now to you she can no more be given.

HEROD

She's dead! Hell take her murderers! She was fair,
Oh what a hand she had, it was so white,
It did the whiteness of the snow impair;
I never more shall see so sweet a sight.

NUNTIO

'Tis true, her hand was rare.

HEROD

Her hand? Her hands.
She has not singly, one of beauty rare,
But such a pair as here where Herod stands,
He dares the world to make to both compare.
Accursed Salome, hadst thou been still,[23]
My Mariam had been breathing by my side.
Oh never had I, had I had my will,
Sent forth command that Mariam should have died.
But Salome, thou didst with every envy vex
To see thyself out-matched in thy sex.
Upon your sex's forehead Mariam sat,
To grace you all like an imperial crown;[24]
But you, fond fool, have rudely pushed thereat,
And proudly pulled your proper glory down.
One smile of hers, nay, not so much, a look
Was worth a hundred thousand such as you.
Judea how canst thou the wretches brook,[25]
That robbed from thee the fairest of the crew?
You dwellers in the now deprived land,
Wherein the matchless Mariam was bred,
Why grasp not each of you a sword in hand
To aim at me, your cruel sovereign's head?
Oh, when you think of Herod as your king
And owner of the pride of Palestine,
This act to your remembrance likewise bring:
'Tis I have overthrown your royal line.
Within her purer veins the blood did run,
That from her grandam[26] Sara[27] she derived,
Whose beldam[28] age the love of kings hath won –
Oh that her issue had as long been lived!
But can her eye be made by death obscure?[29]
I cannot think but it must sparkle still;
Foul sacrilege to rob those lights so pure
From out a temple made by heavenly skill.
I am the villain that have done the deed,
The cruel deed, though by another's hand.
My word though not my sword made Mariam bleed;
Hyrcanus' grandchild died[30] at my command;
That Mariam that I once did love so dear,
The partner of my now detested bed.
Why shine you sun with an aspect so clear?
I tell you, once again, my Mariam's dead!
You could but shine if some Egyptian blowze,[31]
Or Ethiopian dowdy[32] lose her life.
This was – then wherefore bend you not your brows? –

The King of Jewry's fair and spotless wife!
Deny thy beams, and Moon refuse thy light,
Let all the stars be dark, let Jewry's eye
No more distinguish which is day and night –
Since her best birth did in her bosom die.
Those fond idolaters, the men of Greece,
Maintain these orbs are safely governed;
That each within themselves have gods a-piece,[33]
By whom their steadfast course is justly led.
But were it so, as so it cannot be,
They all would put their mourning garments on;
Not one of them would yield a light to me,
To me, that is the cause that Mariam's gone.
For though they feign[34] their Saturn melancholy
Of sour behaviours and of angry mood,
They feign him likewise to be just and holy,
And justice needs must seek revenge for blood.[35]
Their Jove,[36] if Jove he were, would sure desire
To punish him that slew so fair a lass;
For Leda's beauty[37] set his heart on fire,
Yet she not half so fair as Mariam was.
And Mars would deem his Venus had been slain.[38]
Sol[39] to recover her would never stick,[40]
For if he want the power her life to gain,
Then physic's god[41] is but an empiric.[42]
The queen of love[43] would storm for beauty's sake;
And Hermes[44] too, since he bestowed her wit,
The night's pale light[45] for angry grief would shake
To see chaste Mariam die in age unfit.
But oh, I am deceived. She passed them all
In every gift, in every property;
Her excellencies wrought her timeless[46] fall –
And they rejoiced, not grieved, to see her die.
The Paphian goddess[47] did repent her waste,
When she to one such beauty did allow;
Mercurius[48] thought her wit his wit surpassed;
And Cynthia envied Mariam's brighter brow.
But these are fictions; they are void of sense.
The Greeks but dream, and dreaming, falsehoods tell;
They neither can offend nor give defence,
And not by them it was my Mariam fell.
If she had been like an Egyptian black,
And not so fair, she had been longer lived;
Her overflow of beauty turned back
And drowned the spring from whence it was derived.
Her heavenly beauty 'twas that made me think
That it with chastity could never dwell.
But now I see that heaven in her did link
A spirit and a person[49] to excel.
I'll muffle up myself in endless night,
And never let mine eyes behold the light.
Retire thyself,[50] vile monster, worse than he
That stained the virgin earth with brother's blood.[51]
Still in some vault or den enclosed be,
Where with thy tears thou may'st beget a flood,
Which flood, in time, may drown thee. Happy day
When thou at once shalt die and find a grave;
A stone upon the vault some one shall lay,
Which monument shall an inscription have;
And these shall be the words it shall contain:
'Here Herod lies, that hath his Mariam slain.'
[*Exeunt.*]

CHORUS
Who ever hath beheld with steadfast eye,
The strange events of this one only day:[52]
How many were deceived? How many die,
That once today did grounds of safety lay?
It will from them all certainty bereave,
Since twice six hours so many can deceive.

This morning Herod held for surely dead,
And all the Jews on Mariam did attend;
And Constabarus rise from Salom's bed,
And neither dreamed of a divorce or end.
Pheroras joyed that he might have his wife,
And Babus' sons for safety of their life.

Tonight our Herod doth alive remain,
The guiltless Mariam is deprived of breath;
Stout Constabarus both divorced and slain,
The valiant sons of Baba have their death.
Pheroras sure his love to be bereft,
If Salome her suit unmade had left.

Herod this morning did expect with joy
To see his Mariam's much beloved face;
And yet ere night he did her life destroy,
And surely thought she did her name disgrace.
Yet now, again so short do humours[53] last,
He both repents her death and knows her chaste.

Had he with wisdom now her death delayed,
He at his pleasure might command her death;
But now he hath his power so much betrayed,
As all his woes cannot restore her breath.
Now doth he strangely, lunatically rave,
Because his Mariam's life he cannot save.

This day's events were certainly ordained,
To be the warning to posterity;
So many changes are therein contained,
So admirable strange variety.
This day alone, our sagest Hebrews shall
In after-times[54] the school of wisdom call.
[*Exeunt.*]

FINIS

4 *Cupid's Banishment*

ROBERT WHITE

INTRODUCTION

The title-page of the manuscript of *Cupid's Banishment* identifies it more specifically as 'A Maske Presented to Her Majesty By the younge Gentlewomen of the Ladies Hall In Deptford at Greenwich The 4th of May 1617'. The manuscript seems to have been prepared early in the seventeenth century and lay untouched in the library collection of the well-known diarist John Evelyn until the early nineteenth century when it was purchased by William Upcott. It was Upcott who recognized and noted inside the front cover what appears to be Evelyn's handwriting. Interestingly, Evelyn's annotation provides the earliest dramatic link for the masque. 'Richard Browne, 12 years old,' Evelyn wrote, 'acted herein before Queen Anne'; and Browne's daughter Mary married Evelyn in June 1647. Thus, it has long been the scholarly opinion that the manuscript was passed down from Browne to Evelyn.[1]

The manuscript – which has been preserved in its original vellum binding – is written throughout in one clear, consistent seventeenth-century hand. It bears a dedication to Lucy Countess of Bedford, one of the most distinguished patronesses of the day, a woman whose generosity was remembered in the poetry of Michael Drayton and John Donne, among others. She was appointed one of the Ladies of the Bedchamber to Queen Anne, and, in time, she became the queen's closest friend. Lady Bedford was responsible for assisting in the arrangements that led to Samuel Daniel's masque entitled *The Vision of Twelve Goddesses* (8 January 1604), and she also liked to participate in masquing. With the queen Lady Bedford performed in the brilliant series of masques written by Ben Jonson and designed by Inigo Jones, including the 'Masque of Blackness' (6 January 1605), the 'Masque of Beauty' (1609), and the 'Masque of Queens' (1609).[2] The dedication to *Cupid's Banishment*, in which the author, Robert White, thanks Lady Bedford for her 'honourable furtherance and noble encouragement', suggests that it was not only through her patronage and financial assistance that the masque was made possible, but that it was due to her personal initiative that the masque was written and performed. White explains: 'I thought it injustice to devote the fruits which your honour first sowed to any but yourself.' The existence of the dedication also suggests that the manuscript was, at one time, either being made ready for publication or prepared as a presentation copy for Lady Bedford, even though neither finally seems to have occurred.

The conditions under which the masque was actually performed also raise questions. If the title-page of the manuscript is accurate *Cupid's Banishment* was performed before Queen Anne at Greenwich on 4 May 1617; however, no specific references to the masque exist separately from the manuscript. Payments recorded in contemporary Chamber accounts corroborate the fact that some unnamed entertainment was being prepared during this period. Henry Colborne and eight assistants earned £7 16s for eight days' work, which consisted of 'making ready for a play in the Queen's great chamber and for a masque in the hall' at Greenwich. While nothing further was recorded concerning the 'masque in the hall' it was clearly not of as great significance as those written by Jonson (which tend, by contrast, to be well documented in the Chamber and other household accounts). Jonson's only masque of 1617 – the *Vision of Delight* – was presented several months earlier, in January of the same year, at Whitehall.[3]

Additionally, details of staging remain obscure, although many aspects of the manuscript would suggest that the masque was actually performed at least once – on the occasion for which it was written. Charles Coleman and George Lippet, who are identified in the *dramatis personae* as having played the parts of Hymen and Bacchus, were members of the King's Music in 1617.[4] The stage directions within the manuscript of *Cupid's Banishment* – frequently written in abbreviated, incomplete sentences, and in the present tense – give the reader the sense of present, ongoing action, as though they are literally notes reflecting a performance. Also, the masque seems to have been scheduled for an evening performance: 'Banish base dullness for this night / Revels must be the centre of delight' (l. 56). Not least of all, given the large scale of the masque and the limited resources that Ladies Hall was capable of providing (and in keeping with common performance practice that called for professional performers in the antemasque), actors, singers and dancers were brought in for the event. In all, thirty-one performers were named, including six young men, and nine anonymous 'Bacchanalians' whose names were not recorded. The symbolic Master of the Revels was the character Occasion (acted by 'Mr R W', most probably the author), who symbolically provided the 'occasion' for the performance by writing the piece, and who literally directed the 'occasion' by reading the prologue and epilogue, and remaining on stage throughout the performance. One 'Mr Onslo, tutor to Ladies Hall' choreographed the dancing; and one of the songs used for the performance is preserved in the manuscript as well.

Although little is known about Robert White, it would appear that he was the master of Ladies Hall, a school located south of London in Deptford which has otherwise passed into obscurity.[5] It seems to have been a sort of high-class, private academy that offered both academic studies and training in social skills. The interest in bringing the school's masque to the court seems to have been inspired not only by White's connection with the Countess of Bedford, but also by the fact that two of the queen's goddaughters (Ann Chalenor and Anne Sandilands) attended Ladies Hall and participated in the masque. Near the end of the play the goddess Diana presents the goddaughters to the queen, and they, in turn, present needlework gifts to Anne. These consist of two pictures. On the first is an acorn, and on the second is rosemary. Together, their beginning initials – 'A' and 'R' – symbolize the queen herself (Anna Regina). In addition, the rosemary symbolizes remembrance while the acorn presumably alludes to the queen's strength and steadfastness, the acorn becoming an oak tree in its maturity.

In performing *Cupid's Banishment* the women of Ladies Hall flattered the queen and the aristocratic women of her circle. The young women, in imitation of their elders, were showing their admiration for the masque form (a dramatic form of which Queen Anne was especially fond) and also for Anne's adult circle of female masquers, including Lady Bedford. In terms of social structure the women of Ladies Hall were younger versions of their privileged adult counterparts, for many of the ladies were daughters of men with court appointments. For instance, Elizabeth Cranfield was probably the daughter of Lionel Cranfield, an important official in King James's circle. Ann Chalenor was the daughter of Sir Thomas Chalenor, Chamberlain to Prince Henry; and Lea Watson was the daughter of Sir Thomas Watson, Teller of the Exchequer. Overall, in the thematic content of the masque, and even in the dramatic effect of the young women imitating their elders, the queen and her circle were being set up as models of female virtue to which the young ladies could aspire.

Yet not all of Queen Anne's contemporaries felt that it was proper for women to be performing in dramatic activities. G.E. Bentley pointed to evidence in the dedication and prologue of *Cupid's Banishment* to support the proposition that White had been attacked earlier for the theatrical activities of his young ladies. Otherwise, Bentley argued, White would not have explained in two different places that the central activity of the masque – the choosing of a king and queen by Fortune – was a regular feature of Candlemas Night activities at Ladies Hall. Nor would he have asked, in the dedication, that the masque be allowed to 'triumph in despite of envy's raging winter'. 'But let the envious spit their venom,' White continued, 'and tip their tongues with gall; it matters not. This is my comfort: envy barketh only at the stars, and spite spurns at that she cannot reach.'[6]

Whatever objections White was responding to have become obscured by time. Moreover, there is the possibility that *Cupid's Banishment* was criticized by those outside of the aristocratic circle since the masque remains, in the words of C.E. McGee, 'quite conventional'. McGee continues: 'The theme of the superiority of chaste love recurs throughout Jonson's masques . . . [and] the characters, their costumes, and their properties' are derived largely from standard iconography of the period, that which seems especially to have been influenced by Cesare Ripa's *Iconologia* (1611). Even in matters relating to the set – which features Diana's flowery arbour, or the Mount, which opens to reveal the procession of Hymen with the king and queen of Fortune – McGee notes that 'none of these features of the masque is new'.[7]

How a schoolmaster such as Robert White would have become conversant with the standard conventions of the masque raises interesting questions; but the publication of Jonson's *Works* in 1616, a collection that contained twelve masques, might well provide some of the answers. In many aspects *Cupid's Banishment* imitates the most obvious elements of the Jonsonian masque. Like other masques, *Cupid's Banishment* was truly 'occasional'; that is, it was written for a specific occasion, and there is no evidence that it was ever performed more than once. The masque also functions as both a celebration and an offering: a celebration of the female virtues embodied by Queen Anne and her aristocratic circle, and an offering from Lady Bedford and the young women of Ladies Hall to the queen. The contest presented by *Cupid's Banishment* is between chastity (personified by Diana) and the temptations offered by wanton love (personified in Cupid and other minor characters such as the four drunken Bacchanalians); and while the contrasting possibilities offered by chaste and wanton love are entertained, as is typical of the Jonsonian form, there is finally very little actual debate. Chaste love is shown to reign supreme and, as such, the masque celebrates, in the most generalized way, the strength and virtue of the monarchy, and society's (consequent) well-being. Moreover, the wonderful spectacle associated with the masque is exemplified in many aspects of *Cupid's Banishment*, from costumes and the set to the many songs and dances that occur throughout the imaginative world created by White. Moreover, the emblematic and allegorical character of the masque has been well preserved, not only in the characters White has selected but in his explanations of various aspects of costuming.[8]

The characters of *Cupid's Banishment*, as well as many of their properties, were inspired by one of the standard collections of allegorized myths, Cesare Ripa's *Iconologia* (1611). Ripa's emblem of Chastity standing triumphant over Cupid (p. 74) provides the central theme for White's masque. In the woodcut accompanying Ripa's description Chastity is dressed in a long white gown, with a girdle around her waist on which is written '*Castigo corpus meus*' ('I restrain my body'). In Chastity's right hand is a chastising rod (a short rod with streamers coming from the top) poised ready to strike Cupid. In her left hand she holds a sieve, with only a few drops of water leaking through it. Winged Cupid – wearing a blindfold and carrying his bow and quiver – is seated on the ground. The rod is carried by other characters in Ripa's emblems, including Correction and Terror, and is used for punishment. The sieve, appearing in emblems of the period as well as in one well-known portrait of Queen Elizabeth I (the 'Sieve Portrait', dated 1580), was identified with chastity. The ability to carry a sieve without losing the water in it was meant to confirm a woman's sexual impenetrability.

Cupid was commonly depicted in emblem books and poetry as the instigator of wanton love. (He appears as just this sort of character in Lady Mary Wroth's *Love's Victory* which also appears in this collection.) However, in terms of Renaissance ideology interesting complexities surrounded his character. The various depictions of Cupid in the emblems of Andreas Alciati (published in a variety of languages for almost a century from 1536 onward) provide a broad range of characterizations. One illustration shows winged Cupid standing staunchly upright as thunderbolts (often associated with Jupiter) rain down upon him. Cupid manages to break the thunderbolt with his arrow and fire because love generates such heat that no power can withstand it. The meaning is obvious: regardless of age or sex love makes all people into fools.[9] In a related woodcut a scholar is possessed by love. At the centre the scholar sits on a throne, looking like a king with a long beard and a long robe; he holds a sceptre of office and is flanked by three women usually identified as Athena, Venus and Juno. Thus, Venus, goddess of love, conquers the two goddesses of wisdom.[10]

In later editions of *Emblemata* Andreas Alciati introduced a new series of emblems related to love, including characters such as Anteros, who is depicted as an adult version of Cupid and represents the love of virtue. In one illustration Anteros, with wings and his own quiver, binds Cupid to a tree in a landscape. To the left, a fire consumes the arrows, bow and quiver of Cupid.[11] The next illustration features Cupid running into the arms of his mother, Venus, as he is chased by a swarm of bees. The scene represents bitter-sweet love.[12] The subsequent illustration is accompanied by a poem that argues for the force of love. Contrary to the traditional depiction of Cupid as a blind boy who is naked and small, the poet creates a strong, mature image. He writes:

Why should he go about naked? As if cloaks would
  be lacking to a god
Who possessed all the resources of a conquered
  world!
Or who, I ask you, could pass through snows, the
  Alpine north wind,
And meadows rigid with cold, if he were nude?
If he is a boy, do you call the one who conquered
  Nestor a boy?[13]

In imitation of the Jonsonian masque form, *Cupid's Banishment* is divided into masque and antemasque, the court figures (representing good forces) performing in the former, and the characters of darkness and chaos performing in the latter. The characters of the masque, representing virtue, were costumed in colours traditionally associated with truth, light and the higher powers. Diana, who banishes Cupid in the masque, wears a silver and white gown and a 'very rich girdle about', to show her chastity. Her kirtle is embroidered with gold and she carries a silver wand. She is surrounded with flowers and, as an allegory, her nymphs encircle her so that Diana is 'like the moon among the lesser stars'. Occasion, who assists Diana, wears a robe of the same material as Diana, which has been embroidered with silver. She also wears a crimson mantle and carries a silver wand. Occasion has a 'long lock [of hair] before', and is 'bald behind' to signify the difficulty of recalling Occasion if the precise moment is missed. (If Robert White was indeed the 'Master R W' who played Occasion then he was perhaps cross-dressed.) Fortune completes the triad, dressed in a mantle of variable colour 'to express her incertainty, with a veil before her face to shew her blindness and inequality in disposing of her gifts'. She carries her traditional wheel 'to signify her momentary favour'.

The costumes of two supporting characters in the masque, Mercury and Hymen, are unspecified; however, they probably would have been influenced by their many contemporary depictions. Mercury was commonly an adolescent boy with wings on his helmet, and sometimes at his heels; he carried a caduceus, the symbol of his power and authority. In outward appearance, the wings worn by Mercury associate him with Cupid, who was also a winged, young boy. But Mercury and Cupid also contrast in marked ways. As the masque develops, Cupid's insolence leads to a mock coronation in which Diana crowns him with Actaeon's horns, symbolizing the triumph of chastity. (In classical mythology Actaeon was a hunter who saw Diana bathing, and for this transgression was changed into a stag and torn to pieces by his own hounds. Thus, Actaeon, like Cupid, was brought under Diana's control.) Whereas Mercury is content to be the dutiful servant, Cupid behaves like an indignant child whenever his desires are frustrated.

Associated with both Cupid and Mercury was Hymen, the god of married love. In *Cupid's Banishment* he is called upon by Diana to 'crown our sports with sweet delight'. Also generally portrayed by Renaissance artists as a young man, Hymen's dress was based upon images of vegetation and floral motifs, for he symbolized fertility as well as love between married lovers. In White's masque Hymen's followers complement him with images of the forest, wearing green taffeta robes and playing lutes, the conventional instruments of love.

Bacchus and his children provide the antemasque. Riding first in the procession, Bacchus arrives in a chariot hung with vine leaves and grapes, drawn by a goat (symbolizing lust). He carries a bowl of wine and a truncheon, symbolizing his fake authority. His face is red and pimply, and he wears a flesh-coloured buckram (a coarse linen) suit with a wreath of ivy leaves on his head. He is attended by two boys whose faces are red with wine and merriment, each wearing a similar wreath on his head. Like Mercury, but unlike Cupid, Bacchus accepts the boundaries set for his behaviour by Diana. His first mission is to reconcile Cupid with the virgin goddess; but later in the masque, he serves as master of the revels for the antemasque, a bizarre show acted by four of his drunken children: Swash (a fencer), an ape, a tinker and a man weeping. Each is lavishly dressed, exhibiting a variety of colours and fashions; and each dances in a graceless, awkward display befitting his drunken state. In this way the antemasque contrasts sharply with the masque, and it sets the scene for what will follow – the procession of Diana's nymphs, led by Fortune, who descend from the Mount all dressed in white robes, with elaborate jewellery and coronets, to show their complete defiance of Cupid and the rewards of virtue. Consonant with the dramatic trends of the time, *Cupid's Banishment* shows the broadening popularity of the antemasque and the increasing tendency of authors to expand its grotesque elements.[14]

Despite the conventional nature of *Cupid's*

Banishment, the combination of school revels and court masque is unusual. McGee commented: 'The annual Candlemas ritual of Ladies Hall, in other words, provides the form both for the celebration of Diana's ideal of chastity and for the banishment of Cupid.'[15] Structurally, the plan of the masque differs from that of an ordinary masque in that the masquers, two of whom sing songs, are revealed at the opening of the masque and remain in full view of the spectators until the end, when they descend to dance in formations that represent the names of King James, Queen Anne and Prince Charles.[16]

In his casting of men and women White remained consistent with contemporary performance conventions. The actual women who performed in *Cupid's Banishment* participated primarily as silent dancing masquers, contrasting with the men who played the female roles of Diana and Occasion (who was ordinarily depicted as a woman). The single exception in White's casting was Deborah Draper's portrayal of the player queen, probably a decision that he made because the player king and queen were meant to mirror Anne and her husband, King James.

Apparently, the casting conventions of the time were so carefully observed with respect to gender that even Queen Anne – who openly challenged other elements of the masque – didn't feel free to transgress them. Her earliest dramatic offences were the result of indecorum, most often of costuming. After her first masque, Samuel Daniel's *Vision of the Twelve Goddesses* (1604), Dudley Carleton commented on Anne's costume as Pallas Athena, which he thought too short, for it showed the queen's feet and legs.[17] A year later the queen again scandalized members of the court by appearing with her ladies dressed as blackamoors.[18] However, despite such licence, convention eventually prevailed. In *The Masque of Queens* (1609) Jonson refrained from presenting the queens as active agents. Instead he made them passive; and the part played by Anne 'has no individual merit except as a projection of James'.[19]

By setting up a player king and player queen as a central aspect of the annual school revels, and by crowning Cupid with Actaeon's horns, White created an analogy between two fictional courts and the genuine court for which the Ladies Hall masque was written and performed. In the mirroring of courts *Cupid's Banishment* obviously was meant to show King James's family and his court to be a model in which the ideal of chaste matrimonial love was realized. While the literary origins of these coronations and revels are obscure, the folkloric conventions they present were well established in the conventions of popular drama, providing the basis for earlier entertainments, among them the major entertainment held for Elizabeth I in 1592 at Sudeley. There a 'king and queen of the bean' were chosen by cutting a cake in which a bean and a pea were hidden. The person who got the bean (it was assumed, by the hand of fortune) was the king, while the person who got the pea was queen.

This is only one instance of similarity between the annual revels at Ladies Hall and popular entertainment. There are many other examples. But clearly, wherever these conventions were employed the outcome was intended to be political, to reconfirm the supremacy of the monarchy. At Sudeley and elsewhere, McGee notes, 'the selection of a queen by Fortune's doom was important because it created a situation in which two ruling monarchs were present at once'. As in *Cupid's Banishment*, the shepherds of the Sudeley entertainment, costumed as the player king and queen, converted their meeting with Elizabeth I, the genuine monarch, into a gift-giving ceremony.[20] Consequently, the women of Ladies Hall who performed *Cupid's Banishment* venerated and mirrored the court. The women of Ladies Hall acted the parts of virtues. Similarly, Queen Anne, King James and their children were seen as moral examples, giving their own 'gifts' to their courtiers and the common people because they were living examples of virtue.

Nevertheless, on 4 May 1617, the king was away from the court on his famous Scottish tour, and *Cupid's Banishment* was, in every significant way, a 'queen's masque'. During the king's absence Anne met assiduously with the Privy Council to decide the affairs of state; but, although she was essentially functioning as head of state, her health was beginning to suffer. A year later she was showing symptoms of the congestive heart failure from which she died early in March 1619.[21] Thus *Cupid's Banishment* marked the last masquing occasion prepared specifically for Anne. In retrospect, it might well have been that Lady Bedford realized that the queen was sinking towards her end, and thus had organized the masque featuring the queen's goddaughters in order to celebrate not only Anne's important influence over the masque form, but her personal and political eminence in a period of decline.

THE TEXT

The earliest edition of *Cupid's Banishment* was prepared by John Nichols in volume 3 of *The Progresses, Processions, and Magnificent Festivities, of King James the First* (London: J.B. Nichols, 1828), pp. 283–96. C.E. McGee's more recent edition appeared in *Renaissance Drama*, n.s. 19 (1988), pp. 227–64. The edition presented here is newly transcribed from the manuscript (MS MA 1296) owned by the Pierpont Morgan Library. The layout of the transcription below follows that of the original manuscript.

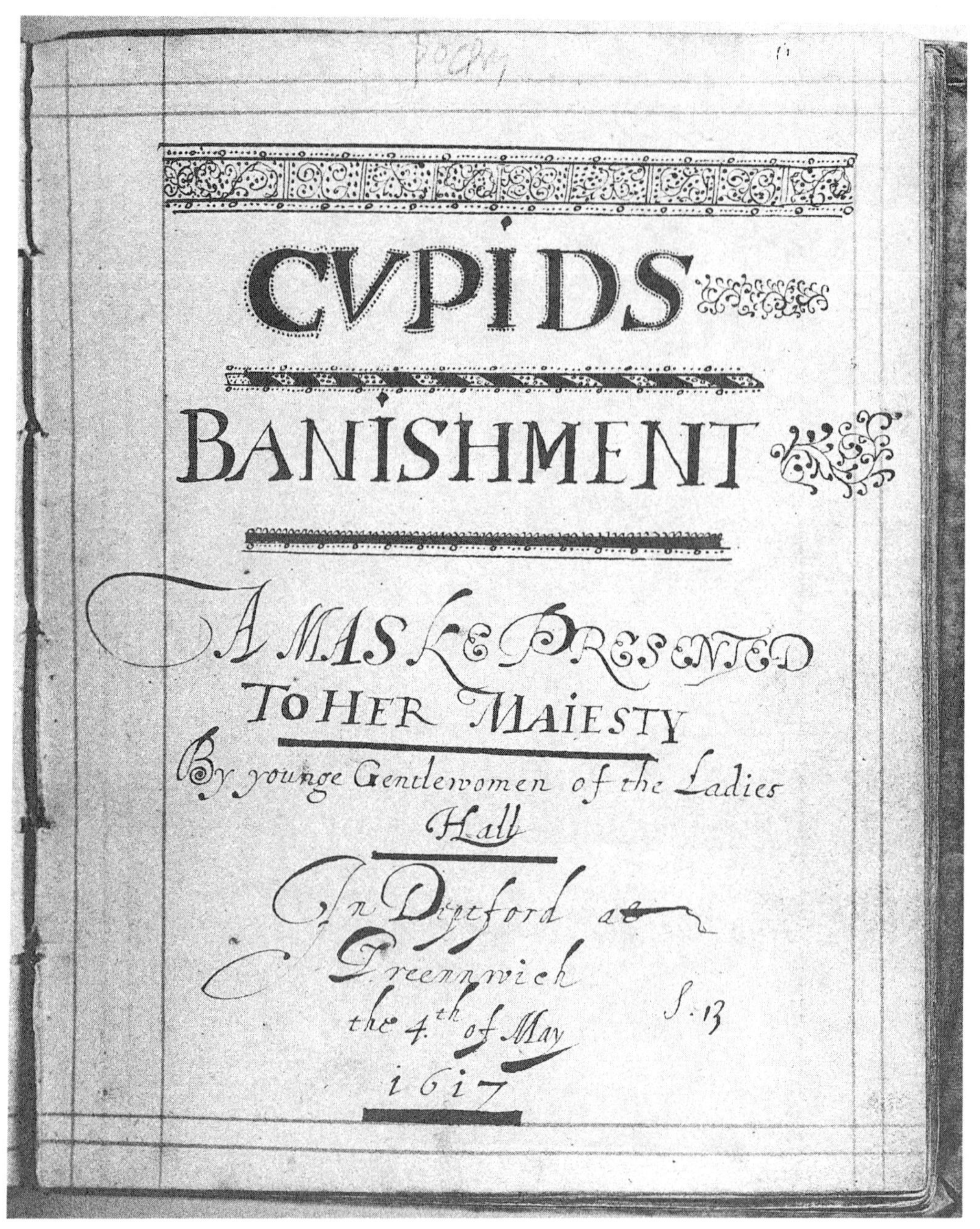

CVPIDS

BANISHMENT

A MASKE PRESENTED
TO HER MAIESTY
By younge Gentlewomen of the Ladies
Hall
In Deptford at
Greenwich
the 4th of May
1617

6 Title page of *Cupid's Banishment*, by kind permission of the Pierpoint Morgan Library

Cupid's Banishment

A MASKE PRESENTED TO HER MAJESTY

By the young Gentlewomen of the Ladies Hall In Deptford at Greenwich The 4th of May 1617

A Note of all the Masquers' Names[1]

Mistress Ann Watkins acted Fortune
Mistress Ann Chalenor[3]
Mistress Ann Libb
Mistress Alice Watkins[6]
Mistress Frances Grant
Mistress Katherine Godschalk
Mistress Katherine Parkinson[7]
Mistress Mary Draper
Mistress Elizabeth Madison[8]
Mistress Elizabeth Cranfield[10]
Mistress Elizabeth Bolton[11]
Mistress Mary Chamber[13]
Mistress Clasie Page[14]
Mistress Lucie Mane
Mistress Ann Sandeland[16]
The Wood Nymphs:
Mistress Jacamote Brussels
Mistress Mary Arls
Mistress Ann Tindall[18]
Mistress Oungelo[19]

Mistress Mary Cramfield[2]
Mistress Elizabeth Jeffs
Mistress Susan Harvey[4]
Mistress Lea Wadson[5]

Master Henry Jennor acted the King
Mistress Deborah Draper the Queen
Master R.W. acted Occasion[9]
John Burreson acted Cupid
Master Richard Browne[12] *acted Diana*
Master Charles Coleman[15] *acted Hymen*
George Lippert, Bacchus
Paul Harbart acted Mercury[17]

To the Honourable and Right Worthy Lady Lucy Countess of Bedford

MADAM:

In regard of the honourable furtherance and noble encouragement your Lady gave us in presenting our masque to Her Majesty, I am bound – if our module[20] of labour may attain to that happiness of desert – to commit this shew[21] to your worthy protection; deeming none more worthy than your Honour to be patroness thereof, for worth is best discerned by the worthy. Base and dejected minds are destitute of that true influence which should [give] vigour to virtue! It is not from affected singularity, or from any conceit of worth in my labours that they durst aspire so high, but a confident opinion of your favourable acceptation,[22] and an absolute resolution of your mild and gracious censure. I confess a lower patronage would have served a higher work, but duty herein only excuses me from presumption. I thought it injustice to devote the fruits which your honour first sowed, to any but yourself. Then from your honourable acceptance let this draw a perpetual privilege, that it may still flourish in the fair summer of your gentle favour, and triumph in despite of Envy's raging winter. But let the envious spit their venom, and tip their tongues with gall;[23] it matters not. This is my comfort: Envy barketh only at the stars, and Spite spurns at that she cannot reach. I hear some curious critic already – whose hungry ears feeds still on other men's provision, and perchance his teeth on other men's tables – hath spied an error and as his perspective informs him, a gross one too! He abruptly demands, 'What should Hymen have to do where Diana is?'[24] Or why there should be a marriage solemnised by the Queen of Chastity? If his refined wit could be confined with reason, I can answer him; but I think hardly satisfy him. The ground of our plot is, choosing of a king and queen by Fortune's doom, which is a sport our little ladies can use on Candlemas night. Again, it was no marriage but a form of uniting chaste hearts to shew a defiance to Cupid and his contracts, and that there could be a chaste combination without his powers. If this will not satisfy I refer him to the speeches; and thus, Madam, holding you no longer with preambles, and superfluous apologies, especially to them that rightly understand me, I rest.

Your Honour's humbly devoted,
Robert White

Cupid's Banishment
Robert White

OCCASION *in a rich garment embroidered with silver, a crimson mantle, and a short cloak of rich tinsie,*[1] *with a white wand to signify her haste, with a long lock before, and bald behind, alluding to the difficulty of recalling her if she be once past: her speech to the* QUEEN.

OCCASION

Gracious and great Sovereigness:
If confidence and royal resolution
Of female worth, and free acceptance
Of noble favour had not armed my breast
With that strong temper of resisting proof
Against Envy's hissing adders,
Time's handmaid had been dumb,
Despair and Fear had overcome our weak
designs;[2]
But bright sphere of greatness[3] thy fair beams
Which shoot with splendour from thy majesty
Revives[4] our fainting[5] Muse with sweet reflection,
And cheers our drooping spirits with unacquainted light.
Thy presence frees each thing that lives in doubt.
No harmless thought now fears the baneful sting
Of fell[6] Distraction, nor here no carping god
Bereaves[7] True Meaning of her worth,
Which the circle[8] of the sacred sphere
Occasion doth repose,
And to this bright audience shews[9]
She was addressed with full attention
Long before this to offer up Time's sacrifice,
Fleeting hours to this fair company;
But worthier objects than they could produce
Diverted their slight purposes;
And yet Occasion cannot shake them off.
Again she is summoned by that lovely crew
Of Ladies Hall, an Academy
Where Modesty doth only sway[10] as governess
These pretty nymphs devoted to your excellence
Present a sport which they yearly celebrate
On Candlemas Night[11] with due solemnity
And with great applause.
They have a King and Queen
Of Fortune's choice,
These be the revels they intend,
Which if your grace will deign to see the end
Occasion thinks herself most fortunate.

OCCASION, *retiring from the presence,* CUPID *meets her and snatches her by the lock.*

CUPID

Come, come Occasion, cease thy old complaints.
Refer thy wrongs unto an equal[12] judge.
Summon young spirits to a jubilee.
Invite fresh youth to some amorous scene.
Banish base dullness for this night;
Revels must be the centre of delight,
With masques and music and sweet harmony,
Each court doth echo forth her melody
With Hymeneal[13] joys and love divine,
Now Kings and Queens do crown the hours of time.
And shall we then be silent where such excellence
Of worth and beauty will give audience,
And where such a chorus[14]
Of lovely nymphs as these shall stand before us?

OCCASION

Peace, foolish boy! Thy blind intrusion
Will not be here admitted. This sacred place
Is only dedicated to chaste Diana[15] and her lovely nymphs.
No wanton[16] subject or immodest strain[17]
Can enter in, for here they do proclaim
Chastity their queen; and to her they sacrifice
Pure thoughts with lust-abhorring eyes.
This is no time nor place for Cupid's wiles.
Thy plots[18] and subtle shifts[19] are all
delusions
To mock mortality and idle fictions
Forged[20] by some poet's fruitless brain.
(OCCASION *shakes him off.*)
Away! Let go! Thou dost deprave my hours
With lust and rape and foul incestuous acts
Under pretence of love. Be gone!
I'll lend thee not a minute to produce
Thy wanton[21] subject and lascivious Muse.
See, thou hast incensed the goddess,
And Fortune with louring[22] beauty frowns.

DIANA *in her arbour, attired all in white to shew*[23] *the purity of chastity, richly decked with jewels, her kirtle*[24] *embroidered with gold, her mantle of silver tinsie, a very rich girdle about called the zone*[25] *of chastity, to shew her defiance to* CUPID *and to signify their chaste meeting, with a silver wand in her hand, her arbour adorned with flowers, encompassed round with her nymphs, like the moon among the lesser stars she shews herself. Whilst the Mount opens the loud music plays, she speaks to* CUPID.

DIANA

Cupid, know thy daring presence doth
offend us,
And thy presumption hath incurred our anger.
We are displeased and do much distaste
Thy rash access[26] without our high command.
Blind Archer, know we are not subject to thy tyranny.
Thy darts[27] and chains[28] are of no power with us;
Nor are we in the compass[29] of thy bow.
We are free from thy bewitching philters,[30]
Thy charms and thy alluring baits.[31]
Our vows are here entire
And are not subject to thy lustful fire.

CUPID
What, are we gods and bear no greater sway?[32]
Is Cupid dead and Venus quite forgot?
Are all my darts grown dull,
My bow so weak that none will stand in awe
But contradict what we command?
Why, dull Time and Lady Chastity,
You know full well that Cupid's conquests
Ring round about the world and will do still
As long as there are things called women.
OCCASION
Boy, leave your waggish[33] wit.
Put up your arrows in your quiver
And be gone.
Fortune is the subject of our scene,
And chaste Diana the mistress of the place
To which fond fancy[34] may not have access.
CUPID
And will all these ladies banish Cupid thus?
Is there never a tender heart that will relent
To thus disgrace me? Do you all consent?
DIANA
Cease, fond idol,[35] thy presence here is tedious.
Steal to some amorous court and tutor
Wanton[36] ladies how to woo
And catch their servants with a nimble glance.
Invent some antic[37] fashion how to please
His mistress' eye with vows and endless protestations.
Make him swear he loves her dearly
Though indeed affecteth[38] nothing less.
These are your practices and chief exploits –
Worthy achievements for a god.
Hence, fond[39] boy!
Thy very breath corrupts a virgin's vow.
CUPID
By all the powers that Cupid can command,
I'll vex you women if I catch you
In my pitfall.[40]
DIANA
Occasion, post away, and shake this copsmate[41] off.
Allot him not a minute space to breath[42] here longer.
(OCCASION *hasteth away and* CUPID *[following] after her.*)
CUPID
Occasion, sweet Occasion, stay.
Grant me but a pair of minutes
To rail with bitter exclamations
Against these milksop[43] ladies.
DIANA
Mercury, with wings of execution,
Finish our command.
Take thy caduseus[44] in thy hand
And summon Hymen[45] to our festival;
But not his fires. Dispatch!
MERCURY
With swiftest expedition I am gone.
Two of DIANA*'s nymphs from the Mount sing, call[ing] for* HYMEN. HYMEN *enters singing,* OCCASION *and* MERCURY *before him, the* KING *and* QUEEN *after him, his followers attending him with lutes and theorbos[46] and excellent voices; the musicians all in green taffety[47] robes.*

THE SONG

Hymen, Hymen, sacred Hymen, that our hearts unite.
Come and crown our sports with sweet delight,
Banish Cupid, that proud boy,
That fills our hearts with deep annoy,[48]
Let us chase him forth our gentle hearts,
His deadly bow and cruel darts.

HYMEN
No spiteful god shall here remain,
To cross[49] our sports and breed[50] our pain.
(*The song being ended,* DIANA *speaks.*)
DIANA
We thank you all with welcome to our court.
Our free acceptance shall declare our heart's affection,
And our joy shall testify your presence acceptable.
See, Fortune congratulates your coming
And smiles with cheerful countenance at your approach.
FORTUNE, *at the bottom of the Mount in a rich mantle wrought with changeable colours[51] to express her incertainty,[52] with a veil before her face to shew her blindness[53] and inequality in disposing of her gifts; her wheel in her hand, to signify her momentary favour.*
FORTUNE
We are engaged[54] to Time for this occasion
That meets our wishes with such good success.
For this great courtesy[55] I'll create
Some unexpected joy to crown thy hours,
Thy minutes, I'll so turn upon this wheel of mine
That men hereafter shall call thee happy Time.
Hymen, Mercury, how welcome you are hither.
We can no more express than we already have.
HYMEN
Chaste and glorious goddesses,
With chastest resolution we are come
To further your intentions,
Clad all in purity,
To shew the blessed chain of amity.[56]

[*Enter*] BACCHUS, *in a chariot hung all with vine leaves and grapes, drawn by a goat,*[57] *riding on a barrel*[58] *with a truncheon*[59] *in one hand and a bowl of wine in the other; two boys, Bacchanalians, with wreaths of ivy, red fiery faces,*[60] *and swelled cheeks, with torches in one hand and bowls of wine in another;* CUPID, *with him, disarmed by* JUPITER, BACCHUS *comes to reconcile the goddess* CYNTHIA[61] *and the god of love and to make a league with the house of love.*

OCCASION
What have we here, more disturbers yet?

BACCHUS
Come, boy, we'll make you all friends,
With a bowl of nectar crowned to the brim.

CUPID
By Venus' apron strings, Bacchus, methinks
I am nobody now I am disarmed. I have a spite
To these squeamish[62] ladies yet for disgracing me.
Would I had my arrows here!

BACCHUS
Come, you'll never leave your wrangling.
I think on my conscience some lawyer was thy
Father and some scolding butterwife[63] thy
Mother. Thou wouldst set all the world
Together by the ears[64] if thou hadst thy will.
Come, boy, submit yourself.

CUPID
Bacchus, I am too stout[65] to yield. Be thou
My orator, good Lyeus,[66] and I'll walk
By like a sheepbiter.[67] Oh, here is fine
Sport for these scornful ladies.
They will laugh me out of my skin.[68]

BACCHUS
Come, take courage boy, and I'll repair unto the throne.
From the spacious court of great commanding Jove, we here
Arrive, the anger to appease, of these incensed goddesses
Against this little boy.

CUPID
You are too familiar, Bacchus.

BACCHUS
Come, you are without your weapons. Now boy,
My father Jupiter who may command,
Entreats a league among his progeny,
A truce, a truce, my little rover.
You know you are confined to use no treachery
Against Cynthia and her train.
Come, let's conclude with love
And drink carouses to the house of Jove.

DIANA
Well, on these conditions we admit you both:
So you contain[69] within the bounds of modesty
And not disturb our sports with rude disorder.

BACCHUS
We do obey,
Yet grant chaste Cynthia that Bacchus may
In a Castalian[70] bowl full fraught with wine
Squeezed in abundance from the swelling vine
Carouse[71] a health unto these ladies round.

DIANA
We are content. Now Fortune it remains
That you do perfit[72] what's by us begun.
Descend, blind goddess, and with some worthy favour,
Drawn from the abundance of thy large lottery,
Grace the happy league[73] of this thy choice.

FORTUNE *and* HYMEN *to the coronation, the* KING *and* QUEEN *seated at the foot of the Mount under* FORTUNE, *the* KING *on her right hand and the* QUEEN *on her left, the* QUEEN *attired all in silver tinsie*[74] *showing that she was one of Diana's train and that their revels did wholly tend to Chastity, being a sport the goddess and her nymphs did use*[75] *in bowers and retired places without any prejudice to virginity or scandal to any entire*[76] *vow.*

OCCASION
Perpetual joy and true delight,
Crown this hour with sweet content.

CUPID *in a white loose garment, girt close to him with a garland of white and red roses, disarmed of his bow and darts,*[77] *falls into a passion because he was excluded from their revels; he stamps and storms.*

CUPID
What, a marriage, and Cupid no actor in it?
What human power can brook[78] this shame?
Shall we that be immortal then contain
And suffer this disgrace,
We that made Apollo rage with love,[79]
Mars[80] mad with doting fancy
And great love,
A captive with the conquering dart of love![81]
Are we now confined, disarmed and scorned
With vildest[82] imputations?[83]
Ye coy dames, I'll make you rave
Like beldames,[84] tear your hair,
And curse your coyness!
Your squeamish, affected niceness[85]
Shall feel the fury of my vengeance!
I'll torment you all!

The goddess, being moved with his insolency,[86] *calleth to her wood nymphs to assist her.*

DIANA
Insolence! Thou dost profane our presence.

Thou shalt find and see
Lust can never conquer Chastity.
Come, all ye that love chaste Vesta[87]
And chase this Bedlam[88] forth.

Enter the DRIADES,[89] *or eight wood nymphs.[They] rush out of a grove adjoining to the Mount, four off one side and four off another – with darts*[90] *in their hands to shew*[91] *they had a dart [that] could conquer* CUPID *– attired all in green garments, the upper part close to their bodies, the lower full and loose with silver and carnation*[92] *lace from the breast to the foot, their arms half naked with bracelets of berries about them, [on] their heads garlands with [a] great variety of flowers, their hair dishevelled, hanging careless about their shoulders, bare with puffs of tiffany*[93] *round about, [and] green pumps and gloves. After the music played over the first strain they fall into their dance. They environ*[94] CUPID *in a figure and put* ACTAEON'S *head*[95] *upon him. They fall off threatening him with their darts when he offers to resist. After many pretty figures*[96] *they chase him forth into the woods by violence and banish him that presence. The nymphs sing in joy.* CUPID *is gone.*

[THE SONG]

Hark, hark, how Philomel[97]
Whose notes no ayre[98] can parallel;
Mark, mark, her melody.
She descants[99] still on chastity
The diapason[100] of her song is Cupid's gone.
He is gone, he is gone, is quite exiled.
Venus's brat, peevish ape,[101] fancy's child,[102]
Let him go with his quiver and his bow.
Let him know we are not subject to him; though
He can command, yet we are free
From Cupid and his tyranny.

After this, OCCASION *speaks to* BACCHUS, *awakens him with her wand, enjoins him to commit no disorder.*

OCCASION

Bacchus, look to it you do contain
Lest you be branded with Actaeon's shame.
Come, leave your roaring, this jovial vein[103]
Delights not ladies. Methinks your vine
Should yield some quick[104] invention to grace
These ladies' revels. Come, be not dull
Nor brainsick[105] now. Rouse up thy spirits!

BACCHUS

By Jove, Occasion, I am horrible sleepy. I could sleep
now with Endymion[106] and snore with Epiminedes;[107] but at
thy entreaty I will awake and show thee some of my
delightful sports. Come, bullies,[108] my brave[109] Bacchanalians,
make the welkin[110] roar with some reeling vein.[111]

Enter a grand BACCHUS, *skipping in with a belly as big as a kinderkin,*[112] *all in flesh-coloured buckram,*[113] *with a wreath of vine leaves about his head, a red swollen face full of pimples with a bass lute in his hand, singing and describing the antimasque. All of Bacchus' children, he describes them particular[ly]*[114] *as they come forth.*

THE SONG

1 Bacchus at thy call
They here come marching roundly,[115]
That will not flinch at all
But take their liquors soundly.[116]

They'll do their parts, they'll drink whole quarts,
A pint with them is but a swallow;
They'll ne'er give o'er, till the welkin[117] roar,
The house run round and the sky look yellow.

Four Bacchanalians

2 Bacchus' children come,
And at their backs they have barrels
With bellies like a tun,[118]
Mulled sack[119] shall end all quarrels.

The Drunk Fencer

Next Swash appears who storms and swears
If that they bring not better wine,
The pots he'll maul,[120] against the wall,
He'll beat my host and break his sign.[121]

The Ape Drunkard

3 Another drunkard skips
Whose head is like a feather.
He'll show as many tricks
As your ape, baboon[122] together.

The Drunk Fiddler

The fiddler's croud[123] now squeaks aloud,
His fuddling strings begin to troll;[124]
He loves a wake and a wedding cake,
A bridhouse[125] and a brave maypole.

The Drunk Tinker[126]

4 Next the roaring tinker,
As furious as a dragon,
He swears he'll be no flincher,[127]
His carouse is but a flagon.[128]
He loves his punk,[129] but when he is drunk,
His muddy brains well mulled[130] with liquor,
He then will roar and call his whore,
And out of door he swears he'll kick her.

The Weeping Drunk

5 Armed all with claret[131]

The weeping drunkard next,
He is very sorry for it,
His soul is sore perplexed.
These are the crew of drunkards true
That do belong to Bacchus' court.

This song being ended the Bacchanalians begin to dance, four of them in flesh-coloured buckram, wreaths of ivy on their heads and girdles[132] *with twists of ivy, barrels at their backs with fiery faces, long hair, great bellies, and red pumps. The* FENCER, *with a sword and dagger, great slops*[133] *guarded*[134] *with yellow and blue cotton, a roaring band*[135] *and a broad-brimmed hat with a low crown buttoned up in the fashion. The* APE DRUNKARD *in red and white cotton, his breeches one side, a slop*[136] *the other side, a trunk,*[137] *with stockings of the same, his short cloak reaching halfway to his back, his hat guarded with yellow and white cotton. The* FIDDLER *with a blue coat with hanging sleeves, on the left sleeve a rat for his cullison,*[138] *playing on a fiddle with a great nosegay*[139] *in his hat. The* TINKER *in a leather pelt*[140] *with a hammer and an old kettle, keeping time with the music, his face all besmeared, his trull*[141] *with a pair of leather bodies,*[142] *her neather*[143] *coat of yellow cotton, a black hat with five wax lights in it, a posy*[144] *pinned to her breast. The* WEEPING DRUNKARD *in blue and yellow cotton, his breeches close, dancing in a melancholy measure and bemoaning his faults. They show the several humours*[145] *of drunkards with many pretty figures befitting the vein.*[146] *The dance being ended,* DIANA *speaks.*

DIANA

So now let these sacred sisters
With their chaste scene begin,
Advance this hour with some sweet passage[147]
And with some whispering measure,[148]
Charm hearts and eyes with never-ending pleasure.

Twelve nymphs descend from the Mount attired all in white tinsie to show their defiance to CUPID; *and to signify their chaste meeting, with rich mantles, six of watched,*[149] *the other six of crimson, their hair dishevelled, their breasts naked [but adorned] with rich jewels and pearls, [and] necklaces, [and] on their heads coronets of artificial flowers with a puff of tinsie rising in the midst, [and also wearing] white pumps and roses and white gloves.* FORTUNE *descends with them to dance, to grace this, her choice, and to signify [that] she is pleased with this chaste festival. She is attired in rich garments of diverse colours, a waistcoat embroidered with gold, many curious flowers wrought with silver and silk with pleasant colours, a rich mantle, a veil before her face, her wheel in her hand. They [the nymphs] pace with majesty toward the presence*[150] *and, after the first strain of the violins, they dance, [forming] Anna Regina [Queen Anne] in letters; [in] their second masquing dance [forming] Jacobus Rex [King James]; [in] their departing dance is [the formation of] Carolus P [Prince Charles] with many excellent figures falling off,*[151] *by Master Onslo, tutor to the Ladies Hall. Having ended their dances, and falling off*[152] *– half off one side, and a half off another –* DIANA *descends from the Mount with two of the* QUEEN*'s* GODDAUGHTERS[153] *and presents them to Her Majesty with this speech.*

DIANA

From our chaste throne we condescend[154]
To greet your Majesty with this my train,
My nymphs retired form the leavy[155] woods
Have left their wonted[156] habits all of green,
Their sportive quivers and their hunting weeds,[157]
Their loose girt[158] garments which they use to wear.
The hills and dales, the brooks and fountains clear,
Decked all in virgin's hue, they come to see
Fair Albion's[159] Queen enthroned in majesty,
And see two of all the rest do seem to show
A Divine duty which they owe
Unto your Highness' grace
Who, to intimate their loves above the rest
Present the timely fruits of their chaste labours
Of which bright shining lamp that in human shape
Show'st heaven's perfection vouchsafe to accept,
And Phoebe with her train,
Devoted to your Grace forever will remain.

This speech being ended, the GODDAUGHTERS *presenting their needlework gifts – one, an acorn; the other, rosemary*[160] *– beginning with the first letters of the* QUEEN*'s name. They retire all, two by two. Making their honours they descend the Mount with this song.*

THE LAST SONG

Thus, Cynthia's triumphs[161] begin to cease
With true love, and joyful peace,
If worth and honour have content
Time's fleeting minutes are well spent
And we shall think what here we do bestow
Are things of duty which we still do owe;
But cruel Time doth slide so swift away
That we must home unto our shady bowers
Where we will ever for your Highness pray
That you in joy may spend your happy hours.

The song, being ended, OCCASION *speaks to the Queen.*

OCCASION

Bright Pallas[162]and royal mistress of our muse,
Occasion hath adventured to bestow
Some nimble minutes which, if they have run
So happily that they have won
The Olympian prize, your gracious favour,
We have achieved a piece of work
Far richer than the golden fleece
Which Jason[163] strove to purchase;[164]
But if vain opportunity
Hath ought[165] profaned your reverent dignity
With tedious time and hath uttered ought
In prejudice of your most noble sex,
Pardon you, glorious company,
You stars of women,
And let the silent rhetoric
Of that gracious look
That works a league[166] betwixt the state of hearts
Vouchsafe to shine upon our childish sports.
We profess [our] stage no Helicon[167]
Our muse is homespun,[168] our action is our own,
Then, bright goddess, with one sweet smile,
Grace all,
Our nymphs, Occasion, and our Ladies' Hall.

FINIS

7 *Lady Mary Wroth*, by kind permission of Lord De L'Isle

5 *Love's Victory*

LADY MARY WROTH

INTRODUCTION

Towards the end of *Love's Victory* the play's heroine, Musella, asks her friend and confidante, Simeana, 'must my wretched end / Proceed from love?' (V.i.2-3). These words could have been uttered by Lady Mary herself, for her life was characterized by conflict and frustration, both in her marriage to Robert Wroth and in her affair with her cousin William Herbert. Perhaps her misfortunes were particularly hard to bear since her childhood had been so happy and auspicious; she was born *c.* 1587 to Sir Robert Sidney and Barbara Gamage, and thus began life as one of the culturally elite Sidney family. After all, her uncle was the renowned author Sir Philip Sidney and her aunt, after whom she was named, was Mary Herbert (née Sidney) the Countess of Pembroke, whose own play, *The Tragedy of Antonie* (1595), is included in this anthology. Indeed, although Lady Mary was married at the age of 17 to Sir Robert Wroth, she retained the Sidney coat of arms.[1] Unfortunately, the marriage appears to have been unhappy from the start; partly this was an inevitability considering the very different lifestyles the couple chose to follow – Mary was inclined to participate in the cultural activities at court: for example, she performed in Ben Jonson's *The Masque of Blackness* (1604), while Robert preferred to hunt on his own lands.[2] However, it is probable that a close affection had already arisen between Mary and her cousin before the marriage to Wroth took place. William Herbert was the son of Mary Sidney, an intelligent and witty man, an author in his own right and the very antithesis of Robert Wroth. Mary Erskine, one of the ladies at court. described him as:

> One of the most agreeable men of his time . . . He has prodigious quick eyes, and a pleasing countenance. He was a graceful and eloquent speaker on all subjects, having not only wit and learning, but judgement to apply them properly.[3]

Perhaps it is significant that such praise came from a lady, for Herbert was also known to indulge in 'pleasures of all kinds, almost in all excesses' and to be particularly susceptible to the charms of women.[4] He had had an affair with one of Elizabeth I's maids of honour, Mary Fritton, and although she became pregnant (a boy was born in 1601), he had refused to marry her. Herbert's own marriage, in 1604 to Mary Talbot, appears to have been a contract between two wealthy families and certainly not a love match. In any case, whatever Herbert's marital relations were like, after Robert Wroth's death in 1616 (Mary's legitimate son died soon after his father in 1616), William Herbert entered into an extended affair with his cousin Lady Mary, and they had two illegitimate children, William and Catherine.

After such scandalous behaviour Mary Wroth was dismissed from court. It is interesting to note that although Herbert remained a valued and respected adviser, she never returned to the social world she had once valued so highly; she was merely able to visit her female friends and relatives. But if Wroth was denied the actual intrigues and excitements of court life, then she began to recreate them in her own writings. Indeed, an awareness of Mary Wroth's biography is essential to the understanding of her work, for the characters in her romances, poems and play represent the people she knew, those she loved and those she despised. During her lifetime her books sometimes aroused interest because of their *roman-à-clef* topicality; even close to her death (*c.* 1651) she was asked by the Earl of Rutland to identify some of the characters in her prose work *Urania*.[5] Of all the authors in this anthology it is Wroth whose life is most intimately bound to her literary productivity.

Like the other women writers referred to here, however, Wroth was perceived as much as a patron of the arts – in other words a patron of male authors – as she was recognized as a writer.[6]

Nevertheless, one of the most apt descriptions of her comes from one of the poets she supported: Ben Jonson. In his collection *Underwood* (28; 1640) he praises her writing, but links it specifically to the world of love:

For in your verse all Cupids Armorie,
His flames, his shafts, his Quiver, and his Bow,
His very eyes are yours to overthrow.
But then his Mothers sweets you so apply,
Her joyes, her smiles, her loves, as readers take
For *Venus Ceston*, every line you make.[7]

Jonson connects Wroth's fascination with the forces of love and desire to her own poetry and, significantly, embodies the double nature of her interests in the personifications of love, Cupid and Venus, the two characters Wroth herself used in *Love's Victory*. But all Lady Mary's works revolve around these central concerns, which are usually epitomized in the heroine and hero of each respective text; in the case of her play, in the characters of Musella and Philisses. But although Jonson openly explains the surface meaning of her writings, he does not uncover the hidden allegories, perhaps not wishing to stir up any rumours of improper behaviour about his patron. Lady Mary Wroth's theme was love, but she conveys the general idea through her own experience of it, and whatever she chose to call her main protagonists they always represent herself and William Herbert – although she sometimes includes Robert Wroth in a minor part (in the play he is the character Rustic). Yet her writing is not overtly personal, its autobiography is hidden beneath a skilful rendition of some of the most complex and self-aware Renaissance literary forms.

Wroth's canon is unparalleled amongst Renaissance women writers; she was the first Englishwoman to write a prose romance, a sonnet sequence and an original pastoral drama.[8] The prose romance, *The Countess of Montgomery's Urania*, exists in two parts: the first was published in 1621 but had to be withdrawn after a complaint was made by Lord Denny who objected to the way he and his family were represented in the text – at one point he is called a 'bla[d]der blowne with wind'.[9] Consequently, the second part was not published in her lifetime, although an edition is currently being prepared from the manuscript version.[10] Not unexpectedly, the *Urania* presents the Sidney family in a more favourable light than Denny and his daughter. For example, Wroth herself becomes the heroine of the romance, Pamphilia, while William Herbert is seen as the charming but unfaithful Amphilanthus. But there is yet another level of contemporary allusion present in *Urania*, for to any Renaissance reader a second type of familial invocation would immediately have been apparent: the title of Wroth's work reflects that of her uncle's prose romance, Sir Philip Sidney's *The Countess of Pembroke's Arcadia* (1590). Not only does Lady Mary draw upon the complex history of relationships within her family, but she also draws upon their writings, so that at times the web of reference, to people and to texts, appears impenetrable. It becomes impossible to determine at which point she has used her uncle's prose romance or his sonnet sequence, her father's poetry, her aunt's translations or her cousin's writings. Moreover, the contemporary allegory inevitably becomes confused along the same lines, so that we cannot say exactly when a particular Sidney relationship is being represented. For example, in *Love's Victory* it is not possible to say that Musella is *only* Lady Mary Wroth, for she may also be Stella, who is a character in Sir Philip Sidney's sonnet sequence, *Astrophil and Stella* (1591), where Stella in turn images the real woman Penelope Rich. Wroth's writing excels at binding together the lives and *œuvres* of the Sidney family, and at inextricably entwining the private and the public identities of men and women alike.

Lady Mary Wroth paid a similar tribute to her uncle in her own sonnet sequence, *Pamphilia to Amphilanthus* (1621), where the two main characters of *Urania* recur, repeating their pattern of unrequited love (Pamphilia means 'all-loving', whereas Amphilanthus ominously signifies 'lover of two').[11] On a simple level, the title may again be seen to recall Philip's *Astrophil and Stella*, while the lovers clearly refer to Wroth and William Herbert.

Initially, Wroth's play, *Love's Victory* (*c.* 1620), appears to be the text least obviously indebted to the work of an earlier Sidney author, although its title, which suggests a derivation from Petrarch's *The Triumph of Love* (*c.* 1360), could be understood as Wroth's attempt to continue the work begun by her aunt, Mary Sidney, who translated Petrarch's *The Triumph of Death* (*c.* 1600).[12]

It is generally considered that Wroth was not particularly vehement in her defences of women, although it is clear that she was aware of the fact that her society's values undermined female independence – indeed, she had personal experience of the double standards applied to sexual relations.[13] Instead, Lady Mary represented the way in which women were contained by the demands made upon them and pointed towards the only escape she knew – close family connections and 'safe' family houses.[14] This type of careful and subdued rebellion against the strictures governing women's lives is exemplified in Wroth's play, *Love's Victory*. Women were not able to write works for production in a public theatre, but they were allowed to write plays for performance within their own homes, the parts being read, and perhaps acted, by members of their family and close friends. Mary Sidney's translation of Robert Garnier's *Antoine* was just such a play, and it is likely that Mary Wroth followed her aunt's example in writing a text intended for dramatic performance within one of the safe Sidney houses which she often visited. There is no evidence that the play was ever acted, although the stage directions in the Penshurst Manuscript suggest that Wroth thought of the work in terms of an actual performance. However, it is possible that *Love's Victory* was one of the plays staged by Sir Edward Dering, who was involved in amateur dramatics during the early 1620s and was also a close friend of the Sidney family.[15] Wroth certainly had experience of private theatricals before writing her play; as has already been mentioned, she performed in Jonson's masques and probably had a part in Jonson's lost play, *The May Lord*.[16] What cannot be questioned is that Lady Mary Wroth was the first Englishwoman to write an original dramatic comedy, and it is essential that in future we consider the play alongside the similar works written by men for the public theatre.

The dates of Wroth's works are mainly uncertain, but since she reuses the same personages it is likely that they were all composed in the early 1620s. Although Pamphilia and Amphilanthus do not reappear in her play (they occur in both the sonnet sequence and the prose romance), there are certain overlaps in terms of character and style with the other texts. The 'Vale of Tempe' in *Urania* II is a pastoral interlude which features a brother and sister who excel at writing poetry, and in which characters called Rustick, Magdaline and Arcas appear. This is clearly expanded in *Love's Victory*, the brother and sister being named as Philisses and Simeana (in reality, of course, Philip and Mary Sidney), and the other characters altered slightly to become Rustic, Dalina and Arcas.[17] The association between the sonnet sequence and the play is evident from the numerous parallels in the love poetry in each of them; for example, the drama's framing device consists of a *deus ex machina* in which Venus and Cupid rule the lives of the shepherds and shepherdesses in the main body of the play, while *Pamphilia and Amphilanthus* begins with a sonnet to Venus and Cupid accusing them of conquering the sonneteer's heart:

> Butt one hart flaming more then all the rest
> The goddess held, and putt itt to my brest,
> Deare sonne, now shutt said she: thus must we winn;
>
> Hee her obay'd, and martir'd my poore hart.[18]

The overall concept of Venus and Cupid triumphing over mortal hearts is derived from Petrarch's *Triumph of Love*, and this is one of Wroth's literary sources, used both in the play and in the poem. More specific to *Love's Victory* are the pastoral dramas: Torquato Tasso's *Aminta* (1580), Samuel Daniel's *Queen's Arcadia* (1606) and John Fletcher's *The Faithful Shepherdess* (1610). A more appropriate term for these plays and for Wroth's *Love's Victory*, however, is 'tragi-comedy', which began to be popular in England at the beginning of the seventeenth century. In Act V of the play Musella and Philisses drink a potion which they and the audience believe to be poison, and Silvesta, who has supplied the drink, proclaims them to be dead:

> Who would outlive them? Who would dying fly?
> That here beheld love and love's tragedy?
> [(V.iv.71-2)]

Of course, the potion has only put the two lovers to sleep, and when they awaken Venus' priests welcome them:

> Philisses, of us take Musella fair,
> We join your hands, rise and abandon care.
> Venus hath caused this wonder for her glory,
> And the triumph of Love's Victory.
> [(V.vii.63-6)]

What was thought to be a sad ending is transformed by Venus' intervention into a happy one, the play shifts from the suggestion of tragedy to the resolution of comedy, and the title of the play is resolutely affirmed to be 'Love's Victory' and not 'love's tragedy'. But while Wroth follows dramatic convention in these concluding manoeuvres, she alters the genre slightly in giving most of her characters equal weight. Although there are some minor figures in the play, such as Climeana and

Phillis, the other couples are given almost the same number of lines. There could be several reasons for this innovation. First, thematically it makes more sense since each couple represents a different kind of love:

True love – Musella and Philisses
Flawed love – Simeana and Lissius
Chaste love – Silvesta and Forester
Comic love – Dalina and Rustic

Wroth, therefore, must give the four couples space in which to express their versions of love, even though a pattern within this larger group clearly does exist. Second, as a woman dramatist Wroth might have been interested in giving more speeches to the female characters, especially in the scenes where they reveal their friendship. Indeed, Barbara Lewalski suggests that the play's emphasis on women reveals it as a 'pastoral adapted to a species of feminist politics'.[19]

However, it is possible to suggest a third reason for this seeming lack of hierarchy – the play's contemporary allegory in which each fictional character has a counterpart in the real world, who in turn might well have been intended to play the part through which they are figured. The contemporary allusions would have been expected within the pastoral genre, since, while evoking an idealized world, pastoral always comments upon the inadequacies of the immediate present.[20] What is different about Wroth's use of pastoral is that she chooses not to refer to late Jacobean society but to her close circle of friends and relations; if inadequacies are revealed they are those of private affairs and individual personalities. Some of the characters are easy to identify, others we have found more difficult to allocate, especially as there are often two periods of allusion. The list below gives some of the possibilities:

Character	*Wroth's contemporaries*	*Earlier generation of Sidney connections*	
Musella	Lady Mary	Penelope Rich (Stella)	
Philisses	William Herbert	Philip Sidney	
Simeana	Susan de Vere	Mary Sidney	
Lissius	Philip Herbert	Matthew Lister	
Rustic	Robert Wroth	Robert Rich	
Dalina		Penelope Rich	(?)
Forester		Robert Sidney	(?)
Silvesta		'Lysa'	(?)

Several of the references are quite clear due to Wroth's use of puns – the names 'Wroth/Worth' and 'Rich' being used quite often – and of quasi-anagrams, such as making *Ma*ry *Sidney* into SIMEANA and *Lis*ter into LISSIUS. Others must remain more tentative; for example, Forester's version of Platonic love is very close to the Neoplatonism incorporated into Robert Sidney's love poems to the unidentified 'Lysa'.[21] Although no final identifications can be made, it is tempting to imagine Wroth writing a play about and for her family and friends. She had, after all, been banished from court, so that her knowledge of the intrigues there might have been somewhat limited. In such circumstances she probably had to focus on those people she considered to be her intimate circle. In her mind Wroth might well have allocated the parts, seeing herself as Musella, her friend Susan de Vere as Simeana, William Herbert as Philisses and his brother Philip Herbert (Susan's husband) as Lissius. As such, she did not perceive her drama as a giving a few actors 'good parts' and the others 'supporting roles', but as a meeting of friends whose mutual pleasure and interest would have been of primary importance. Perhaps this makes Wroth a 'woman dramatist', her concerns focusing upon her family rather than on herself, but it also makes her a Sidney before all else. Lady Mary Wroth is thus the natural heir of the combined voices of her uncle, aunt and father, and her play, *Love's Victory*, is the final tribute to that complex intermixing of text and biography at which the Sidneys excelled.

THE TEXT

Love's Victory exists in only two manuscript versions and one of those is incomplete. The finest copy is the Penshurst Manuscript which is owned by Viscount De L'Isle and has probably remained with the Sidney family since its composition. This version is the basis for Michael Brennan's edition for the Roxburghe Club (1988), which has been of immense use to us in the preparation of our own edition. The other manuscript is now at the Huntington Library (HM 600), but this version is incomplete; it does not have the title-page, I.i.1-38, V.i.68-74, and 103 to the end.[22] Brennan argues, convincingly, that the Huntington *Love's Victory* is the supposedly lost third version, the Plymouth Manuscript. We have referred both to the Penshurst and Huntington manuscripts. We have also made use of the transcripts and editions of the play, obviously drawing upon Brennan, but also incorporating C.H.J. Maxwell's edition of the Huntington version of the play ('"Love's Victorie"', Master's Thesis, Stanford University, 1933), Josephine Roberts's notes on the songs from the Huntington version, and the transcription of parts of the Plymouth manuscript by James O. Halliwell in *A Brief Description of the Ancient and Modern Manuscripts Preserved in the Public Library Plymouth* (1853). Significant differences in the manuscript versions are indicated in the notes. As with the other plays in this collection we have modernized spelling and rationalized punctuation throughout. We have also inserted scene numbers in order to make the play more accessible to a present-day readership and, we hope, audience.

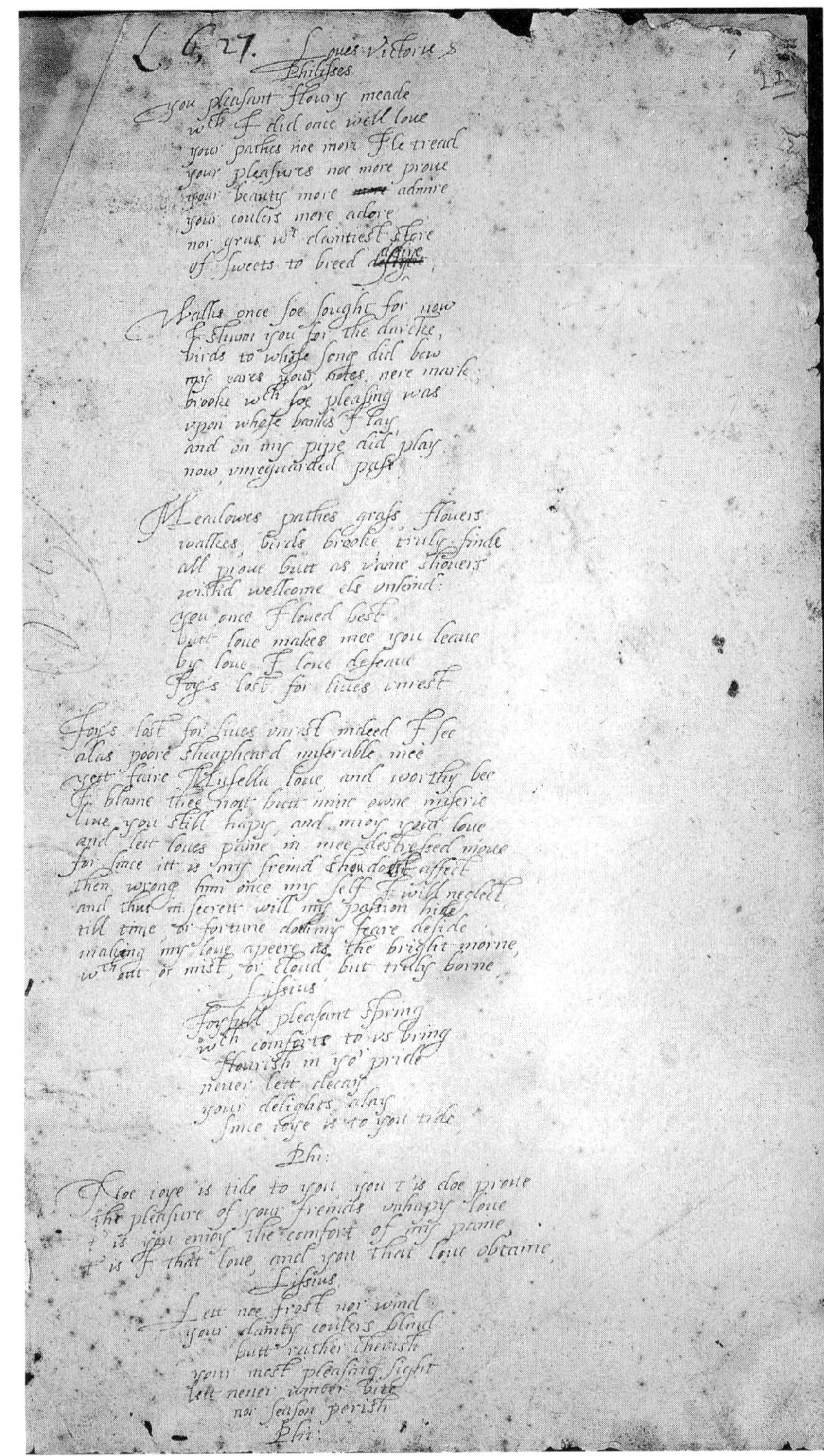

L 6, 27. Loues Victorie s
Philisses

You pleasant flowry meade
wch I did once well loue
your pathes noe more Ile tread
your pleasures noe more proue
your beauty more ~~more~~ admire
your coulers mere adore
nor gras wt daintiest store
of sweets to breed ~~desire~~ desire;

Walks once soe sought for now
I shunn you for the darcke,
birds to whose song did bow
my eares your notes, nere mark;
brooke wch soe pleasing was
vpon whose banks I lay
and on my pipe did play
now vnregarded pass;

Meadowes pathes grass flowers
walkes birds brooke truly finde
all proue butt as vaine showers
wishd wellcome els vnkind:
you once I loued best
butt loue makes mee you leaue
by loue I loue deceaue
Ioy's lost for liues vnrest

Joy's lost for liues vnrest indeed I see
alas poore sheaphierd miserable mee
yett faire Musella loue and worthy bee
I blame thee nott butt mine owne miserie
liue you still happy, and inioy your loue
and lett loues paine in mee destressed moue
for since itt is my freind thou dost affect
then wrong him once my self I will neglect
and thus in secrett will my passion hide
till time or fortune doth my feare deside
making my loue apeere as the bright morne
wth out or mist, or cloud butt truly borne

Lissius

Forsuld pleasant spring
wth comforts to vs bring
flourish in yor pride
neuer lett decay
your delights alway
since ioye is to you tide

Phi:

Noe ioye is tide to you you t'is doe proue
the pleasure of your freinds vnhapy loue
t'is you enioy the comfort of my paine
it is I that loue and you that loue obtaine

Lissius

Lett nee frost nor wind
your dainty coulers blind
butt rather cherish
your most pleasing sight
lett neuer winter bite
nor season perish

Phi:

8 First page of *Love's Victory*, by kind permission of the Huntington Library

Love's Victory

[by LADY MARY WROTH]

[*c.*1620]

List of Characters

Shepherds

Philisses, in love with Musella, and beloved by her
Lissius, in love with Simeana, and beloved by her
Forester, in love with Silvesta
Lacon, in love with Musella
Rustic, in love with Musella, but marries Dalina
Arcas, a villain

Shepherdesses

Musella, in love with Philisses
Simeana, in love with Lissius
Silvesta, has vowed chastity
Climeana, in love with Lissius
Dalina, a fickle lady
Phillis, loves Philisses
Mother to Musella

Temple of Love

Venus
Cupid
Priests

Act I

Scene i

[*Enter*] VENUS, *and* CUPID *with her, in her temple, her* PRIESTS *attending her.*[1]

VENUS
Cupid, methinks we have too long been still,
And that these people grow to scorn our will.
Mercy to those ungrateful breeds neglect;
Then let us grow our greatness to respect,
Make them acknowledge that our heavenly power
Cannot their strength, but even themselves, devour;
Let them not smile and laugh because thine eyes
Are covered, as if blind,[2] or love despise.
No, thou that[3] scarce shalt from thine eyes take off,
Which gave them cause on thee to make this scoff.
Thou shalt discern their hearts, and make them know
That humble homage unto thee they owe;
Take thou the shaft which headed is with steel[4]
And make them bow whose thoughts did lately reel;
Make them thine own, thou who didst me once harm,[5]
Cannot forget the fury of that charm;
Wound them, but kill them not, so may they live
To honour thee, and thankfulness to give;
Shun no great cross[6] which may their crosses[7] breed,
But yet, let blessed enjoying them[8] succeed.
Grief is sufficient to declare thy might,
And in thy mercy glory will shine bright.

CUPID
Mother, I will no cross, no harm, forbear,
Of jealousy for loss, of grief or fear,
Which may my honour touched[9] again repair;
But with their sorrows will my glory rear.
Friends shall mistrust their friends, lovers mistake,
And all shall for their folly woes partake;
Some shall love much, yet shall no love enjoy,
Others obtain, when lost is all their joy.
This will I do, your will and mind to serve,
And to your triumph[10] will these rites preserve.

VENUS
Then shall we have again our ancient glory;
And let this called be 'Love's Victory'.
Triumphs upon their travels[11] shall ascend,
And yet most happy ere they come to end.

CUPID
Joy and enjoying on some shall be set,
Sorrow on others caught by Cupid's net.[12]
[*Exeunt.*]

Scene ii

[*Enter* PHILISSES.]

PHILISSES[13]
You pleasant flowery mead[14]

Which I did once well love,
Your paths no more I'll tread,
Your pleasures no more prove,
Your beauty more admire,
Your colours more adore,
Nor grass with daintiest store
Of sweets to breed desire.

Walks, once so sought for, now
I shun you for the dark;
Birds, to whose song did bow
Mine ears, your notes ne'er mark;
Brook, which so pleasing was,
Upon whose banks[15] I lay,
And on my pipe did play,[16]
Now unregarded pass.

Meadows, paths, grass, flowers,
Walks, birds, brook: truly find
All prove but as vain[17] showers,
Wished welcome, else unkind.
You once I loved best,
But love makes me you leave;
By love I love deceive;
Joys lost for life's unrest.

Joys lost for life's unrest; indeed, I see.
Alas, poor shepherd, miserable me.
Yet, fair Musella, love and worthy be;
I blame thee not, but mine own misery.
Live you still happy and enjoy your love,
And let love's pain[18] in me distressed move;
For since it is my friend thou dost affect,
Then wrong him once, myself I will neglect;
And thus in secret will my passion[19] hide,
Till time or fortune doth my fear decide,
Making my love appear as the bright morn,
Without or mist, or cloud, but truly born.
[*Enter* LISSIUS.]

LISSIUS

Joyful pleasant spring,
Which comforts to us bring,
Flourish in your pride.
Never let decay
Your delights allay,[20]
Since joy is to you tied.

PHILISSES [*Aside.*]

No, joy is tied to you. You 'tis do prove
The pleasure of your friend's unhappy love.
'Tis you enjoy the comfort of my pain,
'Tis I that love, and you that love obtain.

LISSIUS

Let no frost nor wind
Your dainty[21] colours blind,[22]
But rather cherish.
Your most pleasant sight,
Let never winter bite
Nor season perish.

PHILISSES [*Aside*]

I cannot perish more than now I do,
Unless my death my miseries undo.
Lissius is happy, but Philisses cursed,
Love seeks to him, on me he doth his worst.
And do thy worst on me still froward[23] boy,
More ill thou canst not, but poor life destroy,
Which do, and glory in thy conquest got;
All men must die, and Love drew my ill lot.[24]

LISSIUS [*He sees* PHILISSES.]

My dear Philisses. What, alone and sad?

PHILISSES

Neither, but musing why the best is bad.
But you were merry, I'll not mar your song,
My thoughts are tedious, and for you too long.
Exit.

LISSIUS

Alas, what means this? Surely it is love
That doth in him this alteration move;
This is the humour[25] makes our shepherds rave.
I'll none of this, I'll sooner[26] seek my grave!
Love, by your favour, I will none of you,
I rather you should miss,[27] than I should sue.[28]
Yet Cupid, poor Philisses back restore
To his first wits, and I'll affect thee more.
[LISSIUS *retires backstage. Enter* SILVESTA.]

SILVESTA

Fair shining day, and thou, Apollo[29] bright,
Which to these pleasant valleys gives thy light,[30]
And with sweet showers mixed with golden beams
Enrich these meadows and these gliding streams,
Wherein thou seest thy face like mirror fair,
Dressing in them thy curling, shining hair;
This place with sweetest flowers still doth deck,
Whose colours show their pride, free from the check
Of Fortune's frown,[31] so long as Spring doth last;
But then, feel change, whereof all others taste.
As I, for one, who thus my habits[32]change:
Once shepherdess, but now in woods must range
And after the chaste Goddess bear her bow;
Though service once to Venus I did owe,
Whose servant then I was and of her band.
But farewell folly, I with Dian stand,
Against Love's changing and blind foolery,
To hold with happy and blessed chastity.
For love is idle, happiness there's none
When freedom's lost and chastity is gone;

And where on earth most blessedness there is,
Love's fond desires never fail to miss.
And this, believe me, you will truly find,
Let not repentance therefore change your mind;
But change before your glory will be most,
When as the waggish[33] boy can least him boast.
For he doth seek to kindle flames of fire,
But never thinks to quench[34] a chaste
desire;
He calls his foe, he hates none more than those
Who strive his law to shun, and this life[35] chose.
All virtue hates his kingdom's wantonness:
His crown, desires; his sceptre, idleness;
His wounds, hot fires are; his help's like frost,
Glad to hurt but never heals; thinks time lost
If any gain their long-sought joy with bliss;
And this the government of folly is.
But here Philisses comes, poor shepherd lad,
With Love's hot fires, and his own, made
mad.
I must away, my vow allows no sight
Of men, yet must I pity him, poor wight,[36]
Though he, rejecting me, this change hath
wrought,
He shall be no less worthy in my thought.
Yet, wish I do he were as free as I,
Then were he happy, now feels misery.
For thanks to heaven and to the gods above,
I have won Chastity in place of Love.
Now Love's as far from me as never known;
Then basely[37] tied, now freely am mine
own;
Slavery and bondage with mourning care
Were then my living, sighs and tears my fare;[38]
But all these gone now live I joyfully,
Free, and untouched of thought but Chastity.
[*Exit.*]

[*Enter* PHILISSES.]

PHILISSES

Love being missed in heav'n at last was found
Lodg'd in Musella's fair, though cruel, breast;
Cruel, alas, yet whereon I must ground
All hopes of joy, though tired with unrest.
O hearest[39] dear, let plaints[40] which true felt are
Gain pity once, do not delight to prove
So merciless, still killing with despair;
Nor pleasure take so much to try my love;
Yet, if your trial will you milder make,
Try, but not long, lest pity come too late.
But O, she may not, cannot, will not, take
Pity on me, she loves, and lends me hate.

LISSIUS

Fie, my Philisses, will you ever fly
My sight that loves you, and your good
desires?

PHILISSES

Fly you, dear Lissius? No. But still a cry
I hear that says I burn in scorner's fires.
Farewell, good Lissius, I will soon return,
But not to you a rival, like to burn. [*Exit.*]

LISSIUS

Ah, poor Philisses, would I knew thy pain,
That as I now lament, might help obtain;
But yet in love they say none should be used[41]
But self-deserts,[42] lest trust might be abused.

[*Enter*] FORESTER.

FORESTER [*To himself*]

Did ever cruelty itself thus show?[43]
Did ever heaven our mildness thus far move?
All sweetness and all beauty to o'erthrow,
All joy deface and crop[44] in spring-time
love?
Could any mortal breast invent such harm?
Could living creature think on such a loss?
No, no, alas, it was the Furies' charm[45]
Who sought by this our best delights to cross,
And now in triumph glory in their gain.
Where was true beauty found, if not in thee,
O dear Silvesta? But accursed swain[46]
That caused this change. O, miserable me,
Who live to see this day, and day's bright light
To shine when pleasure's turned into
despite.

LISSIUS

Another of Love's band! O mighty Love
That can thy folly make in most to move.

FORESTER

Accursed shepherd, why wert thou e'er born,
Unless it were to be true virtue's scorn?
Cursed be thy days, unlucky ever be,
Nor ever live, lest happiness to see;
But where thou lov'st, let her as cruel prove
As thou wert to Silvesta, and my love.

LISSIUS

If one may ask, what is th'offence is done?

FORESTER

That cursed Philisses hath me quite undone.

LISSIUS

Undone, as how?

FORESTER

Sit down, and you shall know,
For glad I am that I my grief may tell,
Since 'tis some ease my sorrows cause to show,
Disburdning[47] my poor heart which grief doth
swell.
Then[48] know I loved, alas, and ever must,
Silvesta fair, sole mistress of my joy,
Who dear affections were in surest trust
Laid up in flames, my hopes clean to destroy.[49]
For as I truly loved and only she,

She for Philisses sighed, who did reject
Her love and pains,[50] nor would, she cruel, see
My plaints, nor tears, but followed his neglect
With greater passion. I her followed still.
I after both did hie,[51] though for my ill,
Who thus do live all wretchedness to taste.[52]
Long time this lasted, still she constant loved,
And more she loved, more cruel still he grew;
Till at the length thus tyrant-like he proved,
Forcing that change which makes my poor heart rue.[53]
For she, perceiving hate so far to guide
His settled heart to nothing but disdain,
Having all manners and all fashions tried
That might give comfort to her endless pain,
But seeing nothing would his favour turn
From fondly flying of her truest love,
Led by those passions which did firmly burn
So hot as nothing could those flames remove
But still increase, she, for the last resolved
To kill this heat, this hopeless course to take:
Making a vow which cannot be dissolved,
As not obtaining love, will love forsake.
For she hath vowed unto Diana's life[54]
Her pure virginity; as she who could
No more than once love, nor another's wife
Consent to be, nor his now, if he would.
This hath he done by his ungratefulness;
Would it might turn to his own wretchedness!

LISSIUS

O, curse him not, alas, it is his ill
To feel so much as doth his senses kill;
And yet, indeed, this cruelty and course[55]
Is somewhat strange[56] for shepherds here to use.
Yet, see I not how this can prove the worse
For you whose love she ever did refuse;
But much the better, since your suffered pain
Can be no glory to another's gain.

FORESTER

Would it could be to any's gain the most
Of glory, honour, fortune, and what more
Can added be, though I had ever lost
And he obtained[57] the chief of Beauty's store.[58]
For then I might have her sometimes beheld,
But now am barred;[59] for my love placed was
In truest kind, wherein I all excelled;
Not seeking gain, but losing, did surpass
Those that obtain; for my thoughts did ascend
No higher than to look. That was my end.[60]

LISSIUS

What strange effects doth fancy 'mong[61] us prove,
Who still brings forth new images[62] of love?
But this of all is strangest: to affect
Only the sight and not the joys respect,
Nor ends of whining[63] love, since sight we gain
With small ado, the other with much pain;
Doubling the pleasure, having left despair
And favour won, which kills all former care;
And sure, if ever I should chance to love,
The fruitful ends of love I first would move.

FORESTER

I wish you may obtain your heart's desire,
And I but sight, who waste in chastest fire.[64]
Exit.

LISSIUS

These two to meet in one I ne'er did find,
Love and Chastity linked in one man's mind.
But now I see Love hath as many ways
To win as to destroy when he delays. [*Exit.*]

Scene iii

[*Enter*] PHILISSES, DALINA, RUSTIC, LACON, LISSIUS [*and* CLIMEANA].

DALINA

The sun grows hot, 'twere best we did retire.

LISSIUS

There's a good shade.

PHILISSES [*Aside*]

But here's a burning fire.

LACON

Never did I see man so changed as he.

DALINA

Truly nor[65] I, what can the reason be?

PHILISSES

Love, love it is, which you in time may know;
But happy they can keep their love from show.

[*Enter* MUSELLA.]

DALINA

Musella welcome to our meeting is,
Of all our fellows you did only miss.

MUSELLA

Small miss of me. For, oft'nest when I'm here,
I am as if I were another where.
But where is Phillis? Seldom do I find
Her or Simeana missing; yet, the blind
God Cupid late hath struck her yielding breast,
And makes her lonely walk to seek for rest.

PHILISSES

Yet when the pain is greatest, 'tis some ease
To let a friend partake his friend's disease.[66]

MUSELLA

That were no friendly part, in this you miss;
Impart unto your friend no harm, but bliss.

PHILISSES
Some friend will ready be to ease one's smart.
MUSELLA
So to befriend yourself they should bear part.[67]
DALINA
Now we are met, what sport[68] shall we invent
While the sun's fury somewhat more be spent?
LACON
Let each one here their fortunes past relate,
Their loves, their froward chance or their good fate.
MUSELLA
And so discourse the secrets of the mind!
I like not this; thus sport may crosses[69] find.
PHILISSES
Let one begin a tale.
DALINA
Nor that I like.
LACON
What then will please? We see what doth dislike.
PHILISSES
Dislike is quickly known, pleasure is scant.
MUSELLA
And where joys seem to flow, alas, there's want.
CLIMEANA [*Sings.*]
O mine eyes, why do you lead
My poor heart thus forth to range
From the wonted[70]course, to strange
Unknown ways and paths to tread?
Let it home return again,
Free, untouched of gadding[71] thought,
And your forces back be brought
To the ridding of my pain.
But mine eyes, if you deny
This small favour to my heart
And will force my thoughts to fly,
Know yet you govern but your part.[72]
LISSIUS
Climeana hath begun a pretty sport;
Let each one sing, and so the game is short.
RUSTIC
Indeed, well said, and I will first begin.
DALINA
And whosoever's out, you'll not be in![73]
PHILISSES
Sing they who have glad hearts or voice to sing,
I can but patience to this pleasure bring.
MUSELLA
Then you and I will sit, and judges be.
PHILISSES
Would fair Musella first would judge of me.
MUSELLA
Will you then sing?
PHILISSES
No, I would only say [. . .]
MUSELLA
Choose some time else. Who will begin this play?
RUSTIC
Why, that will I, and I will sing of thee.
MUSELLA
Sorry I am I should be your subject be.
RUSTIC [*Sings.*][74]
When I do see
Thee, whitest thee,
Yea, whiter than lamb's wool;
How do I joy
That thee enjoy
I shall with my heart full.
Thy eyes do play
Like goats with hay,
And skip like kids flying
From the sly fox,
So eyelid's box[75]
Shuts up thy sights prying.
Thy cheeks are red
Like ochre[76] spread
On a fatted sheep's back;
Thy paps[77] are found
Like apples round,
No praises shall lack.
MUSELLA
Well you have praises given enough; now let
Another come some other to commend.
RUSTIC
I had much more to say, but thus I'm met
And stayed; now will I harken and attend.
LACON [*Sings.*][78]
By a pleasant river's side,
Heart and hopes on pleasure's tide,[79]
Might I see within a bower[80]
Proudly dressed with every flower
Which the spring doth to us lend,
Venus and her loving friend.[81]
I upon her beauty gazed,
They, me seeing, were amazed;
Till at last upstepped a child,[82]
In his face not actions mild.
'Fly away,' said he, 'for sight
Shall both breed and kill delight.
Fly away and follow me,
And I will let thee beauties see.'
I obeyed him, then[83] he stayed
Hard[84] beside a heavenly maid;
When he threw a flaming dart,
And unkindly struck my heart.
MUSELLA
But what became then of the cruel boy?

LACON
When he had done his worst he fled away.
MUSELLA
And so let us. 'Tis time we do return
To tend our flocks who all this while do burn.
PHILISSES [*Aside*]
Burn, and must burn, this suddenly is said;
But heat not quenched, alas, but hopes
decayed.
DALINA
What have you done, and must I lose my song?
MUSELLA
Not lose it, though awhile we it prolong.
DALINA
I am content, and now let's all retire.
PHILISSES [*Aside*]
And soon return sent by Love's quickest fire.
[*Exeunt.*]

Scene iv

[*Enter*] VENUS *and* CUPID, *appearing in the clouds.*

VENUS
Fie, this is nothing! What? Is this your care?
That among ten the half of them you spare!
I would have all to wail and all to weep;
Will you at such a time as this go sleep?
Awake your forces and make Lissius find
Cupid can cruel be as well as kind.
Shall he go scorning thee and all thy train,
And pleasure take he can thy force disdain?
Strike him, and tell him thou his lord wilt[85]
prove,
And he a vassal[86] unto mighty Love;
And all the rest, that scorners be of thee,
Make with their grief, of thy might feelers be.
CUPID
'Tis true that Lissius, and some others yet,
Are free and lively; but they shall be met
With care sufficient, for 'tis not their time
As yet into my pleasing pain[87] to climb.
Let them alone, and let themselves beguile,
They shall have torment when they think to
smile.
They are not yet in pride of all their scorn,
But ere they have their pleasures half-way
worn,
They shall both cry, and sigh, and wail, and
weep,
And for our mercy shall most humbly creep.
Love hath most glory when as greatest sprites[88]
He downward throws unto his own delights.
Then take no care, Love's Victory shall shine,
Whenas your honour shall be raised by mine.
VENUS
Thanks, Cupid, if thou do perform thine oath,
As needs you must, for gods must want no
troth.[89]
Let mortals never think it odd or vain
To hear that Love can in all spirits reign.
Princes are not exempted from our mights,
Much less should shepherds scorn us and our
rights;
Though they as well can love and like affect,[90]
They must not therefore our commands neglect.
CUPID
Nor shall. And mark but what my vengeance is.
I'll miss my force, or they shall want their bliss;
And arrows here I have of purpose framed
Which as their qualities so are they named:
Love, jealousy, malice, fear, and mistrust,
Yet all these shall at last encounter just;[91]
Harm shall be none, yet all shall harm endure
For some small season, then of joy be sure.
Like you this, Mother?
VENUS
Son, I like this well,
And fail not now in least part of thy spell.
[*Exeunt.*]

Act II

Scene i

[*Enter*] MUSELLA, DALINA, SIMEANA, PHILISSES, LISSIUS [*and*] LACON.

DALINA
Methinks we now too silent are. Let's play
At something while we yet have pleasing day.
[*Enter* SILVESTA *and* FORESTER; *they do not see the others.*]
LISSIUS
Here's sport enough; view but her new attire,[1]
And see her slave who burns in chaste desire.[2]
DALINA
Mark but their meeting.
LISSIUS
She, I'm sure, will fly,
And he poor fool will follow still, and cry.
MUSELLA
What pleasure you do take to mock at love;
Are you sure you cannot his power prove?
But look, he kneels, and weeps.
LISSIUS
And cries, 'Ah me!'
Sweet Nymph[3] have pity, or he dies for
thee.
FORESTER [*To* SILVESTA]
Alas, dear Nymph, why fly you still my sight?

Can my true love and firm affection
So little gain me, as your fairest light
Must darkened be for my affliction?[4]
O look on me and see if in my face
True grief and sorrow show not my disgrace;
If that despair do not by sighs appear;
If felt disdain do not with tears make show
My ever-wailing, ever-saddest cheer,
And mourning, which no breath can
overblow?
Pity me not, else judge with your fair eyes
My loving soul which to you captive lies.

SILVESTA

Alas, fond Forester, urge me no more
To that which now lies not within my might;
Nor can I grant, or you to joy restore
By any means to yield you least delight
For I have vowed, which vows I will obey,
Unto Diana.[5] What more can I say?

FORESTER

O, this I know. Yet give me but this leave
To do as birds, and trees, and beasts may do;
Do not, O, do not me of sight bereave,
For without you I see not. Ah, undo
Not what is yours, o'erthrow not what's your
own,
Let me, though conquered, not be quite
o'erthrown.
I know you vowed have, and vows must stand;
Yet, though you chaste must be, I may desire
To have your sight, and this the strictest band[6]
Cannot refuse, and but this I require.
Then grant it me, which I on knees do seek,
Be not to nature, and yourself, unleek.[7]

SILVESTA

No, no, I ne'er believe your fond-made oath.
I chastity have sworn, then no more move.
I know what 'tis to swear, and break it, both;
What to desire, and what it is to love.
Protest you may that there shall nothing be
By you imagined 'gainst my chastity,
But this I doubt; your love will make you curse,
If you so much do love, that cursed[8] day
When I this vowed; attempt it[9] may be worse.
Then follow not thus hopeless your decay,
But leave off loving; or some other choose
Whose state[10] or fortune need not you refuse.

FORESTER

Indeed, sweet Nymph, 'tis true that chastity
To one that loves may justly raging move.
Yet, loving you, those thoughts shall banished
be;
Since 'tis in you, I chastity will love;
And now depart, since such is your pleasure.
Depart, o me, from joy, from life, from ease,
Go I must, and leave behind that treasure
Which all contentment gives. Now, to displease
Myself with liberty I may free go,
And with most liberty, most grief, most woe.
Exit.

MUSELLA

Lissius, I hope this sight doth something move
In you to pity so much constant love.

LISSIUS[11]

Yes. Thus it moves: that man should be so fond
As to be tied t'a woman's faithless bond![12]
For we should women love but as our sheep,
Who being kind and gentle give us ease,
But cross, or straying, stubborn, or[13] unmeek,
Shunned as the wolf, which most our flocks
disease.

MUSELLA

We little are beholding unto you,
In kindness, less. Yet, you these words may rue;[14]
I hope to live to see you wail and weep,
And deem your grief far sweeter than your sleep.
Then, but remember this, and think on me;
Who truly told, you could not still live free.

LISSIUS

I do not know, it may be very well,
But I believe I shall uncharm[15] Love's spell.
And Cupid, if I needs must love,
Take your aim and shoot your worst.
Once more you rob your mother's dove,[16]
All your last shafts sure were burst,[17]
Those you stole, and those you gave,
Shoot not me till new you have.

PHILISSES

Rustic, faith, tell me, hast thou ever loved?

RUSTIC

What call you love? I've been to trouble moved,
As when my best cloak hath by chance been
torn,
I have lived wishing till it mended were,
And but so lovers do; nor could forbear
To cry if I my bag or bottle lost,
As lovers do who by their loves are crossed,
And grieve as much for these, as they for scorn.

PHILISSES

Call you this love? Why, love is no such thing!
Love is a pain which yet doth pleasure bring,
A passion which alone in hearts do move,
And they that feel not this they cannot love.
'Twill make one joyful, merry, pleasant, sad,
Cry, weep, sigh, fast, mourn, nay sometimes stark
mad;
If they perceive scorn, hate, or else disdain
To wrap[18] their woes in store,[19] for others'
gain,
For that, but jealousy, is sure the worst,

And then be jealous. Better be accursed!
But o, some are,[20] and would it not disclose;
They silent love, and loving, fear. Ah, those
Deserve most pity, favour and regard;
Yet, are they answered but with scorn's reward,
This their misfortune. And the like may fall
To you, or me, who wait misfortune's call.
But if it do, take heed, be ruled by me:
Though you mistrust, mistrust not that she see.
For then she'll smiling say, 'Alas, poor fool,
This man hath learned all parts of Folly's school.'[21]
Be wise, make love, and love though not obtain,
For to love truly is sufficient gain.

RUSTIC
Sure you do love, you can so well declare
The joys and pleasures, hope and his despair.

PHILISSES
I love indeed.

RUSTIC
But who is she you love?

PHILISSES
She who best thoughts must to affection move;[22]
If any love, none need ask who it is.
Within these plains, none loves that loves not this
Delight of shepherd's pride, of this fair place;
No beauty is that shines not in her face,
Whose whiteness whitest lilies doth excel,
Matched with a rosy morning to compel
All hearts to serve her. Yet, doth she affect
But only virtue, nor will quite neglect
Those who doth serve her in an honest[23] fashion,
Which, sure, doth more increase, than decrease, passion.

[*Enter* ARCAS.]

ARCAS
Here are they met, where Beauty[24] only reigns,
Whose presence gives the excellentest light
And brightest, dimming Phoebus,[25] who but feigns
To outshine these, it is not in his might.
Fair troop, here is a sport will well befit
This time and place, if you will license it.

PHILISSES
What is't, good Arcas?

ARCAS
Why stay, and you shall see.
Here is a book wherein each one shall draw
A fortune, and, thereby, their luck shall be
Conjectured.[26] Like you this? You ne'er it saw.

RUSTIC
It is no matter, 'tis a pretty one.
Musella, you shall draw.

MUSELLA
Though choose alone.

PHILISSES
I never saw it, but I like it well.

LISSIUS
Then he, 'chieves[27] best of all, must bear the bell.[28]

RUSTIC
Pray thee, good Arcas, let me hold the book.

ARCAS
With all my heart. Yet, you'll not some lots[29] brook.[30]

RUSTIC [*Takes the book and reads.*]
Fairest, sweetest, bonny lass,
You that love in mirth to pass,
Time delightful come to me
And you shall your fortune see.

MUSELLA
You tell by book, then sure you cannot miss,[31]
But shall I know what shall be, or what is?

RUSTIC
What shall be you need not fear,
Rustic doth thy fortune bear.
Draw, and when you chosen have,
Praise me who such fortune gave.

MUSELLA
And so I will, if good; or if untrue,
I'll blame mine own ill-choice, and not blame you. [*She draws.*]

PHILISSES
Pray, may I see the fortune you do choose.

MUSELLA
Yes, and if right, I will it not refuse.

PHILISSES
None can be cross[32] to you, except you will.[33]

MUSELLA
Read it.

PHILISSES
I will, although it were my ill.
[*Reads.*]
Fortune cannot cross your will,
Though your patience much must be.
Fear not that your luck is ill,
You shall your best wishes see.
Refuse, believe me, no, you have no cause;
Thus hope brings longing,[34] patience, passion draws.[35]

DALINA
I'll try what mine shall be, good Rustic, hold.

ARCAS
A man must follow.

DALINA

I'm still too bold.[36]

PHILISSES

Then I will try, though sure of cruelty. [*He draws.*]
And yet, this lot doth promise good[37] at last;
That, though I now feel greatest misery,
My blessed days to come are not all past.

DALINA

Come, this fond lover knows not yet the play,
He studies[38] while our fortunes run away![39]
What have you got? Let's see, do you this love?

PHILISSES

Read it, but heaven grant me the end to prove.

DALINA [*Reads.*]

You do live to be much crossed,
Yet esteem[40] no labour lost,
Since you shall with bliss[41] obtain
Pleasure for your suffered pain.

Truly, I cannot blame you. Like you this?
So I at last might gain, I well could miss.

MUSELLA

After a rain the sweetest flowers do grow,
So shall your hap[42] be, as this book doth show.

DALINA

Now must I[43] draw. Sweet Fortune[44] be my guide.

MUSELLA

She cannot see. Yet, must your chance abide.

DALINA

Blind or no, I care not, this I take, and
If good, my luck, if not, a luckless hand. [*She draws.*]

PHILISSES

If Fortune guide, she will direct to Love,
They cannot parted be. How[45] now dost move?[46]

DALINA

Move?[47] Did you ever see the like?

PHILISSES

Not I!

DALINA

Nay, read it out, it shows my constancy.

PHILISSES [*Reads.*]

They that cannot steady be
To themselves, the like must see.
Fickle people, fickly choose,
Slightly like, and so refuse.
This your fortune, who can say,
Herein justice bears not sway!

In troth,[48] Dalina, Fortune is proud-cursed[49]
To you without desert.

DALINA

This is the worst
That she can do. 'Tis true I have fickle been,
And so is she;[50] 'tis then the lesser sin.
Let her prove constant, I will her observe,
And then, as she doth mend,[51] I'll good deserve.[52]

ARCAS

Who chooseth next?

LISSIUS

Not I, lest[53] such I prove.[54]

SILVESTA

Nor I, it is sufficient I could love.

ARCAS

I'll wish for one, but Fortune shall not try
On me her tricks, whose favours[55] are so dry.[56]

DALINA

None can wish, if they their wishes love not,
Nor can they love, if that[57] wishings move not.

PHILISSES

You fain would solve this business.

DALINA

Who? Would I?
Nay, my care's past. I, Love and his, deny.

PHILISSES[58]

Love and Reason once at war,
Jove[59] came down to end the jar.[60]
'Cupid,' said Love, 'must have place';[61]
Reason, that it was his grace.[62]
Jove then brought it to this end:
Reason should on Love attend;[63]
Love takes Reason for his guide,
Reason cannot from Love slide.
This agreed, they pleased did part,
Reason ruling Cupid's dart.
So as sure Love cannot miss,[64]
Since that Reason ruler is.

LISSIUS

It seems he missed[65] before he had this guide!

PHILISSES

I'm sure not me, I ne'er my heart could hide
But he it found; so, as I well may say,
Had he been blind[66] I might have stolen away!
But so he saw, and ruled with Reason's might,
As he hath killed in me all my delight;
He wounded me, alas, with double harm,
And none but he can my distress uncharm;
Another wound must cure me, or I die.
But stay, this is enough, I hence will fly
And seek the boy that struck me. Fare you well,
Yet, make not still your pleasures prove my hell. [*Exit.*]

LISSIUS

Philisses now hath left us, let's go back
And tend our flocks, who now our care do lack. [*Aside*]

Yet would he had more pleasant parted hence,
Or that I could but judge the cause from whence
These passions grew; it would give me much ease
Since I perceive my sight doth him displease.
I'll seek him yet, and of him truly know
What in him hath bred this unusual woe.
If he deny me, then I'll swear he hates
Me, or affects[67] that humour[68] which debates[69]
In his kind[70] thought, which should the master be;
But, who the friend is, I will quickly see. *Exit.*

MUSELLA
Well let's away. [*Aside*] And hither soon return
That sun[71] to me, whose absence make me burn. *Exeunt.*

Scene ii

[*Enter*] PHILISSES [*and*] LISSIUS.

LISSIUS
O, plainly deal with me! My love hath been
Still firm to you; then, let us not begin
To seem as strangers. If I have wronged you, speak,
And I'll forgiveness ask; else, do not break
That band of friendship of our long-held love,
Which did these plains[72] to admiration move.

PHILISSES
I cannot change, but love thee ever will,
For no cross[73] shall my first affection kill.
But give me leave that sight, once loved, to shun
Since by the sight, I see myself undone.

LISSIUS
When this opinion first possessed thy heart
Would Death[74] had struck me with his cruel dart.
Live I to be mistrusted by my friend?
'Tis time for me my wretched days to end.
But what began this change in thee?

PHILISSES
Mistrust.

LISSIUS
Mistrust of me?

PHILISSES
I am not so unjust.

LISSIUS
What then? Pray tell, my heart doth long to know.

PHILISSES
Why then, the change and cause of all my woe
Proceeds from this: I fear Musella's love
Is placed in you, this doth my torments move.
Since if she do, my friendship bound to you
Must make me leave for love or joy to sue,[75]
For though I love her more than mine own heart,
If you affect her, I will ne'er impart
My love to her; so, constant friendship binds
My love where truth such faithful biding finds.
Then truly speak, good Lissius, plainly say,
Nor shall a love make me your trust betray.

LISSIUS
O my Philisses! What? Was this the cause?
Alas, see how misfortune on me draws.
I love; but vow 'tis not Musella's face
Could from my heart my freer thoughts displace.
Although, I must confess, she worthy is,
But she, alas, can bring to me no bliss.
It is your sister[76] who must end[77] my care
Now do you see you need no more despair.

PHILISSES
Yet, she may love you, can you that deny?

LISSIUS
And swear I never yet, lest[78] thou[79] could spy.[80]
But well assured I am that she doth love,
And you, I venture, dare doth her heart move.
'Tis true she speaks to me, but for your sake,
Else for good looks from her I might leave take.[81]
Her eyes cannot dissemble, though her tongue
To speak it hazards not a greater wrong;
Her cheeks cannot command the blood,[82] but still
It must appear, although against her will.
Thus have I answered, and advice do give:
Tell her your love, if you will happy live;
She cannot, neither will she, you deny.
And do as much for me, or else I die.

PHILISSES
What may I do that you shall not command?
Then here I 'gage[83] my word and give my hand;
If with my sister I but power have,
She shall requite[84] you, and your sorrow save
With gift of her love.[85] But, once more say this:
From fair Musella hope you for no bliss?

LISSIUS
None but her friendship, which I will require
From both, as equal to my best desire.

PHILISSES
Then, thus assured, that friendship shall remain,
Or let my soul endure eternal pain. *Exeunt.*

Scene iii

[*Enter*] VENUS' PRIESTS TO LOVE, *or his praise,* [*and*] *the* GODDESS *and her* SON, *appearing in glory.*

[PRIESTS]
Cupid, blessed be thy might,
Let thy triumph[86] see no night;
Be thou justly God of Love,
Who thus can thy glory move.
Hearts, obey to Cupid's sway,
Princes,[87] none of you say nay;
Eyes, let him direct your way,
For without him you may stray.
He your secret thoughts can spy,
Being hid else from each eye.
Let your songs be still of love;
Write no satires which may prove,[88]
Lest offensive to his name.
If you do, you will but frame[89]
Words against yourselves, and lines
Where his good, and your ill, shines.
Like him who doth set a snare
For a poor betrayed hare,
And that thing he best doth love
Lucklessly the snare doth prove.
Love, the king is of the mind,
Please him, and he will be kind;
Cross him, you see what doth come,
Harms which make your pleasure's tomb.
Then, take heed, and make your bliss
In his favour, and so miss
No content, nor[90] joy, nor peace,
But in happiness, increase.
Love command your hearts and eyes,
And enjoy what pleasure tries;
Cupid govern, and his care,
Guide your hearts from all despair. [*Exeunt.*]

Act III

Scene i

[*Enter* SILVESTA *and* MUSELLA.]

SILVESTA
Silent woods with desert's[1] shade,
Giving peace.
Where all pleasures first are made
To increase.
Give your favour to my moan
Now my loving time is gone.
Chastity my pleasure is,
Folly fled.
From hence,[2] now I seek my bliss,
Cross love dead.[3]
In your shadows I repose,
You, than[4] Love, I now have[5] chose.

MUSELLA
Choice ill-made were better left,
Being cross.
Of such choice to be bereft,
Were no loss.
Chastity, you thus commend,
Doth proceed but from Love's end.
And if Love the fountain was
Of your fire,
Love must Chastity surpass
In desire.
Love lost, bred your chastest thought,
Chastity by Love is wrought.

SILVESTA
O, poor Musella, now I pity thee;
I see thou'rt bound, who most[6] have made unfree.
'Tis true, disdain of my love made me turn,
And happily I think. But you to burn
In love's false fires[7] yourself, poor soul, take heed,
Be sure before you too much pine,[8] to speed.[9]
You know I loved have, but[10] behold my gain;
This, you dislike, I purchased with love's pain
And true-felt sorrow. Yet, my answer was
From my, then dear, Philisses: 'You must pass
Unloved by me, and for your own good leave
To urge that which, most urged, can but deceive
Your hopes. For know, Musella is my love.'
As then of duty I should no more move;
And this his will he got, but not his mind,
For yet it seems you are no less unkind.

MUSELLA
Wrong me not, chaste Silvesta, 'tis my grief
That from poor me he will[11] not take relief.

SILVESTA
What, will he lose what he did most desire?

MUSELLA
So is he led away with jealous fire.
And this, Silvesta, but to you I speak,
For sooner should my heart with silence break
Than any else should hear me thus much say
But you, who I know will not me betray.

SILVESTA
Betray Musella? Sooner will I die.
No, I do love you, nor will help deny
That[12] lies in me to bring your care to end,
Or service which to your content may tend.
For when I loved Philisses as my life,
Perceiving he loved you, I killed the strife
Which in me was. Yet, do I wish his good,
And for his sake, love you. Though I withstood
Good fortunes, this chaste life well pleaseth me,
And would joy more[13] if you two happy be.
Few would say this, but fewer would it do,
But th'one I loved, and love the other too.

MUSELLA
I know you loved him, nor could I the less
At that time love you. So did he possess
My heart, as my thought all hearts sure must yield
To love him most and best; who in this field
Doth live and hath not had some kind of touch
To like him? But o, you and I too much.

SILVESTA
Mine is now passed. Tell me now what yours is,
And I'll wish but the means to work your bliss.

MUSELLA
Then know, Silvesta, I Philisses love.
But he, although, or that because, he loves,
Doth me mistrust. Ah, can such mischief move
As to mistrust her who such passion proves?
But so he doth, and thinks I have Lissius made
Master of my affections, which hath stayed
Him ever yet from letting me it know
By words, although he hides it not from show.
Sometimes I fain[14] would speak, then straight forbear,
Knowing it most unfit;[15] thus woe I bear.

SILVESTA
Indeed a woman to make love is ill.
But hear, and you may all these sorrows kill;
He, poor distressed shepherd, every morn
Before the sun to our eyes new is born,
Walks in this place, and here alone doth cry
Against his life and your great cruelty.
Now, since you love so much, come here and find
Him in these woes, and show yourself but kind.
You soon shall see a heart so truly won
As you would not it miss to be undone.

MUSELLA
Silvesta, for this love I can but say,
That piece of heart which is not given away
Shall be your own, the rest will you observe
As saver of two hearts, which, too, will serve
You ever with so true and constant love
Your chastity itself shall it approve.

SILVESTA
I do believe it, for in so much worth[16]
As lives in you, virtue must needs spring[17] forth.
And for Philisses, I love him and will
In chastest service hinder[18] still his ill.
Then keep your time, alas, let him not die
For whom so many suffered misery.

MUSELLA
Let me no joy receive if I neglect
This kind advice, or him I so respect.

SILVESTA
Farewell, Musella, love, and happy be. *Exeunt.*

Scene ii

[*Enter* PHILISSES.]

PHILISSES[19]
O wretched man! And thou, all-conquering Love,
Which show'st thy power still on hapless[20] me,
Yet give me leave in these sweet shades[21] to move;
Rest but to show my killing misery;
And be once pleased to know thy wretched fate,
And something pity my ill and my state.
Could ever Nature of the heavens e'er[22] frame[23]
So rare[24] a part[25] so like themselves divine?
And yet that work be blotted with the blame
Of cruelty; and dark be, who should shine
To be the brightest star of dearest[26] prize;[27]
And yet to murder hearts which to her cries,
Cry; and even at the point of death for care,
Yet have I nothing left me but despair.
Despair! O, but despair! Alas, hath hope
No better portion?[28] Nor a greater scope?
Well then, despair with my life coupled be,
And for my sudden end do soon agree.
Ah me, unfortunate; would I could die.
But so soon as this company I fly. *Exit.*

[*Enter*] DALINA, CLIMEANA, SIMEANA [*and*] PHILLIS.

DALINA
Now we're alone let everyone confess
Truly to other what our lucks have been,
How often liked and loved, and so express
Our passions past; shall we this sport begin?
None can accuse us, none can us betray,
Unless ourselves, our own selves will bewray.[29]

PHILLIS
I like this, but will each one truly tell?

CLIMEANA
Trust me, I will, who doth not, doth not well.

SIMEANA
I'll plainly speak, but who shall be the first?

DALINA
I can say least of all, yet I will speak.
A shepherd once there was, and not the worst
Of those were most esteemed, whose[30] sleep did break
With love, forsooth,[31] of me. I, found it thought
I might have him at leisure, liked him not.
Then was there to our house a farmer brought,
Rich and lively, but those bought not his lot
For love. Two jolly youths at last there came,
Which both, methought, I very well could love.
When one was absent, t'other had the name;
In my stayed heart he present did most move,

Both at one time in sight, I scarce could say
Which of the two I then would wish away.
But they found how to choose, and as I was,
Like[32] changing, like uncertain, let me pass.

SIMEANA

I would not this believe if other tongue
Should this report, but think it had been wrong;
But since you speak this, could not you agree
To choose someone, but thus[33] unchosen be?

DALINA

Truly not I. I plainly tell the truth,
Yet do confess 'twas folly in my youth,
Which now I'll mend; the next that comes I'll have,[34]
I will no more be foolish, nor delay,
Since I do see the lads will labour save.
One answer rids them, I'll no more say 'Nay'.
But if he say, 'Dalina, will you love?'
And, 'Thank you', I will say, 'If you will prove'.[35]
The next go on, and tell what you have done.

SIMEANA

I am the next, and have but losses won.[36]
Yet, still I constant was, though still rejected;
Loved and not loved I was, liked and neglected;
Yet, now some hope revives,[37] when love thought dead
Proves like the Spring's young bud when leaves are fled.

PHILLIS[38]

Your hap's[39] the better, would mine were as good,
Though I as long as you despised stood.
For I have loved, and loved but only one;
Yet I, disdained, could but receive that moan[40]
Which others do for thousands;[41] so unjust
Is Love to those who in him most do trust.
Nor did I ever let my thoughts be shown
But to Musella, who all else hath known,
Which was, long time, I had Philisses loved,
And ever would though he did me despise;
For then, though he had ever cruel proved,
From him, not me, the fault must needs arise.
And if, Simeana, thus your brother dear
Should be unkind, my love shall still be clear.[42]

SIMEANA

'Tis well resolved; but how liked she[43] your choice?
Did she, or blame, or else, your mind commend?

PHILLIS

Neither she seemed to dislike or rejoice,
Nor did commend I did this love intend;
But smiling, said,[44] 'twere best to be advised:
Comfort it were to win, but death despised.

SIMEANA

I do believe her. But Climeana yet
Hath nothing said, we must not her forget.

CLIMEANA

Why, you have said enough for you and me!
Yet for your sakes, I will the order[45] keep,
Who though a stranger here by birth I be
And in Arcadia[46] ever kept my sheep.
Yet, here it is my fortune with the rest
Of you to like, and loving be oppressed,
For since I came, I did a lover turn;[47]
And turn[48] I did indeed when I loved here,
Since for another I in love did burn,
To whom I thought I had been held as dear;
But was deceived. When I for him had left
My friends and country, was of him bereft,
And all, but that you kindly did embrace
And welcome me into this happy place.
Where, for your sakes, I meant to keep some sheep,
Not doubting ever to be more deceived;
But now, alas, I am anew bereaved
Of heart, now time it is myself to keep
And let flocks go, unless Simeana please
To give consent, and so give me some ease.

SIMEANA

Why, what have I to do with whom you love?

CLIMEANA

Because 'tis he who doth your passion move.[49]

SIMEANA

The lesser need I fear the winning of his love,
Since all my faith could never so much move.
Yet, can he not so cruel ever be
But he may live my misery to see.

CLIMEANA

And when his eyes to love shall open be,
I trust he will turn pity unto me,
And let me have reward, which is my due.

SIMEANA

Which is your due? What pity's due to you?
Dream you of hope? O, you too high aspire!
Think you to gain by kindling an old fire?[50]

CLIMEANA

My love will be the surer, when I know
Not love alone, but how love to bestow.

SIMEANA

You make him, yet for all this, but to be
The second in your choice.[51] So was not he
In mine, but first, and last, of all the chief
That can to me bring sorrow or relief.

CLIMEANA

This will not win him. You may talk and hope,
But in Love's passages[52] there is large scope.[53]

SIMEANA
'Tis true, and you have scope to change and choose,
To take, and dislike, like, and soon refuse.

CLIMEANA
My love as firm is to him as is thine.

SIMEANA
Yet mine did ever rise, never decline;
No other moved in me the flames of love,
Yet you dare hope as much as I to move.
Folly, indeed, is proud, and only vain,
And you his servant feeds with hope of gain.

CLIMEANA
I love him most.

SIMEANA
I love him best. Can you
Challenge reward, and cannot say you're true?[54]

CLIMEANA
In this you wrong me! False I have not been,
But changed on cause.[55]

SIMEANA
Well, now you hope to win
This second! Yet I, like those, lose no time;
But can you think that you can this way climb
To your desires? This shows you love have tried,
And that you can both choose, and choice divide.
But take your course, and win him if you can,
And I'll proceed in truth as I began.

DALINA
Fie, what a life is here about fond[56] love,
Never could it in my heart thus much move!
This is the reason men are grown so coy,
When they perceive we make their smiles our joy;
Let them alone, and they will seek and sue,[57]
But yield to them and they'll with scorn pursue.
Hold awhile off, they'll kneel, nay,[58] follow you,
And vow and swear. Yet, all their oaths untrue;
Let them once see you coming, then they fly,
But strangely[59] look, and they'll for pity cry;
And let them cry, there is no evil done,
They gain but that which you might else have won.

SIMEANA
Is this your counsel? Why, but now you said
Your folly had your loves and good betrayed,
And that hereafter you would wiser be
Than to disdain such as have left you free.

DALINA
'Tis true, that was the course I meant to take,
But this must you do, your own ends to make;
I have my fortunes lost, yours do begin,
And to cross[60] those could be no greater sin.
I know the world, and hear me, this I advise:
Rather than too soon won, be too precise;[61]
Nothing is lost by being careful still,
Nor nothing so soon won as lover's ill.
Here Lissius comes. Alas, he is love-struck,
He's even now learning love without the book.
[*Enter* LISSIUS.]

LISSIUS [*To himself*][62]
Love, pardon me, I know I did amiss
When I thee scorned, or thought thy blame my bliss.
O, pity me. Alas, I pity crave!
Do not set trophies[63] on my luckless grave,
Though I, poor slave and ignorant, did scorn
Thy blessed name; let not my heart be torn
With thus much torture. O, but look on me,
Take me a faithful servant unto thee!

CLIMEANA
Dear Lissius, my dear Lissius, fly me not;
Let not both scorn and absence be my lot.

LISSIUS
Pray let me go, you know I cannot love;
Do not thus far my patience strive to move.

CLIMEANA
Why, cruel Lissius, wilt thou never mend,
But still increase thy frowns for my sad end?

LISSIUS
Climeana, 'tis enough that I have said,
Be gone and leave me. Is this for a maid
To follow and to haunt me thus?[64] You blame
Me for disdain, but see not your own shame!
Fie, I do blush for you! A woman woo?
The most unfittest,[65] shameful'st thing to do!

CLIMEANA
Unfit and shameful I? Indeed, 'tis true,
Since suit[66] is made too hard;[67] relentless you.
Well, I will leave you and restore the wrong
I suffer for my loving you too[68] long.
No more shall my words trouble you, nor I
Ere follow more, if not to see me die. *Exit.*

LISSIUS
Farewell, you now do right; this is the way
To win my wish. For when I all neglect
That seek me, she[69] must needs something respect
My love the more; and what though she should say
I once denied her, yet my true-felt pain
Must needs from her soft breast some favour gain.

DALINA
Lissius is taken,[70] well said! Cupid, now
You partly have performed your taken vow;

Of all our shepherds, I ne'er thought that he
Would of thy foolish troop a follower be!
But this it is a Goddess to despise
And thwart a wayward boy who[71] wants his eyes.[72]
Come, let's not trouble him,[73] he is distressed
Enough, he need not be with us oppressed.

SIMEANA
I'll stay, and ask him who 'tis he doth love.

DALINA
Do not a pensive heart to passion move.

SIMEANA
To passion? Would I could his passion find,
To answer my distressed[74] and grieved mind.

DALINA
Stay then and try[75] him, and your fortune try;[76]
It may be he loves you. Come let's go by.
Exeunt [DALINA *and* PHILLIS.]

LISSIUS
O, sweet Simeana, look but on my pain!
I grieve and curse myself for my disdain;
Now, but have pity, Love doth make me serve,
And for your wrong, and you, I will reserve[77]
My life to pay, your love but to deserve,
And for your sake I do myself preserve.

SIMEANA
Preserve it not for me, I seek not now!
Nor can I credit this nor any vow
Which you shall make; I was too long despised
To be deceived. No, I will be advised
By my own reason;[78] my love shall no more blind
Me, nor make me believe more than I find.

LISSIUS
Believe but that, and I shall have the end
Of all my pain, and wishes. I pretend
A virtuous love; then grant me my desire,
Who now do waste in true and faithful fire.

SIMEANA
How can I this believe?

LISSIUS
My faith shall tell
That in true love I will all else excel;
But then, will you love me, as I do you?

SIMEANA
I promise may, for you cannot be true!

LISSIUS
Then, you will promise break.

SIMEANA
Not if I find
That as your words are, so you'll make your mind.

LISSIUS
Let me, nor speech, nor mind have, when that I
In this, or any else, do falsify
My faith and love to you.

SIMEANA
Then, be at rest;
And of my true affection be possessed.

LISSIUS
So, dear Simeana, be of me and mine.
Now do my hopes and joys together shine.

SIMEANA
Nor let the least cloud rise to dim this light,
Which Love makes to appear with true delight.
[*Exeunt.*]

Scene iii

[*Enter*] VENUS *and* CUPID.

CUPID
Is not this pretty? Who doth free remain
Of all this flock, that waits not in our train?[79]
Will you have yet more sorrow? Yet more woe?
Shall I another bitter arrow throw?
Speak, if you will, my hand now knows the way
To make all hearts your sacred power obey.

VENUS
'Tis pretty, but 'tis not enough. Some are
Too slightly wounded, they had greater share
In scorning us. Lissius too soon is blessed,
And with too little pain hath got his rest;
Scarce had he learned to sigh before he gained,
Nor shed a tear ere he his hopes obtained.
This easy winning breeds us more neglect,
Without much pain, few do Love's joys respect;
Then are the sweetest purchased with felt grief,
To floods of woe sweet looks give full relief;
A world of sorrow is eased with one smile,
And heart-wounds cured when kind words rule, the while.
That foregone wailings, in forgotten thought
Shall wasted lie disdained, once dearly bought;
One gentle speech more heals a bleeding wound
Than bawlings[80] of pleasure, if from other ground.
Strike then to favour him,[81] and let him gain
His love and bliss by Love's sweet pleasing pain.

CUPID
That shall be done. Nor had he this delight
Bestowed, but for his greater harm and spite;
You shall, before this act be ended, see
He doth sufficiently taste misery.
'Tis far more grief from joy to be down thrown,
Than joy to be advanced to Pleasure's throne.

VENUS
Let me see that, and I contented am;

Such gracious favour would but get thy shame.

CUPID

He and others yet shall taste
Such distress as shall lay waste
All their hopes, their joys, and lives;
By such loss our glory thrives;
Fear not, then all hearts must yield
When our forces come to field. [*Exeunt.*]

Act IV

Scene i

[*Enter* MUSELLA.]

MUSELLA

This is the place Silvesta 'pointed[1] me
To meet my joy, my sole felicity;
And here Philisses is. Ah me, this shows
The wounds by Love given are no childish blows.

[*Enter* PHILISSES; MUSELLA *hides.*]

PHILISSES[2]

You blessed woods into whose secret guard
I venture dare my inward wounding smart,
And to you dare impart the crosses[3] hard
Which harbour in my love-destroyed heart.
To you, and but to you, I durst disclose
These flames, these pains, these griefs, which I do find;
For your true hearts[4] so constant are to those
Who trust in you, as you'll not change your mind.
No echo[5] shrill shall your dear secrets utter,
Or wrong your silence with a blabbing tongue;
Nor will your springs against your private[6] mutter,
Or think that counsel keeping is a wrong;[7]
Then, since woods, springs, echoes, and all are true,
My long-hid love, I'll tell, show, write in you.
Alas, Musella, cruel shepherdess,
Who takes no pity on me in distress.
For all my passions, plaints,[8] and all my woes,
I am so far from gain as outward shows;
I never had could feed least hope to spring,[9]
Or any while least comfort to me bring.
Yet pardon me, dear mistress of my soul,
I do recall my words, my tongue control,
For wronging thee; accuse my poor starved heart,
Which withered is with Love's all-killing smart.
Since, truly, I must say I cannot blame
Thee, nor accuse thee with a scorner's name.
No, no, alas, my pains thou dost not know,
Nor dare I, wretch, my torments to thee show.
Why did I wrong thee then, who all must serve,
And happy he, by thee, thought to deserve?
Who heaven hath framed to make us here below
Deserve, they strive all worth in thee to show,
And doth these valleys and these meads[10] disgrace
When thou art present with excelling grace,
As now, who at this time doth show more bright
Than fair Aurora,[11] when she lends best light.
O, that I might but now have heart to speak
And say I love, though after, heart did break.

MUSELLA [*Aside*]

I fain would comfort him, and yet I know
Not if[12] from me 'twill comfort be or no,
Since causeless jealousy hath so possessed
His heart, as no belief of me can rest.
But why stay I? I came to give relief.
Should I then doubt? No, I may ease his grief,
And help will seek. None should one's good neglect,
Much more his bliss, who for me joys reject.

[*She comes forward.*]

How now, Philisses, why do you thus grieve?
Speak, is there none that can your pains relieve?

PHILISSES

Yes, fair Musella, but such is my state,
Relief must come from her who can but hate.
What hope may I, wretch, have least good to move
Where scorn doth grow for me, for others, love?

MUSELLA

But are you sure she doth your love disdain?
It may be for your love she feels like pain.

PHILISSES

Like pain for me! I would not crave so much.
I wish no more but that love might her touch,
And that she might discern by love to know
That kind respect[13] is fit for her to show.

MUSELLA

Sure this she knows.

PHILISSES

Prove it, and I may live.

MUSELLA

Tell me who 'tis you love, and I will give
My word I'll win her if she may be won.

PHILISSES

Ah me, that doubt in me made me first run
Into this labyrinth[14] of woe and care,
Which makes me thus to wed mine own despair.

MUSELLA

But have you made it known to her you love,
That for her scorn you do these torments prove?

PHILISSES

Yes, now I have; and yet to ease some pain
I'll plainlier speak, though my own end I gain;
And so to end, it were to me a bliss.
Then know, for your dear sake my sorrow is.
It may be you will hate me, yet I have
By this some ease, though with it come my grave.[15]
Yet, dear Musella, since for you I pine
And suffer welcome death,[16] let favour shine
Thus far, that though my love you do neglect,
Yet sorry be I died. With this respect
I shall be satisfied, and so content
As I shall deem my life so lost well spent.[17]

MUSELLA

Sorry? Alas, Philisses, can it be
But I should grieve and mourn, nay, die for thee?
Yet, tell me why did you thus hide your love
And suffer wrong conceits[18] thus much to move?
Now 'tis almost too late your wish to gain;
Yet you shall pity for your[19] love obtain.

PHILISSES

Pity when helpless, 'tis endless given;
Am I to this unhappy bondage driven?
Yet truly pity, and 'twill be some ease
Unto my grief, though all things else displease;
But, do not yet, unless you can affect,
For forced pity's worse than is neglect;
And to be pitied but for pity's sake,
And not for love, do never pity take.

MUSELLA

Well then, I love you, and so ever must,
Though time and fortune should be still unjust;
For we may love, and both may constant prove,
But not enjoy unless ordained above.

PHILISSES

Dost thou love me? O, dear Musella, say,
And say it still, to kill my late dismay.

MUSELLA

More than myself, or love myself for thee
The better much. But wilt thou love like me?

PHILISSES

My only life, here do I vow to die
When I prove false or show unconstancy.

MUSELLA

All true content may this to both procure.

PHILISSES

And when I break, may I all shame endure.

MUSELLA

Nor doubt you me, nor my true heart mistrust,
For die I will before I prove unjust.
But here comes Rustic, whose encumbered[20] brain
With love and jealousy must our loss gain,
For since he hopes, nay, says that I am his,
I cannot absent be but he'll me miss;
But when that is, let day no longer shine,
Or I have life if live not truly thine.
But now, lest[21] that our love should be found out,
Let's seek all means to keep him from this doubt,
And let none know it but your sister dear,
Whose company I keep. So hold all clear,[22]
Then let him watch and keep what he can get,
His plots must want their force our joys to let.[23]
I'll step aside awhile, till you do meet
This welcome man, whose absence were more sweet;
For though that he, poor thing, can little find,
Yet I shall blush with knowing my own mind.
Fear and desire, still to keep[24] it hid,
Will blushing show it when 'tis most forbid.

PHILISSES

None can have power against a powerful love;
Nor keep the blood, but in the cheeks 'twill move,
But not for fear or care it there doth show,
But kind desire makes you blushing know
That joy takes place, and in your face doth climb
With leaping heart like lambkins in the prime.[25]
But, sweet Musella, since you will away,
Take now my heart and let yours in me stay.

Exit MUSELLA.

Could I express the joy I now conceive,
I were unworthy such bliss to receive;
But so much am I thine, as life and joy
Are in thy hands to nurse, or to destroy.

[*Enter* RUSTIC.]

How now Rustic? Whither away so fast?

RUSTIC

To seek Musella.

PHILISSES

Now that labour's past;
See where she comes.

MUSELLA [*Returning*]

Rustic where were you?
I sought, but could not find you.

RUSTIC

Is that[26] true?
Faith I was but, the truth to you to tell,
Marking[27] some cattle and asleep I fell.

MUSELLA[28]

And I was seeking of a long-lost lamb,
Which now I found, ev'n as along you came.

RUSTIC

I'm glad you found it.

MUSELLA

Truly, so am I.

RUSTIC

Now let us go to find our company.

PHILISSES

See where some be.

MUSELLA

It seems too soon, alas,
That love despised should come to such a pass.

[*Enter* LISSIUS *and* SIMEANA.]

LISSIUS [*and*] SIMEANA [*singing*]

Love's beginning like the Spring,
Gives delight, in sweetness flowing;
Ever pleasant, flourishing,
Pride in her brave colours[29] showing.
But Love ending is at last,
Like the storms of Winter's blast.

MUSELLA

Lissius, methinks you are grown sad of late,
And privately with your own thoughts debate.
I hope you are not fallen in love; that boy[30]
Cannot, I trust, your settled heart enjoy!

LISSIUS

'Tis well, you may be merry at my fall!
Rejoice! Nay do, for I can lose but all.

SIMEANA

And so too much! *Exit.*

MUSELLA

Sure, some strange error is.

PHILISSES

Learn you it out.

RUSTIC

We'll leave you.

[*Exeunt* PHILLISES *and* RUSTIC.]

MUSELLA

I'll know this.[31]
Come Lissius, tell me, whence proceeds this grief?
Discover it and you may find relief.

LISSIUS

No, I'll go seek Philisses; he, I'm sure
Will comfort me, who doth the like endure.
Yet, fair Musella, do thus much for me:
Tell fierce Simeana she hath murdered me,
And gain but this, that she my end will bless
With some, though smallest grief, for my distress;
And that she will but grace my hapless[32] tomb,
As to behold me dead by her hard doom.
This is a small request, and 'tis my last,
Whom to obey to my sad end will hast.[33]

MUSELLA

Nay Lissius, hear me. Tell me ere[34] you go
What sudden matter moves in you this woe.

LISSIUS

Alas! 'Tis love of one I did disdain,
And now I seek the like neglect I gain;
Yet at the first she answered me with love,
Which made my passions more increase and move.
But now she scorns me, and tells me I give
My love in equal sort to all; and drive[35]
My sighs and plaints[36] but from an outward part[37]
Of feigned love, and never from my heart;
And when on knees I do her favour crave,
She bids me seek Climeana, where I gave
As many vows as then to her I did;
And thereupon her sight did me forbid,
Vowing that if I did more move or speak
Of love, she would not only speeches break,
But ever more her sight, and would be blind
Rather than in my sight herself to find.
This is the cause, and this must be my end,
Which my sad days to saddest night must lend.

MUSELLA

When grew this change?

LISSIUS

Alas too late, today,
And yet too early[38] for my joy's decay.[39]

MUSELLA

Have no ill tongues reported false[40] of you?

LISSIUS

I know not. But my heart was ever true
Since first I vowed, and that my death shall tell,
Which is my last hope that will please her well.

MUSELLA

Soft, I will speak with her, and know her mind,
And why on such a sudden she's unkind;
Then truly bring you answer what she says.
Till then be quiet, for it can no praise
Bring to your death, when you shall wailing die,
Without so just a cause as to know why.

LISSIUS

But will Musella do thus much for me?
Shall I not of all friends forsaken be?

MUSELLA

Never of me; and here awhile but stay,
And I shall comfort bring your care t'allay.[41]
Exit.

LISSIUS

O no, I know she will not pity me,
Unfortunate and hapless must I be.
And now, thou powerful, conquering God of Love,
I do but thus much crave: thy forces prove
And cast all storms of thy just-caused rage
Upon me, vassal;[42] and no heat assuage
Of greatest fury, since I do deserve
No favour or least grace, but here to starve.
Fed with sharp tortures; let me live to see

My former sin for so much slighting thee;
Death yet more welcome, were it not so meet
I oft should die, who knew not sour from sweet.[43]
Simeana comes! Ah, most ungrateful maid,
Who answers love as one would welcome death:
The nearer that it comes, the more flies, stayed
Ne'er[44] but by limbs that tire wanting breath.
So hastes she still from me whose love is fixed
In purest flames without all baseness[45] mixed.[46]
[LISSIUS *prostrates himself, grief-stricken. Enter* SIMEANA *with* MUSELLA.]

MUSELLA
Simeana, this can be no ground to take
So great dislike, upon one man's report
And what may well prove false, as thus to make
An honest loving heart die in this sort.
Say that he useth others well and smiles
On them, who't[47] may be love of him beguiles;
Or that he used Climeana well, what then?
'Tis all poor soul she gets, who did contemn[48]
And rail at her.

SIMEANA
'Tis true, before my face
He did revile her with words of disgrace.
My back but turned, she was his only joy,
His best, his dearest life, and soon destroy
Himself he would if she not loved him still;
And just what he had vowed his heart did kill,
For my disdain, he shameless did protest
Within one hour to her caused his unrest!
Can I bear this? Who lived so long disdained,
Now to be mocked? I thought I love had gained
And not more scorn; but since thus much I find,
I'm glad joy sank no deeper in my mind!

MUSELLA
Fie, fie, Simeana, leave these doubts, too far
Already grown to breed so great a jar.[49]
'Twas but his duty kindly once to speak
To her, who for him would her poor heart break.
Would you not think it sin quite to undo[50]
A silly maid with scorn! But let these go.
Think you if I did love, and that I saw
He used more well, would I my love withdraw
From him for that? O, no great cause may be
To move good looks; mistrust not, but be free
From this vile humour of base jealousy,
Which breedeth nothing but self-misery.
For this believe, while you yourself are just,
You cannot any way your love mistrust.
Let him discourse[51] and smile, and what of this?
Is he the likelier in his faith to miss?[52]
No, never fear him for his outward smiles,
'Tis private friendship that our trust beguiles.
And therefore let not Arcas' flattering skill
Have power in your breast his[53] deserts to spill;[54]
Lissius is worthy, and a worthy love
He bears to you, then, these conceits[55] remove.

SIMEANA
Arcas did see them sit too privately,
And kiss, and then embrace!

MUSELLA
Well, if he did?

SIMEANA
And in her ear discourse familiarly,
When they did think it should from me be hid.

MUSELLA
Lord, how one may conjecture if one fear;
All things they doubt to be the same they fear.
Though private, must it follow he's untrue,
Or that they whispered must be kept from you?
Fie, leave these follies, and begin to think
You have your love brought to Death's river[56] brink.
Repent, you have him wronged; and now cherish
The dying lad, who else soon will perish.
Go, ask him pardon.

SIMEANA
Pardon, why? That he
The more may brag! He twice hath cozened[57] me!

MUSELLA
Nay, he is past all bragging. Mend your fault
And sorry be you have his torment wrought.
See where he lies, the truest sign of woe;[58]
Go, haste and save him; Love's wings are not slow.[59]

SIMEANA [*She approaches* LISSIUS.]
O, dearest Lissius, look but up and speak
To me, most wretched, whose heart now must break
With self-accusing of a cursed wrong,
Which rashly bred, did win belief too strong.
Ah, cast but up thine eyes, see my true tears,
And view but her who now all torment bears.
Do but look up, and thou shalt see me die
For having wronged thee with my jealousy.

LISSIUS
To see thee die? Alas, I die for thee!
What pleasure can thy death then bring to me?
Yet if I, love, make you say this, then poor I

Shall much more happy and more blessed die.

SIMEANA

Nay, let me end before thy end I see!
Alas, I love you, and 'twas love in me
Bred this great ill, which jealousy confused;
I brought your harm, and my best love abused.[60]

LISSIUS

O joy, which now doth swell as much as grief,
And pleasing yet doth make me seek relief.
Am I myself? No, I am only joy,
Not Lissius, grief did lately him destroy;
I am Simeana's love, her slave[61] revived,
Late hopeless dead, now have despair survived.

MUSELLA

All care now past, let joy in triumph sit;
This for such lovers ever is most fit;
This doth become that happy loving pair,
Who seek to nurse[62] the joys that kill all care;[63]
Let those fall out, mistrust, wrangle and jar,
Who love for fashion[64] not for love; but war
Not you, the couple Cupid best doth love,
Whose troubled hearts his godhead's self did move.

LISSIUS

Musella, you have turned this cloudy day
To sweet and pleasant light; nor can I say
So much as in my heart this kindness breeds,
For now delight all form[65] and speech exceeds.
But let us happy now, unhappy be
When in us least[66] unthankfulness you see.

SIMEANA

Let me myself, nay, my dear Lissius leave,
When I in service or in faith deceive
Musella, sole restorer of this joy;
And jealousy anew strive to destroy
Our loves and hopes, if I forgetful be
Of this increase of lost felicity.
But now, my Lissius, have you me forgiven
My last offence, by love and fearing driven?

LISSIUS

Thou lov'st me, 'tis enough, and now enjoy
All rest, nor bring new doubts to cross our joy;[67]
I all forget, and only hold thee dear,
And from thee all faults past my love doth clear.

SIMEANA

So, let us ever doubtless live and love,
And no mistrust in least sort our hearts move.

LISSIUS

No doubt of thee shall ever stir in mine.

SIMEANA

Nor breed in me so wholly I am thine.

MUSELLA

Happy this time, and blessed be your loves,
And most accursed they that other moves.
Live both contented and live still as one,
Never divided till your lives be done.

[*Enter*] PHILLIS, DALINA, PHILISSES, ARCAS, CLIMEANA [*and*] RUSTIC.

MUSELLA

Here comes the flock.[68]

RUSTIC

We're all here now.

MUSELLA

'Tis true,
We are all here, and one too much by you.

DALINA

Here be our fellows, now let us begin
Some pretty pastime, pleasure's sport to win.
Sweetest Musella, what think you is best?

MUSELLA

That whereunto your fancy is addressed.

DALINA

Mine is to riddling.[69]

SIMEANA

And, indeed that's good.

CLIMEANA

But, methinks, not lest they be understood.

SIMEANA

Understood? Why so shall all be that I make.

CLIMEANA

Tush, you'll say one thing, and another take.[70]

SIMEANA

You'll still be wrangling.

DALINA

Aye, and for a man!
Would I might live till quarrel I began
On such a cause. But pray, now quiet be,
And, fair Musella, first begin with me.

PHILLIS

But must the riddles be expounded?

DALINA

No.

MUSELLA

Then I'll begin, though scarce the play I know:[71]
That I wish, which with most pain
I must gain;
That I shun, which with such ease
Cannot please;
That most easy still I fly,
Barred,[72] I fainest[73] would come nigh.[74]

DALINA

I am the next, mark then what I will say;[75]
Best is, my lovers cannot me betray!
What I seek can never be
Found in me,
Fain[76] I would that try and find,
Which my mind,
Ever yet from my heart kept,

Till away my luck was stepped.

PHILISSES
Let them alone, the women still will speak;
Rustic, come you and I this course[77] will break.[78]
Late I saw a star to shine
Whose light methought was only mine,
Till a cloud came and did hide
That light from me, where light did bide.
Yet, tell me how can these agree:
That light though dimmed, that light I see.
Now Rustic, Fortune's falling on your head,
Bring forth your riddle. Fie, in love, and dead
To such a sport! Think not upon the day,
There is no danger in it, I dare well say.

RUSTIC
Truly, I cannot riddle,[79] I was not taught
These tricks of wit;[80] my thoughts ne'er higher wrought
Than how to mark a beast, or drive a cow
To feed, or else with art[81] to hold a plough,
Which if I knew, you surely soon would find
A matter more of worth[82] than these odd things,
Which never profit, but some laughter brings;
These others be of body[83] and of mind.[84]

PHILISSES
Spoke like a husband,[85] though you yet are none!
But come, what, is this sport already done?

RUSTIC
I cannot riddle.

DALINA
Whistle, 'tis as good,
For you sufficiently are understood!

RUSTIC
What mean you?

DALINA
Naught, but that you are
An honest man, and thrifty, full of care.

RUSTIC
I thought you have meant worse.

DALINA
Meant worse, what I?
Fie, this doth show your doubt and jealousy;
Why should you take my meaning worse than 'tis?

RUSTIC
Nay, I but smile to see how all you miss,[86]
But some shall find when I do seem to smile
And show best pleased, I oft'nest do beguile.[87]

DALINA
Yourself you mean; for few else do respect[88]
Your smiles or frowns; therefore, do not neglect
Your pleasant youth, ill will is too soon got,
And once that rooted, not so soon forgot.

PHILISSES
You grow too wise. Dispute no more. Here be
Others who will let us their hearers be,
And give this sport some life again, which you
Almost made dead.

DALINA
I have done, let joy ensue.

LISSIUS
Guess you all what this can be:[89]
A snake to suffer fire I see;
A fog and yet a clear bright day;
A light which better were away;
Two suns at once, both shining clear,
And without envy hold each[90] dear.

PHILLIS[91]
A Spring I hoped for, but it died,
Then on the next my hopes relied;
But Summer past, the latter Spring,
Could me but former losses bring;
I died with them, yet still I live,
While Autumn can no comfort give.

MUSELLA
Unmannerly,[92] I must your presence leave,
Sent for in haste unto my mother. But
I hope in this sweet place soon to receive
Your most loved companies. And so to put
Good Rustic into better humours;[93] say,
Will you be merry? *Exit.*

RUSTIC
I'll not after stay. *Exit.*

PHILISSES [*Aside*]
No, follow. Shadows never absent be
When sun shines;[94] in which blessing you may see
Your shadowed self, who nothing in truth are
But the reflection of her too great care.
[*To the others*]
What will you further do?

DALINA
Let us depart.

ARCAS
Aye, let's away. [*Aside*] But some ere long will smart.[95]

PHILISSES
When shall we meet again?

DALINA
When day appears.

LISSIUS
No, not till sun, who all foul mists still clears.

PHILISSES
Why, then at sun, and who shall then miss here
A punishment by us ordained shall bear.

DALINA
Let it be so.
PHILLIS
I'm very well agreed.
LISSIUS
So are we all, and sun appear with speed.
[*Exeunt*]

Scene ii

[*Enter*] VENUS *and* CUPID.
VENUS
Now have thy torments long enough endured,
And of thy force they are enough assured.
O, hold thy hand. Alas, I pity now
Those whose great pride did lately scorn to bow.
Thou hast performed thy promise, and thy state[96]
Now is confessed.[97] O, slacken then thy hate;
They humble do their hearts and thoughts to thee;
Behold them, and accept them, and mild be.
Thy conquest is sufficient, save the[98] spoils
And let them only taken[99] be in toils.[100]
But set at liberty again, to tell
Thy might and clemency, which doth excel.
CUPID
I mean to save them; but some yet must try
More pain, ere they their blessings may come nigh;
But in the end most[101] shall be well again,
And sweetest is that love obtained with pain.
[*Enter*] PRIESTS [*to music, singing*].[102]
PRIESTS
Love, thy pow'rful hand withdraw;
And do yield unto thy law,
Rebels, now thy subjects be,
Bound they are who late were free.
Most confess thy power and might,
All hearts yield unto thy right.
Thoughts directed are by thee,
Souls do strive thy joys to see.
Pity then, and mercy, give
To those hearts where you do live;
They your images[103] do prove,[104]
In them may you see great Love;
They your mirrors,[105] you their eyes,[106]
By which they true Love do spy.
Ease[107] awhile their cruel smarts
And behold their humble[108] hearts;
Greater glory 'tis to save,
When that you the conquest have,
Than with tyranny to press,
Which still makes the honour less.
Gods do princes' hearts[109] direct,
Then, to these, have some respect.[110] [*Exeunt.*]

Act V

Scene i

[*Enter*] MUSELLA *and* SIMEANA.
MUSELLA
O eyes, that day can see and cannot mend
What my joys poison, must my wretched end
Proceed from love? And yet my true love crossed,[1]
Neglected for base gain, and all worth[2] lost
For riches?[3] Then 'tis time for good to die,
When wealth must wed us to all misery.
SIMEANA
If you will but stoutly tell your mother
You hate him and will match[4] with any other,
She cannot, nor will, go about to cross
Your liking, so to bring your endless loss.
MUSELLA
Alas, I've urged her, till that she with tears
Did vow and grieve she could not mend my[5] state
Agreed on by my father's will,[6] which bears
Sway in her breast and duty in me. Fate[7]
Must have her courses,[8] while that wretched I
Wish but so good a fate as now to die.
SIMEANA
Wish not such ill, which all we suffer must,
But take some hope the gods are not unjust;
My mind doth give me yet, you shall be blessed,
And seldom do I miss;[9] then quiet rest.
MUSELLA
Rest quiet! O heavens! Have you ever known
The pains of Love and been by him o'erthrown
To give this counsel and advise your friend
T'impossibilities? Why to what end
Speak you thus madly?[10] Can it ere be thought
That quiet, or least rest, can now be brought
To me, while dear Philisses thus is crossed,[11]
Whom missing[12] all my happiness is lost?
SIMEANA
You have not missed, nor lost him yet.
MUSELLA
I must,
And that's enough. Did I my blessings trust
In your kind[13] breasts, you fatal sisters?[14] Now
By your decree to be bestowed, and bow
To base unworthy riches?[15] O, my heart
That breaks not, but can suffer all this smart!
SIMEANA
Have patience.
MUSELLA
I cannot, nor I will not

Patient be! Ah me, and bear this ill lot?
No! I will grieve in spite of grief, and mourn
To make those mad who now to pleasure turn.
[*Enter* PHILISSES.]

PHILISSES
My dear Musella, what is it doth grieve
Your heart thus much? Tell me, and still believe
While you complain, I must tormented be;
Your sighs and tears, alas, do bleed in me.

MUSELLA
I know it, 'tis your loss I thus lament.
I must be married. Would my days were spent!

PHILISSES
Married!

MUSELLA
To Rustic. My mother so commands,
Who I must yield to, being in her hands.[16]

PHILISSES
But will you marry? Or show love to me?
Or her obey, and make me wretched be?

MUSELLA
Alas Philisses, will you this doubt make?
I would my life, to pleasure you, forsake;
Hath not my firmness hitherto made known
My faith and love? Which yet should more be shown
If I might govern but my mother's will.
Yet this last question even my heart doth kill.

PHILISSES
Grieve not my dearest, I speak but for love,
Then let not love your trouble so far move.
You weep not that it wounds not hapless[17] me,
Nor sigh but in me all those sorrows be;
You never cry, but groans most truly show
From deepest of my heart I feel your woe.
Then heap not now more sorrows on my heart,
By these dear tears which taste of endless[18] smart;
No grief can be, which I have not sustained,
And must, for now despair hath conquest gained.
Yet, let your love in me still steady rest[19]
And in that I sufficiently am blessed.
But must you marry? O, those words deny,[20]
Or here behold your poor Philisses die!

MUSELLA
I would I could deny the words I spake,
When I did Rustic's marriage offer take;
Hopeless of you, I gave my ill[21] consent,
And we contracted[22] were, which I repent.
The time now curse, my tongue wish out, which gave
Me to that clown with whom I wed my grave.

PHILISSES
I hear and see my end. O, Love unjust
And careless of my heart put in your trust,
Ungrateful and forgetful of the good
From me[23] received, by whom thy fame hath stood,
Thy honour been maintained, thy name adored,
Which by all others with disgrace was stored.
Is this the great reward I shall[24] receive
For all my service? Will you thus deceive
My hopes and joys?

MUSELLA
Yet, let me one thing crave.

PHILISSES
Ask my poor life, all else long since I gave.

MUSELLA
That will I ask, and yours requite with mine,
For mine cannot be, if not joined to thine.
Go with me to the temple and there we
Will bind our lives, or else our lives make free.

PHILISSES
To die for thee a new life I should gain,
But to die with thee were eternal pain;
So, you will promise me that you will live,
I willingly will go, and my life give.
You may be happy.[25]

MUSELLA
Happy, without thee?
O, let me rather wretched, and thine, be!
Without thee no life can be, nor least joy,
Nor thought but how a sad end to enjoy.
But promise me, yourself you will not harm,
As you love me.

PHILISSES
Let me impose that charm[26]
Likewise on you.

MUSELLA
Content, I am agreed.

PHILISSES
Let's go alone, no company we need.

MUSELLA
Simeana, she shall go, and so may tell
The good or heavy chance that us befell.

PHILISSES
I am content. Your will shall be obeyed
Till this life change and I in earth am laid.

SIMEANA
I fear the worst; but what will you two do?
Both die, and me, poor maiden, quite undo?

PHILISSES
Die? No, we go for evermore to live,
And to our loves a sacrifice to give.

MUSELLA
Our tears and sorrows we will offer there,
And of our offerings you shall witness

bear;
The truest and most constant love there shall
In your sight end, and yet shall never fall.

PHILISSES
Such faith we'll sacrifice as none can touch,
Which once reporting there could be too much.

SIMEANA
I know not what you mean, but I'll along.

PHILISSES
Let's haste, for here come some may do us wrong. *Exeunt.*

Scene ii

[*Enter*] LISSIUS, DALINA [*and*] ARCAS.

LISSIUS
Arcas, is't possible it is today?

ARCAS
It is. Musella now can bear[27] no sway;[28]
Rustic shall have her, he's the blessed man,
Yet cannot get her love, do what he can.

DALINA
I'm sorry for Philisses.

LISSIUS
Truly, so am I.
What than a lost love is more misery?

[*Enter* RUSTIC.]

RUSTIC
Lissius, Dalina, Arcas, well met today!
I must be married; pray be not away,
But see us joined and after dine with us.
Where is Philisses? I hope he'll not miss.
This is a jolly day. This my day is!

LISSIUS
I will not fail. Must we not fetch the bride?

RUSTIC
Yes, marry,[29] from her mother's where w'abide. *Exit.*

DALINA
How well this business doth become this man!
How well he speaks word 'marriage', and began
In as good form his neighbours to invite,
As if he studied manners; yet, at night,[30]
I'll undertake, much mirth will not appear
In fair Musella; she'll show heavy cheer!

ARCAS
This 'tis to look so high and to despise
All loves that rose not pleasing in her eyes;
Now she that soared aloft all day, at night
Must roost in a poor bush with small delight.[31]

LISSIUS
I never knew this in her. But 'tis true
She liked not of the love proffered by you;[32]
And for refusing that she could not like,
No man ought to blame her or her mind dislike.
But you have other qualities to move
A just dislike; you love cross-baits[33] in love.
I was beholding[34] to you when time was;
But I enjoy her now.

DALINA
Come, let that pass.
Arcas is known, and I dare lay my life
You have been meddling and have caused some strife
Lately about Musella. But take heed,
If it prove so, perchance[35] you'll want your meed![36]

LISSIUS
If it be found, thou shalt no longer live,
Than while thou dost her satisfaction give![37]

ARCAS
Be not so choleric[38] till you know the truth;
I have left that foul error in my youth.

DALINA
Hardly, I doubt, for I saw you last day
Sneaking and prying all along this way;
'Twas for no goodness that I'm very sure,
For from a child you could not that endure! *Exeunt.*

Scene iii

[*Enter*] CLIMEANA, LACON [*and*] SILVESTA.

CLIMEANA
Lacon, how fare you now? Musella must
This day be married. Is not Love unjust
To suffer this distasteful match to be
Against her choice, and most against poor thee?

LACON
Not against me. I never hoped, then how
Doth Cupid wrong me, though she marry now?
Yet, thus is Love unjust to let her wed
One who she never sees, but wisheth dead!
So I, although for her I oft have died,[39]
Grieve for her loss, not that I was denied;
I was unworthy of her, and she far
Too worthy for this clown. O, she, the star[40]
Of light and beauty, must she, lovely she,
Be matched to Rustic base, unworthy he?

[*Enter* SILVESTA.]

SILVESTA [*Aside*]
Musella to be forced and made to try
Her faith to one she hates and still did fly?
It should not be, nor shall be. No, no! I
Will rescue her, or for her sake will die!

[*To* CLIMEANA *and* LACON]
Have you yet seen Musella here today?

CLIMEANA
No, but I hear she passed by this way
With fair Simeana, both by break of morn,
With humble minds far from their wonted[41] scorn,
To offer their last rites of maiden thought
To your chaste Mistress.[42] Venus now hath bought
Their future time. How think you of this change?
'Tis better sure than still alone to range!
SILVESTA
It's well you think so, yet methinks you can
Make a clean shift[43] to live without a man!
Exeunt.

Scene iv

[*Enter*] PHILISSES [*and*] MUSELLA *offering in the Temple of Love.*

[PHILISSES AND MUSELLA][44]
Venus and great Cupid, hear,
Take our sacrifices clear!
Where not rites we only give,
But our hearts wherein you live;
Those true relics of firm love
On your altar still to move;[45]
Where none such, none so sincere,
To your triumph light did bear;
Yours they lived while joy had life,
Dying, here will end all strife.
Truer love, or truer hearts,
Never perished by your darts.
PHILISSES
Venus, only Queen of love,
Take these passions which I prove,
Take these tears, this vow take,
Which my death shall perfect make.
But Musella my heart loved,
Her loss hath my joy removed;
Hers I lived, hers now I die,
Crowned with fame's eternity.
Thus your force shall glory have
By Philisses' loving grave.
MUSELLA
Cupid, Lord of love and hearts,
King of thoughts and loving smarts,
Take these offerings which I give,
And my life, which new shall live.
Earth too mean for such a truth,
Shall in death have lasting youth;
No decay, no strife, no fate,
Shall disturb that 'during[46] state.
Life I offer to true love;
Then accept this end, I prove
Time none such did know, nor shall,
See so willingly to fall:
In Philisses I did live,
He departing, life I give.
PHILISSES AND MUSELLA
Fame hereafter swell with pride,
Never love thus lived, thus died.
PHILISSES
Now my Musella, and in death but mine,
Take this last farewell in which glories shine:
Love, but to you, could never be so true,
And death, than life, I choose since 'tis for you;
My life in you I had, my joy, my bliss,
And now for you and by you, my end is.
Yet, keep your promise, ever happy be,
You may be fortunate and outlive me.
MUSELLA
That I believe, when I do thee outlive,
Shame shall, instead of Fame, my triumph[47] give.
I loved as firmly as thou could'st me love,
And can as willingly a death's wound prove.
But you forget the promise you did make,
And since condition made, yourself first break,
I am released; your word forgot and broke,
My hand shall first conclude that blessed stroke
Unto thy love and mine. Since it is thus,
Farewell, poor world, life's living bides in us!
[*She raises a dagger. Enter* SILVESTA.]
SILVESTA
O, hold your hands! I knew your minds and have
Brought fitter means to wed you to your grave.
Let not those hands be spotted with your blood,
But since your destiny is not withstood,
Drink this sweet potion,[48] then take leave and die,
Embracing thus you dead shall buried lie.

PHILISSES
Friendship, what greater blessing, than thou art,
Can once descend into a mortal heart.
Silvesta, friend and priest doth now appear,
And as our loves, let this, thy deed, shine clear.
MUSELLA
Never more fit did friendship meet with need;
Blessed be thy days, most blessed be this deed.
[*They drink the potion and fall.*]
SIMEANA
What, have you killed them? For this you must die!
SILVESTA
And dying for them, I die happily.
Who would outlive them? Who would dying fly,
That here beheld love and love's tragedy?[49]

But first, upon Love's altar let's them lay,
There to abide till their new marriage day;
Then, lead me to those who my life must take,
But ere I die, some joyful heart shall ache.
Exeunt.

Scene v

[*Enter*] RUSTIC *with* SHEPHERDS *and* SHEPHERDESSES, *ready to fetch the bride.*

RUSTIC
Now is the time approached. What think you now,
Is't not a trim[50] day? What cloud shows a brow?
All at my fortune cheer,[51] all smile with joy,
Sheep, goats and cattle, glad that I enjoy.

DALINA
I never loved him; now I hate him! Fie,
To think Musella by this beast must lie!

RUSTIC
Come, let's along, and quickly fetch the bride,
Methinks I long to have her by my side.
[*They see* MUSELLA *and* PHILISSES.]
How now? What, stumble, 'tis not fatal, is't?

LISSIUS
Good luck that you, to him, the ground have missed.[52]

DALINA
A far worse sign than this it doth foretell.

RUSTIC
How, is she married, and thus cozened[53] me?
And dead, and buried? How can all this be?

SILVESTA
Fetch forth her mother, and you then shall know
The cause and actor of this cruel blow.

LISSIUS
O heaven, was she too rare a prize for earth,
Or were we only happy in her birth?

DALINA
Only made rich[54] enjoying of her sight;
She gone, expect we nothing but sad night.

PHILLIS
What glory day did give us was to show
The virtue in her beauty seemed to grow.

CLIMEANA
Sweet love and friendship in her shined bright,
Now dimmed are both, since darkened is her light.

LACON
No worth[55] did live, which in her had not spring,
And she thus gone, to her grave worth doth bring.

RUSTIC
I liked her well, but she ne'er cared for me,
Yet am I sorry we thus parted be.
[*Enter* MUSELLA'S MOTHER.]

SIMEANA
Now hear of me the mournful'st end of love,
That heart for heart could find, and heartless prove.
Philisses and Musella had loved long,
And long unknown, which bred their only wrong.
At last discovered to their greatest joy,
This match came cross their dear hopes to destroy.
But, yet have courage, all things may prove well.

RUSTIC
Nay, pray resolve me, I begin to fear.

LISSIUS
To fear? Fie, man, can trips[56] make hope forbear?
On, on, have mettle,[57] will you now wax[58] faint,
You, who to us a happy life must paint?

RUSTIC
This is not all. This morn a cow did low,
And that ill-luck foretells, I truly know.

DALINA
Had she not lost her calf?

RUSTIC
Her calf? Fie, no,
She had a dainty one, as I will show
At my return, and they together came,
And while she lowed the youngling sucked her dam.[59]

LISSIUS
And so might hurt her, whereat she did cry,
And for your help did low so bitterly.

RUSTIC
Well, come what will, we now may not go back.

DALINA
Yes, very well, for her consent you lack.

RUSTIC
Come then, away, the precious time doth waste.

SIMEANA
Hear first my news, for it may stay your haste;
Your bride, a bridegroom new, with joy hath gained,
And both for wedding-bed a tomb obtained.
Here is the priest that married them to death,
And I the witness of their passing breath.
For she,[60] alas, despairing of her bliss,
Agreed to marry Rustic and to miss
No cross,[61] nor froward[62] hap,[63] which sure with him

She must encounter if in this stream swim.
When this was done they knew each other's heart,
And by it knew the thread[64] which led to smart.[65]
They yet awhile rejoiced in their love,
But too, too soon, there followed this remove.
Her mother hasty to conclude her will,
Appointed this sad day, should that fulfil
Which hath indeed fulfilled a greater harm
Than Spite[66] itself could purchase with her charm.
Musella, finding that her given consent
Proved thus her hell, her soul did then lament.
Yet could not gain release, but that she must
Look as her mother liked. O force unjust!
Yet, so it was, and this procured her end;
Her mother grown her foe, and death her friend;
Her friend she chose. Philisses, who did love
As much as she, and she as much did prove
Of love and pain, as he who felt all smart,
Vowed since they might not join but rather part,
They yet as most unfeigned[67] lovers would
Lovingly die; and so firm lovers should.
Unto the Temple then they took their way,
Together wept, together did they pray,
Together offered. Now Silvesta, you
Must tell the hapless end which did ensue.

SILVESTA
And so I will. Their loves they gave and lives,
Which should have finished been by too-sharp knives,
Provided closely those two to have killed,
Who have the world with love and wonder filled.
But I came in and hindered that sharp blow,
Though not their wills, more honour I did owe
To that in love alone, unhappy pair,
And brought their ends more quiet and more fair.
A drink I gave them made their souls to meet,
Which in their clayey cages[68] could not. Sweet
Was their farewell, while sorrow then used art
To flatter joy, till they no more should part.
Their bodies, likewise joined by us, are placed
Upon Love's altar, nor from thence displaced
By vow must be, till all you lovers lay
This love-killed couple in their biding clay.[69]
This I have done, and here am I to die,
If so you please, and take it willingly.

RUSTIC
Nay, if she loved another, farewell, she!
I'm glad she by her death hath made me free.

LISSIUS
Is this your care?[70] O clownish part,[71] can you,
For shame, not sorrow when our hearts do rue?

RUSTIC
I'm free, I care not.

SILVESTA
The like is she then now.

RUSTIC
She is for me, and here I disavow
All promises which have between us passed,
Or have been made by her, at first, or last,
To me, and thus I do release her. Now,
May I seek one and please myself in love;
I'll none but such whose heart my love shall move. *Exit.*

SILVESTA
She's happy, yet in death, that she is free
From such a worthless creature. Can this be?
Such virtue should in her fair breast abound,
Yet to be tied where no worth[72] could be found?

LISSIUS [*To* MUSELLA'S MOTHER]
Thus have your years your happiness outworn
And brought untimely death to your first-born;[73]
Can you endure this change, and hear us say
Your forced marriage brought her funeral day?

MOTHER
If the true grief I feel could be expressed
By words, or sighs, I should myself detest;
Sorrow in heart and soul doth only bide,
And in them shall my woe be justly tried.
Yet, justice do I crave of this vile pair,
Which were the founders of my endless care.
Arcas first plotted it with skilful art,
To ruin[74] me and, living, eat[75] my heart;
He told me that Musella wantonly[76]
Did seek Philisses' love. Alas, only
The speech of that did inly[77] wound me so,
As stay I could not, nor the time let go.
But sent for her and forced her to consent
To finish that which makes us all lament,
And me to die, o me, with grief and shame,
That thus deservedly I bear this blame.
Silvesta, who their lives brought to an end,
Must also suffer. Death alone, my friend,
Shall me release, these things I hope you'll do,
Which done with age and grief, I'll suffer too.

LISSIUS
These must and shall be done, and rites
Performed to their dear bodies and their sprites.[78]
Now to the temple and their bodies view,
Then give these judgement. Biding joy adieu!
Exeunt.

Scene vi

[*Enter* FORESTER.]

FORESTER
Under a hedge all dead to rest I laid

My body, by despair wholly decayed;
When sleep no sooner did my eyelids close
But half distracted with a dream, I rose.[79]
Methought I saw Silvesta's fair hands tied
Fast[80] to a stake, where fire burned in all pride,
To kiss with heat those most unmatched[81] limbs,
Where Virtue with her shape like habits trims
Herself with her.[82] While she, alas, fair she,
Should to those flames a sacred offering be.
This dream persuaded me to seek her out
And save her, or to free me from the doubt.
And there I see her to the temple go;
I'll after, and my life at her feet throw. [*Exit.*]

Scene vii

The temple, the dead bodies on the altar. Enter the SHEPHERDS *and* SHEPHERDESSES, *casting flowers on them;* VENUS, *[who] appears in glory;* [CUPID *and the* PRIESTS].

SHEPHERDS AND SHEPHERDESSES [*singing*]
Sorrow, now conclude thy hate,
More cannot be done by Fate.
Grief, abandon thy cursed skill,
Love hath now found means to kill.
Lovers here example take:
Faith in Love should never shake;
Only Death hath force to part
Lovers' bodies by his dart;
But their spirits higher fly,
Death can never make them die;
But their souls with pure love's fire
Will to heavenly bliss aspire.

PRIESTS
Now must we judge the offenders for this deed
And each one punish; thus it is decreed.
Silvesta, greatest in the fault, must bend
Her spirit first unto her own sought end;
With flames of fire, as she with flames of zeal
Did act this, she must now her last day seal.
Death she procured, and for death, life shall give.

SILVESTA
'Tis justice. Thus, by death a-new I live!
My name by this will win eternity,
For no true heart will let my merit die.
[*Enter* FORESTER.]

FORESTER
I must enjoy my death ere this be done!
Bright Venus, I beseech thee and thy son,
To look on me, your true, though luckless, slave,
And view the heart my faith to firm love gave.
Save sweet Silvesta, whose youth framed this deed,
Let not her virtue as offences speed.[83]
Or though[84] by law she have deserved this doom,
Let me for her obtain her 'pointed[85] tomb;
I am more fit to die and suffer far,
Life with my sorrows are at endless war;
Besides, the law allows if one will die
For other's fault, his death may their life buy;
Let me first beg it, pay it then with life,
Death for her sake shall please, and end the strife.

VENUS
Poor Forester, thy love deserveth more,
For in thy heart true firmness lived in store.[86]
But since you will her life with your life buy,
You must enjoy death; we can none deny
That this do claim it; she's by you made free;
And you for her must now my offering be.

FORESTER
Goddess of hearts, you thus have done me right;
Now shall my faith, to honour you, shine bright.

SILVESTA
Thanks is your due for saving me from death,
Did I not rather hate, than love, this breath.
Yet, shall this bounty[87] gain in my chaste heart
To your deserts a kind and thankful part.

FORESTER
Death, happy death, since she for whom I die
Doth pity me and weighs[88] my constancy;
Could I live ages, 'twould not be so good,
As now to die with thanks given for my blood.
Then, farewell, world. Death, welcome as new life.
Silvesta thanks me, and gives me this wife.[89]

MOTHER
You sacred priests, perform the latest due
To their dead bodies; and my joys adieu.

PRIESTS
Rustic, before us here disclaim the right
In life was tied to you, now to her sprite.[90]

RUSTIC
I love no sprites, nor those affect not[91] me!
She loved Philisses, therefore she is free.
Were she alive, she were her own to choose,
Thus, here, to her all claim I do refuse.

PRIESTS
Philisses, of us take Musella fair,
We join your hands, rise and abandon care.
Venus hath caused this wonder for her glory,
And the triumph of Love's Victory.[92]
[PHILISSES *and* MUSELLA *arise from the altar.*]

VENUS
Lovers be not amazed! This is my deed,
Who could not suffer your dear hearts to bleed.
Come forth and joy, your faith hath been thus tried,

Who truly would for true love's sake have died.
Silvesta was my instrument ordained[93]
To kill, and save her friends, by which sh'hath[94] gained
Immortal fame, and bands[95] of firmest love
In their kind breasts where true affections move.
Then, all rejoice, and with a loving song
Conclude the joy hath been kept down too long.

MOTHER
Joy, now as great as was my former woe,
Shuts up my speech from speaking what I owe
To all but mine, for mine I joy you are,
And love, and bliss, maintain you from all care.
Pardon my fault, enjoy and blessed be,
And children and their children's children see.

MUSELLA
Pardon me first, who have your sorrow wrought,
Then take our thanks whose good your care hath brought.[96]
Silvesta, next, to you our lives are bound,
For in you only was true friendship found.

PHILISSES
Mother, for so your gift makes me you call,
Receive my humble thanks which ever shall
With faithful love and duty you attend,
Till death our lives bring to a final end.
And chaste Silvesta, take my life when I
Ungrateful prove to your worth-binding[97] tie.

SILVESTA
Venus the praise must have, whose love to you
Made her descend on earth, and your cares view;
She sent the drink hath wedded you to joy,
And in joy live, and happiness enjoy.
Chaste love relieved you, in chaste love still live,
And each to other, true affections give.
For you, kind Forester, my chaste love take,
And know I grieve now only for your sake.
Exit.

FORESTER
My joys increase, she grieves now for my pain,
Ah, happy proffered life, which this can gain.
Now shall I go contented to my grave,
Though no more happiness I ever have.

LISSIUS
Now let me ask my joy, which you must give,
Philisses, you may make me die or live.
Your sister for my wife I seek, alone
I crave but her, and love makes her mine own;
Two bodies we are, yet have but one heart,
Then rather join than let such dear love part.

PHILISSES
Myself from bliss I sooner will divide
Than cross your loves. Then, henceforth, thus abide
Joined in firm love, and happiness attend
Your days on earth until your lives do end.

DALINA
Rustic, what think you; is this called fair play?

RUSTIC
When Venus wills, men cannot but obey.
Yet this I'll swear, I'm plainly cozened[98] here!
But 'tis all one, the bargain may prove dear.

DALINA
Yet you have not lost all: this wreath[99] you see
Is proved your garland, this fair willow tree[100]
You now must reverence[101] and bravely wear.

RUSTIC
I'll sooner die than such disgrace to bear!
Nay, sooner marry, and that now I deem
Far worse than death, though slighter in esteem.

DALINA
I would I might but name the happy maid
Should be your wife.

RUSTIC
Yourself name, and all's said.

DALINA
Will you have me then?

RUSTIC
Rather than my life!

DALINA
In troth,[102] agreed! I'll prove a loving wife.

RUSTIC
'Tis all I seek. Now, God give you all joy,
And blessed am I who this sweet lass enjoy.

MUSELLA
A good exchange, and everyone agreed.

PHILISSES
And as we love and like, so let us speed.

VENUS
Now, sing a song, both Priests and all, for joy;
And cursed be, they your blessed states annoy.[103]

CUPID [*Sings.*]
Now my wars in love hath end,
Each one here enjoys their friend;
And so all shall henceforth say
Who my laws will still obey.
Mother, now judge Arcas' fault,
All things else your will hath wrought.

VENUS
Arcas, think not your villainy's forgot!
But since each now enjoys, the better lot
Doth fall to you: you here must still abide
In these fair plains, where you shall never hide
The shame of falsehood printed in your face;[104]
Nor hence remove, but in the self-same place
You did commit that error foul and ill,
There your days left, with grief and shame shall fill

Your gnawing conscience. This shall be your doom.

ARCAS

O sacred Goddess, let my heart's-suit[105] come
Before your eyes. Rather, o, let me die,
Than here remain with shame and infamy.
This dying life, alas, than death is worse,
Nor can you lay on me a greater curse.

VENUS

Your doom is given, it may not be recalled,
But with your treachery you must be thralled.[106]
And now all duties are performed to Love;
Look that no more our powers by scorn you move,
But be the treasures of Love's lasting glory,
And I, your princess, crowned with victory.

ARCAS

Thus still is sin rewarded with all shame,
And so let all be that deserve like blame.
I have offended in the basest kind,
And more ill do deserve than ill can find.
I traitor was to Love, and to my love,
Those who shall thus offend, like me, shame prove. *Exeunt.*

FINIS

6 *The Concealed Fancies*

LADY JANE CAVENDISH AND LADY ELIZABETH BRACKLEY

INTRODUCTION

Jane Cavendish (1621–69) and Elizabeth Brackley (1616–63) were sisters. They were the daughters of William Cavendish, Duke of Newcastle, by his first wife, Elizabeth Bassett, the great-granddaughters of the infamous Bess of Hardwick, and the stepdaughters of the prolific author, Margaret Cavendish.[1] When they wrote *The Concealed Fancies* Elizabeth was already married, to John Egerton, Viscount Brackley, who was later to become the second Earl of Bridgewater and who had played the part of the elder brother in the first performance of Milton's *Comus.* This early marriage accounts for the authors' use of the initials JC (Jane Cavendish) and EB (Elizabeth Brackley) on the manuscript version of the play. The literary productivity of the two sisters should not, therefore, be read as an isolated excursion into the world of literary creativity, but as a contribution to a familial discourse in which women were capable of asserting an independent subjectivity and, moreover, had the freedom to articulate their identities through textual inscription.[2] As such, the Cavendish family should be considered alongside the Sidneys, as a literary grouping which encompassed both male and female authors. As Sue Wiseman comments in her essay 'Gender and Status in Dramatic Discourse' (1992): 'In their private entertainments the women of this family shift from mere actors to authors, from ciphers filled by the discourse to manipulators of the codes.'[3] Like other seventeenth-century noblewomen, however, Jane and Elizabeth were expected, before all else, to accept that their most important roles would be those of wife and mother. Indeed, Elizabeth became Brackley's wife in 1636 when she was just 15 (he was 19), but she was allowed to remain with her family because she was 'too young to be bedded'.[4] At the outbreak of the Civil War she was still at the Cavendish home, Welbeck Abbey, where Elizabeth Bassett and her three daughters – Elizabeth, Jane and their younger sister Frances – remained, while the Duke and his two sons, Charles, Lord Mansfield, and Henry, later the Earl of Ogle, served with the Royalist forces. On the death of their mother (April 1643), the sisters continued at Welbeck, aiding the King's cause as best they could; for example, by sending military information to the King's commanders at Oxford. They also attempted to sustain their father's fortunes, by saving his silverware and Van Dyck paintings when Welbeck was sacked, and sending him money when he was in debt. The women needed to be enterprising because Welbeck was captured by the Parliamentary forces on 2 August 1644, notwithstanding letters sent by them to Lord Fairfax, the Parliamentary General, which reveal that they were treated with respect and consideration.[5] Although Welbeck was recaptured briefly by a Royalist detachment in 1645, it was finally surrendered in November of that year and the family left their home with what goods they could salvage. It was during this period that Jane and Elizabeth appear to have occupied their time with writing: they wrote several works together, including a play, *The Concealed Fancies*, a pastoral masque, *A Pastorall*, and several poems.[6] The works were probably composed at Welbeck itself, although Nathan Comfort Starr suggests that the play could have been written after the authors had left Welbeck, retiring to Ashridge, one of the Brackley properties.[7] This seems an unnecessary hypothesis, since there is clear evidence to show that Elizabeth and Jane were living together at Welbeck, while none exists to link them to Ashridge, Starr's only evidence being that one of the play's scenes is set in a convent and Ashridge had formerly been a religious house. Moreover, it is clear from the contemporary allegory, that the play was written, and probably performed, before Newcastle remarried in December 1645, and this would suggest a date commensurate with the sisters' residency at Welbeck. What is perhaps more significant is that,

9 *Newcastle and his Family*, after Diepenbeek, by kind permission of the Sidney Jones Library, Liverpool University

by locating the period of composition to the peace time occupation of Ashridge, Starr is able to comment: 'It is quite possible that if the two authors were sojourning at Ashridge, they found the house and grounds so interestingly arranged that they could not resist putting on a play.'[8] This romanticized version of events transfers the authors from their isolated imprisonment at Welbeck, which certainly demanded both independent fortitude and ingenuity, to the cosy environment of Brackley's home, where the two sisters could be protected by Elizabeth's husband. In addition, the play itself becomes a recreational pursuit devised for the amusement of others (note that Starr writes 'putting on' instead of 'writing'), rather than as an effort of joint literary productivity which developed out of the women's personal and political circumscription by the Civil War.

The overall tone of the play is dominated by the problems of the Civil War. The siege at Welbeck, for example, specifically provides the backdrop for the play's subplot, in which three cousins are trapped by Parliamentarian troops at the castle of Ballamo. Indeed, even though the comedy concludes conventionally with a series of marriages, there is a certain lack of resolution and a postponement of any secure future. The play's political allegory is also underlined by the fact that both events and characters have their real-life counterparts. Just as Welbeck Abbey is transformed into Ballamo Castle, so the three besieged cousins represent Jane, Elizabeth and Frances, although the first two sisters are also mirrored in the play's heroines, Luceny and Tattiney. The two Cavendish brothers become the two Stellows, the Duke of Cavendish appears as Lord Calsindow, and, most cruelly, Margaret Lucas (the sisters' future stepmother) is satirized in the figure of Lady Tranquillity. Lucas herself had fled with Queen Henrietta Maria to Paris, where she subsequently met and married the Duke, who was thirty years older than her. It is unlikely that Jane or Elizabeth had met Margaret Lucas when they created the vain and self-advancing figure of Lady Tranquillity; for example, they depict her as older than either Luceny or Tattiney, when in fact, she was approximately the same age as the authors, being born in 1624. The sisters probably received their information from the two Cavendish brothers, who had returned from France and would certainly have brought back gossip about their father's 'inappropriate' courtship.[9] Margaret Lucas, however, seems to have been a fitting consort to the Duke; interested as she was in intellectual pursuits, Lucas was well able to contribute to the familial discourse of literary productivity. Cavendish himself wrote several plays and he certainly encouraged all his progeny, daughters and sons alike, to produce writings of their own. To Jane, he wrote:

> Sweet Jane, I know you are a rare inditer,
> And hath the pen of a most ready writer,

and to Elizabeth:

> Bess, you must write too; write but what you think.
> Now you're a girl, dissemble when you link,

and to Frances:

> Frank, prithee write to me thy running hand
> That none can read, and all less understand.[10]

Cavendish certainly played a powerful role in the women's lives, and *The Concealed Fancies* is both dedicated to him and ends with a speech which calls for his approval of their play:

> But if you like not, I pray let me know,
> The pen and ink shall have a fatal blow . . .
> But if you like, you will me cordial give,
> And so, as witty, I shall ever live.
>
> (Epilogue 103–8)

No records exist of an actual performance of the play, and, although it was so clearly written with William Cavendish in mind, a staging before his new bride Margaret Lucas would have proved indelicate and problematic. On the other hand, dramatic performances in private houses did continue throughout the Interregnum, and the play was obviously intended for presentation, not merely a reading aloud of parts.[11] A cast of nine would have been sufficient, even though this would demand a fair amount of doubling for six of the performers. Indeed, if an original cast-list could be drawn up those most involved would presumably have been Elizabeth, Jane, Frances, their two brothers, and Egerton. The scene directions also suggest that the authors had considered the use of stage machinery; for example, in Act V scene ii Courtley and Presumption descend from the sky disguised as gods. This form of entry is reminiscent of the masques performed at court, where elaborate devices were evolved in order to impress and astonish the audience, and the courtiers dressed up as various idealized figures.[12] The Cavendish family would certainly have been present at some of these shows, allowing Jane and Elizabeth to incorporate aspects of them in their own play.[13] It is significant, however, that *The Concealed Fancies*, as a Civil War play, undercuts any sense of courtly idealism, since the audience is well aware that the two 'gods' are Courtley and Presumption, and that their disguises have been devised in order to trick Luceny and Tattiney, rather than to symbolize their noble natures. The play exists, therefore, at a point of transition. It was written within the intimate environment of a noble family, which still paid lip service to a devalued court ideology, but at the same time, the play cannot help but represent the authors' sense of loss, as well as their sharp disillusionment.

When the two sisters left their father's home, they inevitably ceased to benefit from his open encouragement of their literary skills. Although Elizabeth and Jane continued to write, in future their work would consist of private meditations and personal poetry, not the public drama they had produced with the encouragement of their father, and the freedom which, somewhat ironically, their imprisonment at Welbeck had given them.

When her husband succeeded to the title in 1649, Elizabeth became the Countess of Bridgewater, and she seems to have retired to their country estates, where she lived a secluded and deeply religious life, devoted to her husband and children. The marriage was a happy one, both partners professing a profound love for one another: Elizabeth in her 'Considerations Concerning Marriage' speaks of 'the happyest condition, a friendship never to be broke', and John Egerton stated at his wife's death that he 'did enjoy all the happiness that a man could receive in the sweet society of the Best of Wives'.[14] Upon Elizabeth's death, Egerton collected her unpublished writings under the title 'Loose Papers Left by the Right Honourable Elizabeth, Countess of Bridgewater', and had them copied for each one of their children. This text includes several prose meditations and prayers on childbirth, as well as individual addresses to her offspring. Unfortunately, Elizabeth's misgivings about childbearing were all too prescient: she died in premature labour during her tenth pregnancy in 1663.

In 1654 Jane married Charles Cheney, later the first Viscount of Newhaven and Tory MP for Amersham. Like her sister's marriage, Jane's also appears to have been happy, her comments upon the actual state of married life being surprisingly close to the ideal she anticipated, but doubted, in *The Concealed Fancies*. In the play Luceny defines her notion of a good marriage as:

> My happiness, when I am in the condition of his wife, is still to imagine him Courtley and I Mistress Luceny. (II.iii.54–6)

The distinction Luceny draws between being lovers and being husband and wife is not unlike Jane's comments upon her own marriage: 'Did I not know myself Maried, I should think by what hee writs, that hee was still a woer.'[15] Again, like her sister, Jane continued to write, and she is said to have completed several volumes of manuscript poetry, although these are currently lost to us.[16] All we have extant is the poignant verse she wrote on her sister's death in 1663:

On the death of my dear sister the Countess of Bridgewater, dying in childbed, delivered of a dead infant,
a son, the 14th day of June 1663.

O God thy judgement unto sinful eye
Were great when I did see my sister die;
Her last look was to heaven, from whence she came,
And, thither going, she was still the same,
No discomposure in her life or death,
She lived to pray, prayer was her last breath.
And when Death's heavy hand had closed her eyes,
Me thought the world gave up its ghost in cries,
What ere relations' choice, or nature made,
Lost their best light, and being in that shade,
For none can give example like her life
To friendship, kindred, family or wife.
A greater saint the earth did never bear,
She lived to love, and her last thought was care:
Her new-born child she asked for, which ne'er cried,
Fearing to know its end, she bowed and died.
And her last vale to heaven appeared to all,
How much she knew her glory in the call.[17]

Jane died five years after her sister from a series of epileptic fits.

THE TEXT

This edition of *The Concealed Fancies* is based on the Bodleian Library manuscript version, Rawlinson MS Poet. 16. A transcript of the text with a brief introduction was published by Nathan Comfort Starr in *PMLA* 46 (1931), pp. 802–38.

THE *Concealed Fancies*

A Play by

LADY JANE CAVENDISH

and

LADY ELIZABETH BRACKLEY

[*c.1645*]

The Concealed Fancies

A Play by Lady Jane Cavendish, and Lady Elizabeth Brackley [*c.* 1645]

List of Characters

Calsindow household

Luceny *Tattiney*	*young ladies, the daughters of Lord Calsindow*
Elder Stellow *Younger Stellow*	*young gentlemen, the sons of Lord Calsindow*

Lord Calsindow, their father
Colonel Free, cousin to Luceny and Tattiney
Courtley, suitor to Luceny
Presumption, suitor to Tattiney
Corpolant, rejected suitor to Luceny
Boy, Courtley's page

Care, an old woman *Pretty, a young wench*	*two maidservants*

Luceny's maid

Lady Tranquillity's household

Lady Tranquillity
Toy, her gentlewoman
Pert, her chambermaid

Ballamo, the besieged castle

Cicilley, beloved of the younger Stellow *Sh., beloved of the elder Stellow* *Is.*	*three cousins*
Mr Proper *Mr Friendly* *Mr Devinity*	*gentlemen ushers*
Caution *Discretion*	*two stewards*
Sage *Grave*	*two waiting women*

The smith

Action *Moderate*	*two captured soldiers*

Gravity, the cook
Jack, the kitchen boy

Others

Two Poor Men
Two Poor Women
An Angel

A prologue to the stage

Ladies, I beseech you blush not to see
That I speak a prologue, being a she;[1]
For it becomes as well if votes cry, aye,
Why then should I, a petticoat, cry, fie!
Gentlemen if so you allow, is wit,
Why then not speak, I pray your patience, sit;
And now to tell you truth[2] of our new play:
It doth become a woman's wit the very way,
And I did tell the poet plainly truth,
It looks like eighteen or twenty-two youth,
Or else it would not be, as 'tis but well;
I'll say no more until your hand-plays[3] tell.

The second prologue

Spoken by a woman.
Though a second prologue spoke to our play,
I will speak truth: 'tis woman all the way;
For you'll not see a plot in any act
Nor any rigid, high, ignoble fact.
Fearing you'll censure me now, full of tongue,
It's not fit that I should speak too long.

A particular prologue to your Lordship[4]

My Lord:
If that your judgement doth approve of me,
I pray you smile, that all may truly see
You like, and do approve, of what we say,
And then each one will freely give their pay;
If then your quicker wit doth crown[5] our play,
'Your health' shall be our word today.

Act I

Scene i

[*Enter* COURTLEY *and* PRESUMPTION.]

COURTLEY
Prithee dear companion, tell me in what humour[1] is thy mistress?

PRESUMPTION
Faith, my misfortune is, she knows her scene-self[2] too well.

COURTLEY
What mean you by that?

PRESUMPTION
That is, she will not lessen herself at all by valuing me.

COURTLEY
What, does she scorn you?

PRESUMPTION
No, nor she does not admire me.

COURTLEY
And that's your grief.

PRESUMPTION
Aye, for I would have her possessed with a little Cupid[3] if I could.

COURTLEY
O, then you're not for matrimony, if you pretend Cupid.

PRESUMPTION
Yes but I am, for I hope Cupid will be the gentleman usher[4] to Hymen.[5]

COURTLEY
Fie, that's not becoming to have a boy to usher in the gods.

PRESUMPTION
Well then, allow him to be a page; so she were in love, I care not. Now I have confessed so largely to you, freely relate[6] your mistress to me, and let me know her humour.

COURTLEY
By god, mine's so courtly-coy,[7] I know not what to make of her; for when she smiles I know not whether 'tis a scorn or a grace!

PRESUMPTION
Does she speak much?

COURTLEY
No, but she is so full of her neglecting silence, as I am almost in despair.

PRESUMPTION
But I see you have some relics of hope left you.

COURTLEY
Were it not for that, I should be absolutely nothing.

PRESUMPTION
Tell me her name.

COURTLEY
Tell you her name! Will you be secret then?

PRESUMPTION
Or may I never be happy, if I speak of yours till you shall reveal mine.

COURTLEY
But my curiosity is to know yours first.

PRESUMPTION
What! Must I be St George?[8] First both in her humour and her name. I will not be made so much your fool.

COURTLEY
Well I'll speak her name in a soft whisper: Luceny.

PRESUMPTION
Sister to mine, i'faith.

COURTLEY
If so, she values Cupid no more than if he were her footboy, and her language is the torture to a lover's soul.

PRESUMPTION
Faith by your description, I perceive they are sisters! For my mistress values courtship and a rich suit,[9] no more than signs to catch dotterels[10] withal.

COURTLEY
Certainly they educate one another, for my mistress is in the same humour.

PRESUMPTION
Come let's go to them and see how they will act their scenes.[11]

COURTLEY
Agreed. I'll see your mistress, and you shall see mine, in their posture of coyness.

PRESUMPTION
Content. But let me know before you go,
For wife what mistress you would woo.

COURTLEY
My mistress truly I would have
A pretty monkey,[12] yet seem grave,
Her face I'd have it plump to kiss
And that is as my heart doth wish,
Her stature I would have each see
A wife or mistress she may well then be,
In private know no matrimony law
In public all should think I did her awe,
Her petulance I'd only have with me
With others stately for to be,
I would not have her think of wife
Nor me as husband to make strife,
But justly have her fraught with wit,
So by me, pretty man, may sit.

PRESUMPTION
You have declared your mistress, life of day,
But I'd have mine, me more, for to obey.

[*Exeunt.*]

Scene ii

[*Enter*] LADY TRANQUILLITY[13] *and* [TOY], *her woman.*

LADY TRANQUILLITY
Toy, come hither. I will tell you, though I am up, yet my design is for all, I am well to keep my bed; therefore resolve, Toy, to dress me neatly.

TOY
I will madam, so well as my education will give me leave.

LADY TRANQUILLITY
Toy, tomorrow I intend to go to my wits.[14]

TOY
Who are they?

LADY TRANQUILLITY
Monsieur Calsindow's daughters. Therefore my keeping of my bed is to plump up my face, Toy.

TOY
But truly, madam, in my opinion those ladies look as if they would not mind much, they're too young.

LADY TRANQUILLITY
O, Toy, but they can give such characters as to make a lady appear, or not appear; besides, I am in love with their father, so I would have them like me.

TOY
But your ladyship will not let them know so much.

LADY TRANQUILLITY
Thou art an ass Toy! For, of my faith, I will. They shall not be ignorant of my love, for then I hope Monsieur Calsindow will know; and, in respect to him, I will see the two lady cousins,[15] and will carry one of the Stellows, or both, for then I know I shall be welcome; for they are their servants and 'tis thought will marry them. But what say'st thou to that quiff[16] and pinner[17] that hath the gillyflower,[18] and my best smock-band;[19] will they not agree well together?[20] Speak! What, art thou in a study of my marriage to their father?

TOY
I was thinking of the laces, and truly your ladyship has matched them very well. If your ladyship please I will fetch them.

LADY TRANQUILLITY
No, stay. What o'clock is't?

TOY
'Tis almost ten, madam.

LADY TRANQUILLITY
That's well, for I have time to talk and dress. Five hours without interruption! Now, what say you Toy to the best dress for the face? Do you not think pomatum[21] will do well, and rub it over with scarlet[22] after, and then use Mr Tantram's stilled water[23] – and there are rarer cordials[24] in that water to plump up the face, Toy.

TOY
Truly, madam. But I conjecture with myself, the scarlet will take too much of the pomatum off, and will not suffer that stilled cordial water to give a gloss.

LADY TRANQUILLITY
What, thou would'st have me use an oiled mask?[25] A pox on it! I saw a lady the other day that leaned her face to the glass of a window and her face took dust! So I knew, 'twas that left so much grease, so 'tis nasty.

TOY
Madam, you have left out your white satin waistcoat.

LADY TRANQUILLITY
O impertinent dull brain! Dost thou think I would have forgot that! Come Toy, away, I'm resolved to take my bed. [*Exeunt.*]

Scene iii

[*Enter*] GRAVITY *and* [JACK,] *the kitchen boy.*

GRAVITY
Jack, what o'clock? Is not the bill for dinner gone to my lady? Speak, have your lost your tongue? Speak I say!

JACK
Yes sir, the bill was carried to the ladies.

GRAVITY
Know how they like dinner! Now, there's no tart!

JACK
Mistress Sage told me they were not up.

GRAVITY
Fie, fie, as I am an honest man those wits will ne'er be housewives, and nothing angers me, but they'll neither chide nor commend.

JACK
Yes, under favour, sir. I remember they chid you for not making a quince tart sweet enough.

GRAVITY
Before God, that's true! Come good memory, tell me when they praised me? Speak, or I'll make you remember!

JACK
Why good sir . . . why good sir . . . when a lady was here.

GRAVITY
When a lady was here? Speak, or my stick shall be about your ears!

JACK
Why, if you could remember the lady's name, I could then tell you how they praised you!

GRAVITY
The lady's name?

JACK
Indeed, the lady's name is a hard one.

GRAVITY
I'll have it out, or I'll pluck you for dinner, and send you up as a black bird!

JACK
Why, it begins with 'Tray'.

GRAVITY
Trayvand?

JACK
No, 'Tran'.

GRAVITY
Tran? Speak!

JACK
Tran . . . Tran . . . Tranquillity!

GRAVITY
And what by that lady?

JACK
Why, you made a great dinner, such one as my lady liked.

GRAVITY
But what said she?

JACK
Why she sent you a twenty-shilling piece,[26] and her woman spoke as well as she could to let you know my lady was pleased, and I thought twenty shillings was great commendations!

GRAVITY
The next time I stand in expectation for your no-piece-of-flattery, I'll be sent up as a Friday dinner! For, God knows, I can pretend to nothing but a lean pike, and were that of a poet's dressing,[27] the ladies would like me.
[*Exeunt.*]

Scene iv

[*Enter*] *the two sisters,* LUCENY *and* TATTINEY.[28]

LUCENY
Sister, pray tell me in what humour thou wert with thy servant yesterday? Prithee, tell me how you acted your scene?

TATTINEY
I beg your excuse, a younger sister cannot have the confidence to teach an elder.

LUCENY
Well, then I'll begin first. I dressed myself in a slight way of carelessness which becomes as well, if not better, than a set dress; and when he made his approaches of love, by speaking in a formal way, I answered him: I could not love so dull a brain as he had, always to repeat he loved me. I had rather have him say he hated me, for that would be some variety!

TATTINEY
But what said you, when he expressed himself by oaths and execrations?

LUCENY
I told him I wondered he had the confidence, seeing I kept my chamber, to trouble me with his impertinent language, which ever produceth my vexation. For I will tell you sister, it is impossible to answer him to what he speaks, but he will catch some handle to blow up his ambitious wishes. Therefore I put him off with a sharp reply, as I have told you before; and then said, my face could be no ways inevitable for his affection; therefore I did not desire to be his courting-stock[29] to practise with, against[30] he comes to his mistress; and therefore told him, if he would not make an honourable retreat out of the house, I would proclaim him a malignant,[31] or cause Mr Steward to make him make his retreat with more confusion; so, bid him think of some visit, for here I was resolved he should not stay!

TATTINEY
Pray sister, is he a good fortune?

LUCENY
Yes, and a very good title.

TATTINEY
Then I perceive your discretion likes him.

LUCENY
Aye, and his discretion may very well like me! For my father intends to give me a great portion. Therefore, I shall not know whether 'tis his wisdom or affection that makes choice of me.

TATTINEY
And will you continue this way of discretion with him when you're married?

LUCENY
Why do you think 'I take thee' shall alter[32] me?

TATTINEY
I hear their coming! I'll them defeat! [*Exit.*]

LUCENY
Leaving me only to their cunning cheat!
[*Enter* COURTLEY.]

COURTLEY
Madam, your admirer attends you.

LUCENY
And thinks to be accepted for your new suit.[33]
COURTLEY
Still in your insulting way.
LUCENY
'Tis tyranny indeed. To tell you truth, you are so conscious to yourself,[34] as you think you are the only object of perfection.
COURTLEY
No madam, I am the object of misfortune, not having the least hope of your ladyship's good opinion.
LUCENY
I should think myself debased should I lend you a thought, for as I hear you are the only libertine in the town; and I wonder you can be so great an imposture in your pretended love, as to contract that face of freedom to so serious a piece of formality.
COURTLEY
No madam, it is your sweeter face of innocence that converts the rudest peasant even into modesty.
LUCENY
Aye, but when the species[35] returns back, my face methinks should be converted into debaseness.[36] Now, will not your next posture be to stand with folded arms? But that posture now grows much out of fashion. That's altered to a serious look of admiration, as if your face was so terrible as to turn men to statues.
COURTLEY
I wish damnation, madam, rather than thus to be tormented by your unkinder love.
LUCENY
Away! Away, with your hypocritical language, for I am not yet so vain as to believe your dissembling romances.
COURTLEY
Well I'm gone, and am resolved to be no more!
LUCENY
What, you'll give out[37] you're dead, to try what vanity of love I may be possessed withal?[38] Go, take what resolution you please.
COURTLEY
Ho! I'll love myself better then to die for one that hates me! But, I could be a willing martyr to her that loves me.
LUCENY
Ha, ha, ha! I think so! You would be a willing martyr to her that loves you? And do you think that is a high expression of love? This shows how much you hated her, that would quit her so soon, besides leaving her this legacy: to die of a consumption[39] for your sake!
COURTLEY
Madam, am not I worth that ribbon you hate worst, and that will I contemplate upon with adoration?
LUCENY
I thought you had learned better manners than to offer to plunder me of my favours.
COURTLEY
Give me leave, then, passionately to beg a salute, and I will never see you more, unless I may be answered with more mildness. For now every word you speak is a rack[40] unto my soul; therefore give me one more leave to beg the favour of your lips.
LUCENY
When did you hear my lips were so rude as to come within distance of your sex? And to confirm you there is nothing I hate more then a country gentleman, who must ever salute coming and going or else he will whisper to his next neighbour, I am proud and, I swear, I would rather cut my lips off than suffer you a salute! [*Exit.*]
COURTLEY
What a misfortune's this to me,
To court a wench that doth so truly see. [*Exit.*]

Act II

Scene i

[*Enter* PRESUMPTION *and* COLONEL FREE.[1]]
COLONEL FREE
Presumption, I know thou dost presume of thy own wit[2] and fancy. Therefore, prithee, tell me thy loved humour of mistress.
PRESUMPTION
You think to catechise[3] me at your pleasure; if you take me to be your boy, where's your reward of plum?[4]
COLONEL FREE
Come, prithee, be good natured and let thy voice relate
Thy mistress of thy sweet-loved fancy's fate.

THE SONG

PRESUMPTION
My mistress I would have love's book,
Yet innocent should be her look;
In company she should thus be
A stately pretty thing to see;
Then should she bee, that when I kiss,
Thoughts make me swear, I still do miss;
And then to me a toy,[5] and witty,
Making me mad for herself pretty.

COLONEL FREE
I see sweet Tattiney in your song.

PRESUMPTION
O, that loved name's a cordial[6] to my tongue.

Enter COURTLEY *and* CORPOLANT;
[Free *retires to the back of the stage.*]

CORPOLANT
O Courtly, my pouch of gold, with my way of craft, shall gain your mistress from you!

COURTLEY
Do you think your bank of sordidness can make her misunderstand herself?

CORPOLANT
Why sir, what can she wish, but she shall have! If title please her I'll lay out twenty thousand pounds for what honour or name she likes best; and I know her discretion is not taken with a rich suit or a fair face that appears like one of your polished pictures.[7]

COURTLEY
No Sir, nor she is not taken with your piece of deformity of fat, whose face appears as your worst rustic! Have you ever spoke to her in the way of marriage?

CORPOLANT
No, but I intend first to speak to her cousin to make the way, and then to her father.

COURTLEY
You're mistaken. Because she carved you once a leg of a capon and gave you sauce to boot, your puffed-up bladder[8] thinks to marry her, by reason she gave you the civility of the house, as being her father's friend, which modest courtesy blows your brain up as gunpowder into folly. But, pray you sir, do me the favour: after you have spoke to her in the way of a suitor, let me know your opinion.

CORPOLANT
I will sir, and doubt not of success.

COURTLEY
Of being counted an impertinent ass!

PRESUMPTION
Come Corpolant, if you be in love, I'll put you into a consumption.[9] What do you take my friend to be?

CORPOLANT
A fine piece of vanity in a rich suit.

PRESUMPTION
Ho, Corpolant, Corpolant! You're deceived; he hath a good estate, besides a rich suit,[10] and that mistress Luceny knows.

CORPOLANT
I believe you not youth, I believe you not.

PRESUMPTION
It concerns you to have no faith in that.

[COLONEL FREE *comes forward.*]

CORPOLANT
Here's her cousin. Come, now we have good company. Let's drink Mistress Luceny's health. If she would but love, she should have all my wealth.

COLONEL FREE
I have other business than to drink.

CORPOLANT
What have you to do?

COLONEL FREE
To give order for the army.

CORPOLANT
Nay, then I will command your stay.
Orders belong to me, so me you shall obey;
Bring sack[11] and claret that we may
Make this my mistress' holiday!

COURTLEY [*Aside*]
And I to see my mistress' health belched out in several tuns![12] I'll stay to give her an account, and so revenge myself of him, for I hate he should think of her.

COLONEL FREE
What think you of the taking of Ballamo?[13]

CORPOLANT
'Tis a very strong place.

COLONEL FREE
The best is to watch them tame![14]

CORPOLANT
Aye, but I would correspond[15] first.

[COURTLEY *and* PRESUMPTION *step aside.*]

PRESUMPTION
And recognos[16] till you be so drunk as you cannot give orders.

COURTLEY
Now he's drinking, I'll put myself in the habit of one of my mistress' servants and see if I can cozen[17] him of his pouch of gold.

PRESUMPTION
It will be worth your change of habit.

[*Exit* COURTLEY.]

COLONEL FREE
Come now, let's have a tun.

PRESUMPTION
Our senses sweetly to perfume.

CORPOLANT
I love a canny brave Scotch jig,
And afterwards a wench by me to lig.[18]

Enter COURTLEY *in the habit*[19] *of one of his mistress'*[20] *servants,* [*going across the stage.*]

CORPOLANT
O, call that fellow back. [*To* COURTLEY] Where are you going? How doth your mistress?

COURTLEY
Very well.

CORPOLANT
Set him a chair. [*To* COURTLEY] You're very welcome. Set him a seat or I'll commit[21] some of you.

COURTLEY
I hope I shall not drink so much, but I may stand.

CORPOLANT
In troth, first I took you for a sage.[22]
Pray, what's your business here?

COURTLEY
Faith sir, my mistress has sent me to borrow money for a jewel she has a mind to buy.

CORPOLANT
How much wants she?

COURTLEY
She sent me to borrow a thousand pounds.

CORPOLANT
Here take this bag.

COURTLEY [*Aside*]
By god, I have cozened him!
[*To* CORPOLANT] Well sir, I'll let my mistress know your kindness.

PRESUMPTION [*Aside*]
What an old doting fool is this to part with his money.

COURTLEY [*To* PRESUMPTION]
But he's drunk; for were he in his right sense he would know my mistress would rather starve than receive the money he had looked upon. When he's sober, I'll let him see his drunken act.

CORPOLANT
Come, let's go.

COLONEL FREE
You mean carried! [*Exeunt* CORPOLANT *and* COLONEL FREE.]

COURTLEY
Now will I to my mistress and let her see.

PRESUMPTION
What you have made Corpolant to be. [*Exeunt.*]

Scene ii

Enter PRESUMPTION *and* TATTINEY.

PRESUMPTION
Are you in better humour today? Will you give me leave to speak?

TATTINEY
Your tongue's at liberty!

PRESUMPTION
Faith, so 'tis, but did not know whether you would suffer your lover of admiration to express himself your perpetual servant.

TATTINEY
O, sir, now I understand you: you spoke this yesterday to your mistress, and think to confer the same upon me, and I to believe so foolish a romance.

PRESUMPTION
Are you still pleased to neglect your honourer?[23]

TATTINEY
How you mistake yourself. Did I ever keep you so much company, as you[24] to take the freedom, as to title yourself my servant or my honourer?

PRESUMPTION[25]
I beseech your sweetness to account of me, as of your sad creature and vassal.

TATTINEY
How now, your still[26] is nothing but full of impudence!

PRESUMPTION
What, will you be always my tyrant?

TATTINEY[27]
Now, do you think the pulling down your hat and looking sad, shall make me believe your speech for truth? But you are deceived. Therefore begone to your mistress and let her know, to make mirth, that you have been with me, and how rarely you have acted your part. And what a fine fool you will make her, if you can, to be confident of your affection.

PRESUMPTION
By the gods, you would make me mad! And when I was, you would not pity me.

TATTINEY
There's no danger of your distraction, since you can have that ejaculation.[28]

PRESUMPTION
I desire you will be pleased to give me the happiness to salute[29] your hand, and then I will be gone.

TATTINEY
How I vow I hate you. Begone rude creature! [*Exit.*]

PRESUMPTION
I swear this coy wench makes me not the same,
But she takes the right way to make me tame. [*Exit.*]

Scene iii

Enter LUCENY *and* COURTLEY.

COURTLEY
Look you, here's Corpolant's pouch of gold; for when he was in his drunken fit, I named but your name and he gave it me.

LUCENY
Ha, now piece-of-confidence, I'll make you know you shall not make mirth with me, and so to

find out my humour; and I am so far from being merry, as I am very angry, as to think you should understand my wit, no higher than to laugh at your cheat. Besides, he was not himself so you have no reason to brag.

COURTLEY
Never of your favours, but I thought you had hated Mr Corpolant.

LUCENY
You mean contemn[30] him, for I never thought him so valuable as to hate.

COURTLEY
It seems me you do.

LUCENY
Sure your vanity thought my extreme hate to him, would have made me express love to you.

COURTLEY
Was there ever such a tyrant, she,
As to make nothing of brave gallant, me? [*Exit.*]

Enter TATTINEY.

TATTINEY
Sister, have your heard of Corpolant's folly?

LUCENY
Aye, and his indiscretion, besides his over[31] great bounty to Courtley.

TATTINEY
No more than Courtley?

LUCENY
What, hath he made you for him? Or that twattling lady,[32] that thinks you govern me?

TATTINEY
Aye, and Presumption too thinks you do govern me. Do you not mind how his sister[33] courts you? Aye, but I know who governs us both.

LUCENY
Who prithee? Let me hear.

TATTINEY
Monsieur Calsindow.

LUCENY
Ho! My father, indeed. And that gentleman shall be my alpha and omega[34] of government.

TATTINEY
What, shall not Mr Courtley be your governor when you're married?

LUCENY
How often, sister, have your read the Bible over, and have forgotten man and wife should draw equally in a yoke?[35]

TATTINEY
I warrant you, sister, I know that text as well as you.

LUCENY
How impertinently then dost thou speak?

TATTINEY
I wish with all my heart Corpolant would come.

LUCENY
Whenever he comes, I will not speak to him.

TATTINEY
What will you lay[36] of that?

LUCENY
My destruction or my happiness.

TATTINEY
What's that?

LUCENY
My destruction is that when I marry Courtley I shall be condemned to look upon my nose[37] whenever I walk; and when I sit at meat, confined by his grave wink,[38] to look upon the salt; [39] and if it be but the paring of his nails,[40] to admire him.

TATTINEY
Your happiness then?

LUCENY
My happiness, when I am in the condition of his wife, is still to imagine him Courtley and I Mistress Luceny – and now you shall have no more of me.

[*Enter* CORPOLANT.]

TATTINEY
O my wish! Corpolant is here.

CORPOLANT
Ladies, you look fair today.

TATTINEY
Speak to your ambition, sir.

LUCENY
Alas, he understands not. You must name my name, or else his dull brain understands not.

TATTINEY
Speak to my sister, sir.

CORPOLANT
How do you fair lady? Not a word pray you, make your servant happy. For if you say nothing, I shall then understand you think 'Aye',[41] and so you will make me very happy by your neglecting silence.

LUCENY [*Sings.*]
I prithee, fool, not speak no more
For I cannot thee like,
Thy folly hath been great enough
For me to laughing slight;[42]
Thy face a black, bruised honeycomb,
Thyself, an ugly sot,[43]
Besides, you are a clog of dun,[44]
So I'll not be your lot.

There's none, without it be a hag,
Will ever be your wife,
And for companions, you are such,
As they will not be rife;[45]
Then all your recreation is

A full good cup of sack,
And that your drunkenness doth sip,
Which makes you beastly fat.

You're only fit for witch's like,
For looks of horror, you,
Then she, to oint,[46] and make a flight,
In this to swear she's true;
For sordid acts is your own life,
And this each one doth see;
Thus devil you do make a strife,
Then witch take you for me.

[*Exit* CORPOLANT.]

TATTINEY
Sister, I swear I infinitely commend your wit. I confess you have won your wager, but who must pay it to you?

LUCENY
Myself.

TATTINEY
I swear I long to see it.

LUCENY
Nay, prithee do not speak without a pretty oath.

TATTINEY
Why, as I hope to continue Tattiney! I long to see thee married, but I'm so feared you will prove a fool.

LUCENY
Do you not doubt Luceny, but mind Tattiney. For my observation is that Presumption doth throw his cloak as if he intended to govern you.

TATTINEY
Aye, but as I hope to continue my own, I will make him lay his cloak off[47] if his carriage[48] be to slight me.[49] For do you think, sister, the words[50] saying in the church shall make me mind him more than I do now? He is my servant, for I intend to be his mistress.[51]

LUCENY
You're right, for I intend to be the same with Courtley.

TATTINEY
But sure you do not resolve to let him know so much.

LUCENY
O, I understand you, that is to say, the wife, but the mistress to make his love continue the longer. Aye, but Tattiney shall show obedient when my Lady Knowall[52] visits her.

TATTINEY
And so I believe will you be when Mistress Courtley, your mother-in-law, sees you.

LUCENY
Yes, faith, will I; but though I look obedient and civil to her, I will let her discretion understand in silence, that I know myself, and that I deserve thanks for coming into her family. Therefore I will not lessen my conversation for her piece of sobriety.

TATTINEY
Aye, sister, but I do not like that word some ladies here in town are much acquainted with, the language of friendship and conversation, as they will think.

LUCENY
What, for as I hope for happiness I will continue my innocent freedom with Courtley, and he shall have a true piece of virtue of Luceny; and you need not be more jealous, sister, of Luceny's language, than you are of yourself, of making who I please believe I am an obedient fool.

TATTINEY
Do you not wonder that Courtley and Presumption are held wits? For methinks there are no such miracles in their language.

LUCENY
Why, that's because we have been brought up in the creation of good languages, which will make us ever ourselves.

TATTINEY
And I protest, Presumption shall never see me out of order when I am married – but in a morning, and at night, in my several satin petticoats and waistcoats, and always in my careless garb.[53]

LUCENY
Come, let us go, for I do fear
If at the door they may us hear. [*Exeunt.*]

Act III

Scene i

Enter MR PROPER, MR FRIENDLY *and* MR DEVINITY.

PROPER
Come, what, a siege?[1]

FRIENDLY
By God, I think so; but where's the relief? I'm sure our party[2] is now as flat as a flounder.[3]

PROPER
And this garrison flatter than any.

FRIENDLY
Pox on it![4] I know that. Where's our officers?

PROPER
Why, the old man[5] is at the works.[6]

FRIENDLY
Have we not more?

PROPER
Yes, his clerk who, you know, is an ancient.[7]

FRIENDLY
What wilt thou do?

PROPER
Fight as well as a gentleman usher[8] shall.
And what wilt thou do with thy bulk?[9]

FRIENDLY
Stand in the Half Moon,[10] and swear you all 'into heart'[11] and, now and then, fight. By God, I think the ladies have a mind to see how I shall look without an eye!

PROPER
If I should want a leg I were cashiered[12] from gentleman usher.

FRIENDLY
Then you must have a pension, and if it be a good one it will buy sack and claret enough in time to make you as big as I.

PROPER
But our ladies do not use to keep[13] their gentlemen ushers; so my desire must be to beg as a lame soldier of the king's and the king's lame soldier.

FRIENDLY
Come, Devinity, what sayest thou?

DEVINITY
Faith, I've been measuring, and the works are not made high enough for the enemies, if shot will enter into every chamber of the house.

PROPER
Why, will you not tell our engineer governor[14] so?

DEVINITY
I have, but he is so confounded.

FRIENDLY
Why? Doth he doubt his works?

DEVINITY
No, he cannot understand well English, nor I his language. But I think Mr Discretion[15] will have no siege, having no possibility of relief.

PROPER
Come, Mr Proper, let us go drink,
And afterwards to bed and wink.[16] [*Exeunt.*]

Scene ii

Enter LUCENY *and* TATTINEY, *melancholy.*

LUCENY
Sadness I chide you, thou art slow and dull,
'Tis grief with passion, makes a heart as full
Of gallant actions, and love gives the challenge
So life's not weighed in this world's harder balance;
Then go on wisely on a resolute ground,
And make no question, but go on the round,
And do not make delays, nor go about,
But shortly put unquiet life quite out.

TATTINEY
Grief, I wonder you should angry be with me,
Thou didst not see me till after I was thee,
But patience I have considered with myself, and can
Tell you, sadness is the best, which I'll be and am;
Yours is a madness, for quiet will you see,
But I'll grieve to the bone, anathema[17] will be.

Enter AN ANGEL.[18]

ANGEL
Stay, be not angry, suffer with your friends,
In like fortune yourself to them lend,
For I do hope the happy gain will be,
And that ere long you joyfully shall see.
So I'm assured you shall not make these ends,
For happy shall you be in your blessed friends.
[*Exeunt.*]

Scene iii

Enter COURTLEY *and* PRESUMPTION.

COURTLEY
What, are you upon[19] marriage?

PRESUMPTION
Aye, and I am daily contemplating how to make Mistress Luceny fit to entertain my mother and friends in the country.

COURTLEY
That will be a hard design.

PRESUMPTION
Faith, but I'll tell you the way I think of: as soon as I am married I will let her know I am her husband.

COURTLEY
How do you mean? She knows that.

PRESUMPTION
Aye, but I mean to follify[20] her all I can, and let her know that garb, that doth best become her, is most ill-favoured. So she shall neither look, walk, or speak, but I will be her perpetual vexation; then send her into the country, where I will stay with her a month, then tell her my occasion draws me to town, and so leave her to contemplate me in my absence, and to obey my family.

COURTLEY
O Presumption, thou wilt be a devilish husband! Prithee, more of this, that I may learn by thee to know the word 'husband'.

PRESUMPTION

Why then, whoever my wife fancies I will not esteem of, though a female; for men servants she shall neither dare to speak to them, nor so much as to employ them, were it but to know who it was that came last into the house.

COURTLEY

You'll be over-jealous.

PRESUMPTION

'Tis but careful, besides she shall not stay with her own friends or family after she is married, not three days. Then, once a year, I'll bring her down a gown in fashion, which with continuing long in the country, she shall not know how to put on; then all my discourse shall be to praise the ladies in London. And, if she do but behave herself ugly, then I'll tell her that was like a good wife and an honourable stock to bear children on withal.[21] I would have her take the week books,[22] which is the only way to make her incapable of discourse or entertainment. And, if she do not give respect to my mother and sisters, I will tell her she hath not deserved to enter into my honourable old house. And, I know, continually seeing old long-beards[23] make legs[24] to me, will teach her the fashion to obey.

COURTLEY

Well companion, you deserve the title of a husband; but if you'll have my opinion, Mistress Tattiney looks as if she were prepared for the rigidness of a husband.

PRESUMPTION

Why do you think so?

COURTLEY

By reason she looks as if she did not care for the word, part;[25] and rather than continue her own unquietness, she would live with her friends. You know her father is an understanding gentleman; his discourse uses not to be dull, catechising;[26] and they very much with him.

PRESUMPTION

A pox on you for your opinion! It hath done me much hurt. Prithee, how pretend you?

COURTLEY

Faith, I pretend to possess my sweet Luceny of my sincere affection, and if I can to make her passionately love me, and so to gain her father's friendship, and then by love to gain her observancy, which I will return with great respect, and all her friends shall command me.

PRESUMPTION

And she too?

COURTLEY

No, she shall love me so well, as she shall think me worthy of my freedom, and so we will continue the conversation and friendship of lovers, without knowing the words of man and wife.

PRESUMPTION

This I understand to be one of your courtships[27] to her.

COURTLEY

No, faith,[28] shall be my continual practice.

PRESUMPTION

Sure then, you have great designs upon her father.

COURTLEY

No, faith, I understand gallantry better than to have any design but to serve him. Your way with your wife is to educate her just so, as to hate her within two or three years, or else you are so proud as you would have yourself the only valuable piece of perfection. Believe it. Believe it. Your mistress and mine, though they have great portions,[29] are not to be tutored like a rich citizen's daughter, or a great heir. They are of other breedings.

PRESUMPTION

Well, I'll see in what garb[30] I can bring her to, and tell you a certainty for your opinion.

COURTLEY

And when you find I say true, what will you say?

PRESUMPTION

Why, I'll say I am wiser than you, for I have endeavoured the best I can to make my wife a fool, and you never had so high a design.

COURTLEY

Faith, I hold that no design to make my wife a fool.

PRESUMPTION

We shortly shall be married, then each shall see
Which of us a true kind husband.

COURTLEY

That's me!

Enter a boy, PAGE *to* COURTLEY.

[COURTLEY *continues.*] O my boy, of hope art thou come? What news? Is all well? What, sad? I prithee[31] relate, I care not for a frown so she be well, or if she threw my letter down.

BOY

Sir, your prophecy is true: I have brought your letter back.

PRESUMPTION

Come, give it me; and tell me, prithee boy, thy progress. Hast thou not met a bugbear,[32] thou still looks so sad?

BOY

I have another letter, which I'd have you read, not my master.

PRESUMPTION
Companion, shall I read thy loved fancy[33]of letter?

COURTLEY
Aye, but I saw the boy give you another from your mistress.

PRESUMPTION
[*Reads silently to himself, then speaks.*]
I doubt I never shall enjoy my dear,
For she my rigid[34] thoughts certain did hear,
Could she be mine I'd dedicated be
To her and give her leave for to be free.
Can any wench enter into my head,
If ever have her once into my bed?
When married, my soul shall not think of wife,
For she shall be my mistress, joy of life.

COURTLEY
A sudden change.

PRESUMPTION
A sudden change indeed.

COURTLEY
Pray, speak, are they married? Read that letter! Are they dead?

PRESUMPTION
Read that letter. [*Continues to read in silence.*]
And I am now in deep despair
Never again to see my fair. [*Exeunt.*]

Scene iv

Enter [CICILLEY, SH. AND IS.[35]] *three cousins.*

SH
O cousins, our neighbouring peasants . . .

CICILLEY
Or our pedantical servants, have given us up for a prey to the enemy.

SH
Pray, how did I look in the posture of a delinquent?[36]

CICILLEY
You mean how did you behave yourself in the posture of a delinquent? Faith, as though you thought the scene[37] would change again, and you would be happy though you suffered misery for a time. And how did I look?

SH
As yourself; that's great, though in misfortune.

CICILLEY
So did you.

SH
How should I do otherwise, for I practised Cleopatra[38] when she was in her captivity, and could they have thought me worthy to have adorned their triumphs.[39] I would have performed his gallant tragedy and so have made myself glorious for time to come. Come, prithee, let's talk no more of our captivity. I wish I could not think, that I might not remember, I had been once happy.

CICILLEY
I am not in your opinion, for then I should remember nothing but misery, therefore, let's recreate[40] ourselves with other discourse.

SH
And make ourselves happy by promising hopes of our absent friends.

CICILLEY
But cousin, what shall we do today? I'm loath to[41] learn French, I'm so dulled with grief.

SH
And I am stupefied with a continuation of misery. But I'll tell you, we'll look for our friend's cordials.[42]

CICILLEY
But where are the keys?

SH
I have them! Prithee, sweet cousin, bid Joan, bring them quickly, for we hate delays.

CICILLEY
Now we shall see what rare cordials he hath for restoration of health, and making one young.

SH
Come let's go open the box; what's this?

CICILLEY
'Tis quintessence of mint and magisterium[43] of pearl.

SH
Take one of these cakes, and you cousin, they're very good ones.

CICILLEY
We never saw these before, come we'll put them up.[44]

SH
No take another, he'll never want them.

IS
Truly, if he knew he would wonder how we durst offer to look of them.

SH
I wish he saw us in a prospective.[45]

IS
But 'tis a great way for him to look in a prospective.

CICILLEY
'Tis no matter, 'tis a wish. See, cousin, what receipt's[46] this? I swear 'tis a letter, and one of his mistress' seals.[47]

SH
You're mistaken, you judge wrong, 'tis a cordial seal.

CICILLEY
Here are pots of [ ][48] and accodeshdry.[49]

SH
And pots of preserved nutmegs and morabollans[50] and a whole box of my Lady Kent's cordials.[51]

CICILLEY
And rather essences of all sorts, cabinets of all manner of spirits, Gilbert's water,[52] and curious balmsomes.[53] I am weary with repeating, we'll put them up.

SH
Come cousin, this place is very cold, and we have seen all his cordials; I'll take this half pot of morabollans and so quit them.

CICILLEY
No, take a whole one.

SH
No, I'll have no more than this half pot, for you have more need of cordials than I, so this day shall be yours, and tomorrow mine.

CICILLEY
How yours?

SH
Why I'll invite you.

CICILLEY
To what?

SH
To what? Why, I'll pick his cabinet locks, and there you shall see his magazine[54] of love. I dare swear you shall see locks of all manner of coloured hairs, and favouring ribbons in as many colours as the rainbow.

CICILLEY
How know you that?

SH
'Tis my strong imagination, and if this fancy of mine should prove true, we shall have rarer recreation to look on them.

CICILLEY
Well, on with your design tomorrow.

SH
Faith, so I will if no impertinent lady hinder me.

CICILLEY
Aye, but I doubt a design of so much pleasing consequence will be defeated. [*Exeunt.*]

Scene v

Enter COLONEL FREE *and* MR CORPOLANT.

COLONEL FREE
I'll tell you news, Mr Corpolant. Monsieur Calsindow's daughters, my cousins, are become nuns upon the grief of our departure.[55]

CORPOLANT
Upon the grief of my departure.

COLONEL FREE
What a self-loved piece of fat you are! Do you not know, nor remember, how angry you were when she scorned you, and do you think she is in love with you? Now you are too partial.

CORPOLANT
By your leave Colonel Free, absence increaseth like, sometimes.

COLONEL FREE
I wonder what fancy my wife will be possessed withal, for she can neither be nun, nor vestal,[56] she hath so many children.

CORPOLANT
But the sweet lady will be in a consumption for your sake.

COLONEL FREE
Did you see our sweet young Stellows today?

CORPOLANT
Yes, and in my knowledge of conceit[57] they are very melancholy, and they would not let me know the reason, so I doubt they are in love. Are not you in the same opinion?

COLONEL FREE
They have reason to be sad: their mistresses are captives, and their sisters are nuns in melancholy and, they say, gives[58] blessing to each poor body that comes to be healed of melancholy of the mind.

CORPOLANT
I wonder people can be so simple to come to be cured of them, that cannot cure themselves. [*Exeunt.*]

Scene vi

Enter ACTION *and* MODERATE, *two prisoners.*[59]

ACTION
Sir, brought as a prisoner?

MODERATE
Yes, sir.

ACTION
Pray, what news?

MODERATE
Alas, sir, I wish there were no news, but that my cow had newly calved, or how much cream makes a pound of butter. I'm only brought in by reason they have a thought I am rich.

ACTION
They would have money of me too. A pox take them all[60] and the devil go with them, for they are a company of knaves.

MODERATE
Aye, sir, but pray take heed, for since you are of

our party, I must give you counsel, and desire you not to be so liberal of your tongue. It may do you hurt, and our party no good.

ACTION
'Tis true, for I was put into such a room for talking, as I had no bigger a window to take breath at than the bigness of my little finger, and no more to piss at.[61]

MODERATE
Sure your imprisonment hath made you mad.

ACTION
Faith, so it has, to them in hatred. Come let's go drink a health to the good success of our party and to the rogues' condemnation.

MODERATE
This would be a very good health, but not in this garrison, and thus much known may hang you.

ACTION
Tut, I'll venture my neck but I'll be revenged. You're all upon the salvation of your money, and I have none to lose.

MODERATE
If you have not, you should go upon the ground of keeping your health.

ACTION
Why so I do, for I walk daily in the garden and, when I see the rogues go by me in scorn, will not put off my hat! Let's now handsomely send to our party, to come to take their horses, and if possible, to take this house.[62]

MODERATE
By my faith of my body, I will not be of this high-flown, no-design.[63] Go sir, and sleep, for this can prove nothing.
[*Exeunt.*]

Act IV

Scene i

Enter LUCENY *and* TATTINEY [*as*] *two nuns.*

LUCENY
Where are the innocent souls?

TATTINEY
They're coming.

Enter TWO POOR MEN *and* TWO POOR WOMEN, *kneeling.*

LUCENY
What's your grief?

FIRST POOR MAN
Love.

LUCENY
In what kind?

FIRST POOR MAN
One that I loved as my soul rejected me.

LUCENY
Take this [*she gives him something*],[1] and be assured, you shall grow wiser or have your mistress love you. What's yours?

FIRST POOR WOMAN
Love.

LUCENY
In what kind?

FIRST POOR WOMAN
My friends, who I held more dear than my life, are in a far country.[2]

LUCENY
I have no remedy for that; but take this, it is such as I wear – it is a bow of hope.[3]

SECOND POOR MAN
And my grief is I loved a woman and she would not marry me.

LUCENY
Take this as a scourge to whip your folly away.

SECOND POOR WOMAN
And I have almost lost my wits by plunder.[4]

LUCENY
Take this laurel[5] as a promising hope of conquest.

TATTINEY
Now I will grind upon this holy stone:[6]
Your doubts, mixed altogether, not alone,
Your griefs,
Your fears,
Your sighs, and your sad tears.

LUCENY
May you all happy be; but I bless and wish
That you your friends again may see.
And pray you, pray that prayer for me.

COURTLEY *and* PRESUMPTION [*are discovered*].

COURTLEY [*Sings.*]
I swear as you are fair
And chaste as is the air,
Since that I saw you first
Myself could never be;
But still I'm offering at your shrine,
And you will not allow to see
Which makes my anger's not to tell,
What is my fortune well;
But I will never cease
To offer pay my hopeful vows,
Therefore I'll not despair to see a day
Wherein I may
Most happy be
And mortals envying me to see.

LUCENY [*Sings.*]
I wonder what's the cause about you go,
Thus to profane my sacred priesthood so,
As to name me wantonly fair,
Chaste that I am; and it shall be my care

Your stealing language further shall not creep
Into my sacred church, where I will weep;
Praying that all may truly, honest keep,
For my ambitious store in votes[7] ascends
For my loved, dear and absent friends,
That each upon their temples truly may
Wear several laurels, of each sweeter bay;[8]
At their return then happy shall I be
In that blessed day, I once them more do
see.

PRESUMPTION
And I have found thy most sacred self here,
Whose presence turns all sex to joy, not fear.
So I'll kneel with adoration to thee
And never think the time too long, to see
Thy purer face, of angel beauty fair,
But look and imagine what piece you are
So stands with admiration, that a she
Should thus so like a pure just goddess be.

TATTINEY
Bless me what spirit possesses you
To speak to me as if I were not true?
But I am just and will be just to grief
And now without my friends have no relief.
[*Exeunt.*]

Scene ii

Enter the two STELLOW *brothers,*[9] *the eldest passionate.*

ELDER STELLOW
My lady and mistress[10] captive, a prisoner! Can Stellow suffer that? I'll her relieve!

YOUNGER STELLOW
But how can you, brother?

ELDER STELLOW
Name 'how'? And thy mistress[11] in the like condition!

YOUNGER STELLOW
But though I'm in love, I am not out of sense.

ELDER STELLOW
By God, thou art out of sense, if thou canst think any impossibility an impossibility to gain your mistress' liberty, though at the rate of your life!

YOUNGER STELLOW
I am resolved to hazard myself would that relieve her, but to die and not to release her, and then my corpse can have no possibility of enjoying her, and what doth that profit me?

ELDER STELLOW
Why, it doth profit me if she could see me blown in a thousand pieces to show I die her martyr, and in that piece of service I shall account my grave, my eternal, happiness.

YOUNGER STELLOW
By God brother, I should rather account her bed of love eternal happiness.

ELDER STELLOW
Thou art all for thyself.

YOUNGER STELLOW
But methinks, you neither for yourself, nor her.

ELDER STELLOW
Well, I am resolved of my design.

YOUNGER STELLOW
What's that? Prithee, let me know.

ELDER STELLOW
That is, I will either ruin myself or gain her. Wilt thou go with me? I am not for demurs.[12] Speak!

YOUNGER STELLOW
I'm not for merry calls.[13] If a possibility, I go.

ELDER STELLOW
Hang that word, 'possibility'. I love – then what is impossible?

YOUNGER STELLOW
So do I, and yet methinks all things are impossible. But tell me who's of your design?

ELDER STELLOW
Love and Courage to that hight.[14] As thou appear'st to me like a bedridden fellow, or at best a frozen statue of ice, that ere long will consume by my heat of love, you had best keep at distance.

YOUNGER STELLOW
Well, I dare love as well as thee,
Therefore my mistress I will die but see.

ELDER STELLOW
Then let us go all danger to embrace,
So we may see their sweeter face. [*Exeunt.*]

Scene iii

Enter [CICILLEY, SH. *and* IS.,] *the three lady cousins.*

SH
Cousin, I long with great impatience till the smith[15] come.

CICILLEY
It may be he that knocks. Come in.
[*Enter the* SMITH.]

SH
I have my wish. Hark you friend, you know your master's cabinets' locks, they are very good ones; do you think you can open them?

SMITH
Yes, of my life, madam, I can.

CICILLEY
There are some books there we would read to pass away this sad and solitary life we're in.
[*Exit* SMITH *and*] *enter* SAGE, *a waiting woman.*

SH
Ha! Now impertinent! What have you to do here?
SAGE
Mr Steward, Madam, is come with the books[16] and say'th you have not seen them this fortnight.
SH
Go formality, and tell his formalityship I have other business than to stupefy my brain with how many quarters of malt is bought, and in that how much I am cozened,[17] neither care I how many scores of sheep have been plundered from me.
SAGE
I shall tell him so, madam.
SH
No, stay. It is better to please him, and tell him I do not suspect his honesty. Therefore he needs not bring the books so soon, and let him know this was his plot to see whether I suspected him, and to let him see I confide in him, I will not take the books this month.
[*Exit* SAGE *and*] *enter* GRAVE, *another* [*waiting woman*].
CICILLEY
Ha, now another!
SH
Now fool, what comes your piece of gravity for?
GRAVE
The Lady Tranquillity is come.
CICILLEY
A pox go with you for your ill news! I'll teach you better manners than to bring me word of my vexation. Where is she?
GRAVE
The lady is in the next chamber.
CICILLEY
I thought this was too happy a design[18] to prove prosperous.
SH
Well cousin, content yourself, the boxes are here, and the smith lives not far off, so I hope we are not totally defeated.
[*Exit* GRAVE *and*] *enter* LADY TRANQUILLITY.
SH
Sweet madam, how long hath your Ladyship been here? How chance I heard not sooner?
LADY TRANQUILLITY
I have not been here long. Your Ladyship need not be angry.
SH
Lord, madam, how happy am I that your Ladyship can think me worthy of a visit. Will your Ladyship go into my bed chamber?
LADY TRANQUILLITY
I shall attend your Ladyship. [*Exeunt.*]

Scene iv

[*Enter*] COURTLEY.
COURTLEY [*Sings.*]
Being in shops of sadness now I cry:[19]
Ladies, what lack you? Pray you of me buy
Melancholy hoods,[20] or pendant tears of pearl,[21]
Which if condensed will wash each finer girl;
Or fine sweetwater sighs,[22] for to perfume
your closet chamber,[23] or so any room;
If like a fucus,[24] take my crimson heart
'Twill finely red your cheeks before you part,
And when you please, it will you panting tell
How it doth pray for you and wish you well;
And if doubt's multiplying glass[25] you'll have,
I've one that adds, most rarely brave;
Besides a prospective,[26] wherein you'll see
My griefs of fuller moan, like rocks to be.
What, will you nothing of me buy?
Truly sweet ladies, you are very shy.
But I do hope, ere long, that Fortune's cap[27]
Will turn about, and hug me in her lap.
Then do not doubt, but have great store
Of lady customers to haunt my door.
Enter PRESUMPTION *with his mistress' picture.*
PRESUMPTION
Look on this picture where you'll see
A face of pure divinity;
Adore it with a jealous view
Since it appears an angel true;
The face is absolute true fair
As if 'twas made of select air.
'Tis sin if look, and not adore,
For such a one was ne'er before.
COURTLEY *falls into the like passion with fancying his mistress' face.*
COURTLEY
My mistress' picture, it doth make
A study to express each feature's take,
And when but view her sweeter smile I say,
I've seen celestial happiness today.
Then, when but see her quicker eye, 'tis such
That all sex swears they cannot look too much.
Thus she appears my innocent delight,
So I will call her my true virtue's light.
[*Exeunt.*]

Scene v

Enter TOY *and* PERT, *a chambermaid.*
TOY
Come Pert, I'll tell you news: who do you think makes love to me? Come, think, and tell me.

PERT
Faith,[28] Mistress, I cannot say your lord, for you have none, for your Lady's a widow; but the Lord of Lords may.

TOY
God bless my courtship, I'm not so divine yet, to have the Lord of Lords make love to me!

PERT
You mistake me, Mistress; I can explain myself.

TOY
Why, prithee, do then, or I vow to God I'll make my Lady angry with you for not starching her band[29] well. Therefore you had best please me.

PERT
By my troth, Mistress, I'll please you, for I'll be as secret to your counsels as you can wish.

TOY
Good wench, speak then who thou thinks.

PERT
Faith, I'm loath to speak, for fear you'll think I'll tell my Lady.

TOY
Faith, I'll think nothing but what you'll have me; and this is enough for my Lady's gentlewoman to speak to her chambermaid; therefore, with a pox to you, speak.

PERT
Why then, I think my Lord Calsindow loves my Lady a little, to love you more; and now I have spoke.

TOY
Thou'st spoke with a vengeance! But, by God, if you tell my Lady, in hope of a gentlewomanship, my careful way of not dressing myself fine when his Lordship comes, i'faith may pull you down to a washermaid.

PERT
How's that? Pray that again, I did not hear you.

TOY
Why I'll tell thee. I have no other way so good to disguise our loves, than to dress my Lady fine and myself ugly.

PERT
Ha, ha, ha! If I did not think so, I'm a very rogue. But hark you Mistress, what would you do with a lady that understands the world, and if she were married would say to her husband: 'Prithee, take my woman. Faith, I'm weary of your husbandly loved conversation.' What would you do then? Now do you speak.

TOY
Faith, such a careless thing of knowledge, I think I should serve best.

PERT
I believe you, but you would have a hard task, whether to please my Lord or my Lady.

TOY
No faith, but I should not, for which pleased best my humour of please, I would please.

PERT
Faith, but I know some ladies that will be so much of the wench with their husband, that thou would prove at best but a cold mouldy pie, and this in plain English is true.

TOY
But I'll tell thee then, I would be the wife with that lady's husband, and make him fond that way.

PERT
A pox of thy no wit, this lady that I mean will have her several scenes,[30] now wife, then mistress, then my sweet Platonic soul,[31] and then write in the like several changes of mistress, not only to confirm love, but provoke love, then dress themselves always as a pretty sweet wife or mistress. What says Mistress Toy to serve one of these?

TOY
Pox on you, I know whereabouts you are, but I'm not like to serve either of these you mean. But I'll tell you, faith, they used me very kindly the last time they saw me. But God knows, they're not in condition now to see anybody, God comfort them.

PERT
Forsake, sake,[32] thou givest pity; but what say you to a gentlewomanship to one of those wits?[33]

TOY
I thank you for nothing; I'll serve none of your she-wits. They will not court me. I'm for your he-wits, or a lady that doth not know me. Let me alone to choose a lady to serve if I part with my good Lady Tranquillity; I'll have a lady of the times, if I can get her, or one that thinks it an honour for me to serve her. [*Exeunt.*]

Scene vi

Enter MR CAUTION *and* MR DISCRETION.

DISCRETION
Did our ladies[34] chide you today? Come let's walk.

CAUTION
No faith,[35] I value no chiding by them, but to say truth they gave me sharp apprehension[36] and, stately,[37] gave me a little no respect;[38] and when we talked, they spoke of some designs against

them, and so put a dislike upon me; and in good faith, I said I knew of no design, nor had design against them, but I would serve Monsieur Calsindow the best I could. They said I might very well study and plead that pretence, as being the only handle[39] I had and so convert them to a belief: 'since we honour him as our father, we can say nothing to you in that concern'. Then they swore my wisdom should not alter their resolution, and in good faith, I know not their resolutions, neither can I imagine.

DISCRETION

I see you call nothing, chiding, unless they had power to put out a servant or in a servant into the estate. But in good faith, sir, they trouble us unexpressedly to govern them to do themselves good, find you not that?

CAUTION

I do not find they trouble me at all, but they trouble business, and I love not interruptions.

DISCRETION

Once I had a design to vex them, since they will not be pleased: I made one of the grooms say, one of their coach-horses was plundered and that, I knew, would passionately vex them.

CAUTION

And were they angry?

DISCRETION

No. They're quick at fancy, and knew it was a plot of me.

Act V

Scene i

Enter [CICILLEY, SH. *and* IS.] *the three lady cousins* [*singing*].

SH

Instead of men's drink,

CICILLEY

Let us merrily think.

IS

Now we're at liberty,[1]

CICILLEY

What we shall wish to thee,

IS

'Gainst we you married see.

CICILLEY

Think not of beauty,

IS

Nor of duty,

CICILLEY

But, resolve to be –

IS

A pretty toying she!

Enter the two Stellows.

SH

O friend, I have been in hell!

ELDER STELLOW

No, sure your goodness cannot that place tell.

SH

O yes, this world doth imitate the other;
But this a secret, let it go no further.

ELDER STELLOW

Well, on with your discourse.

SH

I will,
And tell you how they good souls kill:
They have their tarrier[2] devils to betray
Each honest soul, that loves the true right way.

ELDER STELLOW

I know all this, but tell what fires they have,
And when they're burned, how pitiful they rave.

SH

Fires, that's fancy, by a hotter flame,
And having no joys, swears grief burns them lame;
As for bleared eyes, 'tis neither fire, nor smoke,
But crying and sad grief them smothering choke.
For darkness, that their melancholy self,
If happy, they not want of waggish elf.[3]

ELDER STELLOW

They say hell's low.

SH

How can it other be?
For when misfortune, then you hell do see.

ELDER STELLOW

When you were there, would you your friends there wish?

SH

No, she devils I would not have them kiss.

YOUNGER STELLOW

[*To* CICILLEY]
Madam, do you this catechism[4] know?
I like it not, I pray you let us go.
[*Exeunt.*]

Scene ii

Enter [LUCENY *and* TATTINEY *as*] *two nuns.*

LUCENY

When I in sadness am and then do think,
I'm lulled asleep in melancholy wink;
Each chamber ceiling doth create true sad,
Yet tempered so as I am quiet, glad.
Then when I walk nuns' gallery round,
My thoughts tell me I'm falling in a swound,[5]
And when that flowers fine I have,
Then sure I'm decked for my grave.

So if each one will have a fine-loved death,
Enter your self in sadness, sweeter earth;
Then, when my quiet soul desires to walk,
The gardens do revive my tongue to talk.
So in white sheet of innocence I pray,[6]
Each one that wishes me to see,
For ghosts do love to have their own delights
When others think they have designs of frights.
So even as they, I wish no fear to none,
But on my friends, contemplate alone.

TATTINEY[7]
My grief doth make me for to look
As if life I had quietly forsook;
Then for my fine delitive[8] tomb,
Is my seeled chamber and dark parlour room.
Then when my spirit in the gallery doth walk,
It will not speak, for sin to it is talk.
At night I rise from tomb to see
My friends pure well, but sleeping that must be;
This is my truer soul of glad;
And ghost's contentment, now you see, is sad.

[*Enter*] COURTLEY *and* PRESUMPTION [*disguised as gods and singing*] *coming down out of the sky.*[9]

COURTLEY AND PRESUMPTION
Hark, hark, and hear,
And put off fear.
Resolve and come away,
And make no stay.
Your sainted prayers ever came to we,
So we're resolved your father you shall see.

LUCENY [*Sings.*]
At your commands we make no stay.

TATTINEY [*Sings.*]
But you, great gods, we will obey.

COURTLEY
These garments we you bring,

PRESUMPTION
To usher you to your joyed spring

[LUCENY *and* TATTINEY *remove their nuns' habits and put on the ordinary cloaks presented by* COURTLEY *and* PRESUMPTION.]

LUCENY
Can I so soon forget a nun?

COURTLEY
Aye sure, and bring love's happy sun.

TATTINEY
How do I in this habit look?

PRESUMPTION
As love's divinity of book.

[*The four are drawn up, repeating the following song, which is sung in parts, until they disappear.*]

COURTLEY
Now let us cut each way away.

PRESUMPTION
And make rude winds to us obey.

LUCENY
To bring us to our happy day.

TATTINEY
Then blessings will be our rich pay.
[*Exeunt.*]

Scene iii

Enter CORPOLANT *and* LADY TRANQUILLITY.

CORPOLANT
Come madam, you shall be my antidote against Mistress Luceny. Wit,[10] how like you my proffer?[11]

LADY TRANQUILLITY
What, do you mean your bag of gold? Very well.

CORPOLANT
Faith, and you shall have my bag of gold if you'll have me to boot.

LADY TRANQUILLITY
And what say you Mr Corpolant, to be my garrison[12] of profession against all the world?

CORPOLANT
Faith, madam, and I love you so well as I dare marry you and let the world say what they will, you'st[13] be my only fort.

LADY TRANQUILLITY
Excuse me sir, you rather appear mine.[14]

CORPOLANT
Come, in a word, if you'll me have. You shall have title, coach, and all things that is brave.

LADY TRANQUILLITY
Sir, you look a great plump bag I swear,
So if I shake you well I need not care.
[*Exeunt.*]

Scene iv

Enter [*at opposite sides*] MONSIEUR CALSINDOW [*and,*] *at the other door,* LUCENY *and* TATTINEY *in their change of habits, and* COURTLEY *and* PRESUMPTION *still in the habits of gods.*

COURTLEY
Look, look and see!

PRESUMPTION
Your daughters, here they be!

LUCENY
We you a blessing ask.

COURTLEY
Then we'll put off our mask.[15]

COURTLEY *and* PRESUMPTION [*remove their disguises.*]

CALSINDOW
What, am I surprised with joy of please!
But pray you daughters who are these?

COURTLEY
Your servant, Courtley.

PRESUMPTION
Yours, Presumption.
LUCENY
Are you god-cheaters?
TATTINEY
Or are we not ourselves?
COURTLEY
Madam, we can create,
PRESUMPTION
And, if your father please, we are your fate.
CALSINDOW
I thank you both, for now I see,
You love my daughters, then you must love me.
[*Exeunt.*]

Scene v

Enter [CARE *and* PRETTY].
CARE
Passion of God, these young flirts vex my soul out of my body! Did not I tell thee, thy carelessness would spoil the linings[16] against[17] the marriage of my lord Calsindow's daughters? I tell thee again, brides' linings[18] ought to be had a care of, but thou art afraid thy fair face should be burnt, or thy hands too rough. Marry gep,[19] with a vengeance! Come out!
PRETTY
I am sure I have burnt my fingers with smoothing.[20]
CARE
Burnt your fingers, and if you had burnt them off, God would have blessed you never a whit the worse. But i'faith, i'faith, you're a flirt; you stand when my lord's men courts you and say'th 'away, fie'. You speak not as you think, and with this dallying discourse never minds your business. I'faith the world's turned upside down since I was young.
PRETTY
Why forsooth, would you have me believe them?
CARE
Well, well, I know what I know, and Care will say no more; but thy very name, Pretty, hath undone thee.
PRETTY
Truly Mistress, but that name could never undone you.
CARE
Thou dost provoke me, but I will not chide you, for a reason best known to myself, but i'faith I could tell.
PRETTY
Pray you tell my lord then.
CARE
You had best tell him yourself, for I am not so familiar with his lordship. I will do him faithful and true service, for by my troth, I cannot be a flirt. Honesty shall ever be my worst, and none shall say worse of me.
PRETTY
I think it was always the worst with you.
CARE
The worst with me? Take heed my worst be not better than your best.
Take heed, I say, take heed,
If beg, I will not ask you, at my need. [*Exeunt.*]

Scene vi

Enter LUCENY *and her* [*maid, who carries a mirror; looking in the mirror,* LUCENY *loosens her hair and*] *sings.*
LUCENY
What is't they say, must I a wife become?
MAID
Yes, madam, that's the vote[21] as I do hear it run.
LUCENY
Why then, a wife in show appear,
Though monkey[22] I should dare;
[23]And so upon the marriage day
I'll look as if obey.
Enter [ELDER] STELLOW, *singing.*
ELDER STELLOW
Now do I hear the ladies, what wagers they will lay,
Saying, surely you'll disallow obey;
Truly I know not what you mean, cry you and look away,
What act you mean to be the scene,[24] lost wagers each must pay.
LUCENY
Now do I view myself by all so looked upon,
And thus men whispering say, faith she's already gone,
For wit[25] or mirth I plainly see,
That she a wife will be.
No sir, say I, a wit[26] above
Is Hymen's[27] monkey love.
Enter YOUNGER STELLOW.
YOUNGER STELLOW
Well sister, for all your reply of song, I saw an ill sign today.
LUCENY
What was it?
YOUNGER STELLOW
Faith, a very careless garb[28] in Courtley.
LUCENY
In what particular?

YOUNGER STELLOW
In putting on his hat.

LUCENY
Faith, brother, but as I hope to continue my innocent freedom of Luceny, he shall put his hat off before he make me observe his actions, for I was never born to be his dancing master to have four pounds a month to observe his garb. But did not I give him the like return of my allegiance?

ELDER STELLOW
Yes, I was infinitely pleased to see you, but I'm afraid he should contract your face to several forms of ridiculousness when you're married, as I dare not name marriage.

LUCENY
Pray you fear yourself, and leave me to the world, that is, a husband.

[*Exeunt* ELDER *and* YOUNGER STELLOWS.] *Enter* CALSINDOW, TATTINEY, COURTLEY, PRESUMPTION, CORPOLANT, LADY TRANQUILLITY *and* TOY.

CALSINDOW
Sir, take you Luceny to your wedlock wish.
And you, Tattiney, for a marriage kiss.

Enter the two STELLOWS *with their mistresses.*

ELDER STELLOW
My lord, I have brought my mistress through with my life,
And if you please she shall be now my wife.

CALSINDOW
Son, since you love truth, so truly know
With all my heart you to the church may go.

YOUNGER STELLOW
Brothers and sisters married now I see,
If I have your leave, I now may married be.

CALSINDOW
Madam, if that my younger son you'll have,
You will, as heaven, him surely save.

CORPOLANT
Now I will tell you news of me:
My Lady Tranquillity my wife will be.

LADY TRANQUILLITY [*Sings.*]
Mais de van que Je vous marriez,
Je vous die que Je nemiey.[29]

CALSINDOW [*He turns to* TOY.]
All here I married see,
Excepting you and me;
Now, Madam,[30] I will take
Your woman for my mistress mate.

[*An* ANGEL *descends, singing.*]

ANGEL
Fie, fie, let marriage life
Plant virtue in you; take a wife
That's truly virtuous and fair,
Handsome and innocent as the chaste air.
Then since the gods makes you this choice
Marry, marry to rejoice.

CALSINDOW [*Sings.*][31]
This change I like, i'faith, 'tis very fine,
No sin commit, and yet this wench is mine.
Angel you're paid in that you will relate
Unto the gods, that virtue is my fate.
Then, Toy, you may be gone, for I'll be true,
My conscience bids me not to look of you.

[*Exeunt all except* LUCENY *and* TATTINEY, *music playing.*]

Epilogue

TATTINEY
As you love me sister, now you are married, tell me how you agree, did you never fall out?

LUCENY
As I hope to continue my own thou'rt grown a fool! Did not we resolve to fall out with our husbands?

TATTINEY
Yes, but I thought he had altered you. But pray, sister, did he never chide you?

LUCENY
No, but he hath given me very good counsel.

TATTINEY
O, I understand you, but I wonder you will suffer him to be so imperious.

LUCENY
Will you judge before you hear?

TATTINEY
Why, tell me then.

LUCENY
According to your commands, I'll tell you upon his first good counsel: I looked soberly, as if I would strictly observe him, yet dressed myself contrary to his instruction, and my behaviour was according to my dress, so much as he said, sweet heart, do you go abroad today? I said, no, is your desire I should? No, said he, but methinks you're very fine. And though I knew I was, yet I said, fie, why will you reproach your own so much, but I am glad you said so, for now I shall understand you by contraries. So, sister, I knew he was to seek about again for a new good counsel.

TATTINEY
Come, dear sister, tell me his next humour.[32]

LUCENY
Swear you will tell your husband's humour and your own, otherwise you shall have me no more your liberate fool.

TATTINEY
What oaths you please I'll swear.

LUCENY

Well I'll trust you. Faith, all that day he was in a conflict, betwixt anger and melancholy, not knowing whether my behaviour proceeded from neglect or ignorance. Then he declared himself by allegory,[33] and praised a lady, obedient fool, in town, and swore her husband was the happiest man in the world. I replied, she was a very good lady, and I accounted him happy that was her husband, that he could content himself with such a mechanical[34] wife. I wish, said he, she might be your example, and you have no reason to slight her, for she is of a noble family. I know that, said I, and do the more admire why she will contract her family, nobleness and birth, to the servitude of her husband, as if he had bought her his slave, and I'm sure her father bought him for her, for he gave a good portion,[35] and now in sense who should obey?[36] Then he came with his old proverb and said he would teach me another lesson, and so with a forced kind of mirth, went out of the room, and I understood he had nothing else to say so was never angry.

TATTINEY

But is he never higher?

LUCENY

Yes once, when he thought to make me cry; but i'faith, I observed him in his own way, and told him his tearing oaths should not fright me, and for part,[37] I valued at the same rate[38] he did, for I had no design upon him, but to love him and pray for him. I would yet, if in either of these I was inconvenient to him, I could lay those contemplations[39] at his feet, and would not weep.

TATTINEY

Ha, ha, ha! How I am pleased to see Courtley become Presumption after marriage.

LUCENY

And Presumption, Courtley?

TATTINEY

No, faith, he gently sleights[40] as being mad in love.

LUCENY

How prithee? Let me hear!

TATTINEY

Why thus, when I am in company with him he becomes a compound of he-knows-not-what, that is, he doth not appear my husband; neither is his garb[41] my servant.

LUCENY

Now I wonder, sister, how you can call this a sleight, for in this he appears himself. But I see you would have him fond in company.

TATTINEY

By wit,[42] I hate see a fond[43] fool, let it be he or she. But in a word I knew I had angered him, therefore took this, his silence, as a neglect, yet I swear, by you, I was myself, and held my petulant garb. Once he spoke in company according to a discreet husband, then I gave him a modest return of wife, and yet appeared his mistress.

LUCENY

How write you to him?

TATTINEY

In as several humours as I will dress myself. His mistress, this you may see is an equal marriage, and I hate those people that will not understand matrimony is to join lovers.

LUCENY

But thinks husbands are the rod of authority![44]

TATTINEY

Or a marriage clog![45]

LUCENY

That puts me in mind of my epilogue:

Luceny's epilogue

Truly the conflicts I did see within,
Which for to tell you even would be a sin;
The several ways and fancies of their fears,
And yet they dare not speak for their ears.
Now I am charged not a word more to say
But beg your likes and then 'tis holiday.

TATTINEY

Tattiney's epilogue

And I was sent in all haste to you here,
For to assure you there is a great fear,
Not knowing how the comedy doth please,
Disliked there will be a white hoods'
decease;[46]
Ladies from you I beg a smile of like,
If hats[47] the poet's happy in this might.

An epilogue, in particular to your Lordship[48]

LUCENY

Now since your excellence hath thought it fit,

TATTINEY

To stay a three hours' comedy of sit;

LUCENY

And so but speak of it as like,

TATTINEY

Then are our scenes even happy in your sight.

LUCENY
And though we have smiles and hats, if you dislike,
TATTINEY
We're totally condemned, for tonight.
Have you now read, my lord, pray do not speak,
For I'm already grown so faint and weak,
Not knowing how you will now censure me,
As rash to think no wit a present be.
But if you like not, I pray let me know,
The pen and ink shall have a fatal blow;
If you not pleased it will impression make
In my vain self, for indiscretion sake;
But if you like you will me cordial[49] give,
And so, as witty, I shall ever live. [*Exeunt.*]

FINIS

PART 2

Documents

Introduction

The following collection of material is meant to introduce readers to some of the documentary evidence representing women as collaborators in Renaissance theatre – as spectators, performers, employees, patrons and theatre owners. It includes examples relating to both private and the public theatre. It also presents some commentary illustrating contemporary attitudes concerning women's involvement in theatrical activity. Selections are divided between fairly well-known materials (for instance, the description of Moll Frith, the female transvestite who frequented the Swan and Fortune Playhouses) and less familiar sources (such as the indenture between Edward Alleyn, the owner of the second Fortune Playhouse, and Marie Bryan for ownership of one twelfth share in that playhouse).

Traditional wisdom has held that English women were generally excluded from the public stage.[1] There has therefore been a tendency to assume that they were prohibited from taking part in all theatrical activity with the exception of the court masque. However, Stephen Orgel raises an important distinction:

> the English stage was a male preserve, but the theatre was not. The theatre was a place of unusual freedom for women in the period. . . . The fact of the large female audience must have had important consequences for the development of English popular drama.[2]

The central question of Orgel's essay concerns the reasons as to why the English popular stage was an all-male preserve when women actors didn't seem to be a point of contention for other European societies; however, his suggestion that many female spectators attended the public playhouses reminds us that women had a genuine influence on the English Renaissance theatre. In many ways, both the public and private theatre need to be re-evaluated as a place of freedom for women. Women actually held a proprietary interest in the theatre both as influential spectators and, as will be discussed later, as financial investors.[3]

The first section of documents presented here is gathered under the heading 'Attitudes towards Women's Attendance at the Playhouses'. John Northbrooke (2)[4] complains that plays teach women bad morals (1577). Stephen Gosson (3) asserts that women spectators participate in libel and defamation because the 'libel and rebuking' cannot be in earnest (1590). In Samuel Rowlands's poem *The Bride* (1617), the author describes the wife's most important duties, including caring for her house, entertaining her husband's friends, and managing finances frugally in order to preserve her husband's wealth (1). But, Rowlands admonishes, the modest wife will never be seen at the public playhouses. John Rainolds (4), whose broader purpose was to expose what he perceived as the vanity of plays, argues against women who claimed that they could be edified as well at plays as at sermons (1599). Therefore women, apparently, not only attended the playhouses in significant numbers, but they participated – if not openly, at least covertly, Rainolds implies – in the debate surrounding the social and moral influences of the playhouses, a controversy that was to coexist with the playhouses throughout this period up to 1642 when overwhelming puritanical sentiment forced their closure.[5]

What was the experience of women as spectators? Accounts are mixed. The personal statements of some women, such as Mary Rich, Countess of Warwick, reconfirm the prejudices of the times: plays are 'vain and foolish pastimes' (6).[6] But quite aside from moral pronouncements, playgoing was more complicated for women than it was for men. Lady Anne Halkett recounts the convoluted arrangements she and four of her friends made in order to preserve their reputations when they decided to attend a play without the accompaniment of a male escort (7). (As the anonymous author of *The Actor's Remonstrance* (1643) reminds us, women who come 'lawfully' to the playhouses are those attended by their husbands;

all others are 'harlots' (11). Consequently, John Chamberlain was annoyed by requests for him to provide the requisite escort service (9).) Yet, given even these few statements, it is interesting to note that women don't seem to have felt vexed by the moral issues associated with the theatre by so many of the men, like John Northbrook, who condemned it as inappropriate for women. Twenty years after *The Actor's Remonstrance* was published fashions had changed. By 1667, Margaret Cavendish could write of playgoing as just another of the city's recreations, equal to walking in Hyde Park or dining on barges on the Thames (5).

While the formal etiquette surrounding playgoing at the public theatres was of some concern to aristocratic women, Thomas Cranley claimed that lower-class women attended plays in order to imitate their betters (10). In Henry Fitzgeffrey's *Satyres* he describes an audience at Blackfriars with its many interesting characters; for example, the loose Cheapside woman who, disguised as a man, sneaks into the gallants' row to fondle the men seated there. Fitzgeffrey good-naturedly pokes fun at the ways in which both men and women are acting out in the audience. 'Playhouse observation!' he comments, 'Fruits of the vacant hours of a vacation!' (8). Lastly, Sir John Harington tells the humorous story of a woman who manages to foil some thieves in the audience from stealing her jewels (13); and Henry Peacham recounts a wonderfully raucous tale of a tradesman's wife who returns home from a play indignant at the loss of her purse. But as her husband questions her about the incident she wittily seems little bothered by the fact that the thieves have fondled her beneath her skirts (12). At court, where audiences appear quieter and more self-possessed, at least according to John Finet's narrative, seating at table was carefully arranged, and the play part of a well-choreographed evening (14).

Whatever theatrical activity women undertook has not been well documented. However, they were generally restricted to private or non-professional, public situations. An informal, rural May Day entertainment, featuring a local woman as May Queen, was recorded in Oxfordshire in 1598 (15). Court performances were recorded by court commentators and foreign ambassadors, some of whom were appalled at the liberty enjoyed by aristocratic women who dressed up as blackamoors (17-18). The preparations for masques (16) and the detailed expenses for building the queen's dancing chamber at Whitehall are preserved among the Exchequer records (19). In William Prynne's well-known treatise *Histriomastix* (1633), the author opposed women performers and boys dressed as women in plays (20), and Richard Baker countered Prynne's arguments (21). Yet one infamous woman – Moll Frith – dressed as a man and flaunted her clothes at the Swan and Fortune playhouses in rebellion against social norms of the period.

Although women never achieved status equal to men in theatrical affairs, it would be erroneous to assume that they were wholly disconnected from the enterprise of playing. Some aristocratic women issued patents to playing companies, women served as gatherers at the public playhouses (occasionally acting in minor roles), and several women became shareholders in various playhouses. The patronage of playing companies by women was a trend begun by Queen Elizabeth I. In 1583, the company that came to be known as Queen Elizabeth's Men was formed by twelve players chosen at the request of Secretary of State, Sir Francis Walsingham (23). (Previously Elizabeth I had maintained players, called 'players of interludes' in documents of the period; however, these early companies were not major influences upon the theatrical history of the period.) The Queen's Men became the best known of the London companies during the decade of the 1580s, both performing at court and touring various provincial towns, including Norwich, Bristol, Leicester, Gloucester, Aldeburgh, Nottingham and Shrewsbury. Two of the actors – Richard Tarlton and Robert Wilson – were particularly famous at the time, the former as a clown and improviser, the latter as a writer known for 'learning and extemporal wit'. During their most active years the Queen's Men certainly performed *The Troublesome Reign of King John* (1591). Nine other plays, thought to be theirs, found their way into publication in 1594–5, including *A Looking Glass for London and England, King Leire, The Famous Victories of Henry V, The True Tragedy of Richard III*, and *The Old Wives Tale*.[7]

During the reign of King James I all acting companies adopted royal patronage. Consequently, three companies – Queen Anne's, Lady Elizabeth's (Queen of Bohemia's) and Queen Henrietta's – acquired patents from women patrons between 1603/4 and *c.* 1625 (24). As in the case of the other companies patents gave a company of players licence to perform in public; but the patent did not bring with it regular payment, as did the patents for court offices, for instance. Instead, when the players performed at court, usually during the Christmas holidays and often following Easter, they were paid a fee. Yet this did not replace the income they lost by vacating their usual London venue during these times, nor did royal patronage guarantee the financial success of a company. Rather, the payments for holiday entertainment were apparently more tokens of gratitude than salary. Moreover, although there are rare accounts of companies appealing to their patrons for intervention (especially in political affairs relating to the London authorities with whom they were sometimes at odds), patents did not seem to give their patrons control over the dramatic and artistic affairs of the companies. Many theories have been offered to explain the move to royal patronage under King James, none of them totally convincing. What is significant, however, is that the women at court were perceived as equal to their male counterparts in this regard. Playing companies were not allowed to exist unless they acquired a patent, and female royals offered this privilege to the players.

The final two documents in this collection represent women who were involved in theatrical affairs in a more traditional business context. In 1634 William Browne – an actor who was probably introduced to his profession by his stepfather Thomas Greene, a well-known comedian – bequeathed his share in the Red Bull company, and whatever proceeds were earned from them, to his mother Susan Baskervile (25).[8] Interestingly, Browne acted in accordance with family precedent: his mother inherited her husband's share in Queen Anne's company in 1612. When she attempted to collect what was owed her on the share (valued at £80), and for an additional debt (£37), several arrangements for future payment were made, on all of which the company defaulted. Finally, the company broke up, some scholars have argued, largely due to the debt they owed Mrs Baskervile. For our purposes here, it is important to note that Mrs Baskervile's inheritance gave her genuine financial control over Queen Anne's company. The arrangements made subsequent to her husband's death were all cases in which she invested additional sums of money in return for a promise that she would receive a pension for each day that the company performed in repayment of their debt.[9]

The arrangements outlined in the indenture between Edward Alleyn and Marie Bryan (26) differ somewhat from the situation involving Susan Baskervile in that Bryan initiated her own investment in the playhouse instead of inheriting it. In 1621 the First Fortune Playhouse burned down, and the next year Alleyn reconstructed a new playhouse. However, he did not want to assume the whole financial burden for the theatre himself. Consequently, he issued shares and half-shares (for a total of twelve full shares) to a variety of investors, not all of them actors. Three players in the Palsgrave's company (who performed in the First Fortune) purchased shares. But the other shareholders consisted of several tradesmen, Alleyn himself, and two women – Mary Bryan, a widow, and Margaret Gray, also a widow. Gray purchased a half-share and Bryan purchased a whole share, both of which were substantial investments. Each shareholder paid a ground rent of £10 13s 10d *per annum* and an assessment of £83 6s 8d for the construction of the playhouse. The leases ranged from 49½ to 50 years.[10]

Women also entered the financial sphere of the theatrical world by serving as gatherers who were responsible for collecting money from spectators. In the mid-1580s Margaret Brayne served temporarily as a gatherer at the Theatre. In 1612 Robert Browne, probably the actor, wrote to Philip Henslowe (Alleyn's father-in-law and co-owner of the First Fortune Playhouse) to request a gatherer's place for the wife of 'Mr Rose', a player with the Prince's Men. There has also been some conjecture that gatherers, including the women, performed minor roles in plays on rare occasions; but it has also been argued that in these circumstances the gatherers were all men.[11]

Even a cursory reading of the evidence presented in this collection of documents reveals that the materials from which we write theatre history are varied both in content and kind. Some evidence – such as Browne's will or the Alleyn–Bryan indenture – are legal documents. By nature these are public writings meant to provide a record of a binding agreement. Other pieces – Vincent's letter to Benson (17), to cite one example – are drawn from private correspondence; while Henry Peacham's account of the tradesman's wife who was groped at the playhouse (12) is anecdotal. Because of these differences, documents carry their own historicity; that is, they present historical knowledge that is mediated by their authors (their motivations and own histories as individuals) and the circumstances that existed when they were created.[12] Consequently, the collection of materials presented here provides a diverse range of types of evidence for reconstructing the place of women in relation to the English Renaissance theatre.

7 *Attitudes towards Women's Attendance at the Playhouses*

1. Samuel Rowlands, *The Bride* (1617), E1^{r}-E1^{v}.[1]

A modest woman will in compass[2] keep,
And decently unto her calling go,
Not diving in the frugal purse too deep,
By making to the world a peacock show:
Though they seem fools, so yield unto their wives,
Some poor men do it to have quiet lives.

Fourth duty is, to love her own house best,[3]
And be no gadding gossip up and down,
To hear and carry tales amongst the rest,
That are the news reporters of the town:
A modest woman's home is her delight,
Of business there, to have the oversight.

At public plays[4] she never will be known,
And to be tavern guest she ever hates,
She scorns to be a street-wife (idle one),[5]
Or field-wife[6] ranging with her walking mates:
She knows how wise men censure of such dames,
And how with blots they blemish their good names.

2. John Northbrooke, *A Treatise wherein Dicing, Dauncing, vaine Playes, or Enterluds, with other idle Pastimes, &c., commonly used on the Sabbath Day, are reproved by the Authoritie of the Word of God and auntient writers* (1577), J3^{v}–J4^{r}, K2^{r}–K2^{v}, L1^{r} [pp. 62–3, 67–8, 73].[1]

Therefore let the people, and especially women, give ear to pagan Ovid,[2] if not to Christian precepts, speaking of those common resortings unto plays, sayth:

> They come to see, and eke for to be seen,
> Full much chastity quailed[3] thereby had been.

Juvenal the poet sayth also: that no wives or maidens, that list to content and please sad and honest men, will be found and seen at common plays, dancings, or other great resort of people.[4] For the plays be the instruments and armour of Venus and Cupid, and to say good sooth, what safeguard of chastity can there be, where the woman is desired with so many eyes, where so many faces look upon her, and again she upon so many? She must needs fire some, and herself also fired again, and she be not a stone; for what maid can be pure and whole among such a rabblement,[5] and not spotted with any lust?

. . . If you will learn how to be false, and deceive your husbands, or husbands their wives, how to play the harlots, to obtain one's love, how to ravish, how to beguile, how to betray, to flatter, lie, swear, forswear, how to allure to whoredom, how to murder, how to poison, how to disobey and rebel against princes, to consume treasures prodigally, to move to lusts, to ransack and spoil cities and towns, to be idle, to blaspheme, to sing filthy songs of love, to speak filthy, to be proud, how to mock, scoff, and deride any nation, like unto Genesius Aralatensis,[6] etc., shall you not learn then as such enterludes[7] how to practise them?

Therefore great reason it is that women (especially) should absent themselves from such plays. What was the cause why Dina[8] was ravished? Was it not her curiosity? The maiden would go forth and understand the manners of other folks. Curiosity then no doubt did hurt her, and will always hurt women. . . . And therefore St Cyprian[9] vehemently inveigheth against those which, contrary to nature and the law, do attire themselves being men, in women's apparel, and women in men's apparel, with swans' feathers on their heads, silks, and golden apparel, etc., showing forth in their plays very Venus itself, as if they were fully in the kingdom of Satan.

3. Stephen Gosson, *Plays Confuted in Five Actions* (1590), sigs C5r–C6r, D1r, E5r, G6r–v.[1]

The argument of tragedies is wrath, cruelty, incest, injury, murther[2] (either violent by sword, or voluntary by poison); the persons [are] gods, goddesses, juries, fiends, kings, queens, and mighty men. The ground work of comedies is love, cosenage, flattery, bawdry, sly conveyance of whoredom; the persons [are] cooks, queens, knaves, bawds, parasites, courtesans, lecherous old men, amorous young men . . . .

Sometime you shall see nothing but the adventures of an amorous knight, passing from country to country for the love of his lady, encountering many a terrible monster made of brown paper, and at his return, is so wonderfully changed, that he cannot be known but by some poesy in his tablet,[3] or by a broken ring, or a handkircher,[4] or a piece of cockle shell. What learn you by that? When ye[5] soul of your plays is either mere trifles, or Italian bawdry, or wooing of gentlewomen, what are we taught?

. . . If the common people which resort to theatres being but an assembly of tailors, tinkers, cordwainers, sailors, old men, young men, women, boys, girls, and such like, be the judges of faults there painted out, the rebuking of manners in that place is neither lawful nor convenient, but to be held for a kind of libelling, and defaming.

. . . The proof is evident, the consequent is necessary, that in state plays[6] for a boy to put on the attire, the gesture, the passions of a woman; for a mean person to take upon him the title of a prince with counterfeit port,[7] and train, is by outward signs to shew[8] themselves otherwise then they are, and so within the compass of a lie, which by Aristotle's judgement is naught of itself and to be fled. . . .

As at first, so now, theatres are snares unto fair women. And as I told you long ago in my *School of Abuse*, our theatres and playhouses in London are as full of secret adultery as they were in Rome. In Rome it was the fashion of wanton young men to place themselves as nigh as they could to the courtesans, to present them pomegranates, to play with their garments, and to wait on them home when the sport was done. In the playhouses at London it is the fashion of youths to go first into the yard, and to carry their eye through every gallery, then like unto ravens where they spy the carrion thither they fly, and press as near to ye fairest as they can. Instead of pomegranates they give them pippins,[9] they dally with their garments to pass the time, they minister upon all occasions, and either bring them home to their houses on small acquaintance, or slip into taverns when the plays are done. He thinketh best of his painted sheath,[10] and taketh himself for a jolly fellow, that noted of most to be busiest with women in all such places. This open corruption is a prick in the eyes of them that see it, and a thorn in the sides of the godly when they hear it. This is a poison to beholders, and a nursery of idleness to the players.

Most of the players have been either men of occupations, which they have forsaken to live by playing, or common minstrels, or trained up from their childhood to this abominable exercise and have now no other way to make their living.

4. John Rainolds, *Th'overthrow of Stage Playes* (1599), sigs A2r–A4r.[1]

The vanity and unlawfulness of plays and interludes hath been often spoken against by the holy men of God. The danger and hurt that cometh by them hath been plainly laid open by sundry fruitful treatises of this our age. Further it seemeth that the Lord himself by sundry his visible judgements from heaven hath pronounced a sensible [way?] against them even in the face of the world. Witness Paris Garden[2] and other places where diverse have been grievously hurt, wounded, and maimed; and some by lamentable [?] and destruction utterly cast off and consumed. These and such like warnings and examples going before should (a man would think) have been a fearful precedent to the succeeding age that came after. But alas our practice sheweth it to be far otherwise, the usual flocking and gadding that we see daily before our eyes to these playhouses and idle places of intercourse (many leaving their houses and sundry necessary duties unperformed, yea not sparing the very Sabbath itself, nor fearing the profanation thereof, so they may therein serve their unruly appetites and affections) what mettle[3] we are made, and wherein the treasure of our heart consisteth . . .

Surely for mine own part, I am persuaded if this present discourse be read, marked, and digested as it should be, the gentlewoman that sware[4] by her troth[5] that she was as much edified at a play as ever she was at any sermon, etc., will, ere she die, be of another mind, though it may be she said true then, in regard of her own negligence and backwardness in not giving ear to the word of God with reverence. The like may fall out also to those men too that have not been afraid, of late days, to bring upon the stage the very sober countenances, grave attire, modest and matronlike gestures and speeches of men and women to be laughed at as a scorn and reproach to the world, as if the very hypocrisy of Judas[6] (if it were brought upon the stage) could any whit disgrace the apostles of our saviour Christ, and yet if these men had but thus far exceeded, kept themselves there, and gone no farther to the foul profaning and abusing of the holy scriptures of God, their sin had not been so great as it is.

8 *Women as Spectators*

5. Margaret Cavendish (Duchess of Newcastle), *Nature's Pictures Drawn by Fancy's Pencil* (1667), p. 285.[1]

[Margaret comments on her sisters' entertainments:]

But to rehearse their recreations. Their customs were in winter time to go sometimes to plays, or to ride in their coaches about the streets to see the concourse and recourse[2] of people; and in the spring time to visit the Spring Garden,[3] Hyde Park, and the like places; and sometimes they would have music, and sup in barges upon the waters. These harmless recreations they would pass their time away with; for I observed they did seldom make visits, nor never went abroad with strangers in their company, but only themselves in a flock together, agreeing so well that there seemed but one mind amongst them. And not only my own brothers and sisters agreed so, but my brothers and sisters in law, and their children, although but young, had the like agreeable natures and affectionable[4] dispositions. For to my best remembrance I do not know that ever they did fall out, or had any angry or unkind disputes. Likewise, I did observe that my sisters were so far from mingling themselves with any other company, that they had no familiar conversation or intimate acquaintance with the families to which each other were linked by marriage, the family of the one being as great strangers to the rest of my brothers and sisters as the family of the other.

6. Mary Rich, Countess of Warwick, *Autobiography* (1672?) (British Library, Add. MS 27, 357, fols 4v–5v).[1]

About this time [*c.* 1638] my fourth brother, Master Francis Boyle then (afterward Lord Shannon), was by my father married to Mistress Elizabeth Killigrew, daughter to my Lady Stafford;[2] and my brother being then judged to be too young to live with his wife, was a day or two after the celebrating [of] the marriage (which was done before the King and Queen) at Whitehall (she being then a maid of honour to the Queen) sent into France to travel, and his wife then brought to our house where she and I became chamber-fellows, and constant bed-fellows; and there then grew so great a kindness between us, that she soon had a great and ruling power with me; and by her having brought me to be very vain and foolish, enticing me to spend (as she did) her time in seeing and reading plays and romances, and in exquisite and curious dressing.

7. Anne, Lady Halkett, *Autobiography* (c. 1677–8) (British Library, Add. MS 32, 376, fols 2r–v).[1]

What my childish actions were I think I need not give account of here, for I hope none will think they could be either vicious or scandalous. And from that time till the year 1644 I may truly say all my converse[2] was so innocent that my own heart cannot challenge me with any immodesty, either in thought or behaviour, or an act of disobedience to my mother, to whom I was so observant that as long as she lived I do not remember that I made a visit to the nearest neighbour or went anywhere without her liberty.[3] And so scrupulous I was of giving any occasion to speak of me, as I know they did of others, that though I loved well to see plays and to walk in the Spring Garden[4] sometimes (before it grew something scandalous by the abuse of some), yet I cannot remember three times that ever I went with any man besides my brothers; and if I did, my sisters or others better than myself was with me. And I was the first that proposed and practised it, for three or four of us going together without any man, and everyone paying for themselves by giving the money to the footman who waited on us, and he gave it out at the playhouse. And this I did first upon hearing some gentlemen telling what ladies they had waited on to plays, and how much it had cost them; upon which I resolved none should say the same of me.

8. Henry Fitzgeffrey, *Satyres: and Satyricall Epigrams, with Certain Observations at Blackfriars* (1617), sigs F1r–F2v, F7r–v.[1]

from 'The Third Book of Humours Entitled Notes from Blackfriars'

But stay! See here (but newly entered),
A Cheapside dame, by the tittle[2] on her head!
Plot! (Villain!) Plot! Let's lay our heads together!
We may devise perchance to get her hither.
(If we together cunningly compact)
She'll hold us doing 'til the latter act.
And (on my life) invite us supper home,
We'll thrust hard for it, but we'll find her room,
Here, Mis——! (Pox on't! She's past, she'll not come o'er.
Sure[3] she's bespoken for a box before.)
Now, Mars defend us! See'st thou who comes yonder?
Monstrous! A woman of the masculine gender.[4]
Look! Thou may'st well descry her by her growth.
Out! Point not man, lest we be beaten both!
Eye her a little, mark but where she'll go,
Now, by this hand,[5] into the gallants' row.
Let her alone! Whate'er she gives to stand,
She'll make herself a gainer, by the hand.[6]
  What think'st thou of yon plumed Dandebrat,[7]
Yon Lady's shuttle-cock,[8] Egyptian Rat,[9]
Yon Musk-ball,[10] milk-sop,[11] yon French sycophant,[12]
That ushers in, with a coronto[13] grace.
Yon gilded marchpane,[14] yon all vardingale,[15]
This is the puppet, which the ladies all
Send for of purpose and solicit so
To dance with them. 'Pray, sir, a step or two.
A galliard or a jig?'[16] 'Pox on it!' cries he,
'That ere I know this toiling faculty.'
Yet mark! No sooner shall the cornets blow,
But ye shall have him skipping to and fro. . . .
Others may chance (that know me not aright),
Report (injuriously) all my delight,
And strength of study I do wholly bend
To this loss-labour[17] and no other end.
To these I wish my scandaled Muse reply
In as plain terms as may be: ''Tis a lie,
Here's but pate-pastime![18] Playhouse observation!
Fruits of the vacant hours of a vacation!'
Then[19] (say all what they can) I am sure of this:
That for a play-time it is not spent amiss!

9. John Chamberlain, from a letter to Sir Dudley Carleton (*Calendar of State Papers, Domestic Series*; 21 August 1624, PRO/SP14/171/66).[1]

I doubt not but you have heard of our famous play of Gondomar,[2] which hath been followed with extraordinary concourse, and frequented by all sorts of people old and young, rich and poor, masters and servants, papists and puritans, wise men, etc., churchmen and statesmen, as Sir Henry Wotton,[3] Sir Albert Morton,[4] Sir Benjamin Rudier,[5] Sir Thomas Lake,[6] and a world besides; the Lady Smith[7] would have gone if she could have persuaded me to go with her. I am not so sour nor severe but that I would willingly have attended her, but I could not sit so long, for we must have been there before one o'clock at farthest to find any room. They counterfeited his person to the life, with all his graces and faces, and had gotten (they say) a cast suit of his apparel for the purpose, and his litter, wherein, the world says, lacked nothing but a couple of asses to carry it and Sir G Peter or Sir T Matthew[8] to bear him company. But the worst is, in playing him they played somebody else, for which they are forbidden to play that or any other play till the King's pleasure be further known; and they may be glad if they can so scape scot-free. The wonder lasted but nine days, for so long they played it.

10. Thomas Cranley, *Amanda, or the Reformed Whore* (1635) sigs F2r–v.[1]

The places thou dost usually frequent,
Is to some playhouse in an afternoon.
And for no other meaning and intent,
But to get company to sup with soon,
More changeable and wavering than the moon,
  And with thy wanton looks, attracting to thee,
  The amorous spectators for to woo thee.

Thither thou comest, in several forms and shapes,
To make thee still a stranger to the place:
And train new lovers, like young birds to scrapes.[2]
And by thy habit so to change thy face.
At this time plain; tomorrow all in lace.

Now in the richest colours may be had
The next day, all in mourning black and sad.

In a stuff[3] waistcoat, and a petticoat
Like to a chamber maid, thou com'st today.
The next day after thou dost change thy note,
Then like a country wench, thou com'st in grey,
And sittest like a stranger at a play.
The morrow after that, thou comest then,
In the neat habit of a citizen.

The next time, rushing in thy silken weeds,
Embroidered, laced, perfumed, in glittering show,
So that thy looks an admiration breeds,
Rich like a Lady, and attended so,
As brave as any Comtess[4] dost thou go.
Thus, Proteus-like strange shapes thou ventrest on,
And changest hue, with the Chameleon.

The play once ended, to some tavern near,
Thou, and thy Copes-mates presently resort,
Where the best wine and most costly cheer,
Must be provided in the neatest sort,
For thy choice palate, else thou car'st not for't.
And when thou hast it, yet thou canst not eat
Without a noise of fiddlers to thy meat.

11. Anon., *The Actor's Remonstrance* (1643), p. 8.[1]

To conclude, this our humble complain great Phoebus,[2] and you nine sacred sisters,[3] the patronesses of wit, and protectresses of us poor disrespected comedians, if for the present, by your powerful intercessions we may be reinvested in our former houses, and settled in our former calling, we shall for the future promise, never to admit into our six-penny rooms those unwholesome enticing harlots, that sit there merely to be taken up by prentices[4] or lawyers' clerks; nor any female of what degree soever, except they come lawfully with their husbands, or near allies: the abuses in tobacco shall be reformed, none vended, not so much as in three-penny galleries, unless of the pure Spanish leaf. For ribaldry, or any such paltry stuff, as may scandal the pious, and provoke the wicked to looseness, we will utterly expel it with the bawdry and ungracious poets, the authors to the Antipodes.[5] Finally, we shall hereafter so demean ourselves as none shall esteem us of the ungodly, or have cause to repine at[6] our action or interludes: we will not entertain any comedian that shall speak his part in a tone, as if he did it in derision of some of the pious, but reform all our disorders, and amend all our amisses, so prosper us Phoebus and the nine Muses, and be propitious to this our complaint.

12. Henry Peacham, *The Art of Living in London* (1642), sig. A4^{r}.[1]

Keep out of the throngs and public places, where multitudes of people are, for saving your purse; the fingers of a number go beyond your sense of feeling. A tradesman's wife of the Exchange[2] one day when her husband was following some business in the City, desired him he should give her leave to go see a play, which she had not done in seven years. He bade her take his prentice along with her, and go; but especially to have a care of her purse, which she warranted him she would. Sitting in a box among some gallants and gallant wenches, and returning when the play was done, returned to her husband, and told him she had lost her purse. 'Wife,' quoth he, 'did I not give you warning of it? How much money was there in it?' Quoth she: 'Truly, four pieces, six shillings, and a silver tooth-picker.' Quoth her husband, 'Where did you put it?' 'Under my petticoat, between that and my smock.'[3] 'What,' quoth he, 'did you feel nobody's hand there?' 'Yes,' quoth she, 'I felt one's hand there; but I did not think he had come for that.' 'So much for the guard of your purse!'

13. Sir John Harington, *Epigrams* (1618), sigs. 16^{r-v}.[1]

A lady of great birth, great reputation,
Clothed in seemly and most sumptuous fashion:
Wearing a border[2] of rich pearl and stone,
Esteemed at a thousand crowns alone,
To see a certain interlude,[3] repairs,
Through a great press, up a dark pair of stairs.
Her page did bear a torch that burnt but dimly.
Two cozening[4] mates, seeing her decked so trimly,
Did place themselves upon the stairs to watch her,
And thus they laid their plot to cunny-catch[5] her:
One should as 'twere by chance strike out the light;
While th'other that should stand beneath her, might
Attempt (which modesty to suffer loathes),
Rudely to thrust his hands under her clothes.

That while her hands repelled such gross
disorders,
His mate might quickly slip away the borders.
Now though this act to get to her was most
displeasant,[6]
Yet being wise (as women's wits are present),
Straight on her borders both her hands she cast,
And so with all her force she held them fast.
'Villains,' she cried, 'you would my borders have!
But I'll save them, t'other itself can save!'
Thus, while the page had got more store of
light,
The cozening mates, for fear slipped out of sight.
Thus her good wit, their cunning over-
matched,
Were not these conycatchers conycatched?

14. Sir John Finet, from his notebook (19 November 1629), Book 3, fol. 58^{r-v}.[1]

On the birthday of the King, being the 19 of November [1629], the Queen had prepared a feast for the entertainment of his majesty and other lords and ladies at Somerset House. The two dukes (of Württemberg and Saxony) expressed their desires to be there for the sight of it. But I, by oblique ways propounding their invitation to their Majesties, not only for sight but participation also of it, if it be permitted, and the King expressing his consent, the Queen withstood it, saying she should be less happy than any common country gentlewoman if she would not make one meal in a year without the presence of unknown faces. So as the dukes appeared not at it, either as partakers or spectators. Whereas it was offered they might, if they thought fit, be there after supper, and at the play, then prepared, they would not appear at all with this reason, that if other thought fit they should not be present as guests at supper, they themselves thought it unfit to be present at the entertainment after supper.

The French ambassador was there, as an invited guest, together with diverse lords and ladies seated at their majesties' table. The king and queen in the midst, and on their left hand (with the distance of one seat) sat the ambassador, on their right (with like distance) the Lady, Marquess of Hamilton, and so answerably the rest of the lords and ladies round about the table, except only in the opposite of their majesties (where room was left) for their carver, sewer,[2] etc. At a long table in another room were bestowed the inferior ladies and the maids of honour together with the French ambassador's servants. After supper was a play, with divers[3] changes of the scene, answerable to the subject in action. The third act ended there was brought a banquet of boxes of sweetmeats brought in chargers[4] and here and there distributed among the ladies and strangers.

9 *Women Performing*

15. Anon., report of an incident in Oxford, from Hatfield House, Hertfordshire (Cecil Papers, MS 62/16, 9 June 1598).

The inhabitants assembled on the two Sundays before Ascension Day,[1] and on that day, with drum and shot and other weapons, and men attired in women's apparel, brought into the town a woman bedecked with garlands and flowers, named by them the Queen of May. They also had morris dances[2] and other disordered and unseemly sports, and intended the next Sunday to continue the same abuses. Details the proceedings taken by the University officers, and the riotous conduct of the inhabitants, in armed resistance to arrest, discharging volleys of shot, and using seditious speeches. The Vice-Chancellor on his return sent to entreat the Mayor to meet him, to which message the Mayor made a frivolous and dilatory answer, and in the meantime preferred an unjust and scandalous complaint against the University.

16. From the Declared Accounts of the Office of the Works (PRO, Exchequer Accounts, E351/3243, Whitehall, 1 October 1607–31 March 1609).[1]

. . . making a stage three foot high from the ground upon trestles all the length and breadth of the hall, making the hallpace[2] railed about under the King's state being all made ready for plays in the hall, setting up degrees[3] and boarding them in the great chamber for the Queen's dancing chamber, making a great number of degrees on either side of the banqueting house both below and in the galleries above, making of a great stage four foot high from the ground upon trestles, making a great hall under the king's state and making a great throne of cants[4] borne in the midst by a great pillar with diverse wheels and devices for the moving round thereof, framing and setting up of a great stage four foot high whereon the same frame was placed, framing and setting up of a dormer with seven lights in the roof over the tilting gallery, setting up the judgehouse in the tiltyard, boarding the floor and sides thereof and making a pair of stairs under the King's window, there making of hallpaces, trestles, forms, tables, cupboards, etc., both for the chapel and diverse other offices against St George his day, mending the terrace and making diverse steps of boards there for the better passage of the Knights of the Garter from the great chamber to the banqueting house . . . working and setting a great quantity of cornices[5] over the heads of the columns in the banqueting house, planing and setting up of a great quantity of thin deal in the frieze over the said columns to fasten the carved work unto, then sitting and setting up of diverse kinds of beasts, arms, pendants, and roses about the lower frieze in the banqueting house, fitting up of diverse running scaffolds, framing and setting up of a great stage for a masque, all the height of the banqueting house with a floor in the middle of the same being made with sundry devices with great gates and turning doors below and a globe and sundry seats above for the Queen and ladies to sit on and to be turned about, framing and setting up a hallpace under the King's state and a great number of degrees on both sides of the said house with rails before the same and taking down thereof after the masque was ended, etc.

17. Vincent to Benson, *Calendar of State Papers, Domestic Series* (PRO, SP14/12/14, 10 January 1605).[1]

Our news here can be nothing but of feasting, revelling, and munificence. . . . But one of the holidays – Sir Philip Herbert's wedding – was kept at court where it is incredible to tell what bravery[2] there was of all parts. Upon Twelfth Day[3] the king's second son, the Lord Charles, was created Duke of York with much ceremony and magnificence. . . . At night there was a sumptuous shew[4] represented by the Queen and some dozen ladies all painted like blackamoors, face and neck bare, and for the rest strangely altered in barbaresque mantles to ye half leg, having buskins all to be set with jewels, which a wave of the sea (as it was artificially made and brought to the stage by secret engines)[5] cast forth out of a scallop shell to perform the residue of the device of dancing, etc., which I saw not, nor harkened after further. But tell it to you only for this: that you discern the humour of the time. It cost the King between £4[000] and £8000 to execute the Queen's fancy. The Spanish ambassador was there, which bred a great quarrel, for the French ambassador thought himself, and consequently his Master, to have received a great affront thereby. . . .

Concerning the same event Sir Dudley Carleton wrote to Ralph Winwood on 6 January 1605 (Boughton House, Winwood Papers III, Northamptonshire Record Office):

At night we had the Queen's masque at the banqueting house, or rather her pageant. There was an engine at the lower end of the room, which had motion, and in it were the images of sea-horses with other terrible fishes, which were ridden by Moors. The indecorum was, that there was all fish and no water. At the further end was a great shell in form of a scallop, wherein were four seats; on the lowest sat the Queen with my Lady Bedford;[6] on the rest were placed the Ladies Suffolk, Derby, Rich, Effingham, Ann Herbert, Susan Herbert, Elizabeth Howard, Walsingham and Bevil. Their apparel was rich, but too light and curtizanlike[7] for such great ones. Instead of vizzards[8] their faces, and arms, up to the elbows, were painted black, which was disguise sufficient, for they were hard to be known; but it became them nothing so well as their red and white, and you cannot imagine a more ugly sight than a troop of lean-cheeked moors. . . .

18. Zuane Pesaro, Venetian ambassador in England, in a letter to the Doge and Senate, *Calendar of State Papers Venetian Series* (6 March 1625/6 (24 February, English)).[1]

On Shrove Tuesday the Queen and her maidens represented a pastoral, followed by a masque, with rich scenery and dresses, and remarkable acting on her part. The King and court enjoyed it, those present being picked and selected, but it did not give complete satisfaction because the English objected to the first part being declaimed by the Queen.

Of the same occasion John Chamberlain noted (*Calendar of State Papers, Domestic Series* (PRO, SP16/22/40, 7 March 1626):[2]

On Shrove Tuesday the Queen and her women had a masque or pastoral play at Somerset House, wherein herself acted a part, and some of the rest were disguised like men with beards. I have known the time when this would have seemed a strange sight, to see a Queen act in a play, but *tempora mutantur et nos*.[3]

19. Declared Accounts of the Office of the Works (Exchequer Accounts, E351/3266, 1 October 1631–30 September 1632, Denmark House).[1]

Also allowed to the said accountant for money by him issued, paid, and defrayed for setting up a new house of timber and dealboard[2] in the paved court at Denmark House, fitting it with degrees[3] and making a scene there with diverse engines and motions[4] for a pastoral and masque to be performed by the Queen and her ladies for performance whereof sundry emptions & provisions have been made which with their quantities, rates & prices together with charges of carriages,[5] wages of artificers, workmen, and labourers, taskwork,[6] rewards,[7] and other charges hereafter ensue: viz.[8] for emptions and provisions, viz. timber (2 lo: 29 foot: at 37s 6d[9] the lode) £4 16s 9d, dealboards (viz. 30 at 16d apiece, 40s). . . . bomspars[10] (20 at 16d apiece, 16s 8d), capravens[11] (20 at 5d the piece, 8s 4d) . . . nails of sundry sorts (£19 12s 11d), ironwork of diverse kinds (£4 20d), hoops and ashen poles (3s 6d), a tub (4s 6d), bassrope[12] (18 pieces at 14d apiece, 21s), whiterope (14lbs. at 8d the pound, 9s 4d), steel pack-needles (4, 12d), baskets (12, 4s), wooden pullies (4, 3s), soap (12lbs., 3s 3d), candles (29 dozen lbs at 6s the dozen lb, £8 13s), pitch (£3 12d), pails (8, 8s), brooms and mops (5s), packthread (16lbs at 9[d?] the lb, 12s), pack-thread lines (3, 4s), wire (£2 12s), and billets[13] (27s) . . . in all for the said emptions and provisions £58 15d. Carriage of diverse of the said provisions with boathire (57s 6d), wages viz. of carpenters at 11d, 18d, 20d, and 22d *per diem* (£79 12s 6d),[14] sawyers at 2s 6d the 100th, (11s 10d), labourers at 12d *per diem* and 8s *per noctem* (£39 17s 6d), and Andrew Durrant, Clerk of the Works at 20d *per diem* (81s 8d), in all the said wages £128 14s 6d. Taskwork viz. to Richard Ryder, carpenter, for framing and raising a great house of firtimber and dealboards in the paved court (76 foot long, 36 foot wide, and 25 foot high) with two outlets at the end where the scene was, putting up degrees in the said house and joisting[15] and boarding the lower room (he finding all manner of stuff and workmanship, £14 10s), making a large scaffold all of his own stuff over all the lower part of the said house to put up the cloth in the ceiling and to put up the state (10s), taking down the degrees at the lower end of the said house after the said pastoral were performed, altering them for more conveniency of the house and inlarding the room with joisting and boarding it for a masque, he finding all manner of stuff and workmanship (£7), framing and putting up two outlets (38 foot long), the piece with two floors to them over the degrees on the sides of the said house, [he] finding all materials and workmanship (£13 6s 8d), fitting and putting up rails about the stage at the foot of the degrees, he finding stuff and workmanship (12s), and for the loan of 100 Norway dealboards which were used about the masque and pastoral (20s in all, £118 8s 8d), and to a joiner for planing . . . leaves of slit dealboards at 18d the score (6s 9d), in all for the said taskwork (£118 15s 5d) and in rewards viz. to John Damport, carpenter, for his extraordinary pains in directing the rest of the carpenters for the furtherance of the said work by the space of four months (40s), and to labourers and porters for taking up of timber and boards at diverse times (7s 6d), in all for rewards (47s 6d). In all the charges of the said works done for the pastoral and masque aforesaid performed at Denmark House . . . the sum of £310 16s 2d.

20. William Prynne, *Histriomastix* (London, 1633), pp. 214–16, 414–15.[1]

And so by consequence the plays themselves which are acted in such apparel (as all our masques and stage plays for the most part are) must questionless be sinful, yea abominable, as men's putting on of women's apparel is. Thus, the fore-alleged councils, fathers, authors do from hence conclude, and so must I from all the premises.

If any now object, that it is far better, far more commendable for boys to act in women's attire, then to bring women-actors on the stage to personate female parts, a practice much in use in former times among the Greeks and Romans, who had their *Mima*, their *Scenicae mulieres*,[2] or women-actors (who were all notorious impudent, prostituted strumpets), especially in their Floralian[3] interludes,[4] as they have now their female players in Italy, and other foreign parts, and as they had such French-women actors, in a play not long since personated in Blackfriars Playhouse,[5] to which there was great resort.

I answer first, that the very ground of this objection is false, unless the objectors can manifest it to be a greater abomination, a more detestable damning sin, for a woman to act a female's part on the stage, than for a boy to put on a woman's apparel, person and behaviour, to act a feminine part; which the Scripture expressly prohibits, as an abomination to the Lord our God, or unless they can prove an irritation, an inducement to sodomy, or self-pollution (in thought, if not in act), a lesser sin, a more tolerable evil, then mannish impudency, or a temptation to whoredom, and adultery, which none can evidence. Secondly, admit men-actors in women's attire are not altogether so bad, so discommendable[6] as women stage-players; yet since both of them are evil, yea extremely vicious, neither of them necessary, both superfluous as all plays and players are; the superabundant sinfulness of the one, can neither justify the lawfulness, nor extenuate the wickedness of the other. It is no good argument to say adultery is worse then simple fornication. Sodomy with such other unnatural wickednesses are far more abominable then adultery. Therefore fornication and adultery are lawful and may still be tolerated (as they are in beastly Rome, the very sink, the stews and nursery of all such uncleanness; which should cause all Christians to detest this whore, together with the pope, her supreme pander) because the transcendent badness of the one, doth neither expiate nor extenuate the sinfulness of the other. Yet this is the present objection in effect. Female actors are worse then male actors arrayed in women's apparel. Therefore they are tolerable, if not lawful. Whereas this should rather be the conclusion (with which I will close up this scene). Both of them are abominable, both intolerable, neither of them laudatory or necessary, therefore both of them to be abandoned, neither of them to be henceforth tolerated among Christians. . . . But there is no man who discerns how great the stains of sin are. For because we fear not things that are to be feared, therefore we fear those things which have no cause of fear in them. But what is this so great noise of theatre men? What these diabolical clamours? What this Satanical apparel? One, being a young man, hath his hair combed backward, an effeminating nature in his countenance, apparel, pace, and such like, strives to deduce it to the similitude of a tender virgin. Another, on the side, being an old man, having his hair and all modesty shaven off with a razor, standing by girt,[7] is ready to speak and act on all things. Women also, with a naked and an uncovered head, speak to the people without shame, and usurp impudency to themselves with so great premeditation, and infuse so great lasciviousness into the minds of hearers and spectators that all may seem, even with one consent, to extirpate[8] all modesty out of their minds, to disgrace the female nature, and to satiate their lusts with pernicious pleasure. For all things that are done there are absolutely most obscene, the words, the apparel, the tonsure, the pace, the speeches, the songs, the ditties, the turnings and glances of the eyes, the pipes, the flutes, and the very argument of the plays, all things (I say) are full of filthy wantonness.

21. Sir Richard Baker, *Theatrum Redivivum, or, the Theatre Vindicated* (1662), pp. 15–19.[1]

For his [Prynne's] dislike of plays now (though with the interposition of some extravagant conceits,[2] which he calls reasons; and will fitter take their place afterward) is because of their clothes. He thinks it is not lawful for men to wear women's clothes, or for women to wear men's; and, because this is often done in plays and masques, he utterly condemns them. Yet this is well; there is some moderation in this, for this reason puts not plays to death, but only confines them. For, notwithstanding this reason, they may be lawful enough amongst the Indians[3] who go naked; and, not to go so far, they may be lawful enough too amongst the Irish, where one kind of garment serves men and women. But though we can be content to cross the water to the Bankside,[4] yet we should be loath to cross the Irish seas to see a play; and can we not see one here because of their clothes? Indeed, he cites a text of scripture for it, Deut. xxii. 5: 'The women shall not wear that which pertaineth to the man; neither shall a man put on a woman's raiment.' A pregnant place indeed; but where finds he this precept? Even in the same place where he finds also that we must not wear clothes of linsey-woolsey;[5] and seeing we lawfully now wear clothes of linsey-woolsey, why may it not be as lawful for men to put on women's garments? But if he will have this precept to stand in force, though it be no part of the moral law, yet because it may have a moral construction; how will he then defend his own eating of black-puddings[6] against the precept for eating of blood? For this precept against eating of blood hath a stronger tie than that for wearing of garments. For that, as given only by Moses, may, with just probability, be thought to end with Moses; but this against eating of blood is continued after Moses's time by the Apostles themselves. And why then should it trouble Mr Prynne's conscience to see a boy wear women's garments against the precept of Moses when it troubles not his conscience to eat black-puddings against the precept of the Apostles? But howsoever it trouble his conscience, it need not trouble anybody's else; seeing his reason proves it no more unlawful to see a play than to eat a pudding, and so, upon the matter, is not worth a pudding. But if it be so great a sin for men to put on women's garments, what is it for men to put on women's conditions? Which is indeed the very moral of this precept: as Clemens Alexandrinus[7] and St Cyril,[8] of old and of late, amongst others, Macchabæus Alpinas (a writer Melancthon[9] exceedingly commends) expound it. And if it be so, then is this man the true breaker of the precept, and not players; at least, if we may call it women's conditions, to do nothing else but scold and rail; for what is all his book but a bundle of scolding invectives and railing, instead of reasoning? But to give a full answer to this argument, do but hear what eminent divines conceive of this precept. And, that I may not do, as this man useth to do (to shew a bee, bring in the whole swarm) I will name you one of many, yet not *unum è multis*,[10] Martin Luther[11] whose words upon this place are these: *Hic non prohibetur, quin ad vitandum periculum, aut ludendum joco, vel fallendum hostes, Mulier possit arma Viri, & Vir uti veste muliebri; sed ut seriò, & usitato habitu talia non fiant; ut decora utrique sexui servetur dignitas.* It is not (saith he) forbidden by this precept; but that to avoid danger, or to play and sport, or to deceive an enemy, a woman may wear a man's apparel, and a man a woman's; but that it be not done in earnest, and as useful habit; that so decent comeliness in both sexes may be observed.[12] And who knows not that Luther, when time was, did greater matters in the world than making good the exposition of a single text. But lest you should think it a Lutheran opinion, or that Luther herein were singular by himself, I will join one with them, that had as lieve[13] die, as be joined with him, if he could otherwise choose, the learned Jesuit, Lorinuse[14] who, reciting great variety of interpretations upon this text, makes choice of this, as the soundest, that *Dissimulatio vestis potest interdum sine peccato fieri, vel ad representandum comicè tragicéve personam; vel ad effugiendum periculum; vel in casu simili*;[15] for representing a person in comedy or tragedy; or for avoiding of danger, or in such like cases, a woman may lawfully put on a man's apparel; and a man a woman's.[16] Thus these men allow that in plays, for which this man [Prynne] allows not plays. And is it not strange that Mr Prynne, with all his great reading, should never meet with any of these?

22. Consistory Court of London, Correction Book, fols 19–20 (27 January 1612).[1]

This day & place the said Mary appeared personally & then & there voluntarily confessed that she had long frequented all or most of the disorderly & licentious places in this City as namely she hath usually in the habit of a man resorted to alehouses, taverns, tobacco shops & also to playhouses, there to see plays & prizes & namely being at a play about 3 quarters of a year since[2] at the Fortune[3] in man's apparel & in her boots & with a sword by her side, she told the company there present that she thought many of them were of the opinion that she was a man, but if any of them would come to her lodging they should find that she is a woman & some other immodest & lascivious speeches she also used at that time. And also sat there upon the stage in the public view of all the people there present in man's apparel & played upon her lute & sang a song. And she further confessed that she hath for this long time past usually blasphemed & dishonoured the name of God by swearing & cursing & by tearing God out of his kingdom if it were possible, & hath also usually associated herself with ruffinly,[4] swaggering, & lewd company as namely with cut-purses, blasphemous drunkards & others of bad note & of most dissolute behaviour with whom she hath to the great shame of her sex oftentimes (as she said) drunk hard & distempered her head with drink. And further confesseth that since she was punished for the misdemeanours aforementioned in Bridewell[5] she was since upon Christmas Day at night taken in Paul's Church with her petticoat tucked up about her in the fashion of a man with a man's cloak on her to the great scandal of diverse persons who understood the same & to the disgrace of all womanhood. And she sayeth & protesteth that she is heartily sorry for foresaid licentious & dissolute life & giveth her earnest promise to carry & behave herself ever from hence forward honestly, soberly, & womanly & resteth ready to undergo any censure or punishment for her misdemeanours aforesaid in such manner & form as shalbe assigned her by the Lord Bishop of London, her Ordinary.[6] And then she being pressed to declare whether she had not been dishonest of her body & hath not also drawn other women to lewdness by her persuasions & by carrying herself like a bawd, she absolutely denied that she was chargeable with either of these imputations. And thereupon his Lordship thought fit to rend her to Bridewell from whence she now came until he might further examine the truth of the misdemeanours enforced against her without laying as yet any further censure vpon her.

10 *Women in Theatrical Affairs*

23. Edmund Howes's addition to John Stow's *Annales* (1615), p. 697.[1]

Comedians and stage-players of former time were very poor and ignorant in respect of these of this time: but being now grown very skilful and exquisite actors for all matters, they were entertained into the service of divers great lords: out of which companies there were twelve of the best chosen, and, at the request of Sir Francis Walsingham,[2] they were sworn the Queen's servants and were allowed wages and liveries as grooms of the chamber: and until this yeare 1583, the Queen had no players. Among these twelve players were two rare men, viz.[3] Thomas Wilson,[4] for a quick, delicate, refined, extemporal[5] wit, the wonder of his time. He lieth buried in Shoreditch.

[In a note Howes writes: 'He [Tarlton][6] was so beloved that men use his picture for their signs.']

24. Chancery Records, Draft Patent for Queen Anne's Men (1603–4), PRO/SP14/2/100.[1]

James, by the grace of God, King of England, Scotland, France, and Ireland, defender of the faith, &c., To all Justices of Peace, mayors, sheriffs, vicechancellors of any our universities, bailiffs, headboroughs, [and other our officers,] constables, and to all other our officers, ministers, and loving subjects to whom it may appertain, greeting. Know ye that we of our special grace, certain knowledge, and mere motion have licensed and authorized, and by these presents do license and authorize Thomas Green, Christopher Beeston, Thomas Heywood, Richard Perkins, Robert Pallant, John Duke, Thomas Swynerton, James Holt, Robert Beeston, & Robert Lee,[2] servants unto our dearest [and welbeloved] wife the Queen Anna, with the rest of their associates, freely to use and exercise the art and faculty of playing comedies, tragedies, histories, interludes, morals, pastorals, stage plays, and such other like as they have already studied, or hereafter shall use or study, as well for the recreation of our loving subjects as for our solace and pleasure, when we shall think good to see them, during our pleasure. And the said comedies, tragedies, histories, interludes, morals, pastorals, stage plays, and such like to exercise publicly when the infection of the plague shall decrease to the number of thirty weekly within our city of London and the liberties thereof, as well within their now usual houses called the Curtain and the Boar's Head, within our county of Middlesex, [or] as in any other playhouse not used by others, by the said Thomas Green elected, or by him hereafter to be built, and also within any town halls, or moothalls,[3] or other convenient places, within the liberties and freedoms of any city, university, town, or borough whatsoever, within our said realms and dominions, willing and commanding you and every [one] of you, as you tender our pleasure, not only to permit and suffer them [herein] to use and exercise the said art of playing without any your lettes,[4] hindrances, or molestations, during our said pleasure, but also to be aiding and assisting unto them, if any wrong be to them offered, and to allow them such [former] courtesies, as hath heretofore been given unto any men of their qualitie. [And also what further favour, any of our subjects shall shew to these our dear and loving wive's servants, for our sake, we shall take kindly at your hands. Yeoven[5] at the day of In the year of our reign of England, &c:][6] fc Gyven &c.

[Endorsed] The Queen's Players

25. Last will and testamant of William Browne (23 October 1634), PRO/PCC/PROB11/166, fols 317^{v}–318^{r}.[1]

I, William Browne of the parish of St James Clerkenwell, in the county of Middlesex, gentleman, being at this present sick and weak

. . . [direct my body] to be buried . . . in the chancel of the parish church of St James Clerkenwell aforesaid so near as may be conveniently to my father Greene. . . . I give and bequeath unto my father Robert Browne, haberdasher, the sum of £5 of lawful money of England, and also my best suit of apparel (vizt.) hose, doublet, and cloak, and the same to be paid and delivered him within one month next after my decease. Item, I give and bequeath unto the three children of the said Robert Browne the sum of £10 of lawfull money of England to be shared amongst them, part and part alike. And my will and mind is that if any of my said brother's children shall depart this life before they shall accomplish their full ages of one and twenty years, then his, or their part so dying to remain to the survivor of them; and if they shall (all of them) die before the accomplishment of their said ages of one and twenty years then I will the same shall remain unto my said brother. Item, I give to my brother-in-law Thomas Bond my best black stuff suit and cloak, my wrought gold cap, my best half shirt and my best band, and my white beaver hat, to be paid and delivered to him immediately after my decease. Item, I give and bequeath unto my sister Susan Bond, wife of the said Thomas Bond, the sum of £4 to be paid her within three months next after my decease. And I do also release, acquit, and discharge my said sister of the debt of 20s which she oweth me. Item, I give and bequeath unto my dearly beloved mother Susan Greene alias Baskerville all such sum and sums of money, debts, duties, claims, challenges, and demands whatsoever as either is, ought, or shalbe due owing, or belonging unto me forth, out of and from the Red Bull Playhouse scituate in St John Street in the County of Middlesex whereof I am a member, and a fellow sharer, or of or by any of the shares or other person or persons, players there, or owners thereof, and of, in, or to any house or houses to the said playhouse adjoining. And also all bonds, bills, debts, and other things as I have formerly granted or assigned unto my said mother, or wherein by deed I have declared any trust to be reposed in me for the use and benefit of my said mother. Item, I further give and bequeath unto my said mother my house clock, my pocket watch, my gold seal ring, my best beaver hat, and all my wearing apparel, as well linen as woollen, not otherwise herein and hereby given, disposed, willed, or bequeathed. Item, I give to the said company of players 20s to buy them black ribbons to wear in remembrance of me. Item, I give unto Philip Massam, my son-in-law, the sum of £10 of lawful money of England to be paid him at his age of one and twenty years if he shalbe then living. And my will and mind is that if my said son shall depart this mortal life before he shall accomplish his age of one and twenty years aforesaid that then the said £10 which should have been paid to him shalbe paid within one month next after the said Philip's decease unto my foresaid brother Robert Browne, his executors, or assigns. Item, I give to the poor of the said parish of St James Clerkenwell the sum of 20s to be distributed amongst them at the discretion of my executrix hereafter named. And all my other goods, chattels, cattell, plate, ready monies, debts, and whatsoever else of mine, and not herein or by deed under my hand and seal otherwise disposed (of my due debts being first paid and my funeral expenses and legacies discharged) I give unto my wife, Anne Browne. And I do make and ordain my said mother, Susan Baskerville alias Greene, full and whole executrix of this my testament and last will. And I do hereby revoke and disannul all former wills and this only to stand for, and as my last will and testament. In witness whereof I, the said William Browne, have hereunto set my hand and seal, yeoven[2] the day and year first above written, *per me*,[3] William Browne . . .

26. Indenture between Edward Alleyn and Marie Bryan for one twelfth of the second Fortune Playhouse (24 March 1623), Dulwich College, MSS Second Series, Number 23.[1]

This indenture made the four and twentieth day of March 1623, and in the years of the reigns of our Sovereign Lord James, by the grace of God, King of England, Scotland, France, and Ireland, the one and twentieth, and of Scotland the seven and twentieth, between Edward Alleyn of Dulwich in the county of Surrey, Esquire, of one part, and Marie Bryan of Clerkenwell in the county of Middlesex, widow, of the other part. Witness that whereas the said Edward Alleyn the day of the date of these presents is seized in his demesne[2] as of fee, of and in one new playhouse or building called the Fortune with a taphouse belonging to the same, being a tenement now in the occupation of Robert Hart and three tenements thereto also belonging, which are part of and built in the said playhouse of building, and also seized of, and in two other messuages[3] or tenements, the one in the tenure or occupation of William Peadle . . . and the other in the tenure or occupation of Edward Deakyn . . . scituate on the north side of the way leading to the said playhouse or building, all scituate and being between Whitecross Street and Golding Lane in the parish of St Giles without Cripplegate in the county of Middlesex. Now this indenture further witnesseth that the said Edward, as well for and consideration of the yearly rent and covenants hereafter in these presents expressed which on the tenants or leases part during the terms here under granted are, and ought to be paid, done, and performed as also for diverse other good causes and considerations, him the said Edward Alleyn hereunto especially moving hath demised, granted, and to form letten, and by these presents doth demise, grant, and to form let unto the said Marie Bryan one part of the new playhouse or building and premises in twelve equal parts to be divided with all easements, passages, profits, and commodities thereunto belonging, or in any wise appertaining, to have and to hold the said one part of the said new playhouse or building and premises in twelve equal parts to be divided as aforesaid with all and every the appurtenances unto the said Marie Bryan, her executors, administrators, and assigns, from the feast day of the Annunciation of our blessed Lady St Marie the Virgin next ensuing, the date hereof unto the full end and term of nine and forty years and one quarter of a year from thence next ensuing and fully to be complete and ended, yielding and paying therefore, for the first quarter of a year of the said term unto the said Edward Alleyn, his heirs, or assigns the sum of three and fifty shillings and five pence, half penny, of lawful money of England, at or in the said college called God's Gift in Dulwich aforesaid; And yielding and paying therefore also yearly, and every year during the residue of the said term of nine and forty years and one quarter of a year unto the said Edward Alleyn, his heirs, or assigns, £10 13s and 10d of lawful English money at four most usual feasts or terms in the year, that is to say, the Nativity of St John Baptist, with Michael th'archangel, the birth of our lord, and the Annunciation of our lady with Marie the Virgin, by even and equal portions, at or in the said college called God's Gift at Dulwich aforesaid . . . [and Marie Bryan, along with the other shareholders] shall repair, uphold, sustain, fence, maintain, and keep and the pavements and passages leading to the said new playhouse or building and premises . . . [and the building shall be inspected twice yearly to determine necessary repairs, for which the shareholders shall be financially responsible].

Notes

PART I TEXTS

1 Elizabeth I, *Hercules Oetaeus*

Introduction

1 Christopher Hibbert, *The Virgin Queen*, p. 25.
2 Ibid., pp. 26–7.
3 Quoted in John Nichols, *The Progresses and Public Processions of Queen Elizabeth*, vol. I, p. ix, n. 2.
4 Queen Elizabeth I, *The Poems of Queen Elizabeth I*, p. xiv.
5 Ibid., pp. xiv–xv, and *Queen Elizabeth's Englishings*, orig. ser., vol. 113, pp. vii–viii.
6 The manuscript gathering of Boethius, Horace and Plutarch is PRO, Domestic Elizabeth 289. See Queen Elizabeth I, *Poems*, pp. xiv–xv.
7 *Queen Elizabeth's Englishings*, pp. x–xii.
8 Queen Elizabeth I, *Poems*, p. 80.
9 Ibid., *Poems*, p. xiv.
10 My rendering from the Latin text as presented in Seneca, 'Hercules Oetaeus' in *Tragedies*, trans. Frank Justus Miller, p. 240. Elizabeth's translation roughly corresponds to ll. 604–99 in this edition.
11 Horatio Walpole, *A Catalogue of the Royal and Noble Authors of England, Scotland, and Ireland; with Lists of their Works*, vol. I, pp. 84–109. In addition to those translations discussed earlier Walpole also identified as Elizabeth's 'a translation of a dialogue out of Xenophon in Greek between Hiero, a King, yet sometime a private Person, and Simonides a Poet, as touching the Life of the Prince and Private Man' (p. 86).
12 Ibid., p. 109.
13 Ewald Flügel, 'Die Gedichte der Königin Elisabeth', *Anglia*, 14 (1892), pp. 346–52.
14 R.A. Foakes and R.T. Rickert (eds), *Henslowe's Diary*, pp. 28–9, 34, 89, 93, 185, 318, 324.
15 See, for example, Jean Wilson, *Entertainments for Elizabeth I* and David M. Bergeron, *English Civic Pageantry*.

Hercules Oetaeus

1 Burden.
2 Scarce, uncommon.
3 The Latin should be translated 'thou'. This is probably a scribal error.
4 Swords (rare form of singular 'glaive').
5 Crowd. The MS reads 'rool', probably a scribal error. The Latin original translates *tot populis*, 'whole nations'.
6 The Latin original refers to a 'gilded gate' here, and to 'doors' in the next line. 'Ledge' seems to be an awkward translation of Latin *limen*, 'a threshold, sill, lintel'.
7 Deceit, trickery.
8 Probably an error for 'passage'.
9 The MS reads 'thee'.
10 The 'gift' is the wisdom that follows.
11 More often.
12 The rising sun.
13 Suddenly surprised, confounded.
14 Slippery.
15 Labour.
16 Abate.
17 Hister, the lower course of the Danube river.
18 A country in western Asia Minor.
19 Spain.
20 The west wind.
21 A river flowing west through central Spain and Portugal.
22 A river in Thrace.
23 A tributary of the Indus river. The Latin original translates: 'and rich Hydaspes should be added to his fields'.
24 A river flowing south-east from the Himalayas to the Bay of Bengal, sacred to the Hindus.
25 Persons.
26 The sentence is awkward. It should probably read: 'For greedy men all of nature is

insufficient [to satisfy their desires]' ('*Avidus, avidus natura parum est*').

27 A 'hind' is a farm labourer, here 'crooked' ('bent', 'deformed') from hard work.
28 Lumps of earth, turned up through ploughing.
29 Meadows.
30 Defeated, checked.
31 The moon in its earliest phase when it is new ('newed').
32 Soft.
33 City on the Phoenician coast, famous for its crimson dye called 'Tyrian purple'.
34 Golden.
35 Fears.
36 Lofty successes.
37 'Bruttium', related to the inhabitants of the southern part of Italy.
38 This is a mistranslation of 'Corus', the north-west wind.
39 'Franched' literally means 'to devour, feed greedily upon'. Hence, the 'franched mind' is tormented.
40 The Latin original of this line translates: 'The poor man's heart is free from care.' It would seem that the heart, freed from care in Seneca's rendition, becomes, perhaps incorrectly, the anxious mind in this translation.
41 Cup carved from the wood of a beech tree.
42 Obtained.
43 Cares.
44 Swords girded on thighs.
45 Tied.
46 Labour.
47 Red.
48 Weight, pull of gem-laden earrings.
49 The dawn; metaphorically, the Orient.
50 Hindrance.
51 City of ancient Phoenicia (modern Saida), famous for its production of purple dye.
52 The Lydian (Maeonian) women were well known for their embroidery.
53 Cleft stick on which wool was wound.
54 Suspicion, expectation.
55 Scribal error for 'with'.
56 Erinys, a Fury, an avenging spirit.
57 Scribal error for 'adorned'.
58 Crowd.
59 Turned to the side, distorted.
60 Balk: unploughed ridge, raised path between fields, i.e., 'he who eschews the middle way is destined to travel the difficult, distorted path'.
61 Phaethon, son of Helios (the sun), who borrowed his father's chariot for a day and drove so dangerously that he was struck down by Zeus.
62 Also.
63 Chariot.
64 Customary.
65 Worn, familiar.
66 Unknown.
67 The sun.
68 In classical mythology an Athenian architect who built the labyrinth for Minos and made wax wings for himself and his son (Icarus) so that they could escape. Icarus, through his pride, flew too close to the sun. His wings melted and he fell into the sea.
69 Purpose, goal.
70 Now called the Icarian Sea, part of the Aegean.
71 Fly, escape.
72 Shelter.
73 Frail.
74 The translation of this line seems to be in error. The Latin reads: 'Let my frail boat keep close to shore.'
75 Most central, open.

2 Mary Sidney, *The Tragedy of Antonie*

Introduction

1 Biographical information about Mary Sidney may be found in Frances B. Young, *Mary Sidney, Countess of Pembroke*; Gary Waller, *Mary Sidney, Countess of Pembroke: A Critical Study of her Writings and Literary Milieu*; and Margaret P. Hannay, *Philip's Phoenix: Mary Sidney, Countess of Pembroke.* For a full Mary Sidney bibliography see Josephine Roberts's excellent compilation in Kirby Farrell *et al.* (eds), *Women in the Renaissance: Selections from 'English Literary Renaissance'*, pp. 245–58 and 265–9.
2 Descriptions of the dedications may be found in Michael Brennan, *Literary Patronage in the English Renaissance: The Pembroke Family*, pp. 59–82, and Mary Ellen Lamb, *Gender and Authorship in the Sidney Circle*, pp. 28–71.
3 See Josephine A. Roberts, *The Poems of Lady Mary Wroth*, p. 11. Mary Sidney's name has often proved problematic for twentieth-century critics and historians since she was known during her lifetime by both her maiden (Sidney) and married (Herbert) names.

4 Grief at the death of her brother and parents is often cited as the reason for Mary's literary endeavours; see, for example, Michael Brennan, *Literary Patronage*, p. 59.
5 John Aubrey, *Brief Lives*, pp. 138–40.
6 The Countess of Pembroke has traditionally been seen as at the centre of a school of writers at Wilton, but this view has been successfully challenged by Mary Ellen Lamb in 'The Countess of Pembroke's Patronage' and 'The Myth of the Countess of Pembroke: The Dramatic Circle'.
7 Waller, *Mary Sidney*, p. 77.
8 Mary Sidney, *The Psalms of Sir Philip Sidney and the Countess of Pembroke*, ed. J.C. Rathmell.
9 Katharina M. Wilson (ed.), *Women Writers of the Renaissance and Reformation*, p. 483; see also, Elaine V. Beilin, *Redeeming Eve: Women Writers of the English Renaissance*, pp. 121–50, and Waller, *Mary Sidney*, pp. 152–256.
10 G.F. Waller (ed.), *The Triumph of Death and Other Unpublished and Uncollected Poems by Mary Sidney, Countess of Pembroke (1561–1621)*; Diane Bornstein (ed.), *The Countess of Pembroke's Translation of Philippe de Mornay's Discourse of Life and Death; for The Tragedy of Antonie* see below, pp. 19–42.
11 Sir Philip Sidney, *The Countess of Pembroke's Arcadia*, ed. Maurice Evans. Evans bases his edition on the 1593 version of the *Arcadia* which was produced under the Countess's auspices, rather than the 1590 version undertaken by Fulke Greville.
12 'The Doleful Lay of Clorinda' first appeared in Edmund Spenser's *Colin Clout's Come Home Again* (1595); for a modern edition see Waller, *Triumph of Death*, pp. 176–9; 'To the Angel Spirit' is included with the psalms; see Waller, *Triumph of Death*, pp. 190–2; 'A Dialogue' first appeared in Francis Davison's *Poetical Rhapsody* (1602): see Waller, *Triumph of Death*, pp. 181–3; 'Even Now That Care' is also included with the psalms: see Waller, *Triumph of Death*, pp. 88–91; manuscript letters: BL MS 12506 and Salisbury MSS.
13 Criticisms of *Antonie* include: V.W. Beauchamp, 'Sidney's Sister as Translator of Garnier', *Renaissance Notes*, pp. 8–13; Beilin, *Redeeming Eve*, pp. 121–50; Hannay, *Philip's Phoenix*, pp. 119–29; Tina Krontiris, *Oppositional Voices. Women as Writers and Translators of Literature in the English Renaissance*, pp. 69–78; Lamb, *Gender and Authorship*, pp. 129–32; and Wilson, *Women Writers*, pp. 481–521.
14 Waller, *Mary Sidney*, pp. 111 and 118–9. For example, stichomythia (dialogue in alternate lines): II.314–27; anaphora (beginning successive lines with the same word): II.158–62; and apostrophe (an address to a person or object not present): II.152–75.
15 E.K. Chambers, *The Elizabethan Stage*, vol. II, pp. 128–34, and Hannay, *Philip's Phoenix*, p. 124.
16 Sir Philip Sidney, *An Apology for Poetry*, ed. Geoffrey Shepherd, pp. 133–6.
17 For discussions of this 'group' of neo-Senecan tragedies see: David M Bergeron, 'Women as Patrons of English Renaissance Drama' in Guy Fitch Lytle and Stephen Orgel (eds), *Patronage in the Renaissance*, pp. 274–90; Brennan, *Literary Patronage*, pp. 75–80; Nancy Cotton, *Women Playwrights in England c.1363–1750*, pp. 30–1; and Waller, *Mary Sidney*, pp. 110–11.
18 Philip Sidney, *Apology*, pp. 134–5.
19 Samuel Daniel, 'To the Lady Mary Countess of Pembroke' in *Daniel's The Tragedie of Cleopatra*, ed. M. Lederer, pp. 3–7.
20 T.S. Eliot, 'Seneca in Elizabethan Translation', pp. 92–3.
21 Brennan, *Literary Patronage*, p. 80.
22 Waller, *Mary Sidney*, p. 107; Daniel's *Cleopatra* went through six editions in five years (see Hannay, *Philip's Phoenix*, p. 120).
23 Hannay, *Philip's Phoenix*, p. 127.
24 Ibid., pp. 125–6 and 129, and Waller, *Mary Sidney*, pp. 115–16.
25 For a discussion of Cleopatra's character see: Krontiris, *Oppositional Voices*, pp. 69–72; Lamb, 'The Countess of Pembroke and the Art of Dying' in Mary Beth Rose (ed.), *Women in the Middle Ages and the Renaissance*, pp. 213–20, and *Gender and Authorship*, pp. 130–2; Waller, *Mary Sidney*, pp. 112–15.
26 Krontiris, *Oppositional Voices*, p. 71.
27 Hannay, *Philip's Phoenix*, p. 201.
28 See below, p. 90–4.
29 *The Tragedie of Antonie. Doone into English by the Countesse of Pembroke Imprinted at London for William Ponsonby 1595.*

The Tragedy of Antonie

THE ARGUMENT

1 More commonly known as Augustus Caesar (he was given this name by the Senate in 27 BC), Octavius originally governed the Roman republic in a triumvir with Antony and Lepidus, but by 31 BC had defeated both his rivals to become undisputed emperor of the Roman world. It was his sister, Octavia, who married Antony (n. 2 below).

2 Mark Antony (83–30 BC), the titular protagonist of the play, was one of the main supporters of Julius Caesar, whom he attempted to succeed; he was foiled by the intervention of Caesar's adopted son, Octavius (later Augustus Caesar). Although the two rivals came to an uneasy agreement (Antony married Octavius' sister), forming a triumvir with Lepidus, their alliance finally crumbled when Antony deserted his wife and nation for Cleopatra, the queen of Egypt. He was finally defeated by Octavius at the battle of Actium (31 BC), and committed suicide with Cleopatra the following year when Octavius besieged Alexandria. The play roughly follows these events. Within the playtext we follow Mary Sidney and use both 'Antonius' and 'Antonie'; in the notes, the modern spelling 'Antony' is used.

3 A semi-nomadic military nation who originally occupied a small district of western Asia; they later ruled an empire extending from the Euphrates to the Indus. The Parthians fought a series of wars to protect their territory from the advancing Romans.

4 Marcus Licinius Crassus (115–53 BC) was a triumvir, along with Pompey and Julius Caesar, known for his wealth and influence. He was slain by the Parthians and his head was sent to the Parthian king, Orodes, who had gold poured into the corpse's mouth to signify Crassus' greed when alive.

5 Cleopatra (69–30 BC) became joint heir, with her brother Ptolemy, to the Egyptian throne at the death of her father, but she was expelled from the rulership and only regained her position with the aid of Julius Caesar, by whom she had a son. She was renowned for her beauty and intelligence and, in 41 BC, when she met Antony she had little difficulty in winning him away from his wife, Octavia. In the ensuing war with Octavius she supported Antony, but her flight from the battle of Actium hastened his defeat and they were forced to return to Alexandria, where both committed suicide. The play traces the latter part of her life.

6 Country on the south-east coast of Asia Minor.

7 City on the north coast of Egypt, near the mouth of the Nile; founded by Alexander the Great.

8 Promontory in the south of Epirus off the west coast of Greece, site of the famous sea battle between Octavius and Antony, at which the former was victorious.

9 1595 edition reads 'hard off', a misleading spelling.

10 Plutarch (*c.* AD 46–120) was an eminent Greek biographer, historian and philosopher whose *Parallel Lives* (of twenty-three prominent rulers and statesmen) concentrated upon the moral character of his subjects. The most famous translation of the *Lives* was that produced by Sir Thomas North (1579), made from the French version *Amyot* (1559). North's translation was followed closely by Shakespeare in *Antony and Cleopatra*.

ACT I

1 An engine is a machine; here, metaphorically, the wheel of fortune.

2 Fitting.

3 City in lower Egypt, lost to Octavius, supposedly with Cleopatra's collusion.

4 Enticements.

5 The Fates; three supernatural sisters from classical mythology who determined the destinies of men and women.

6 Throw Antony's corpse to the wolves to be eaten by them.

7 One of the three Furies, horrific figures from classical mythology who enacted pitiless punishment on human wrongdoers. They were usually depicted as winged maidens with serpents in their hair and blood dripping from their eyes.

8 Cupid is the Roman god of love; his fire would be one of desire, unlike the darker passions envisaged by Antony.

9 Antony identifies his passion with the emotional turmoil suffered by Orestes, who in Greek mythology murdered his mother and was consequently pursued, and eventually driven mad, by the avenging Furies.

10 Pertaining to the river Styx, which in classical mythology conveys the souls of the dead to the underworld. What is suggested here

is that Orestes sees his mother's ghost.

11 A bay or laurel wreath was worn by Roman generals celebrating their victories.

12 In contrast to the military bay wreath, the myrtle tree was sacred to Venus, the goddess of love.

13 Defiled.

14 Sword.

15 Piece of armour; specifically a breast-plate and back-plate which buckled together.

16 Restored.

17 River in south-west Asia.

18 For Parthians see Argument, note 3.

19 Medes, governed by the Parthians and then the Persians, lived in Media, a land located south-west of the Caspian Sea.

20 Hyrcania, a province of the Persian empire and summer dwelling-place of the Parthians.

21 Phraates, king of Parthia and, hence, Media.

22 Siege machines.

23 Frames again.

24 Becomes again.

25 The River Nile.

26 Parched.

27 The white marble lighthouse on the island of Pharos at Alexandria, one of the seven wonders of the world.

28 Plutarch records that Cleopatra entered into lengthy negotiations with Octavius after Actium. Garnier alters this so that Cleopatra never betrays Antony, although he doubts her. Sidney follows Garnier.

29 In the late sixteenth century it was almost universally accepted that women were, by nature, intellectually inferior to men. One of the most virulent attacks against women in the English Renaissance is Joseph Swetnam's *The Arraignment of Lewd, Idle, Froward and Unconstant Women* (1615), which accuses women of being fickle and wanton.

30 In imitation of Horace, *Odes* II.ix, in which the speaker urges a truce with sorrow, offering consolation in the face of adversity and loss.

31 In Roman mythology the ruler of the gods, traditionally armed with thunderbolts.

32 Heads.

33 People of Scythia, a country in northern Asia.

34 People of Massagetae, a country in central Asia.

35 Phoebus Apollo, in classical mythology, the god of the sun; here, metaphorically, the sun beating down.

36 The name generally given in Greek mythology to the rebellious children of Uranus, the original ruler of the gods; however, it was also an epithet used for their less mutinous offspring, such as the sun.

37 Follow upon, succeed.

38 Blessed.

39 In Greek myth a demi-god, who made men and women out of clay, stole fire from Olympus, and subsequently taught humanity how to use it; he was punished by Zeus, who chained him to a rock where his liver (magically restored) was eaten out daily by a vulture.

40 Stab, prick.

ACT II

1 Flash, rain down.

2 In classical legend the Gigantes (giants) were huge and terrifying beings who made war upon the gods; they were defeated with the help of Hercules and imprisoned beneath volcanoes.

3 Destruction, ruin.

4 King of Lapithae, known for his ingratitude to Jove and his attempt to seduce Hera, Jove's wife.

5 In Garnier the character is named as Salmoneus, who imitated lightning by burning torches, thereby incurring the wrath of Zeus, who killed him with a real thunderbolt.

6 Mythical king of Phrygia who angered the gods and was punished by being cursed with a terrible hunger and thirst, which he was magically prevented from quenching despite being within reach of food and drink. Hence, the verb 'to tantalize'.

7 Atreus, the mythical king of Mycenae, took revenge upon his brother, Thyestes, for seducing his wife, by killing Thyestes' children and serving them to him at a banquet. On realizing that he had eaten his own children Thyestes fled in horror, and Atreus was cursed by the gods. In some versions Thyestes and Atreus are uncle and nephew.

8 The sun god's chariot was pulled across the sky by winged horses.

9 Seizing.

10 Egyptian goddess, wife of Osiris identified with the earth and moon.

11 Mercifulness.

12 Ulcerate, causing ill health.

13 Paris who, by stealing the beautiful Helen away from her Greek husband, Menelaus, initiated the Trojan war, in which the Greeks

defeated the Trojans and burned down the city of Troy.

14 More.

15 The list of names represents the Trojans who died in the war against the Greeks and whose red blood coloured the river Scamander. Priam, the king of Troy, was slain by the Greeks when they captured the city; his sons, Hector, Troilus and Deiphobus, were killed in the battle; Glaucus, a commander in the Trojan army, and Memnon, the king of Ethiopia who had come to Priam's aid, were also slaughtered by the Greeks.

16 Like the plague.

17 Changed the aspect of, distorted.

18 Sacred bull worshipped by the Egyptians.

19 Formerly.

20 The Roman god of wine and pleasure, his feasts were renowned for their wild and dissolute character.

21 Where Bacchus was raised and, hence, sacred to him.

22 The laments are roughly based upon the lists in Seneca's *Agamemnon* 664ff. and his *Hercules Oetaeus* 184–208.

23 The nightingale (Garnier names her as Philomela). The story behind this reference continues with the allusion to Procne at l. 98 below: Procne was married to Tereus, king of Thrace, but he conceived a desire for her sister, Philomela, and subsequently raped her. After the assault Tereus cut out Philomela's tongue so that she would not reveal the crime. But Philomela informed Procne by means of words woven into a tapestry. In retaliation, Procne stabbed her son Itys and served up his flesh in a dish for Tereus to eat unawares. Procne and Philomela then fled, but were soon overtaken by Tereus; the two sisters prayed to the gods and the three protagonists were transformed into birds. There is some uncertainty as to which sister became a nightingale and which a swallow, but here Philomela is the nightingale, the queen of the singing birds, while Procne becomes the swallow with her harsher chattering cry; Tereus was transformed into a hoopoo. The story was most commonly known from Ovid's *Metamorphoses* vi.459–679.

24 See note to l. 92 above.

25 Empty.

26 Halcyons are kingfishers, taking their name from Alcyone, Ceyx's wife, who, when he drowned, tried to kill herself and was transformed by the gods into a kingfisher. The source is Ovid, *Metamorphoses* xi.410–752.

27 The swan; Cycnus was metamorphosed into a swan while dying on the banks of the Menander river; here, Sidney refers to the legend that a swan sings as it dies.

28 Alarms.

29 The daughters of Phoebus Apollo, the Greek god of the sun, wept for the death of their brother Phaeton, who had died when he was unable to control his father's chariot of the sun and fell into the Padus river (the Po in Italy). As they grieved they were transformed into poplar trees and their tears became amber. The story comes from Ovid's *Metamorphoses* ii.31–332.

30 Niobe, who in classical myth, proud of her numerous progeny, boasted that she was superior to Leto (one of the Titans), who had borne only two children, Artemis and Apollo. Whereupon, the two latter gods murdered all of Niobe's offspring, leaving her to grieve; she was transformed by Zeus into a stone on Mount Sipylus which in the summer is said to shed tears. The story is derived from Ovid's *Metamorphoses* vi.145–317.

31 Myrrha fell in love with her father and deceived him into having sex with her. As a result of this incestuous union she became pregnant (with Adonis) and was transformed into a myrrh tree to hide her shame. She 'gave birth' to her son when her bark was cut open. The story is found in Ovid's *Metamorphoses* x.298–518.

32 The goddess Cybele fell in love with a young shepherd, Attis. However, he proved unfaithful to her and in anger she drove him mad; he finally castrated himself and as he lay dying was transformed into a fir tree. The priests of Cybele's cult likewise castrated themselves.

33 A nymph in Greek mythology who was transformed into an 'echo' by Hera for distracting her attention away from Zeus' sexual liaisons with constant chatter. Echo then fell in love with Narcissus, but her love was not returned and she grieved until nothing remained of her but her voice. See Ovid, *Metamorphoses* iii.338–400.

34 Although the overall structure of the play would suggest that the act should end after the chorus speaks, Sidney here follows Garnier in continuing Act II through to the next chorus intervention.

35 Flash down upon.

36 The River Nile.

37 Fortune.
38 Charon's barge conveyed the souls of the dead to the underworld.
39 Complain.
40 Spirit.
41 Scythians: a nomadic tribe inhabiting a region extending over a large part of European and Asiatic Russia.
42 See Argument, note to l. 3. The Parthians were renowned for their ability as horse-archers; they would attack quickly, but never engage in prolonged combat, instead preferring to retreat while shooting their arrows backwards upon the enemy.
43 North African nomads.
44 The following lines (231–6) are an example of stichomythia, that is, line-by-line rhyming dialogue. This rhetorical device was derived from Seneca and was commonly used in Renaissance tragedies. See also ll. 311–18 below.
45 Neptune, the god of the sea, supposedly built the walls of Troy (Ovid, *Metamorphoses* xi.199–206). The following reference (ll. 259–70) is to the Trojan war.
46 The eldest son of Priam, king of Troy, Hector was the leader of the Trojan forces and the bravest of the warriors at the siege of Troy.
47 Inciting.
48 Ruined.
49 Ruin.
50 Goodwill, friendship.
51 The Stygian lake (see above, l.62); the waters of the river Styx across which the souls of the dead were carried to the underworld.
52 Welfare, well-being.
53 See note above, ll. 231–6.
54 Inhuman, without the natural kindness and pity of human beings.
55 Escapes.
56 One of the major south Asian rivers, which was thought to be the wellspring of humankind.
57 Fearing, reverencing.
58 Pluto was the god of the underworld; his mansion therefore would be the house of the dead.
59 Albeit, although.
60 Alcestis who, in classical mythology, died in place of her husband, Admetus.
61 Moistened.
62 Artemesia was the wife of Mausolus, king of Caria (an Asian country); the Mausoleum was built as his tomb, and it became one of the seven wonders of the world.
63 Engrave.
64 To make or construct, probably in the sense of words, i.e. to tell of.
65 The site of the battle between Julius Caesar and Pompey at which Antony commanded the left wing.
66 River in Thessaly close to the site of the battle of Pharsalia.
67 The city of Mutina was held by Brutus against a siege undertaken by Antony.
68 Outlive.
69 Carried.
70 Innocent, harmless.
71 Maturing.
72 Large cask or barrel.
73 Posterity.
74 Befits.
75 Diminish.
76 One of the Fates, classical divinities who supposedly determined the lives of men and women; Clotho is often depicted with a spindle spinning out the thread of life.
77 Belongs.
78 Without cause.
79 Understanding.
80 In Egyptian religion, the jackal-headed god who conducted the souls of the dead to the region of immortal life.
81 Apis, the sacred bull of Egyptian religion, was the incarnation of Osiris, the most worshipped of Egypt's gods; he was the husband of Isis and represented male fertility.
82 Confirmation.
83 With even greater contentment.
84 The merit, that which deserves reward.
85 City in Macedonia where Octavius and Antony defeated Brutus and Cassius.
86 The ruler of the gods, armed with a thunderbolt, often became enamoured of mortal women.
87 Pale; as white as alabaster.
88 Dyes.
89 Ovid, *Metamorphoses* i.395–451.
90 The mud of the Nile.
91 Spew.
92 The chief river of central Italy on which the city of Rome stands.
93 Thick foam.
94 A proconsul was a governor or military commander of a Roman province; his symbol of office was a fasces, a bundle of rods enclosing an axe.

95 Pronounced as two syllables.
96 Pilfered.
97 Unchanging, i.e. end fastened to end.

ACT III

1 Stichomythia; see above, note to II.231–6.
2 A city in lower Egypt, lost to Octavius, supposedly with Cleopatra's collusion.
3 Thyrsus was appointed by Octavius to negotiate personally with Cleopatra, who honoured him conspicuously. Antony became jealous and had Thyrsus flogged and then sent back to Caesar.
4 Alexas of Laodicea was the servant of Cleopatra and active in Rome against Antony. Stylistically inspired by Seneca, *Agamemnon*, 589–92 and 598–600.
5 Stabs, pricks.
6 Albeit, although.
7 Destruction.
8 Modern Modena, the city where Brutus was besieged by Antony (44–43 BC).
9 The consuls were two annually elected magistrates who exercised supreme authority in the Roman republic; the title persisted into the empire, but ceased to carry any power. The two consuls mentioned here are Pansa and Hirtius, who fought against Antony at Mutina.
10 Revenge.
11 Antony is here invoking the absent Octavius Caesar.
12 See above, note to II.374–5.
13 Cassius and Brutus played leading roles in the conspiracy and assassination of Julius Caesar; they were defeated by the combined forces of Antony and Octavius at Philippi (42 BC).
14 Antony compares the fickle love of women with the constancy of men; see above, I.145–8.
15 Lucilius had saved Brutus' life by surrendering himself to Antony in the pretence that he was Brutus; Antony, impressed by Lucilius' honourable loyalty spared his life, and Lucilius henceforward became Antony's true servant.
16 Fortune was personified as a woman, Dame Fortuna, in the Renaissance, hence the reference to 'She' in the following line (107). This perpetuates the gender division of men as constant and women as fickle begun above, III. 99–109.
17 One million.
18 Shake hands, make a bargain.
19 Changes position (and disposition).
20 Rotating sphere; the goddess Fortune was often depicted with a constantly turning globe or wheel to signify the instability of fate.
21 Fixed position.
22 Octavius was the *adopted* son of Julius Caesar.
23 Towards you.
24 Antony had actually made this request, but it was denied by Octavius.
25 Lucius Antonius had conspired with Antony's wife, Fulvia, against Octavius, but had surrendered and been pardoned in 40 BC, becoming governor of Spain.
26 One of the triumvirs with Octavius and Antony, he was defeated by Octavius and stripped of his power, but Lepidus was allowed to retire with dignity to Rome.
27 Spain and Portugal.
28 Complain.
29 Express discontent.
30 Fortune.
31 Mars, the Roman god of war; Antony accuses Octavius of being inexperienced in, and afraid of, warfare.
32 In classical mythology the name given to Hercules, the son of Zeus by Alcmene; he was the most famous of all the Greek heroes and was renowned for his numerous victories and feats of strength.
33 The battles at Pharsalus and Philippi.
34 The following list describes the great heroes of Rome: Camillus (fl. 403–365 BC) was one of the renowned figures of the Roman republic; Claudius Marcellus (fl. 222–208 BC) was an illustrious Roman general and conqueror of Syracuse; Scipio Africanus (234–*c.* 183 BC) was one of the most famous Roman generals, who defeated Hannibal and conquered the Carthaginians; Julius Caesar (100–44 BC), apart from ruling Rome and her provinces, firmly established Roman rule in Gaul and extended Roman governance to Britain; Pompey (106–48 BC) was part of the first triumvirate, with Julius Caesar and Crassus, but he independently made numerous conquests in Asia.
35 Suffer.
36 Intertwined in combat.
37 Spears.
38 In Homer's *Iliad* Ulysses (Odysseus) is presented as energetic, forceful and, at times, cunning. In some of the tragedies, Euripides' for example, his cunning makes him unscrupulous.

39 Mutina; the two consuls, Pansa and Hirtius, were both killed supporting Octavius at the battle of Mutina against Antony. Octavius thereupon took control of their armies and returned to Rome, persuading the senate to elect him consul.
40 Lepidus: see above, note to III.174. Although Lepidus landed in Sicily to support Octavius in his battle to control the island, Octavius used the opportunity to subdue Lepidus and strip him of his power.
41 The goddess Fortune was often depicted with a turning wheel to signify the vacillations of fate.
42 The Roman goddess of war.
43 A frequenter of ladies' chambers, one who values the arts of love above all else.
44 Heedless.
45 The Roman goddess of love.
46 Spirits.
47 Deceptive.
48 Greedy, with a possible suggestion of lechery. Garnier's use of 'friande' (small cake, delicacy) in this context, suggests a lust for rich food, as well as other appetites.
49 Rob.
50 Marrow.
51 Foolish.
52 Sennacherib, who led a fruitless and self-indulgent expedition against Egypt, while back in Assyria the Medes began a rebellion and won their independence.
53 The most renowned hero of classical legend, Hercules performed twelve labours: the ones referred to here are: his capturing the oxen of Geryones; his descent into Hades to bring the dog Cerberus into the upperworld; his destruction of the nine-headed Lernean hydra; and, in order to obtain the golden apples of the Hesperides, he held the world on his shoulders while Atlas took the fruit for him. Hercules performed other heroic feats besides the twelve labours; the ones mentioned here are: his defeat of the giant Antaeus; his murder of his companion Lichas, who he wrongly believed had poisoned him; and his killing of the river god, Achelous, in a contest for Deianira, who then became Hercules' wife. However, the hero also succumbed to the power of love when he became the servant of Omphale, queen of Lydia. Omphale and Hercules were said to have exchanged clothes and occupations, so that he put on the garments of a woman and spun wool.
54 A cleft stick on which wool or flax was wound.
55 Gnawing, devouring.
56 Plaything.
57 Inspired by Seneca, *Agamemnon*, 589–92 and 598–600.
58 To keep our life from passing quickly.
59 Cowardly.
60 Superficial, empty.
61 Appearance.
62 A river in the underworld. The following description of hell is based upon Virgil, *Aeneid* vi.
63 A wig.
64 The boatman who conveys the souls of the dead to the underworld.
65 Souls of the deceased, ghosts.
66 Alecto was one of the three avenging furies who punished the misdeeds of humankind; they were usually depicted with snakes entwined in their hair and carrying torches.
67 An allusion to Cerberus, the monstrous, three-headed dog who guarded the entrance to the underworld.
68 The mythical personification of the north wind.
69 Irrational, rough, lacking control.
70 Tumult, battle.
71 Mad.
72 Jove, the mythical ruler of the gods, was often depicted carrying a thunderbolt.
73 Moist.
74 In confusion.
75 Lake Avernus was one of the doorways to the underworld; here it is referred to metaphorically as concealing death.
76 King of Egypt, Psammetichus returned from exile to defeat his foes and become sole monarch of the land.
77 King of Egypt, Amasis was renowned for his prosperous rule.
78 Macedonian Greek dynasty that ruled Egypt from the death of Alexander the Great in 322 BC until the Roman conquest, under Octavius, in 30 BC.
79 Formerly.

ACT IV

1 The Roman goddess of war.
2 Good fortune and misfortune.
3 Jove, in Roman mythology, the ruler of the gods; he was armed with a thunderbolt, and was believed to determine the course of all human affairs.
4 Sets up a statue.

5 Phoebus Apollo, the sun god.
6 The Garamante tribe were a people living in the southernmost region of north Africa.
7 The north wind.
8 Of a deep sky-blue, possibly with a suggestion of serenity.
9 Shields or bucklers.
10 Javelins, spears.
11 Glauce was one of the Nereides, in classical mythology, the marine nymphs of the Mediterranean; here her name is used generically.
12 The Tritons were mythical sea figures, who were half-man and half-fish.
13 The site of the decisive sea battle between Octavius and Antony.
14 Destruction.
15 The following allusion is to the legend of the Gigantes, a race of giants who grew from the earth on the spot where Uranus' blood had been spilt. They made an attack upon Mount Olympus, the seat of the gods, by piling two other mountains (Pelion and Ossa) upon its slopes. They were defeated and buried under volcanoes.
16 Two of the giants involved in the rebellion against the gods.
17 In classical mythology Phoebe was the moon goddess and sister to Phoebus (Apollo) the sun god; they were the children of Zeus and Leto (called Latona by the Romans). According to Plutarch (36) Antony named his two children by Cleopatra after the two divinities.
18 After finally deserting Octavia for Cleopatra, Antony honoured Cleopatra with various kingdoms he conquered in her name; one of these was Judaea, the king of which (Antigonus) he unceremoniously beheaded, giving the kingdom to Herod.
19 The following list denotes the countries given by Antony to Cleopatra (Plutarch 36).
20 A list of peoples and countries in Asia Minor conquered by the Romans.
21 Artabazus had originally betrayed Rome when he deserted with his troops in a battle against the Parthians. When Antony captured him, he was taken as a prisoner before Cleopatra in Alexandria, which was interpreted as an insult to Rome, where his capture should rightfully have been celebrated.
22 Mythical founder of Rome.
23 A celebrated city in north Africa, Carthage was a rival power to Rome; but the Carthaginians were defeated by the Romans in the three Punic wars (265–201 BC).
24 Gaul, a country roughly coinciding with present-day France, subjugated by Julius Caesar (59–50 BC).
25 Samnium was a country in central Italy that had been one of the first Roman conquests; the Samnites, however, also struggled unsuccessfully for their independence in 82 BC.
26 Pyrrhus (319–272 BC), the king of Epirus, was a renowned warrior who defeated the Romans on two occasions.
27 Mithridates the Great (fl. 120–63 BC), king of Pontus, was involved in three wars against the Romans; during the first one (88–84 BC) he massacred all the Roman citizens living in his state.
28 The Parthians ruled an empire from the Euphrates to the Indus, and fought a series of battles against the advancing Romans.
29 General good, here derived from being under the governance of Rome.
30 The temple of Jupiter/Jove in Rome, one of the most imposing buildings in the city playing an important part in the city's ceremonies and festivals.
31 Pitiful.
32 Pale.
33 Javelins, spears.
34 Agrippa had been in command of part of the fleet at Actium.
35 Funeral canopies or curtains.
36 Wrapped up, packed up.
37 The body; either alive or dead.
38 In disorder.
39 It seems to me.
40 Octavius' captain and envoy.
41 Strife.
42 Here used in the sense of 'to bathe in blood'.
43 Hard, unfeeling.
44 The god of the sea.
45 The dye 'Tyrian purple' was obtained from certain molluscs from the Phoenician coast near the city of Tyre.
46 Quarrelling, discord.
47 Pallas Athena, the Greek goddess of wisdom, was associated with the olive tree, a symbol of peace and fertility, unlike the bay (laurel) wreath, which was used by the Romans to signify military victory and martial prowess.
48 The god of war.
49 Janus, the Roman god usually depicted with two faces, had a temple in Rome whose doors were kept open in times of war and closed to signify peace.
50 Helmet.

51 Hook.
52 The Germans, Parthians, and inhabitants of Biscay (Spanish) are the future foes prophesied by the Roman soldiers.
53 The Parthians fought on horseback, pretending to retreat while simultaneously shooting backwards over their shoulders.
54 Spaniard's.

ACT V

1 Pernicious.
2 Torch, as in Cupid's torch, the fire of passion.
3 Capable of being buried.
4 The three Fates who in classical mythology spin out the destinies of human beings.
5 A river in the underworld.
6 The river which flowed around Tartarus in the underworld. The allusion is to Virgil's *Aeneid* vi.
7 It seems to me.
8 Pitiful.
9 The fields of the underworld where the souls of the dead wander; the allusion is to Virgil, *Aeneid* vi.
10 Rigid, rather than cold.
11 Locks of hair.
12 Chain of high mountains in Asia.
13 Chief of the Egyptian female divinities, and wife to Osiris.
14 Hercules, the most famous of all heroes in classical mytholgy; see above, III.201–2 and 347–72.
15 Niobe was metamorphosed into a stone on Mount Sipylus; see above, note to II.127–33.
16 Phaeton's sisters were transformed into alder (in some stories, poplar) trees; see above, II.121–6.
17 Calamitous.
18 Venus, the Roman goddess of love (Greek, Aphrodite); she was said to have been born from the sea off the coast of Cyprus near the town of Paphos. Julius Caesar had promoted the worship of Venus since he claimed descent from Aeneas, who was believed to be the son of Mars and Venus, and the founder of the Roman race. The allusion is to Virgil, *Aeneid* i.
19 Antony was the son of Julius Caesar's aunt, Julia, and therefore could claim descent from Aeneas as well as Caesar.
20 A person resembling a block of wood, i.e. inert, dead.
21 Sorrows and misfortune.
22 Love, close relationship.
23 Her brother Ptolemy, whom she defeated with the help of Julius Caesar.
24 From.
25 The scene is of Elysium, taken from Virgil's *Aeneid* vi.
26 Complaints.
27 Salt-water.

3 Elizabeth Cary, *The Tragedy of Mariam*

Introduction

1 This quotation is taken from Richard Simpson (ed.), *The Lady Falkland: Her Life: from a MS in the Imperial Archives at Lille*, p.9. There are two other biographies of Elizabeth Cary: Georgianna Fullerton's *Life of Elizabeth Lady Falkland (1582–1639)* and Kenneth B. Murdoch's *Sun at Noon: Three Biographical Sketches*, pp.6–40. Margaret Ferguson and Barry Weller append a new edition of *The Lady Falkland: Her Life* to their recent edition of *Mariam*, pp.183–275.
2 *State Papers* (Ireland), 63, 242/280; quoted in Barbara Kiefer Lewalski, *Writing Women in Jacobean England*, p.185.
3 Lady Denby was one of Elizabeth Cary's closest friends and had herself flirted with the idea of Catholicism; it is likely that her actions were not those of deliberate betrayal, but self-preservation in case she became implicated in the affair.
4 See above, note 1, and Ferguson and Weller, pp.1–2.
5 Dedications in: Michael Drayton, *Englands Heroicall Epistles* (1597); John Marston, *Works* (1633); and Richard More, *Englands Helicon* (1614).
6 Davies, *The Muses' Sacrifice*, p.5.
7 The following is a chronological list of Cary's works that remain extant: *Abraham Ortelius' 'Mirroir du Monde'* (*c.* 1600); *The Tragedy of Mariam* (pub. 1613); *The History of the Life, Reign, and Death of Edward II* (*c.* 1627–8); 'An Epitaph upon the death of the Duke of Buckingham by the Countesse of Faukland' (*c.* 1628); *The Reply of the Most Illustrious Cardinall of Perron, to the . . . King of Great Britaine* (1630). The other works are known about mainly through *The Lady Falkland: Her Life*. For a detailed account of Cary's canon see Ferguson and Weller, pp.10–16.

8 sig. C2; quoted in Betty Travitsky, *The Paradise of Women. Writings by Englishwomen of the Renaissance*, p.220.

9 For detailed critical discussion of the play see: Ferguson and Weller's exhaustive Introduction to their recent edition of the play, pp.1–59; Elaine V. Beilin, *Redeeming Eve: Women Writers of the English Renaissance*, pp.157–76; Betty Travitsky, 'The *Feme Covert* in Elizabeth Cary's *Mariam*' in Carole Levin and Jeanie Watson (eds), *Ambiguous Realities*, pp.184–96; and Lewalski, *Writing Women*, pp.179–211. For a more general treatment of Cary's contribution to Renaissance drama see: Tina Krontiris, 'Style and Gender in Elizabeth Cary's *Edward II*' in Anne M. Haselkorn and Betty S. Travitsky (eds), *The Renaissance Englishwoman in Print*, pp.137–53; and Maureen Quilligan, 'Staging Gender: William Shakespeare and Elizabeth Cary' in James Grantham Turner (ed), *Sexuality and Gender in Early Modern Europe*, pp.224–30.

10 Mary Sidney's *The Tragedy of Antonie* immediately precedes Cary's drama in this collection; see above, pp.13–42.

11 Thomas Lodge, *The Famous and Memorable Workes of Josephus* (1602).

12 Maurice Valency, *Tragedies of Herod and Mariamne*, pp.88–91, discussed by Travitsky in *Paradise of Women*, pp.212–16. For a further analysis of the play's indebtedness to Josephus, see Beilin, *Redeeming Eve*, pp.165–73.

13 Dympna Callaghan points to the issue of race in the play as a further way in which Mariam appears to be idealized in that the queen's 'fairness' is persistently emphasized, while Salome is referred to as dark-skinned ('Re-Reading Elizabeth Cary's *The Tragedie of Mariam, Faire Queene of Jewry*' in Margo Hendricks and Patricia Parker (eds), *Women, "Race," and Writing in the Early Modern Period*, pp.163–77).

14 Ferguson and Weller suggest that the importance of divorce to the play occurs because of Cary's interest in Henry VIII's divorce from Catherine of Aragon in order to marry Anne Boleyn (pp.30–5). Although they produce persuasive arguments for this, there was nearly a century between the historical event and the writing of the play, and the other works they cite as being influenced by the event were all published in the 1540s.

15 The comparison between Salome and Graphina is discussed in Beilin, *Redeeming Eve*, pp.167–9. Catherine Belsey discusses Salome's role in the play in *The Subject of Tragedy*, pp.171–5.

16 Quoted in Lewalski, *Writing Women*, p.187.

17 See ibid., pp.190–4.

18 Germaine Greer *et. al.* (eds), *Kissing the Rod*, pp.54–60.

19 See Ferguson and Weller, pp.41–3; Quilligan, '*Staging Gender*'; and Travitsky, *The Paradise of Women*, p.213.

20 Simpson, *The Lady Falkland*, p. 9.

The Tragedy of Mariam

TO DIANA'S ETC. / NAMES OF THE SPEAKERS / THE ARGUMENT

1 The sonnet is dedicated to a 'Mistress Elizabeth Cary' who was probably the sister-in-law of Elizabeth Cary the dramatist and author of *Mariam*. The latter was the wife of Sir Henry Cary, who is represented in the sonnet as the sun, and the former was the wife of Sir Henry's brother, Philip Cary, who is depicted as the moon.

2 The sun god in Greek mythology.

3 A place on the opposite side of the globe; as the sun sets on one horizon, so the moon rises on the facing skyline. Also an allusion to Sir Henry Cary, who was absent on military service (1602–6).

4 One of the names ascribed to the goddess of the moon; a female Phoebus.

5 The sun.

6 Like the moon.

7 Cary's first play, now lost, was set in Syracuse, Sicily; the line suggests that it was probably dedicated to Henry Cary.

8 Illuminate.

9 The sun god in Roman mythology.

10 The moon goddess in Roman mythology.

11 The 1613 edition has 'Salome', which is a typographical error.

12 The 1613 edition omits this character.

13 Syrian.

14 Mariam was the granddaughter of Hyrcanus II; Cary's mistake is derived from *Antiquities* (I.614). The relationship is corrected below.

15 Herod had Mariam's brother, Aristobolus, killed when they went swimming together. Some of Herod's servants ducked the young man under the water pretending it to be a game, but they held him under until he drowned. Herod also had Hyrcanus II,

Mariam's grandfather, put to death on a charge of treason (see, *Antiquities* I.596–8 and 608–10).

16 Marcus Antonius (c. 82–30 BC), the triumvir, who with Octavian and Lepidus, ruled the Roman world; close associate of Caesar and lover of Cleopatra.

17 Octavian (also Gaius Octavius, 63 BC – AD 14), with Mark Antony and Lepidus, one of the triumvirate who ruled Rome, but later known as Caesar Augustus, the first of the Roman emperors.

ACT I

1 Julius Caesar (Plutarch, *Caesar*, bk XLVIII).

2 Line two syllables short.

3 Prevent.

4 Freedom of desire; Herod has tried to assure Mariam's faithfulness by restricting her freedom. Weller and Ferguson suggest that the repetition of 'range' (to roam) implies a pun on heart/hart, thereby evoking the conventional Renaissance link between hunting and amorous desire.

5 Bore.

6 Tears, which dry up, that is, become 'unmoistened'.

7 Dunstan suggests 'louelyest', i.e. 'loveliest'.

8 Pity.

9 Spirit.

10 Imprisoned, entombed.

11 The 1613 edition reads 'maide'; Dunstan suggests 'minde'.

12 Inseparable.

13 Forerunner, precursor.

14 Distress be seen, be evident.

15 Murderer's. The 1613 edition has 'murthers'; Dunstan suggests 'murthrer's'.

16 Person.

17 Edom was the land of the Edomites, who were supposedly descended from Esau and, therefore, the foes of Jacob's descendants who inhabited Israel.

18 The descendants of Jacob, who wrestled the birthright away from his elder brother Esau and thus became the founder of the Israelites (Genesis 25: 24–34). Thus, Alexandra is claiming god-given ancestry for her son, but condemns Herod as a usurper.

19 Become king of the Jews. David, despite being the youngest son of Jesse, was made king of the Jews (2 Samuel). Although he can therefore be seen to overturn the order of primogenture, like Jacob, he is generally regarded as the model of a divinely appointed king.

20 The Jewish race.

21 1613 edition has 'fain'd'; Dunstan suggests 'fam'd'.

22 Hyrcanus was one of the last descendants of the noble Hasmonean dynasty, who ruled Judea 142–63 BC. This dynasty was usurped by Herod.

23 Wretch.

24 'Edom' may mean 'red'; see Genesis 25: 30.

25 Turned.

26 One of the vestments of a Jewish priest, it was slit at the sides and fastened with a girdle at the waist.

27 Dunstan suggests 'Herod'.

28 Spasmodic inclinations.

29 Perhaps.

30 1613 edition has 'Nuntio', but Mariam is clearly the speaker in this instance.

31 Not at all.

32 Third king of Israel (*c.* 961–922 BC), celebrated for his wisdom.

33 One of the famous kings of the Hasmonean dynasty from whom Mariam was descended. However, it could also be read as 'Alexandra's', since Mariam was her daughter. Both meanings affirm that Mariam is direct heir to the throne.

34 In defiance of, or in opposition to, Herod's power.

35 The personification of good fortune.

36 Mourning robe.

37 Tolerate, endure.

38 Portrait.

39 In this speech (ll. 161–98) Alexandra tells how she sent a double portrait, of Mariam and her brother Aristobolus, to Antony, who finds the girl and boy equally attractive. Cary here diverges from her source, Josephus, who writes that Antony sent only for Aristobolus, to emphasize heterosexual desire.

40 Favourites'.

41 Carried.

42 Plentiful.

43 Thinks fit.

44 1613 edition has 'leeke'; Dunstan suggests 'seeke', while Ferguson and Weller have 'like'.

45 Gone alone.

46 Cleopatra (69–30 BC) was the queen of Egypt and renowned for her beauty.

47 Thinned, withered.

48 A market-place.

49 Dunstan suggests 'apart', while Ferguson and Weller prefer 'past' (surpassed).

50 Let us withdraw.
51 Is it.
52 1613 edition has 'discontent'; the plural form makes more sense in relation to the rhyme scheme.
53 Anger.
54 Inflammatory.
55 Half-caste: half Jewish and half Edomite.
56 Reproach, taunt.
57 Here the symbolic father of all humanity.
58 Open.
59 The 1613 edition has 'suspitious'; Dunstan suggests, 'suspitions'.
60 1613 edition has 'Josephus'; Dunstan suggests, 'Josephs', which is more faithful to the metre.
61 Use.
62 Judge.
63 See Matthew 7: 17–20.
64 1613 edition has 'allyes'; Dunstan suggests 'all eyes'.
65 Hindrances.
66 The Renaissance phrase 'to stand upon one's points' meant to insist upon a strict code of behaviour, or, more generally, to be punctilious.
67 A blush.
68 A formal or legal document which entitled man and wife to separate; in the Bible it may only be initiated by men (Deuteronomy 24: 1).
69 Salome's attitude appears somewhat in advance of her time, in that she sees marriage as repressing women and divorce as a road to freedom. However, she only wishes to leave Constabarus in order to marry Silleus. Although she had only been married for a short time when she wrote *Mariam*, Cary was herself to become estranged from her husband.
70 The name 'Baba' occurs in other forms in the play ('Babas'/'Babus'); we use 'Baba' throughout. Weller and Ferguson prefer 'Babas'.
71 Constabarus has concealed the sons of Baba; see below, Act II.87–214.
72 Place.
73 Constabarus had tried to escape Herod's rule by asking Cleopatra to intercede for him with Antony; on hearing of this supposed 'disloyalty' Herod threatened to execute Constabarus, and spared him only because Salome begged for his life.
74 Bound fast.
75 Inborn.
76 Moses'.
77 1613 edition has 'do'es', i.e. 'do is'. To align with the metre the two words must be said as one syllable.
78 1613 edition has 'Solleus'.
79 To dash, to beat against.
80 Crown.
81 King Obodas of Arabia was a weak monarch who allowed his affairs to be managed by Silleus (*Antiquities* II.21). Hence, Silleus acts as his presence on earth in the same way that an oracle tells the wishes of the gods.
82 Ferguson and Weller suggest that, since the sense of ll. 354–6 is difficult to follow, there may be some textual corruption at this point.
83 1613 edition has 'home'; Dunstan suggests 'whom'.
84 Hush.
85 Someone is prowling like a wolf nearby, and therefore able to overhear the conversation.
86 The fortress of the pre-Israelite city of Jerusalem, conquered by David and made his capital; a place of sacred ceremony.
87 Constabarus' description of how unchaste women were condemned is representative of conventional Renaissance attitudes towards women; the ideal was chastity, silence and obedience to their husband's will. This particular allusion comes from Proverbs 12: 4.
88 Dunstan suggests adding 'to' or 'by', which would make the line metrically regular.
89 Babus.
90 Makes my anger stay within limits.
91 Do not care for.
92 The social and cultural roles of men and women in the Renaissance were generally considered to be natural and immutable. The particular inversion of nature suggested by Constabarus was commonly used in the pamphlet wars about the virtues and vices of women during the early seventeenth century. Two important texts which relate to the following speech are *Hic Mulier* (1620) and *Haec Vir* (1620), the former attacking masculine women and the latter condemning feminine men.
93 Turned upside-down.
94 1613 edition has 'beastes, swine', but 'swim' (suggested by Dunstan) makes more sense in relation to the previous 'fishes graze'.
95 Mounts upwards.
96 People, men or women.
97 Joshua, the famed military leader of the Old Testament, swore peace with the Gibeonites, then condemned them to perpetual servitude.

98 The Ark of the Covenant, containing the stone tablets on which the Ten Commandments were written, was a box of acacia wood with a cover of gold, at the opposite ends of which were two winged cherubim.
99 Egypt.
100 A reference to the last of the ten plagues with which God smote the Egyptians (Exodus 12: 29); 'the land of Ham' is a biblical term for Egypt. Moses did not personally slay the first-born, but he was instrumental in the release of the Jewish nation from their Egyptian captors in which the plagues play an essential role. The Israelite houses were spared the plague since the Lord 'passed over' them, hence leading to the Feast of Passover when the 'holy lamb' is eaten.
101 Mosaic Law.
102 1613 edition has 'vowd'; Dunstan suggests 'vow'.
103 As opposed to 'farewell': see below, ll. 471 and 472.
104 Wreck, destruction.
105 To come upon by chance.
106 Foolish.
107 Contentment.
108 Eagerly.
109 Leap.
110 1613 edition has 'Of'; Dunstan suggests 'If'.

ACT II

1 Cary probably took the name from 'Glaphyra', who is not loved by Pheroras, but used by him to stir up enmity against Herod in *Antiquities* II.20.
2 Pheroras' inability to cry parallels Mariam's lack of tears at the beginning of Act I.
3 By violence.
4 Pheroras was betrothed to Herod's young daughter (*Antiquities* II.19).
5 Dunstan suggests adding this word in order to regulate the metre.
6 Benefited.
7 With this.
8 Begrudged.
9 The followers of the God of Love.
10 Inclined.
11 Wondered at.
12 Pun on 'weaker vessel', a biblical term for a woman which was commonly used in the Renaissance (1 Peter 3: 7).
13 Then don't all these favours require careful thought.
14 Repaid.
15 Careful consideration.
16 Firm.
17 Exult.
18 Receive.
19 Dare.
20 An earlier time of idyllic perfection in classical mythology.
21 Nobly, as well as without reserve.
22 During the Renaissance, the relationship between David (Jesse's son) and Jonathan (Saul's son) was seen as the ideal model of friendship (1 Samuel 18 – 2 Samuel 1).
23 Buried alive.
24 Obtained.
25 The cuckoo is well known for laying its eggs in the nests of other birds. When the young cuckoo hatches it proceeds to eject any of the true eggs and/or fledglings from the nest.
26 Dunstan suggests 'safety'.
27 Babus.
28 Forewarning.
29 To be set free.
30 1613 edition reads 'leare'; Dunstan suggests 'feare'.
31 Broad sword.
32 This line is two syllables short.
33 Began.
34 1613 edition has 'live'; Dunstan suggests 'lie' which allows for the rhyme with 'I', l. 177 above.
35 Gaius Octavius (also, Caesar Augustus) was the adopted nephew of Julius Caesar.
36 Julius Caesar's.
37 Features. Physiognomy was the art of telling characters or fortunes according to facial attributes.
38 Anger.
39 1613 edition has 'set', which is probably a typographical error.
40 Prophet.
41 Coward's.
42 The line is hypermetrical; Ferguson and Weller suggest that 'a' is an unauthorized insertion.
43 1613 edition has 'Your'; Dunstan suggests 'You'.
44 Give room to her. Ferguson and Weller suggest 'stoop'.
45 The Feast of the Passover, during which unleavened bread (i.e. flat, that which has not fermented) was eaten (Leviticus 23 and Exodus 12).
46 Before.
47 1613 edition has 'oath'; Dunstan suggests 'oaths'.

48 Kneeling.
49 Previous.
50 It makes no great difference in what way.
51 1613 edition has 'expectation'; Dunstan suggests 'exception'.
52 Anything.
53 1613 edition has 'Salom', but the metre suggests 'Salome' to be a more accurate reading.
54 Ready, willing.
55 Hack, cut.
56 ll. 315–34: an attack drawn from the early seventeenth-century pamphlet debate which enumerated charges against and defences for women. Similar material may be found in Joseph Swetnam's *The Arraignment of Lewde, idle, froward and unconstant women* (1615). See above, I.396 and 421, and below, IV.309–49.
57 Envy you.
58 It would be as impossible to try to hold the wind as to make Salome stay. This is again a common attack against women during the period.
59 A tomb, but in the Bible specifically used to refer to someone whose fair outward appearance masks inner corruption.
60 1613 edition has 'filed' which gives the sense of 'defiled' as well as replete.
61 See Matthew 23: 27.
62 Name.
63 Begins.
64 Physiognomy, face.
65 Like, choose.
66 This line is hypermetrical; Ferguson and Weller suggest condensing the first two words to 'Thou'st'.
67 Predict.
68 Listen.
69 A pun on life (to breathe) and a pause (to take a breath).
70 1613 edition has 'I, I, they fight', which is probably a corruption of the original stage direction. However, it is important to note that Cary included information for performance as it confirms she envisaged her play being acted, which would have been unusual for a woman playwright of her time.
71 Finds no way of obtaining.
72 Dunstan suggests 'too'.
73 Open.
74 Haste.
75 That have already made their judgement.
76 See Deuteronomy 16: 19.
77 Abate, diminish.
78 Offer any arguments against.
79 Succeed.

ACT III

1 Does not aspire to, as well as, not influenced by.
2 You are.
3 Expect.
4 Preparations.
5 Affect with pain, torture.
6 Line short by two syllables.
7 In losing.
8 Taken.
9 Marry.
10 Protection.
11 1613 edition has 'her'; Dunstan suggests 'here'.
12 A region probably in south-west Arabia (Genesis 10), famous in the Old Testament for its gold, but also for all exotic and specialized goods, including frankincense.
13 An ancient Phoenician seaport, renowned for its magnificent buildings.
14 Dunstan suggests 'doom'd'.
15 Dunstan suggests 'we'.
16 Dunstan suggests 'our'.
17 See above, note to I.84.
18 Countenance.
19 A grey-blue colour, as when affected by fear or dismay.
20 1613 edition does not ascribe l. 124 to Mariam, but it is clearly her speaking.
21 Says.
22 A stickler was one who stood by to part combatants when victory could be determined without bloodshed.
23 Away from.
24 Says, it is said.
25 Plotted and joined together.
26 From classical mythology: comprising the heavens (ruled by Zeus), the seas (ruled by Poseidon), and the underworld (ruled by Hades).
27 Self-restraint, mental balance.
28 Desert.
29 An allusion to the sword which was suspended by a single hair over Damocles' head; Dionysius punished the overly effusive Damocles in this manner to show him the instability of fate.
30 Commands.
31 1613 edition has 'Alexanders'; Dunstan suggests 'Alexandras'.
32 A reference to the fort built by Herod, but renamed 'David's Tower' in the eleventh century by the crusaders.

33 An allusion to the plagues of Egypt and to the parting of the Red Sea (Exodus 10 and 14).
34 Joshua made the sun stand still in one of his battles (Joshua 10: 12–13); see below, IV.16.
35 Reversed in its course.
36 An allusion to Cupid the winged god of love, who often represented erotic desire in Renaissance iconography.
37 A tablet on which the sacred laws were inscribed (Exodus 31:18).
38 The Chorus affirms the Renaissance concept of an ideal woman as not only being chaste, but also appearing to be so, which is relevant to both Mariam and Salome in this Act. However, the definition of that chastity, which forbids women to 'be by public language graced' (l. 240), implies that Cary is aware of the risk she runs herself of being condemned for writing a play.
39 Endure.
40 Only.
41 Private.
42 Had she not directed herself to this.

ACT IV

1 The line is a syllable short; Dunstan suggests adding 'How?', which is also adopted by Ferguson and Weller.
2 Soon.
3 Cover.
4 Candle; Herod is referring to the sun.
5 In one of his battles Joshua makes the sun and moon stand still (Joshua 10: 12–13).
6 Rome.
7 Roman magistrates who superintended the city's games and pageants.
8 Wife of Octavius Caesar.
9 Herod addresses ll. 33–6 to his eyes.
10 Herod's brother who, when captured by the Parthians, committed suicide.
11 Alike.
12 1613 edition has 'you'; Dunstan suggests 'your'.
13 Babus.
14 1613 edition has 'Salom', but 'Salome' agrees metrically.
15 Spirit; 1613 edition has 'spirit', but should be read as 'sprite' to rhyme with 'requite' (l. 83).
16 Clothes.
17 Fine, unclouded.
18 An allusion to Josephus' account of how Herod raided the tomb of David and Solomon after Mariam's death.
19 Never.
20 Weller and Ferguson submit that the gap in the rhyme scheme suggests that a line is missing.
21 Liked.
22 Aristobolus.
23 Dunstan notes that the rhyme-line is missing.
24 Perverse, rebellious; a term often used during the Renaissance to describe women who did not obey their husbands, as in Joseph Swetnam's *The Arraignment of Lewde, idle, froward, and unconstant women* (1617).
25 Strange imaginings.
26 Rely.
27 Scold, reprove.
28 Plot.
29 1613 edition has 'passion'; Dunstan suggests 'poison', which makes more sense in narrative terms.
30 It was believed in the Renaissance that a 'white devil', that is one which is concealed, was worse than a black devil, that is one which is obviously evil.
31 A herb mentioned in the Bible; it was used in the Jewish religion for ceremonial purification.
32 Reveal secrets.
33 Waited.
34 The inner substance of a plant, referring to the resin of the cedar tree.
35 The cedar wood was prized for its smell and texture, and was often used for elaborately carved boxes, but its resin is poisonous.
36 1613 has 'never' inserted at this point; Dunstan suggests that the word be omitted, which makes sense grammatically as well as metrically.
37 The image of an ever-turning wheel commonly represented the instability of fate, which showed that those who resided at the top of the wheel (i.e. had good fortune) would soon fall from their positions of eminence.
38 Pitch black.
39 Make a fool of.
40 1613 edition has 'heauy'; Dunstan suggests 'heaunly'.
41 In spite of.
42 1613 edition has 'looke'; Dunstan suggests 'locke'.
43 Dispatched.
44 Who leave.
45 Ordered.
46 1613 edition has 'boue'; Dunstan suggests 'loue'.

47 Mariam is given a Christ-like identity as the Lamb of God (John 1: 29).
48 Black.
49 1613 edition has 'caules'; Dunstan suggests 'causeles'.
50 A reference to Abel; see Genesis 4: 10.
51 Pages.
52 Possibly the book described in Daniel 12: 1–4.
53 Achitophel, a counsellor to David, betrayed the king and joined forces with his son, Absalom. When Absalom subsequently altered his allegiance and accepted the counsel of Hushai, Achitophel hanged himself.
54 1613 edition inserts 'not' at this point; Dunstan suggests the word is omitted and 'didst' changed to 'didest' to retain the metre.
55 Vulgar and low trade, with the sense of 'traffickers', those who carry out such commercial negotiations.
56 1613 text has ''Tis'; Dunstan suggests 'Thus'; we have followed Ferguson and Weller who suggest 'This'.
57 1613 text has 'your'; Dunstan suggests 'our'; we have followed Ferguson and Weller, who suggest 'her'.
58 1613 edition has 'Were by'; this is probably a typographic error since 'Whereby' makes more sense.
59 For this ideal of friendship see John 15: 13.
60 Person. What follows is an archetypal attack upon women drawn from the debate literature of the English Renaissance, on the virtues and vices of women; see, for example, Edward Gosynhill, *The Schoolhouse of Women* (*c.* 1541) and Joseph Swetnam, *The Arraignment of Lewde, idle, froward and unconstant women* (1615). Constabarus is presented as a stereotypical 'woman-hater', while Salome may be seen as the conventional 'shrew'. See also: I.261–324, 396 and 421, II.315–334.
61 Here Constabarus groups all women together as a female commonwealth.
62 Chase away.
63 An allusion to the common belief that hyenas weep hypocritically for their prey.
64 Opposed to.
65 Inwardly.
66 1613 edition has 'many'; Dunstan suggests 'man', which is metrically correct.
67 An allusion to God's covenant with mankind that there should not be another flood (Genesis 9: 11).
68 Inconstant, fickle.
69 1613 edition has 'You'; Dunstan suggests 'Your'.
70 Perverse; see note to IV.141.
71 1613 edition has 'he', which is clearly a typographical error for 'she'.
72 Foolishness.
73 The curse of Cham (Ham) was that of servitude; this was brought about when he saw his father, Noah, lying naked in a drunken stupor and, instead of covering him, Cham went to tell his two brothers (Genesis 9: 21–7). Here Constabarus conflates Cham's sin with Eve's (original sin), pronouncing women to be subservient to men (Genesis 3: 16).
74 Supplied.
75 Those who disturb quiet.
76 In spite of all.
77 Curtal-axe; a broad cutting sword.
78 Repel.
79 Regret.
80 Broad sword. 1613 edition has 'fanchions' which is probably a typographical error.
81 Blunt.
82 Latin: once, formerly.
83 An end.
84 A lime-bush was coated with a sticky substance so that birds would become entangled and therefore caught. The allusion to crimson suggests the use of cosmetics to colour the cheeks in order to appear more alluring. The metaphor is sustained throughout the subsequent exchange between Herod and Salome.
85 Stain.
86 A mass of hair; an allusion to the highly prized golden fleece of classical legend.
87 1613 edition has 'Troy' and 'Helens', which are probably typographical errors.
88 Helen of Troy, renowned for her legendary beauty, but also the cause of the Greeks' shame (she was seduced by the Trojan prince, Paris); she also precipitated the downfall of Troy when it was burned by the Greeks in revenge.
89 Line is two syllables short, emphasizing Herod's ironic tone.
90 Cosmetic powder; the 'beauty' of Mariam's words is not natural, instead relying upon the artifice of make-up. Ferguson and Weller suggest the allusion is to gunpowder.
91 Herod repeats the accusation made by the chorus at the end of Act III, that female chastity should be equated with silence, and

that women who spoke freely to others should be regarded as promiscuous. While the charge is made against Mariam, the judgement obviously has significance for a female author who does speak to 'every stranger's ear'.

92 Matters.

93 Black.

94 A fixed star; it was thought that some stars were fixed, even though the majority moved.

95 Chatter, prattle.

96 A black-skinned African (with depreciatory force).

97 Cosmetic devices.

98 Deceiving.

99 Unjust. Lines 472–4 are ambiguous; 'you both' could as well refer to Sohemus and Mariam as to 'Earth and heaven'.

100 David, known for his musical talent, seduced Bathsheba while her husband, Uriah the Hittite, was away at war. When she became pregnant, David surreptitiously arranged for Uriah to die at the siege of Rabbath, and afterwards the king married Bathsheba (2 Samuel 11).

101 Solomon, who was renowned for his numerous wives and concubines (1 Kings 11: 3).

102 Ahasuerus, the Persian king, mounted a splendid banquet and called his wife (Vashti) to show herself to his guests in order to impress them with her beauty. When she refused, he sought for another wife, finally choosing the humble Jewish maiden, Esther (Esther 1–2).

103 Balance.

104 Lure.

105 Unfortunate.

106 Follows upon.

107 In classical mythology Ate was the goddess of all evil who aroused jealousy among the gods. Jupiter dragged her away by the hair and sent her to dwell on earth where she was thought to incite people to wickedness, precipitating conflict among them.

108 Cary herself used this same method of dispelling grief (*Life of Lady Falkland*, p.196).

109 1613 edition has 'At'; Dunstan suggests 'As'.

110 Stories concerning the Egyptian queen, Cleopatra, characterize her as powerful, but deceitful and self-interested.

111 Test, make trial of.

112 The following use of anaphora to describe Cleopatra's face indicates Mariam's ironic tone.

113 Venus, traditionally born from the sea-foam on the shores of Paphos, near the south-west coast of Cyprus.

114 Taken; i.e. mistaken.

115 Destruction.

116 Carelessly.

117 Takes account of.

118 Fortune.

119 The first of the Old Testament matriarchs and wife of Abraham; hence, the female equivalent of Abraham's bosom (meaning to be in heaven) is said to be Sara's lap.

120 Giving birth to.

121 Possibly the cup of God's fury (Isaiah 51: 17) or of God's wrath (Revelation 16: 19).

122 1316 edition has 'Gerarim'; Dunstan has 'Gerizim', which makes more sense since Mount Gerazim was, according to Samaritan tradition, the peak on which Abraham sacrificed his son Isaac.

123 Burdened.

124 Seldom. Ferguson and Weller alter the punctuation of this line to read: 'Great hearts are task'd beyond their power but seld,'.

125 Treated leniently.

126 A reference to the 'marriage debt', where the couple 'owe' one another sexual gratification (1 Corinthians 7: 3–5).

127 Dunstan suggests 'In', but we have followed Ferguson and Weller who suggest that the original 'Is' may be retained if l. 660 is end-stopped.

ACT V

1 Chosen.

2 It had.

3 Phoenix's nest; the phoenix, a mythical Arabian bird, makes a nest every five hundred years, and immolates itself. From the ashes of the nest arises a new phoenix; hence, the bird became a symbol of resurrection. Metaphorically, the sun admires Mariam in that she goes to her death phoenix-like. Moreover, the image of the phoenix rising from its ashes was often used as a metaphor for Christ's resurrection. Thus, Mariam's death makes her into a Christ-like martyr; this allegory is reinforced below, V.77–8 and 103–10.

4 1613 edition has 'darke'; Dunstan suggests 'darken' for metrical reasons.

5 Flatterer.

6 1613 edition ascribes these two words to Nuntio, but to make sense they must be spoken by Herod.

7 Precisely.
8 This line is two syllables short.
9 Swans reputedly sang as they died.
10 1613 edition has 'made'; Dunstan suggests 'mad'.
11 In the sense of Mariam's speech, but also an allusion to the order for her death.
12 It is predicted that Mariam will rise Christ-like after three days (see: Matthew 27: 63–4). See above, V.26.
13 1613 edition has 'divided', but 'divide' makes more sense in terms of both metre and rhyme.
14 Is it.
15 Like Judas Iscariot (Matthew 27: 3–5); part of the representation of Mariam as a Christ-like martyr (see above, V.26).
16 1613 edition has 'she'; Dunstan suggests 'he'.
17 See Proverbs 31: 10.
18 Crushed, smashed to pieces.
19 Half, portion.
20 Rebuked.
21 Second son of Adam and Eve, slain by his brother and renowned for his righteous character; he was often identified as a prefiguration of Christ (Genesis 4: 1–15).
22 Dress, garments.
23 Quiet.
24 See Proverbs 12: 4.
25 Endure.
26 Grandmother, or more generally a female ancestor.
27 The wife of Abraham and the first matriarch in the Old Testament (Genesis 12 and 20).
28 A remote ancestress, or an aged woman.
29 Dark, without life.
30 1613 edition has 'did'; Dunstan suggests 'died'.
31 Most commonly a ruddy, fat-faced girl, but, used in conjunction with 'dowdy', more probably a common wench, possibly a prostitute.
32 A shabbily dressed woman, a common and vulgar female.
33 In classical mythology each planet was supposedly governed by a different god; e.g. the planet Mars was controlled by the god Mars.
34 Pretend to, represent in fiction. Ferguson and Weller point out that the extant copies of *Mariam* are equally divided between those that read 'faine' (feign) and those which have 'fame'. We have followed their decision to adopt 'feign' on the grounds that it follows the drift of Herod's speech more closely.
35 The god Saturn was the Roman deity equivalent to the Greek Kronos and the ruler of the gods until he was usurped by his son Jupiter (Zeus). However, in astrological lore the planet Saturn (governed by the god) was associated with melancholy and gloom, as well as with a harsh and unforgiving wisdom; it was said to confer these qualities on those born under its planetary influence.
36 Another name for the Roman god Jupiter, the ruler of the gods after he dethroned his father Saturn. Generally, the supreme god.
37 One of the beautiful women seduced by Jupiter, who on this occasion disguised himself as a swan.
38 The amours between Mars and Venus, the Roman gods of war and love, were popular subjects in Renaissance literature; here Mariam's beauty is compared favourably with Venus' legendary attractions.
39 The sun.
40 Remain stationary, without action.
41 The Greek god Apollo was the divine protector of physicians as well as being the deity of the sun (Sol).
42 A quack.
43 The goddess Venus whose beauty was supposedly without equal.
44 The Greek deity Hermes was messenger to the gods and was also renowned for his articulacy and intelligence; he was, hence, the bestower of wit.
45 Possibly a reference to Cynthia, the goddess of the moon, since she is alluded to again at l. 234 below. She was also the goddess of chastity.
46 Untimely.
47 Venus; see ll. 219 and 223 above.
48 Mercury was the Roman name for the Greek god Hermes; see l. 224 above.
49 Body.
50 Herod is addressing himself.
51 Cain, the elder son of Adam and Eve, slew his brother Abel thereby committing the first murder (Genesis 3: 9–16).
52 This refers to the rule of the unity of time adopted in classical drama (see above, Introduction, p. 47).
53 States of mind, moods.
54 The future.

4 Robert White, *Cupid's Banishment*

Introduction

1 Richard Browne was the grandson of Richard Browne, Clerk of the Green Cloth in 1604, and son of Christopher Browne, Esq., of Deptford, where the Ladies Hall was located. Browne became eminent as a foreign diplomat and statesman, and was created baronet in 1649. He resided in the manor-house of Sayes Court in the parish of St Nicholas, Deptford, which he bequeathed to his daughter and her husband, John Evelyn.

2 On the relationship between Queen Anne and the Countess of Bedford see Barbara Kiefer Lewalski, *Writing Women in Jacobean England*, pp. 22–4, *passim*. See also R.C. Bald, *John Donne*, pp. 170–80, *passim*.

3 F.P. Wilson, 'Dramatic Records in the Declared Accounts of the Office of Works, 1560–1640', *Malone Society Collections*, 10 (1977), 27–8.

4 Andrew J. Sabol, *Four Hundred Songs and Dances from the Stuart Masque*, vol. 3, 285. Apparently singers were regularly drawn from the King's Music.

5 Deptford is probably best remembered as the place in which Christopher Marlowe was slain and buried. The earliest Deptford records date from the eighteenth century, and are of no assistance in learning more about Ladies Hall. In *The History of Deptford*, Nathan Dews identifies the school with a thoroughfare 'leading from the Globe Inn to the Water-gate' (p. 177).

6 G.E. Bentley, *The Jacobean and Caroline Stage*, vol. 5, pp. 1257–8.

7 C.E. McGee (ed.), 'Cupid's Banishment: A Masque Presented to Her Majesty by Young Gentlewomen of the Ladies Hall, Deptford, May 4, 1617', *Renaissance Drama*, n.s. 19 (1988), 227–64.

8 Two excellent discussions of the basic characteristics of the masque, from its beginning in the Tudor period through their sophistication at the Jacobean and Caroline courts, can be found in the introduction to David Lindley (ed.), *The Court Masque*, pp. 1–15, and Jerzy Limon, *The Masque of Stuart Culture*, pp. 17–91. Also considered standard sources are Stephen Orgel, *The Jonsonian Masque*; Stephen Orgel and Roy Strong, *Inigo Jones: The Theatre of the Stuart Court*; and Enid Welsford, *The Court Masque*.

9 *Emblemata* (Paris, 1542) and *Imprese* (Lyons, 1551), cited as 'The Power of Love'.

10 *Emblemata* (Paris, 1542) and *Imprese* (Lyons, 1551), cited as 'The Scholar Captured by Eros'.

11 *Emblemata* (Padua, 1621) cited as 'Anteros, the Love of Virtue, overcoming the other Cupid' (Emblem 111).

12 *Emblemata* (Padua, 1621), cited as 'Sweet Things Sometimes Become Bitter' (Emblem 112).

13 *Emblemata* (Padua, 1621), cited as 'On a Statue of Eros' (Emblem 114).

14 Welsford, *The Court Masque*, p. 198.

15 McGee, 'Cupid's Banishment', p. 231.

16 Welsford, *The Court Masque*, p. 197.

17 Suzanne Gossett, '"Man-maid, begone!": Women in Masques' in *Women in the Renaissance*, p. 120.

18 Gossett, '"Man-maid, begone"', p. 120. See also Marion Wynne-Davies, 'The Queen's Masque: Renaissance Women and the Seventeenth-Century Court Masque'.

19 Gossett, '"Man-maid, begone"', pp. 122–3.

20 McGee, 'Cupid's Banishment', pp. 231–2.

21 Otto J. Scott, *James I*, pp. 368–9.

Cupid's Banishment

MASQUERS' NAMES/TO THE HONOURABLE ETC

1 Little is known concerning the young women and men who performed in the masque; however, many were probably children of various court officers. In the following notes the most likely candidates are identified.

2 Probably related to Elizabeth (see below), daughter to Sir Lionel Cranfield.

3 Daughter of Sir Thomas Chalenor, tutor to Prince Henry.

4 Daughter of William Harvey, physician to King James from 1610.

5 Daughter of Thomas Watson, Teller of the Exchequer.

6 Daughter of David Watkins, granted the Controllership of the Works at Windsor Castle in 1618.

7 Daughter of John Parkinson, Apothecary to King James I.

8 Daughter of Sir Ralph Maddison, active at court in the 1620s.

9 Robert White, author of the masque.

10 Daughter of Sir Lionel Cranfield, appointed Lord High Treasurer in 1621.

11 Daughter of Edmund Bolton, who suggested

that King James create a royal academy in 1617; or perhaps daughter of Robert Bolton, Fellow of Brasenose College, Oxford, and a governor of Elizabeth I's grammar school.

12 His daughter married John Evelyn to whom the manuscript of *Cupid's Banishment* was passed.

13 Daughter of Sir James Chambers, a physician to King James.

14 Probably daughter of Samuel Page, poet and divine, who served as vicar of St Nicholas, Deptford, the parish in which Richard Browne, his daughter, and later son-in-law, John Evelyn, lived.

15 Probably, in later life, the court musician and contributor to the children's masque presented in 1636, 'The King and Queen's Entertainment at Richmond'.

16 Daughter of Sir James Sandilands.

17 Possibly the offspring of some member of the well-connected and extensive Herbert family.

18 A relation of John Tindall, Master Gunner, who was granted a Gunner's place in the Tower for life.

19 Related to Signior Angelo, a Prince's musician.

20 Model.

21 Show, entertainment.

22 Favourable regard, approval.

23 Bitterness.

24 Hymen was the god of marriage, and Diana was the goddess associated with chastity, characteristics that would seem diametrically opposed to each other.

THE PLAY

1 Rich material of silk or wool interwoven with gold or silver thread.

2 Enterprise.

3 Queen Anne.

4 '. . .beams . . . revives' reads this way in White's manuscript.

5 Fading.

6 Cruel, fierce, deadly.

7 Robs.

8 The revolving shell in which heavenly bodies were thought to be set.

9 Shows, demonstrates.

10 Have under control, rule as a sovereign, manage.

11 Feast of the purification of the Virgin Mary (2 February) when candles were blessed.

12 Equitable.

13 Hymen was the god of marriage, frequently represented as a handsome youth bearing a torch.

14 The young women of Ladies Hall who form a group of dancers on this occasion.

15 The classical goddess of virginity associated with the moon.

16 Lewd.

17 Tendency.

18 Crafty plans.

19 Underhanded stratagems.

20 Made, both in the sense of genuine and of counterfeit creation.

21 Lewd.

22 Frowning, threatening.

23 Show, demonstrate.

24 Outer petticoat.

25 Belt, girdle.

26 Approach.

27 Arrows.

28 Because Cupid metaphorically binds hearts.

29 The curved path taken by an arrow in flight.

30 Love potions, charms.

31 Enticements. A common image in Renaissance literature in which Cupid symbolically lures people into his power and traps them.

32 Influence.

33 Mischievous, lewd.

34 Fond fancy was another term for foolish love.

35 Foolish pretender, false god.

36 Lewd.

37 Grotesque, vulgar.

38 Is fond of.

39 Foolish.

40 A concealed pit prepared as a trap for people or animals.

41 Copesmate, adversary, a person with whom one copes.

42 Breathe.

43 Effeminate, spiritless.

44 Rod of office carried by Mercury, who was the messenger of the gods.

45 God of marriage.

46 Large lutes with double necks and two sets of strings.

47 Taffeta, a lustrous silken cloth.

48 Pain, distress.

49 Disrupt.

50 Increase, with sexual undertones.

51 Loose, sleeveless cloak of cloth that varies in appearance with light and/or movement.

52 Uncertainty, with various senses (changeability, fickleness).

53 Fortune's blindness and her revolving wheel were legendary.

54 Bound by gratitude.
55 Favour, kindness.
56 Friendly relationship.
57 A common symbol of lechery in the Renaissance.
58 A keg of wine, representing his drunkenness.
59 Staff symbolizing Bacchus' authority.
60 Red from the effects of alcohol.
61 Goddess identified by the Romans with Diana, characterized as a virgin huntress and associated with the moon.
62 Coy, modest, prudish.
63 A woman who makes and sells butter; proverbially renowned for her outspokenness.
64 Set at odds, start fighting.
65 Stubborn.
66 Another name for Bacchus meaning 'the one who sets [people] free' (here, from cares and sadness).
67 A dog which worries or bites sheep, and consequently is kept at a distance.
68 Perhaps, into nakedness, an appropriate image for Cupid.
69 An unusual use of the verb meaning 'to hold oneself', 'remain'.
70 From the area around the Castalia (a fountain on Mount Parnassus associated with Apollo or, more generally, with the Muses).
71 Drink deeply and frequently.
72 Perfect, complete.
73 Alliance.
74 A rich material of silk or wool interwoven with gold or silver thread.
75 Practise.
76 Sincere, unreserved.
77 Arrows.
78 Tolerate, endure.
79 Cupid's mastery of the other deities is discussed, among others, by Hesiod, *Theogeny*, 120–2.
80 God of war.
81 Cupid's arrow.
82 Vilest, most base.
83 Reports, opinions, reputation.
84 Old hags, the opposite of the young women of Ladies Hall.
85 Modesty.
86 Improper behaviour.
87 Virgin goddess of health, often associated with chastity and purity.
88 Literally the popular name of an insane asylum (St Mary of Bethlehem) in London; but here used figuratively as a scene of wild confusion and disorder.
89 Deities or nymphs of the woods.
90 Arrows, spears.
91 Show.
92 Rose pink.
93 Transparent silk or muslin.
94 Form a ring around, surround.
95 A hunter who, for seeing Diana bathing, was changed by her into a stag and torn to pieces by his own hounds.
96 Dance movements.
97 Frequently the generic name for a shepherdess, with probable allusion to mythological Philomela, daughter of Pandion (a king of Athens) who was violated by her brother-in-law and turned into a nightingale (hence, her association with song).
98 Archaic form of 'air', a sprightly tune, a part-song.
90 Sings melodiously on a theme.
100 A full, rich outpouring of song.
101 Mischievous, spiteful mimic.
102 The child of blind affection.
103 Style, manner.
104 Lively, vigorous; here, the sense is applied to the capacity wine has to enliven.
105 Foolish, muddle-headed.
106 Zeus gave Endymion eternal life and youth by allowing him to sleep perpetually.
107 A teacher and wonder-worker of Crete reported to have fallen asleep for fifty-seven years.
108 Affectionate term for 'fine fellows'.
109 Stout-hearted.
110 The heaven.
111 Lively style.
112 Half a barrel.
113 Strong, coarse linen.
114 Individually.
115 Directly, promptly.
116 To the fullest, deeply.
117 The heaven.
118 Large cask or barrel.
119 Wine made into a hot drink with sugar and spices.
120 Batter, strike.
121 The host of a tavern, and its outdoor sign, identifying it as an inn.
122 Terms of abuse.
123 Violin, fiddle.
124 Move nimbly.
125 A bridehouse, house where a wedding is held.
126 Mender of pots.
127 One who shrinks from an undertaking.
128 Large bottle.

129 Prostitute.
130 Stupefied, dulled.
131 Red wine, especially from Bordeaux.
132 Belt worn around the waist to secure garments.
133 Wide, baggy breeches.
134 Trimmed.
135 A collar or ruff (band) of loud colours signifying the Fencer's noisy, disorderly behaviour.
136 Unspecified outer garment, as a loose jacket, tunic, or gown.
137 Trunk-hose, full baggy breeches covering the hips and upper thighs.
138 Crest, badge.
139 Small bunch of flowers.
140 Undressed skin of sheep or goat.
141 Whore.
142 Bodice.
143 Archaic form of 'nether coat', a coat worn under other garments.
144 Flower, bouquet.
145 Various states of mind and/or mood.
146 Manner, style.
147 Short part of book, poetry, or piece of music.
148 Probably a light dance.
149 Light blue cloth.
150 Queen Anne.
151 Dance formations coming together and dividing (as directed by Master Onslo, dancing master to Ladies Hall).
152 Dividing, half (of the dancers) to one side; the other half to the opposite side.
153 Probably two of the four young ladies among the performers who were named Ann (perhaps Ann Chalenor and Ann Sandeland).
154 Descend.
155 Leafy.
156 Customary, usual.
157 Apparel.
158 Belted.
159 Britannia, the ancient Roman name of England, especially the southern part where the early Roman provinces were. The word 'Albion' (related to the Latin *albus* or 'white') also alludes to the white cliffs of Dover, and therefore associates Queen Anne with the girls in white.
160 Rosemary was given for remembrance; the acorn, which grows to maturity as an oak, is a symbol of strength. Together, the initial letters of each – 'A' and 'R' – allude to 'Anna Regina', Queen Anne.
161 Solemn procession.
162 Pallas Athena, patron goddess of Athens known for her wisdom, chastity and martial skill.
163 Mythological leader of the Argonauts and husband of Medea, who managed to obtain the golden fleece in spite of the fire-breathing bulls and the dragons guarding it.
164 Gain possession of.
165 Aught, anything.
166 Agreement for mutual benefit.
167 Part of Mount Parnassus, home of the Muses.
168 Rustic.

5 Mary Wroth, *Love's Victory*

Introduction

1 For a biography of Lady Mary Wroth and the description of her coat of arms see Josephine A. Roberts, *The Poems of Lady Mary Wroth*, pp. 3–40. Until recently this was the authoritative 'life', but Gary Waller's *The Sidney Family Romance: Mary Wroth, William Herbert, and The Early Modern Construction of Gender* provides excellent ancilliary material.
2 For a description of Mary Wroth's involvement in Jonson's masque see Marion Wynne-Davies, 'The Queen's Masque: Renaissance Women and the Seventeenth-Century Court Masque'.
3 Waller, *Sidney Family Romance*, pp. 55–6.
4 Ibid., p. 56.
5 Roberts, *Poems*, p. 29, and Barbara Lewalski, *Writing Women in Jacobean England*, pp. 245–6.
6 A list of those writers to whom Mary Wroth acted as patron may be found in Lewalski, *Writing Women*, pp. 266–7.
7 C.H. Herford and Percy Simpson (eds), *Ben Jonson*, vol. 1. VIII, p. 182.
8 For a comprehensive listing of Wroth's work see Lewalski, *Writing Women*, pp. 243–307.
9 Wynne-Davies, 'Queen's Masque', p. 94.
10 Josephine Roberts, who is probably the foremost Wroth scholar working at present, is editing *Urania II* from the manuscript in the Newberry Library, Chicago (Case MS fols 1565 W 95); it will be published by the English Renaissance Text Society.
11 *Pamphilia to Amphilanthus* may be found in Roberts, *Poems.*
12 *Lord Morley's 'Tryumphes of Fraunces Petrarcke'. The First English Translation of the 'Trionfi'*, ed. D.D. Carnicelli, pp. 80–108. Mary Sidney, *The Triumph of Death and*

Other Unpublished and Uncollected Poems, ed. Gary Waller.

13 Wroth is, however, one of the women writers currently being 'restored' to the canon and a number of criticisms have been forthcoming. Ones of note, apart from those directly referred to here, are: Naomi J. Miller and Gary Waller (eds), *Reading Mary Wroth: Representing Alternatives in Early Modern England* and Carolyn Ruth Swift, 'Feminine Self-Definition in Lady Mary Wroth's *Love's Victorie* (*c.* 1621)'.

14 For a discussion of Wroth as a 'feminist' writer, or not, see Beilin, *Redeeming Eve: Women Writers of the English Renaissance*, pp. 208–43; Krontiris, *Oppositional Voices. Women as Writers and Translators of Literature in the English Renaissance*, pp. 126–32; Lamb, *Gender and Authority in the Sidney Circle*, pp. 142–93 (it is to Lamb that we owe the idea of the Sidney 'safe' house); and Swift, 'Feminine Identity in Lady Mary Wroth's Romance *Urania*', pp. 173–4.

15 For a discussion of the evidence for this performance see Michael Brennan's edition of *Love's Victory* for the Roxburghe Club, pp. 13–14; we are deeply indebted to this edition and regret that the expense of the book makes it inaccessible for the majority of readers.

16 Herford and Simpson, *Ben Jonson*, I p. 143. See also Lamb, *Gender and Authority*, pp. 151–2.

17 Wroth, *Urania* II, fols 3av–5bv.

18 Roberts, *Poems*, p. 85.

19 Lewalski, *Writing Women*, p. 297.

20 For a discussion of Wroth's use of pastoral see Barbara Lewalski, 'Mary Wroth's *Love's Victory* and Pastoral Tragicomedy' in Naomi J. Miller and Gary Waller (eds), *Reading Mary Wroth*, pp. 88–108. Margaret Anne McLaren in her essay, 'An Unknown Continent: Lady Mary Wroth's Forgotten Pastoral Drama, "Love's Victorie"' in Anne M. Haselkorn and Betty S. Travitsky (eds), *The Renaissance Englishwoman in Print*, argues that Wroth doesn't fully understand the conventions of pastoral so that the characters are 'confined by their author to the never-never world of the pastoral'. However, while Wroth might not allude to contemporary court politics, she certainly alludes to 'family' politics.

21 See Millicent V. Hay, *The Life of Robert Sidney, Earl of Leicester (1563–1626)*, and P.J. Croft (ed), *The Poems of Robert Sidney*.

22 Josephine A. Roberts, 'The Huntington Manuscript of Lady Mary Wroth's Play, *Loves Victorie*'.

Love's Victory

ACT I

1 The first scene of *Love's Victory* is masque-like in its use of Venus and Cupid, the classical goddess and god of love. However, the opening also resembles Wroth's *Pamphilia*, which commences with a similar vision of the deities (P1), and *Urania*, where a group of lovers visit the Temple of Venus. Her source for each was most probably Petrarch's *Triumph of Love* (see above, Introduction, p. 9).

2 Cupid is traditionally depicted with a blindfold signifying that 'love is blind'.

3 The blindfold.

4 The arrow; another of Cupid's traditional possessions, a wound from which incited love.

5 Cupid wounded his mother with one of his arrows thereby increasing her love for the god Mars; Wroth also refers to this story in *Pamphilia* (P58). The sources are Ovid's *Metamorphoses* iv. 171, and Philip Sidney's *Astrophil and Stella* 17.

6 Vexation.

7 Misfortunes.

8 Their troubles.

9 Tainted.

10 Public celebration or show; a term often used to describe court festivities, hence adding to the masque-like nature of this first scene.

11 Pun on 'travels', that is journeys, and 'travails', labours.

12 Trapped by love, caught by a sophisticated argument; the ultimate source is Ovid's *Metamorphoses* iv. 206–28, but Wroth's image also recalls one of William Herbert's poems which refers to being caught in '*Cupid's* net'.

13 The following song is reminiscent of a song in Wroth's *Urania* (U1) and of Philip Sidney's *Certain Sonnets* 18.

14 Meadow.

15 Hunt and Hall; Pen has 'bank'.

16 Pastoral convention in which the shepherd playing on his pipe represents a poetic second-self.

17 Ineffectual.
18 Hunt; Pen has 'love paines'.
19 Hunt; Pen has 'passions'.
20 Weaken, abate.
21 Hunt; Pen has 'daintiest', which doesn't scan as well.
22 Obscure.
23 Wilful, perverse; the traditional characteristics of the Anacreontic Cupid.
24 Object in a game of chance; Philisses suggests that Cupid has drawn a token for him which signifies ill-luck.
25 State of mind, disposition.
26 Hunt and Hall; Pen has 'rather'.
27 Fail.
28 Woo.
29 In classical mythology the sun god; often depicted with golden hair, which represents the sun's rays (see below, I.ii.77–8).
30 Hunt and Hall; Pen has 'Which to thes vallies giv'st thy pleasant sight'.
31 The frown of the goddess Fortune signified ill-luck.
32 Dress, behaviour. Silvesta explains that she has transferred her allegiance from Venus, the goddess of love, to Diana, the goddess of chastity, both in terms of her conduct and of her clothes. Presumably this means that she wears the garments of a huntress and carries a bow in emulation of the nymphs who followed Diana in classical mythology. Silvesta's change of garb is commented on by the other characters (II.i.3), which suggests that Wroth envisaged an actual performance of the play, rather than a simple reading of parts.
33 Roguish.
34 Hunt and Hall; Pen has 'heal'. 'Quench' makes more sense in terms of the fire metaphor.
35 Pen; Hunt and Hall have 'have'.
36 Person.
37 Lowly, with the sense of dishonourably.
38 The conventional Petrarchan image of a lover as the slave of his lady and prostrate with grief is here inverted to describe a woman's experiences rather than a man's.
39 Pen; Hunt and Hall have 'deerest'.
40 Lamentations.
41 Be employed habitually.
42 Rewarding oneself.
43 Hunt; Pen has 'Did cruelty itt self thus ever show'. Hunt corresponds more evenly with the following line.
44 Cut off.
45 In classical mythology the three Furies were figures of vengeance and punishment; the reference to 'charm' is ironic, since 'curse' would be more appropriate.
46 Shepherd; Forester refers to Philisses.
47 Unburdening. Hunt; Pen has 'disburding'.
48 Hunt; Pen has 'They'.
49 Wrecked by the fires of passion and love.
50 Efforts.
51 Hasten.
52 Experience.
53 Regret.
54 To be chaste; see above, I.ii.73–124.
55 Behaviour.
56 Unusual, surprising: Pen; Hunt has 'hard'.
57 Pen; Hunt has 'had gain'd'.
58 A collection, sometimes of people.
59 Prevented from seeing, kept away from.
60 Forester advocates a chaste love based only upon sight; as such he represents one of the 'types' of love described in the play (see above, Introduction, p. 94). In so doing he represents a Neoplatonic ideal in which the sight of beauty is sufficient to inspire love and no physical, and therefore lustful, contact is needed. Wroth's literary source for this exemplar was her father's (Robert Sidney's) poetry, as in his 'Pastoral 8', rather than her uncle's (Philip Sidney's) more sensuous verse.
61 Among.
62 Types.
63 Complaining.
64 Conventional Petrarchan image of the lover burning with desire; frequently evoked by Philip Sidney in *Astrophil and Stella*.
65 Hunt; Pen has 'not'.
66 Trouble.
67 Bear part of the pain: Pen; Hunt has 'you'l make them smart'.
68 Amusement, diversion. Each act of *Love's Victory* depicts a different form of poetic 'sport'; for this device Wroth is indebted to the eclogues which Philip Sidney used to conclude the five books of his *Arcadia* (see above, Introduction, p. 9).
69 Troubles.
70 Accustomed.
71 Wandering.
72 Part of the body.
73 Whoever is not included, you will not be one of them or sing in tune. Dalina employs a pun in order to mock both Rustic's inability to sing and his lack of wit.
74 Rustic's song is a parody of the Petrarchan love poems sung by the other shepherds and

shepherdesses; in this Wroth is indebted to the comic eclogues in Philip Sidney's *Arcadia*.

75 A protective covering; hence, the eyelids encase and shield the eyes.

76 A yellow or red pigmentation used to mark sheep, in order to determine their owners.

77 Breasts.

78 Lacon's song echoes the Lover's vision in Petrarch's *Triumph of Love*.

79 A pun; meaning both, tied to pleasures, as well as carried on a tide of pleasure.

80 Arbour.

81 Mars, the god of war in classical mythology.

82 Cupid.

83 Hunt; Pen has 'when'.

84 Close.

85 Will.

86 Servant.

87 A conventional Petrarchan combination of opposites.

88 Spirits.

89 Be without good faith.

90 Also feel affection.

91 Justice. Pen; Hunt has 'lust'.

ACT II

1 Dressed like the followers of the goddess, Diana, probably as a huntress; see above, I.ii.83.

2 Conventional Petrarchan description of the lover as the servant of his lady.

3 A fair young woman.

4 Conventional Petrarchan image of the lady as the sun which Wroth also uses in *Pamphilia and Amphilanthus* (P23), but her more immediate source was Robert Sidney's 'Sonnet 30'.

5 Goddess of chastity in classical mythology; see above, I.ii.83.

6 Agreement.

7 Unlike.

8 Ill-fated, unfortunate.

9 An attempt to win her love, perhaps causing her to break her vow of chastity.

10 Condition; that is, someone who has not promised to be chaste.

11 The following speech (II.i.65–70) signals that Lissius represents an anti-marriage and anti-woman stance in the play. As such he recalls the pamphlet debate about the virtues and vices of women which occurred at the beginning of the seventeenth century. Lissius, however, will be punished for these sentiments, and shown the value of women and marriage.

12 Hunt; Pen has 'band'.

13 Hunt; Pen has 'and'.

14 Regret.

15 Break the charm of.

16 To furnish his arrows with feathers.

17 Broken.

18 Disguise, conceal.

19 Hoarded, put away in a storehouse.

20 Hunt; Pen has 'be'.

21 The skills – in this instance foolish love – which are taught at Folly's school. The idea of Folly teaching people how to love is repeated by Wroth in *Pamphilia to Amphilanthus* (P72).

22 Incite.

23 Pen; Hunt has 'modest'.

24 Personification of Beauty as a queen; in this instance a courtly compliment to the shepherds and shepherdesses.

25 In classical mythology the sun god; here simply meaning that the group is so beautiful that they outshine the sun.

26 Forecast.

27 Achieves.

28 The one who leads the group; the reference is to the foremost sheep in a flock which wore a bell about its neck; hence it is a fittingly pastoral allusion.

29 Objects in a game of chance; see above, I.ii.60.

30 Tolerate.

31 Make a mistake.

32 Vexatious.

33 Allow them to be.

34 Pen; Hunt has 'lingring'.

35 Brings; but also a pun on 'drawing' a fortune.

36 Dalina appears to chastise herself for being too bold, a quality which would have been considered unbecoming in a woman at the time Wroth was writing.

37 Pen; Hunt has 'promises some joy'.

38 Meditates, thinks hard.

39 Pass quickly by; there is a suggestion that fortune, like time, cannot be halted.

40 Consider.

41 Pen; Hunt has 'joy'.

42 Fortune.

43 Pen; Hunt has 'I may'.

44 Fortune is personified as a goddess (see above, I.ii.81); she is described as blind by Musella in the next line, which echoes the portrayal of Cupid (see above, I.i.8).

45 Pen; Hunt has 'What'.

46 What does it propose.

47 Propose, but with a pun on being emotionally 'moved', that is disturbed.
48 Truly.
49 Cursed by pride, therefore hurtful to Dalina.
50 The goddess Fortune, who was renowned for her changeable nature.
51 Reform.
52 Be entitled to a better fate.
53 For fear that.
54 Have a similar experience.
55 Gifts, aid.
56 Whose gifts and presents are unappealing. However, Arcas' comment has erotic overtones suggesting that Fortune's sexual antics and offers of intimacy are sterile and unattractive.
57 Hunt and Hall; Pen has 'that theyr', which adds an extra syllable.
58 The idea of a debate between Love and Reason also occurs in Wroth's *Pamphilia to Amphilanthus* (P86); the source for both poems may have been the contest between Reason and Passion in the Second Eclogue of Philip Sidney's *Old Arcadia*, but they are also a direct refutation of William Herbert's poetical defence of Love against Reason in 'It is enough, a Master you grant *Love*'.
59 In classical mythology the ruler of the gods and the guardian of justice.
60 Quarrel.
61 Must be given a place of honour.
62 A favour to be awarded.
63 Watch, guard.
64 Do offence.
65 A pun, meaning to miss as in 'to cause offence', as well as in 'to mistake the way'.
66 Here and in the next line Philisses suggests that Cupid is not blindfolded (see above, I.i.8) since his aim is so accurate.
67 Is disposed towards.
68 State of mind.
69 Quarrel. Pen; Hunt has 'debases'.
70 Gracious, affectionate.
71 She refers to Philisses.
72 Flat meadow lands, a suitable setting for a pastoral romance. Pen; Hunt has 'lanes'.
73 Trouble.
74 Like Cupid, Death is often depicted carrying a spear or arrow. Pen; Hunt has 'devils'.
75 To entreat.
76 Simeana. As brother and sister, Philisses and Simeana represent Philip and Mary Sidney (see above, Introduction, p. 93).
77 Pen; Hunt has 'ease'.
78 Unless.
79 Hunt; Pen has 'show'.
80 Observe.
81 Lines 42–3 mean: 'I only get kind looks from her because I know you, I might as well leave rather than wait to receive them for my own sake.'
82 She blushes.
83 Engage.
84 Repay.
85 Pen; Hunt has 'the love you gave / Soe freely to her'.
86 A public festival; see above, I.i, the note to Venus' entrance.
87 Those who rule others, but must themselves be ruled by Love.
88 Write no attacks which will test Cupid's humour and might offend him.
89 Produce.
90 Hunt; Pen has 'noe'.

ACT III

1 Uninhabited, wild.
2 Henceforth.
3 To turn completely against love.
4 Rather than.
5 Hunt and Hall; Pen has 'rather'.
6 Silvesta states that more men have fallen in love with Musella than with any other shepherdess.
7 A conventional image of love as burning desire.
8 Wear away.
9 To be successful.
10 Pen; Hunt and Hall omit 'but'.
11 The use of the word 'will' here and in lines 43, 48, 49 and 50 suggests a possible reference to William Herbert (see above, Introduction, p. 94).
12 Hunt and Hall; Pen has 'What'.
13 Pen; Hunt and Hall have 'yett joy most'.
14 Gladly.
15 It would have been considered improper for a woman to woo a man, since ideally she should appear innocent and chaste.
16 Merit or value, but also a possible pun on 'Wroth', which would identify Musella with the author (it is repeated at IV.i.396, V.i.4, V.v.24–5 and 115, and V.vii.92); see Introduction, p. 94.
17 Hunt and Hall; Pen has 'break'.
18 Delay, prevent.
19 The following speech (ll. 1–20) resembles Sonnet 30 in Wroth's *Pamphilia to Amphilanthus* (P34).
20 Unfortunate.
21 In the quiet shelter of the woods.

22 Ever. Hunt and Hall; Pen has 'bright heav'ns'.
23 Create.
24 Exceptional.
25 Character.
26 Most precious.
27 Value.
28 Allotted destiny.
29 Reveal.
30 Hunt and Hall; Pen has 'who'.
31 In truth.
32 Equally changing, equally uncertain.
33 Pen; Hunt and Hall have 'this'.
34 Hunt and Hall; Pen has 'The next that coms this fault I'le mend, and have'.
35 Put my love to the test.
36 Simeana's love has always been spurned, but also evocation of opposites traditional in Renaissance love poetry.
37 Hunt and Hall; Pen has 'hopes remaines'.
38 Wroth probably used the classical tale of Phyllis and Demophoon in her creation of the following tale of unrequited love, as well as more generally for her character Phillis. In Ovid Phyllis hangs herself when she believes she has been deserted by Demophoon her lover (*Heroides* II).
39 Fortune.
40 Grief.
41 Phillis points out that while others love many times, she has loved only once.
42 Innocent, blameless.
43 Musella.
44 Hunt and Hall; Pen has 'told mee' which adds an extra syllable.
45 Arrangement.
46 Wroth's acknowledgement of the influence of Philip Sidney's *Arcadia* on her own text.
47 Become.
48 Change.
49 Hunt and Hall; Pen has 'prove'.
50 A conventional use of fire as a metaphor for love; it is used here to suggest that it is not possible to love twice, even as a burned-out fire cannot be rekindled.
51 Pen; Hunt and Hall have 'love'.
52 Transactions.
53 Great freedom.
54 Is it possible to claim the reward of love even when you have loved more than once?
55 Forced to change.
56 Foolish.
57 Woo.
58 Hunt and Hall; Pen has 'and'.
59 Pretending to be a stranger, in a reserved and distant manner.
60 Go against.
61 Strict in the observance of rules and propriety. In effect Dalina suggests that women should 'play hard to get'.
62 This apology to Cupid recalls Wroth's similar approach in one of the last poems in *Pamphilia to Amphilanthus* (P76).
63 Emblems of victory, often placed on a tomb.
64 Lissius' comment repeats the assertion that only men should initiate courtship; see above, III.i.77–9.
65 Hunt and Hall; Pen has 'unfitting'st'.
66 To petition.
67 Difficult.
68 Hunt and Hall; Pen has 'soe'.
69 Simeana.
70 Caught by love.
71 Hunt and Hall; Pen has 'that'.
72 On Cupid as blind see above, I.i.8.
73 Lissius.
74 Hunt and Hall; Pen has 'desire'.
75 Test him to discover his feelings.
76 Find out.
77 Keep alive, preserve.
78 Hunt and Hall; Pen has 'reason now, my love'.
79 Who doesn't attend us as followers.
80 Loud cries which contrast with the 'gentle speech' of the previous line.
81 Lissius.

ACT IV

1 Appointed, arranged for.
2 The following complaint resembles Dicus' song in the Fourth Eclogue of Philip Sidney's *Old Arcadia*, although Wroth emphasizes the silence of the trees rather than the grieving sounds suggested by her uncle. She used a similar theme for Urania's first sonnet in her prose romance (*Urania*, U1).
3 Troubles.
4 Dispositions.
5 An allusion to the legend of Echo, a nymph in classical mythology, who pined away through unrequited love until only her voice remained, repeating whatever anyone says.
6 Private concerns.
7 An oblique reference to the Ovidian tale of Midas' ears (*Metamorphoses* xi.174–93); however, it is likely that Wroth used Chaucer's retelling of the tale in 'The Wife of Bath's Tale', where Midas' wife whispers the secret

of his asses' ears to the waters of a marsh.

8 Complaints.

9 I never had that which could feed the least hope to make it Spring.

10 Meadows.

11 In classical mythology the goddess of the dawn.

12 Hunt; Pen has 'doe not know / Whether', which does not scan as well.

13 Pen; Hunt has 'reguard'.

14 Love is described as a labyrinth in the first sonnet of the 'Crown of Sonnets' in Wroth's *Pamphilia to Amphilanthus* (P77).

15 I will die because of it.

16 Pen; Hunt has 'paine'.

17 A Petrarchan use of opposites; hence, that which is *lost* in gambling will *win* Philisses what he wants.

18 Meanings, ideas.

19 Hunt; Pen has 'you'.

20 Obstructed, useless.

21 For fear that.

22 Innocent.

23 Allow.

24 Hunt; Pen has 'conceale'.

25 An expression of endearment, which refers to the bounding of lambs in the morning, but also a sly parody of Rustic's clumsy use of pastoral language. See above, I.iii.55–72.

26 Hunt; Pen has 'Is it'.

27 Tending.

28 In her response to Rustic, Musella makes a covert reference to the newly acknowledged love between Philisses and herself. Such covert allusions recall that the play itself makes hidden intimations of people Wroth actually knew, and this particular speech points to Wroth's (Musella's) love for William Herbert (Philisses) and the couple's mocking disregard for Robert Wroth (Rustic). See above, Introduction, p. 94.

29 Excellent appearance. But also a military or naval ensign, which would suggest the metaphor of a shipwreck in ll. 157–8.

30 Cupid.

31 Pen; Hunt has 'and bring bliss'.

32 Unfortunate.

33 Hasten.

34 Before.

35 Derive.

36 Complaints.

37 The external appearance; or outward show, an act.

38 Too soon for me to have forgotten. Pen; Hunt has 'soone to bring'.

39 Use of Petrarchan opposites, early and late.

40 Pen; Hunt has 'nott some made some false report'.

41 To abate.

42 A pun on 'vassal' that is the lover as his lady's servant, and 'vessel' which refers to the lover as a ship wrecked by the storms of his lady's anger. The latter metaphor was common in Renaissance poetry and Wroth would probably have been aware of several examples, such as Petrarch's *Rime* 189, and Robert Sidney's Sonnet 23; she herself uses it again in *Pamphilia to Amphilanthus* (P68).

43 Hunt; Pen has 'wer't nott in dispit / To punish mee who knew nott day from night'. Hunt retains the food metaphor begun at l. 222.

44 Never.

45 That which is inferior or lowly.

46 Pen; Hunt has 'with justest meaning mixt'.

47 Who it.

48 Refuse scornfully.

49 Quarrel.

50 Ruin.

51 Talk.

52 Fail.

53 Lissius'.

54 To destroy his rewards.

55 Fanciful thoughts.

56 Lethe, the river that carried the dead to the underworld in classical mythology.

57 Fooled, cheated.

58 Lissius lies prostrate with grief, a traditional pose for the spurned lover.

59 A reference to Cupid as a winged god, but also implying that love makes one hurry.

60 Pen; Hunt has 'by . . . abus'de'.

61 A Renaissance convention of describing the lover as his lady's slave.

62 To promote, to foster.

63 Hunt; Pen has 'dispaire', which repeats l. 314.

64 For the sake of show, that is, not true love. Wroth makes a similar comparison in *Pamphilia to Amphilanthus* (P94).

65 Behaviour.

66 The smallest amount of.

67 Pen; Hunt has 'All blis, bring noe doubts now . . .'.

68 Of people, but with a parodic reference to the pastoral setting of the play.

69 The game of 'riddling' at the end of Act IV is similar to that evoked by Philip Sidney in *Astrophil and Stella* (37), where the riddles simultaneously conceal and divulge the real

identities of the fictional characters; for example, Penelope Rich as Stella. Wroth's whole play is, in a sense, a riddle, since most of the characters allude to at least one, but sometimes two, real people; see above, Introduction, p. 94.

70 Assume.

71 Musella's riddle refers to her love for Philisses who she desires but cannot marry, and her distaste for Rustic whom she is betrothed to. On a second level of meaning the riddle alludes to Wroth's love for William Herbert and her antipathy towards her husband, Robert Wroth.

72 Prevented from seeing.

73 Would be most glad.

74 To approach, come close to. Hunt; Pen has 'by'.

75 Dalina's riddle points to her search for constancy in love, which she can never have since she has an innately fickle nature; even her name (Dalina, dalliance) suggests her inconstancy. Dalina's identity in the play's contemporary allegory is more difficult to determine. If Philisses is identified with Philip Sidney, as he sometimes is, then Dalina could be Penelope Rich, who rejected Sidney's love and married Robert Rich, although she later became Charles Blount, Lord Mountjoy's, mistress. For the play's topical allusions see above, Introduction, p. 94.

76 Gladly.

77 Procedure, line of action.

78 Philisses' riddle has three levels of interpretation: first, it refers to his love for Musella which he had thought to be frustrated when she became betrothed to Rustic, but which he now realizes is returned by her regardless. Second, it refers to William Herbert's love for Wroth which, as with the fictional couple, is returned despite the fact that she was married to Robert Wroth. Third, the allusion to 'star' (l. 381) identifies Philisses as Philip Sidney (Astrophil) and his love as Penelope Rich (St*ella*). If this is the case Rich should be linked with Musella (close in sound to Stella) and not Dalina. However, considering the multiple allusions constructed by Wroth, both Musella and Dalina may be connected with the younger and older Rich, as other characters in the play allude to two quite separate people (for example, Philisses as Philip Sidney and William Herbert). See above, Introduction, p. 94.

79 Rustic, who is linked by Wroth with her husband, Sir Robert Wroth, is not allowed to participate in the game of riddles, partly, one imagines, because Wroth excludes him from any connection with her artistic and poetic Herbert/Sidney family. See above, Introduction, p. 94.

80 Powers of imagination.

81 Rustic means 'skill', but Wroth inserts a pun on 'art' as a cultural pursuit, emphasizing Rustic's lack of learning.

82 A pun on 'Wroth'; see above III.i.95, and below, V.i.4, v.24–5 and 115, and vii.92.

83 Material substance.

84 Something wished for, not real.

85 A man who is married, but with a pun on someone who farms, who is skilled in 'husbandry'.

86 Fail to understand.

87 Disguise my meaning.

88 Pay attention to.

89 Lissius' riddle refers to the jealousies and misunderstandings which have occurred between Simeana and himself before they have finally acknowleged their mutual love. The characters of Lissius and Simeana have their counterparts in Wroth's own acquaintences; she probably alludes to Mary Sidney and Sir Matthew Lister – who were reputed to be lovers – since there are close verbal ties between the names. However, considering the close friendship between Wroth (identified as Musella) and Susan Vere, her sister-in-law, Simeana, who is Musella's close friend, might well be associated with Vere, whose relations with her husband, Philip Herbert, were often difficult due to his seeming disregard for affection and love. See above, Introduction, p. 94.

90 Each other.

91 Phillis' riddle alludes to her unrequited love for Philisses. A similar theme occurs in the song of a shepherdess in Wroth's *Pamphila to Amphilanthus* (P7) and in Robert Sidney's song of a shepherd. We have found it impossible to find a counterpart for Phillis in Wroth's circle of friends and relations.

92 Without manners, that is, in haste.

93 Disposition, state of mind.

94 Musella is the sun and Rustic her shadow.

95 But before long someone will suffer.

96 Exalted position.

97 Acknowledged.

98 Hunt and Hall; Pen has 'thy'.
99 Caught.
100 Nets.
101 Pen; Hunt and Hall have 'all', which does not coincide with the narrative resolutions at the end of Act V, when some characters have still not gained their loves.
102 Hunt and Hall have 'Love a god did slander beare / gained his person, and his power butt'.
103 Counterparts, copies of you.
104 Turn out to be.
105 They reflect your concerns, that is, they have become lovers.
106 They see with your eyes, that is, they look with love.
107 Pen; Hunt and Hall have 'Cease'.
108 Pen; Hunt and Hall have 'yeelding'.
109 Pen; Hunt and Hall have 'hands'.
110 Hunt and Hall have a final speech by Cupid to Venus:

CUPID
Now your part comes to play,
In this you must something sway.
So you shall, and I, your child,
When you bid can soon be mild.

ACT V

1 Frustrated.
2 Pun on 'Wroth'; in this speech the author laments her marriage to Robert Wroth. See above, III.i.95 and IV.i.396, and below, V.v.24–5 and 115, and vii.92.
3 A possible pun on Penelope 'Rich', which would link the Philisses/Musella/Rustic plot to Philip Sidney/Penelope/Robert Rich. See above, Introduction, p. 94.
4 Link in marriage.
5 Hunt; Pen has 'any'.
6 While there appears to be no specific contemporary allusion here, in the Renaissance fathers often chose to control their daughters' lives from beyond the grave by making detailed wills; see, for example, the unreasonable demands made upon Portia by her father's will in Shakespeare's *The Merchant of Venice*.
7 Fate is here personified as a goddess.
8 Accepted procedures.
9 Get things wrong. Pen; Hunt has 'faile'.
10 Foolishly. Pen; Hunt has 'idly'.
11 Vexed, thwarted.
12 Being absent.
13 Fitting, appropriate.
14 The Fates in classical mythology were three sisters who determined the course of human life.
15 Possible allusion to Robert and Penelope Rich; see above, l. 5.
16 The duty of children to obey their parents was mostly unquestioned in the Renaissance.
17 Unfortunate.
18 Pen; Hunt has 'all'.
19 Allow your love for me to remain constant.
20 Pen; Hunt has 'MUSELLA: Alas, my dear, I must'.
21 Unfortunate.
22 Betrothed.
23 Pen; Hunt has 'us'.
24 Pen; Hunt has 'we must'; the plural is sustained in the following two lines substituting 'our' for Pen's 'my'.
25 The Huntington MS finishes at this point. See above, Introduction, p. 94.
26 Binding words, but with a sense of magic, that is, she has bewitched him with love.
27 Maintain.
28 Control.
29 An oath; a shortened version of 'By Mary'.
30 Dalina alludes to the sexual consummation of the marriage.
31 The metaphor describes Musella as a bird which was once free to fly where it chose, but which is now forced to nest in a low bush, that is to marry Rustic.
32 Lissius mentions Arcas' love for Musella, which appears to have occurred before the action of the play starts.
33 Malicious or adverse harassments and traps.
34 Indebted, although here used ironically.
35 Maybe.
36 Be without your reward.
37 Atone for your offence.
38 Angry.
39 Dying for love was a commonly used expression in Renaissance poetry.
40 Perhaps referring to Musella as 'Stella', that is, Penelope Rich; see above, Introduction, p. 94.
41 Accustomed.
42 Diana, the goddess of chastity in classical mythology; she is often contrasted with Venus, the goddess of love.
43 Make a complete and total effort.
44 The following song uses religious language ('rites' and 'true relics' ll. 3 and 5) which serves to elevate the love between Musella and Philisses from physical desire to an idealized spiritual union.
45 Incite.
46 Enduring.
47 A pageant or commemorative show.

48 The potion recalls that used by Juliet in Shakespeare's *Romeo and Juliet*.
49 An allusion to the title of the play, but with the significant difference that 'tragedy' here replaces the title's 'victory'; see above, Introduction, p. 93.
50 Fine.
51 Brennan has 'cleere', which seems a mistranscription in terms of the sense.
52 It has been fortunate for you that you have lost out to him.
53 Fooled.
54 Possible pun on the name Rich; see above, Introduction, p. 94.
55 Pun on Wroth, which is repeated at the next line; see above, III.i.95, IV.i.396, V.i.4, v.115, and vii.92.
56 False steps, blunders.
57 Courage.
58 Become, grow.
59 Mother.
60 Musella.
61 Misfortune.
62 Perverse.
63 Fate.
64 That which connected them, bound them together.
65 Pain.
66 A personification of spite and outrage.
67 Not false, therefore true.
68 Earthly prisons, that is, bodies.
69 The earth where they dwell, their graves.
70 Concern.
71 Peasant character.
72 Pun on Wroth; see above, III.i.95, IV.i.396, V.i.4, v.24–5, and vii.92.
73 Wroth was the eldest child of Robert Sidney and Barbara Gamage, although the details of the father's will and the conflict with the mother are not taken from Wroth's own life.
74 Dishonour.
75 Corrode, destroy love and affection.
76 Both without her mother's consent and with a sense of impropriety.
77 Inwardly.
78 Spirits.
79 Forester's dream presents Silvesta as a Christian martyr being burned at the stake.
80 Firmly.
81 So beautiful that they are without compare.
82 Virtue is personified as dressing or adorning her form with the clothing and behaviour of Silvesta, since that chaste maiden is so perfectly virtuous.
83 Be taken for.
84 Although.
85 Appointed.
86 Abundant supply.
87 Goodness.
88 Gives value to.
89 Ironic in that Forester hoped to marry Silvesta.
90 Spirit.
91 Are not fond of.
92 An allusion to the title of the play.
93 The agent appointed by me.
94 She has.
95 Promises.
96 Musella reveals herself to be a dutiful daughter by asking for her mother's forgiveness.
97 The final pun on Wroth in the play; see above, II.i.95, IV.i.396, V.i.4, v.24 and 115.
98 Fooled.
99 Dalina makes a distinction between a wreath which signifies sadness, and a garland (l. 120) which suggests happiness; for example, a funeral wreath and a wedding garland.
100 The willow was a symbol of disappointed love.
101 Have respect for.
102 Truth.
103 A song is missing here in the MS, although space has been left to fill it in later.
104 An allusion to the mark of Cain (Genesis 4: 15).
105 My deeply felt claim and request.
106 Forfeit your liberty.

6 Elizabeth Brackley and Jane Cavendish, *The Concealed Fancies*

Introduction

1 Margaret Cavendish's biography of her husband, *The Life of William Cavendish Duke of Newcastle* (1667), is a useful source of Cavendish family history.
2 For a discussion of the sisters' contribution to the Cavendish 'coterie', see: Margaret J.M. Ezell, '"To Be Your Daughter in Your Pen": The Social Functions of Literature in the Writings of Lady Elizabeth Brackley and Lady Jane Cavendish', pp. 281–96.
3 Susan Wiseman, 'Gender and Status in Dramatic Discourse', p. 161.
4 Germaine Greer *et al.* (eds), *Kissing the Rod*, p. 106; and Betty S. Travitsky, '"His Wife's

Prayers and Meditation"; MS Egerton 607', p. 243.

5 Quoted in Nathan Comfort Starr, '*The Concealed Fansyes*: A Play by Lady Jane Cavendish and Lady Elizabeth Brackley', pp. 803–4. Very little has been written about the play; see: Nancy Cotton, *Women Playwrights in England c. 1363–1750*, pp. 40–2, and Margaret J.M. Ezell, '"To Be Your Daughter"'.

6 Excerpts from *A Pastorall* and three poems are printed in Germaine Greer, *Kissing the Rod.*, pp. 106–18.

7 Starr, '*The Concealed Fansyes*', pp. 804–5.

8 Ibid., p. 836.

9 Cavendish, *Life of William Cavendish*, p. 46.

10 A.S. Turberville, *A History of Welbeck Abbey and Its Owners*, pp. 45–6.

11 Wiseman, 'Gender and Status in Dramatic Discourse', pp. 161–2.

12 Sophie Tomlinson, '"My Brain the Stage": Margaret Cavendish and the Fantasy of Female Performance', pp. 137–9.

13 They could easily have witnessed the two masques presented to Charles and Henrietta Maria at Welbeck and Bolsover by William Cavendish in 1633 and 1634.

14 Betty S. Travitsky, '"His Wife's Prayers"', pp. 241–3.

15 Greer *et al.*, *Kissing the Rod*, p. 108.

16 The only evidence of Jane's continued writing is from a poem on her death by Thomas Lawrence (UNott Portland MS PwV.19).

17 Greer *et al.*, *Kissing the Rod*, p. 118. The original is at the Huntington Library, Ellesmere MS 8353. We have modernized the spelling and punctuation.

The Concealed Fancies

PROLOGUES

1 An attribution for the first prologue is absent, unlike the second, which is specifically ascribed to a woman. However, it is likely that the two Cavendish sisters spoke the opening addresses, introducing the play to their family, in the same way that they conclude the play with two separate epilogues, followed by a joint one explicitly directed towards their father. Such a performance would have been impossible in the public theatre, as may be seen from Rosalind's apologies for speaking the epilogue in Shakespeare's *As You Like It* (V.iv.198ff.), even though her part would have been played by a boy actor. By emphasizing the female gender of the speakers, the authors undermine the dramatic conventions of their day, but it is important to realize that they could do this only within the private theatrical entertainments of a cultured and close family group.

2 By associating women with 'truth', the authors reverse the 'women as deceivers' commonplace.

3 Applause; literally, hand-to-hand encounter.

4 William Cavendish, first Duke of Newcastle, the father of the two authors.

5 To adorn in token of honour.

ACT I

1 Mood, state of mind.

2 Outward self, public identity; with a possible allusion to the actual theatrical nature of the character.

3 God of love.

4 A gentleman acting as an usher (servant) to a person of superior rank; here, acting as a go-between.

5 The god of marriage.

6 Give report of.

7 Polished and refined in her show of shyness.

8 Patron saint of England, but here evoked as an archetypal hero.

9 Clothing: but with a pun on courtship.

10 Species of the plover bird, renowned for its stupidity.

11 Behave, but with a self-aware allusion to the play itself.

12 With an allusion to the animal, a term of playful contempt.

13 The character is based on Margaret Lucas, who was to become the second wife of William Cavendish and, hence, the authors' stepmother. For further details of the play's contemporary allegory see the Introduction, pp. 129.

14 'Wit' was commonly used in the Renaissance to describe the affected cleverness, elegant manners and rhetorical skill admired by the aristocracy; characterized in John Lyly's *Euphues, or the Anatomy of Wit* (1578). Here 'wits' is used as a noun to signify clever ladies (Calsindow's daughters).

15 The cousins who later appear in Ballamo, the besieged castle, at which point their number has increased to three.

16 Lock of hair, probably false.

17 A head-covering with two long flaps hanging down either side of the head and neck, usually pinned into place.

18 Carnation.
19 Collar, to fit a smock.
20 Go well together.
21 An ointment, similar perhaps to today's foundation cream.
22 A red colouring, perhaps like the blusher of today's cosmetics.
23 Distilled water. Lady Tranquillity's cosmetics are not unlike the potions described in *A Choice Manual of Rare and Select Secrets in Physick and Chyrurgery* by Elizabeth Grey, Countess of Kent, a book which is referred to at III.iv.56.
24 Restorative medicines, essences.
25 Ladies of this period often used masks, made of silk or leather, to wear when they went outdoors, especially in the evening. The mask referred to here has been impregnated with oil on the inside, which was supposed to help reduce wrinkles.
26 A coin worth twenty shillings (one pound); at that time a substantial amount of money, more than a token.
27 Rhetoric, literary ornamentation.
28 Based on the two authors Jane Cavendish and Elizabeth Brackley, the parts would probably have been performed by them. Luceny, as the elder sister, would have been played by Elizabeth, and Tattiney by Jane.
29 'Stock' was often used contemptuously to describe an idol or sacred image; here Luceny suggests that Courtley is using her merely as an inert figure on which he can practise his skill at wooing.
30 Before, in preparation for.
31 A person of ill will.
32 With a pun on altar, i.e., marry.
33 A pun on clothing and courtship.
34 Conscious of yourself, self-absorbed.
35 The outward appearance, visible form.
36 Indignity, lowered in value or character.
37 Spread a rumour.
38 With.
39 A wasting disease; wasting away was thought to be one of the outward signs of love.
40 Torment.

ACT II

1 Possibly based upon Colonel Fretchwell who masterminded the brief retaking of Welbeck Abbey for the Royalist cause in 1645.
2 See note above, to I.ii.8.
3 To preach at, especially instructing the young.
4 The fruit, a prized reward; Presumption is referring, ironically, to the nursery rhyme in which Jack Horner 'pulls out a plum' from his pie.
5 Trinket, affectionate term.
6 Restorative liquid, medicine.
7 Cultured images, i.e., feigned.
8 Figurative: inflated ego.
9 A wasting disease, supposedly an outward sign of love; here, a mocking allusion to Corpolant's weight.
10 Corpolant's reference to a 'rich suit' means expensive clothing. Presumption puns on the term's alternative meaning, that of a formal courtship founded on financial security.
11 A Spanish wine.
12 Large casks of wine.
13 Possibly, from the Latin: *bellus* 'charming', *amor* 'love'. Ballamo, a fictional place, probably stands for Welbeck (happy river) Abbey the home of the two authors and where they were actually imprisoned during the siege of 1644–5.
14 i.e. not to take action and fight.
15 Talk with them pleasantly.
16 Reconnoitre.
17 Cheat.
18 To lie with; i.e., have sex with.
19 Dressed as.
20 Luceny's.
21 Engage in combat.
22 A wise man.
23 Admirer.
24 For you.
25 This speech is attributed to Tattiney in the manuscript, but the sense gives it to Presumption.
26 Container for distillation; Tattiney puns on the words 'vassal' and 'vessel'.
27 This speech is given to Presumption in the manuscript, but it makes more sense being said by Tattiney.
28 Statement; in other words, you are in no danger of going mad if you are capable of talking about in that manner.
29 Literally, to come into contact with; here, to kiss.
30 Despise, scorn.
31 Too.
32 Chattering lady, probably a reference to Lady Tranquillity.
33 Lady Tranquillity.
34 Alpha and omega are the first and last letters of the Greek alphabet; here, the beginning and end.

35 Philippians 4: 3.
36 Lay down, as a bet.
37 Keep my eyes lowered.
38 Look.
39 Look down at the table.
40 Cutting his nails, i.e. an insignificant gesture.
41 That you agree to marry me.
42 Put off disdainfully.
43 Fool.
44 A lump of vile matter; in more modern terminology, a piece of shit.
45 Common, many.
46 Anoint, as in marriage.
47 Take his cloak off.
48 Conduct, behaviour.
49 To treat me contemptuously.
50 For example, the phrase 'love, honour and obey' in the traditional wedding ceremony.
51 A pun on 'mistress', which means both a woman in authority as well as a woman who is courted and loved.
52 Presumption's mother; her name, 'Knowall', is a suitable complement to his.
53 Artless, unconcerned dress or demeanour.

ACT III

1 The fictional siege of Ballamo is based upon the historical siege of Welbeck Abbey by the Parliamentarian forces, during which the two authors were held captive. For a discussion of the play's political allusions see the Introduction, pp. 127–9.
2 The Royalists.
3 Without any substance.
4 'A curse on it'; an exclamation of irritation.
5 The governor of the castle.
6 Military barriers.
7 Standard-bearer, ensign.
8 A gentleman acting as a servant to a person of superior rank; since, in this context, Proper refers to his own occupation the term carries overtones of self-disparagement.
9 Body, though a large one, since Friendly is quite fat (see l. 20 below).
10 The name of an inn.
11 Courage; as in 'take heart', possibly a drinking toast.
12 Dismissed.
13 Make a habit of keeping, supporting.
14 The governor of the castle and the constructor of the military barriers mentioned above (III.i.6). The character is based upon Major Jammot, a French commander who, with Colonel Fretchville, retook Welbeck Abbey for the royalists in July 1645, although it appears to have been lost again to the Roundheads by November that year. His poor English is referred to at ll. 33–4 below.
15 The steward.
16 Sleep.
17 Cursed.
18 The introduction of an angel as one of the characters gives the play a masque-like quality; for a further discussion of the play's similarities to these court entertainments see the Introduction, p. 129.
19 Bent upon.
20 To madden her, to make her mad. Presumption's tactics are akin to those exercised by Petruchio against Katherine in Shakespeare's *The Taming of the Shrew*.
21 Moreover.
22 Keep the weekly accounts.
23 Old men; literally, those with long beards.
24 Bow, bend the knee.
25 Or any part of it.
26 Sermonizing, boringly didactic.
27 Ways in which Courtley woos Luceny, with a suggestion of 'courtly' trickery.
28 No, in faith; no, truly.
29 Marriage portions were the money, goods and land given to the husband by his wife's family upon their marriage.
30 Manner, behaviour.
31 Pray thee.
32 Hobgoblin; an imaginary object of terror.
33 A fond delusion; also a reference to the play's title where 'fancy' means 'love' as well as 'devices of the imagination'.
34 Harsh, severe.
35 The names are uncertain: the play gives 'Cicilley' (V.i) and this corresponds with the abbreviation of her name, 'CI.'. The other two are referred to only as 'SH.' and 'IS.'. The three cousins are based on the three Cavendish sisters: Jane, Elizabeth, and their younger sister, Frances.
36 An offender.
37 Surroundings, but with a self-conscious allusion to the the fact that this is a play.
38 Played the part of Cleopatra, perhaps in Shakespeare's *Antony and Cleopatra* since the authors appear to make other allusions to his plays (see above: Prologue and III.iii.10) and refer to 'his gallant tragedy' (below, l. 17).
39 The ceremonial entries of victorious generals into Rome; Cleopatra was intended to adorn Octavius Caesar's triumph. Here, Sh. sees

herself, somewhat melodramatically, as similarly paraded by the Parliamentarian forces who have taken Ballamo.

40 Find recreation for.
41 Disinclined to.
42 Restorative medicines. 'Our friend' probably refers to Calsindow.
43 Concentrated essence, a term associated with alchemy. Referred to in Elizabeth Grey's *A Choice Manual*, which is cited at l. 56–7 below.
44 Store them away, for future use.
45 A crystal ball, offering magical powers of sight. However, Is.'s reply refers to another meaning of 'prospective', that is, a 'telescope'.
46 A formula or prescription, a statement of medicinal ingredients.
47 The impression of a crest left in sealing wax by a seal.
48 A word is missing in the manuscript.
49 A medicinal herb, couch grass (Agrostidaea).
50 Myrobalans, a variety of plum.
51 Elizabeth Grey, Countess of Kent, was the author of *A Choice Manuall of Rare and Select Secrets in Physick and Chyrurgery* (1653); although this was not published until 1653 she was related to the Cavendish family, perhaps providing an opportunity for the authors to see the work in manuscript form. Margaret Cavendish mentions Elizabeth Grey, both as a relative and maker of 'cordials' in *The Life of William Cavendish Duke of Newcastle* (1667).
52 Medicinal water, recalling 'Doctor Stephen's Sovereign Water' and 'Doctor Willoughbies Water' in Elizabeth Grey's *A Choice Manual*, referred to at l. 56–7 above.
53 Balsams, salves.
54 Storehouse, repository.
55 To war, to raise the siege of Ballamo in which the previous scene was set.
56 Virgin; the vestals were the chaste female servants of the Roman deity Vesta, goddess of the hearth.
57 Fanciful sentiments.
58 MS reads 'give's'.
59 Action and Moderate are Royalist prisoners in Ballamo, the castle held by the Parliamentarians; they are impossible to identify as historical personages and are probably typical, rather than individual, men.
60 'A plague upon them all'.
61 Action's coarse language is condemned by Moderate, but it suits his rough, military character. However, the use of such vocabulary in the writings of Renaissance noblewomen would have been considered inappropriate, and shows how independent the authors were of conventional social constraints.
62 To regain Ballamo for the Royalist cause.
63 An ambitious but plotless strategy.

ACT IV

1 Luceny perhaps gives the love-sick man a cordial (medicinal drink) similar to those found in Lord Calsindow's medicine cabinet in III.iv.
2 Suggestive of the exile undergone by many Royalists during the Civil War; for instance, the authors' father, the Duke of Newcastle was, at the time they were writing the play, resident in Paris.
3 A ribbon denoting favour such as is referred to by Sh. (see above, III.iv.75); also, a rainbow: Genesis 9: 12–17.
4 A reference to the Civil War, presumably the lady's home has been ransacked by Parliamentarian forces.
5 Symbol of military victory; a laurel wreath was worn by victorious Roman commanders.
6 Possibly an altar.
7 Votive offerings, prayers.
8 Another name for the laurel, signifying victory.
9 Based on the authors' two brothers, Charles Viscount Mansfield, and Henry, Earl of Ogle.
10 Sh., one of the three cousins besieged in the castle of Ballamo.
11 Cicilley, another of the besieged cousins.
12 Hesitations.
13 Playful summons, i.e. unreal and fruitless calls for action.
14 Commanded, called.
15 Blacksmith.
16 The account books, mentioned as 'week books' by Presumption (III.iii.38).
17 Cheated.
18 Scheme, the plot to break into Calsindow's personal cabinets.
19 Courtley takes on the character of a street vendor singing directly to the audience; the part seems unusual for him since he is presented as the epitome, even if a somewhat mannered one, of gentlemanly behaviour. The song form suggests that this might be a stylized piece which the authors inserted into the play in emulation of mountebank literature; e.g. as in Ben Jonson's *Volpone* (II.ii.191–203) where Volpone disguises

himself as a mountebank and sings a song similar to that of Courtley.

20 A separate head-covering worn by women in the sixteenth and seventeenth centuries; they are fancifully described as 'melancholy' to denote their association with the archetypal grief of a rejected lover. Courtley's other purchasable items are depicted in a similar manner.
21 See 'magisterium of pearl' (III.iv.37–8).
22 Perfumed water, scent.
23 Small, private room.
24 Cosmetic.
25 Magnifying glass.
26 Telescope; see above, note to III.iv.46.
27 The general sense is that Courtley's luck will turn, bringing him good fortune. There is, however, a suggestion that 'Fortune's cap' is not merely her face or head, but a reference to the cap of Fortunatus, a hero of popular legend who is favoured by the goddess Fortune and who possesses a magic wishing-cap. Thomas Dekker wrote a play based upon the story, *Old Fortunatus* (1600).
28 In faith, truly.
29 A white collar.
30 Ways of conducting herself, different characters.
31 Pert's list describes different forms of love: wifely virtue, the passion of courtship, and the idealized union of souls.
32 Merely a repetition.
33 See above, note to I.ii.7.
34 The three cousins; the exchange described by Discretion is that planned by Sh. (IV.iii.21–6).
35 No, in faith; no, truly.
36 They showed keen-witted understanding of my nature.
37 Stately, in a stately manner.
38 Lack of respect.
39 The only way in which he could defend himself.

ACT V

1 The siege has been lifted.
2 Delaying, obstructive.
3 Mischievous behaviour.
4 Lesson, conducted in the form of questions and answers.
5 Swoon, a faint.
6 The manuscript has 'fray', but 'pray' makes more sense in this context.
7 The manuscript attributes this speech to Luciney, but it is clearly Tattiney's reply to her sister.
8 Delightful, pleasant.
9 The use of stage machinery to lower figures onto the stage and the disguises adopted by the two young noblemen are drawn from court masque conventions. The authors were familiar with this genre, having jointly written a masque, *A Pastorall*, which may be found in the same manuscript as *The Concealed Fancies*; for a more complete discussion see the Introduction, p. 129.
10 Namely, that is to say; from an abbreviation of 'to wit'.
11 Proposal, offer.
12 Protection, defence.
13 You would'st.
14 To be mine.
15 A pun on 'masque'; the previous exchange between the four lovers closely resembles one of these courtly dramas, where the courtiers disguised themselves as allegorical figures, often wearing facial 'masks'.
16 Obselete form of 'linens'.
17 Before.
18 Linens, but with a pun on underclothes.
19 A colloquial exclamation or phrase: 'To be sure get along with you'.
20 Ironing.
21 Consensus.
22 To be a mimic.
23 Risk.
24 Whatever form of behaviour (act or scene) you adopt.
25 Intellect; see above, note to II.i.2.
26 A small amount; a pun on whit/wit.
27 Hymen, the god of marriage in classical mythology.
28 Demeanour.
29 'But it's for pride that I marry you, / I tell you that I don't love you.' Lady Tranquillity's French is poor, another aspect of the satire against Margaret Lucas (see the Introduction, p. 129).
30 Lady Tranquillity.
31 In the manuscript the next six lines are attributed to the angel, but they clearly are meant to be spoken by Calsindow.
32 Disposition, state of mind.
33 A narrative with two meanings: the superficial story, and the secondary sense. Here, a story of another woman who Luceny is supposed to admire and emulate.
34 Doltish, stupid.
35 Dowry.
36 Luceny succeeds in turning on its head the Renaissance convention that women should

be 'chaste, silent and obedient'; she points out, with economic astuteness, that the spouse who brings the most money into the marriage should rightfully have control over the other, regardless of gender.

37 Personal attributes.
38 Economic metaphor: to be worth as much.
39 The love and prayers just mentioned.
40 Pretends.
41 Manner.
42 To be sure.
43 Infatuated.
44 A wand or stick symbolizing authority. Luceny refers scathingly to women who assume their husbands should rule over them. However, there is also a sexual pun – rod signifying penis – which is picked up by Tattiney in the next line.
45 Block of wood; Tattiney comments ironically upon Luceny's phrase, questioning both the 'authority' and the sexual potency of husbands.
46 White hoods were commonly worn by women during this period; the most probable meaning is that, if the play is disliked by those with white hoods (the ladies), they will depart.
47 The men in the audience would undoubtedly have worn hats and, perhaps as a gesture of their appreciation of the play, they are encouraged to remove them as a display of courtesy.
48 Addressed to the authors' father, William Cavendish, Duke of Newcastle.
49 Restorative medicine.

PART II DOCUMENTS

Introduction

1 Chambers, *Elizabethan Stage*, vol. 1, p. 371: 'Boys were regularly employed to take female parts, and although it would be going rather too far to say that a woman never appeared on the Elizabethan stage, women were not included in the ordinary companies.'
2 Stephen Orgel, 'Nobody's Perfect: Or Why Did the English Stage Take Boys for Women?', *South Atlantic Quarterly*, 88 (1989), p. 8. In addition, women spectators were addressed directly in some plays. See, for example, the epilogue to John Lyly's *Gallathea* (1592) in which Gallathea urges the women of the audience to succumb to love, or John Fletcher's *Rule a Wife and Have a Wife* (1640) in which women are advised to look to their behaviour and to their reaction to the play, which is set in Spain.
3 By contrast, when Thomas Coryat (an Englishman) visited a playhouse in Venice in 1611 he noted the severe restrictions placed upon female spectators: women attended the theatre in double masks covering the area from their foreheads to the base of their necks. In addition, seating arrangements between men and women were carefully regulated. See Thomas Coryat, 'Crudities' (1611) as excerpted in *Life in Shakespeare's England*, ed. John Dover Wilson, p. 164. See also Jean E. Howard, 'The Materiality of Ideology: Women as Spectators, Spectacles, and Paying Customers in the English Public Theater' in *The Stage and Social Struggle in Early Modern England*, pp. 73–92, previously printed in *Staging the Renaissance* ed. David Scott Kastan and Peter Stallybrass.
4 Numbers in parentheses refer to document numbers in this collection.
5 There is much scholarship on the puritans' antitheatrical prejudice. See, for instance, Jonas Barish, *The Antitheatrical Prejudice* and Margot Heinemann, *Puritanism and Theatre*.
6 The exception to this seems to have been plays at court. In 1617, Lady Anne Clifford wrote in her diary:

> Upon the 25th [of January] I went into the Court. Lord Villiers was created Earl of Buckingham. My Lord, my Lord of Buckingham, and divers other lords bringing them up to the king. Supped with my Lord and Lady Arundel and after supper I saw the play of the Mad Lover in the hall.

The Mad Lover was performed by the King's Men, probably on January 5th at Whitehall. Therefore the 25th – as cited above – might well be a mistake for the 5th, as the court was in transit to Somerset House between 20 January and 17 February.

7 Chambers, *Elizabethan Stage*, vol. 2, pp. 104–15, 342–5, 349–50.
8 Gerald Eades Bentley, *The Jacobean and Caroline Stage*, vol. 2, pp. 382–3.
9 Ibid., vol. I, pp. 158–60.
10 Ibid., vol. VI, pp. 156–7.
11 Chambers, *Elizabethan Stage*, vol. 2, pp. 187, 389. The example of a play that seems to

have required many extra players for minor roles is *Frederick and Basilea*. (See Chambers, *Elizabethan Stage*, vol. 2, p. 150. W.W. Greg argues against the theory of women gatherers as minor actors in *Henslowe Papers*, p. 63, n. 8.

12 For theoretical perspectives concerning revisionary historiography see Hayden White, *Tropics of Discourse: Essays in Cultural Criticism*, chs 1–3, and Dominick LaCapra, *Rethinking Intellectual History: Texts, Contexts, Language*.

7 Attitudes Towards Women's Attendance at the Theatres

1 Samuel Rowlands, *The Bride*, 1617

1 Little is known of Samuel Rowlands (?1570–?1630), despite the fact that he wrote numerous poems and pamphlets. Most of his work could be termed social criticism. Early in his career Rowlands's tone was deemed so offensive to the authorities that two pamphlets were burned in the kitchen of the Stationers' Company. Not surprisingly, one of Rowlands's most common targets was the theatre. *The Bride* is a moral dialogue in which three characters – Cate, Mistress Susan and the Bride – discuss the virtues to which a wife should aspire.

2 Within social limits.

3 Rowlands described the first three duties of a wife as: caring for the house, entertaining her husband's friends, and being frugal so as to preserve her husband's wealth. Readers familiar with Shakespeare's *The Taming of the Shrew* will recognize two of Rowlands's other tenets: a wife should 'observe her husband's disposition' and conform herself 'with weak submission'. She must, Rowlands explains, 'pacify his ire, although she find that he impatient be'.

4 Plays performed at one of the public playhouses (as the First Globe or the First Fortune) at which all manner of society was welcomed (as opposed to plays performed at the private playhouses where high admission prices restricted the audience to the elite).

5 A street-wife was a woman who spent much of her time gadding about on the streets, with the implication of loose sexuality and social impropriety. It was thought inappropriate, at the time, for women to go about on their own unchaperoned and unprotected.

6 A woman who works in the fields.

2 John Northbrooke, *A Treatise* etc., 1577

1 John Northbrooke (fl. 1570), preacher, gained and lost several church appointments during the course of his career. He wrote three religious treatises published in 1571, 1573 and 1577, all of which were popular enough to be reprinted. One of these – from which the excerpts printed here are taken – is the earliest pamphlet to criticize the contemporary theatre in a distinctive, systematic way. For Northbrooke, the only acceptable plays were school plays, for they could be justified 'for learning and utterance's sake, In Latin, and very seldom in English'.

2 Roman poet, banished because of the salacious nature of his writing. The quotation is from Ovid's *The Art of Love*, Book 1, l. 99: '*Spectatum veniunt, veniunt spectentur ut ipsae*'; that is, 'They come to see, they come that they may be seen' (Ovid, *The Art of Love and other Poems*, trans. J.H. Mozley, pp. 18–19).

3 Overpowered.

4 Juvenal was the first great Roman satiric poet. This is probably an allusion to his 'Satire 6', ll. 60ff. in which he asks, 'Can our arcades show you one woman worthy of your vows?' He goes on to describe lewd behaviour in the playhouses, both on stage and off. (Juvenal, 'Satires' in *Juvenal and Persius*, trans G.G. Ramsay, p.89.)

5 The common people, here used with disdain.

6 Glossed in the 1577 edition as 'a common jester and player to Domitian the Emperor, which did mock and scoff most filthy with his gestures the godly Christians'.

7 Interludes.

8 Northbrooke refers his reader to Genesis 4: 1: 'And Adam knew Eve his wife; and she conceived, and bare Cain, and said, I have gotten a man from the Lord.' However, given his reference to 'Dina', he might be conflating Eve with the classical goddess Diana, the huntress who, whilst bathing nude, tempted Actaeon to gaze at her. In punishment, she changed him into a stag and he was torn to pieces by his own hounds. However, Diana was never ravished.

9 Christian saint and martyr.

3 Stephen Gosson, *Plays Confuted in Five Actions*, 1590

1 Stephen Gosson (1554–1624) attended Corpus Christi College, Oxford, and later made his way to London, where he wrote plays and poems, the latter of which were ranked with Sir Philip Sidney and Edmund Spenser as 'the best for pastoral'. He was also said, by some, to have been a player for a short time.

Around 1579 Gosson underwent a change of heart and eventually he began to write elaborate, prudish attacks on the theatre. The best known of these was *The School of Abuse* (1579), an invective that prompted Sidney to write his *Defense of Poetry*.

In the excerpt presented here Gosson is answering a defence of the theatre written by his most formidable opponent, Thomas Lodge, an actor and colleague of Edward Alleyn's. Alleyn – famed for his acting of the bombastic heroes of Christopher Marlowe's plays – was a theatre entrepreneur and a founder of charitable institutions. Interestingly, Gosson (who served as rector of St Botolph's, Bishopsgate, at the time of his death) recommended several parishioners for residence in Alleyn's institutions.

2 Murder.
3 Inscription on the ornament of precious metal or jewellery of a flat form, worn about the person.
4 Handkerchief.
5 The.
6 Plays performed by the boys' companies, sometimes at court.
7 Demeanour.
8 Show, exhibit.
9 Apples.
10 A cover for a dagger, with a pun on phallus.

4 John Rainolds, *Th'overthrow of Stage Playes*, 1599

1 Objections to the playhouses spread even to the universities, spawning a classic debate at Oxford between Dr John Rainolds (1549–1607), an eminent theologian, and Dr William Gager, the Latin dramatist. Rainolds's side of the controversy was first published in 1599. In this pamphlet he argued that plays foster vanity; women cannot be better edified at plays than at sermons.
2 The Bear Garden, located on Bankside near the Rose Playhouse and the site of the First Globe Playhouse. The arena was used for bear-baiting interspersed with acrobatics and other types of carnivalesque spectacle, activities which brought much criticism on moral grounds. An accident that occurred in 1583, during which a scaffold fell down and eight persons were killed, was thought by some opponents to represent God's disapproval.
3 Material, substance.
4 Swore.
5 Truth.
6 The archetypal traitor who betrayed Christ with a kiss.

8 Women as Spectators

5 Margaret Cavendish, *Nature's Pictures* etc., 1667

1 Margaret Cavendish (b. 1623) was the youngest child of a wealthy landowner. Her father died when she was an infant and her mother took over her education. At the age of 20 Margaret was a Maid of Honour to Henrietta Maria, following the queen into exile in France. There she met her future husband, William Cavendish, Duke of Newcastle, a widower nearly thirty years her senior. As a patron of writers and a minor poet and playwright himself, Cavendish encouraged his wife's creative efforts.

Margaret wrote poems, essays, scientific and philosophical tracts; she was interested in a wide variety of subjects including language, natural history, and human behaviour. She also wrote a utopian fiction addressing the oppression of women and two volumes of plays (1662, 1668). In 1667 she wrote *The Life of William Cavendish*, for which she was best known in her time. She was invited to the Royal Society in 1667, a rare event for a woman.

The excerpt printed here is from an autobiography entitled 'A True Relation of my Birth, Breeding, and Life' (Book 11 of *Nature's Pictures Drawn from Fancy's Pencil*). In it she describes the pastimes of young women who, like herself, 'were bred virtuously, modestly, civilly, honourably, and on honest principles'.

Because she was self-conscious about her lack of formal education Margaret was a strong advocate of the importance of women's education. Perhaps that is one one reason why she encouraged her two step-daughters – Lady Jane Cavendish and Lady Elizabeth Brackley – who collaborated in writing a play, *The Concealed Fancies*, which is printed in the first part of this volume.

Margaret Cavendish is buried in Westminster Abbey.

2 Coming and going.

3 A pleasure garden frequented by the public, located near St James's Park.

4 Affectionate.

6 Mary Rich, Countess of Warwick, *Autobiography*

1 Mary Rich, Countess of Warwick, was born in 1625. Her courtship was opposed by her father and, for a brief time, she was banished from home. Finally, Mary and her father were reconciled, but her marriage was a secret. Her autobiography – she claimed – was written in two days in 1672. In it she describes her marriage in idealistic terms; however, the diary which covers the last eleven years of her life renders a very different account.

Three of her works were published in 1686: *Rules for a Holy Life*, *Pious Reflections upon Several Scriptures*, and *Occasional Meditations upon Sundry Subjects*.

Mary Rich died in 1678.

2 Sir Robert Killigrew, courtier and Groom of the Privy Chamber to Queen Elizabeth I, married Mary Woodhouse, niece of Sir Francis Bacon. She survived her husband and subsequently married Sir Thomas Stafford, Gentleman Usher to Queen Henrietta Maria. Her daughter Elizabeth married Francis Boyle, first Viscount Shannon. Of Lady Stafford, the Countess of Warwick wrote: 'She was a cunning old woman who had been herself too much, and was too long versed in amours.' If this is to be believed, apparently Elizabeth followed in her mother's ways, bearing a child by Charles II.

7 Ann, Lady Halkett, *Autobiography*

1 Anne Halkett (1622–99) was the younger daughter of Thomas Murray, who was tutor to the children of King James I and later Provost of Eton College. Anne's mother served as governess to the king's children and, when her husband died, she took over responsibility for her daughter's education. This included French, music, dancing and needlework as well as physic and surgery. Anne also received an extensive religious education shaped by Bible readings, daily prayers and regular church attendance.

Anne's mother forbade her to marry her first suitor because of his modest fortune. A quarrel ensued and was ended only when Anne threatened to enter a Protestant nunnery. Subsequently she became the lover of the Royalist colonel Joseph Bampfield. Together they rescued James, Duke of York (the future James II), from Parliamentary captivity through a plot in which Anne provided one of her dresses for the duke's disguise. Although Bampfield – posing as a widower – proposed marriage to Anne, the existence of his wife was eventually proven.

Following a period in which she practised medicine in Scotland, Anne married Sir James Halkett, a widower with two daughters. Before the birth of their first child she wrote an essay entitled 'The Mother's Will to Her Unborn Child', the manuscript of which is now lost. Following her husband's death she taught the children of nobility, and also received a pension for her services from James II.

Upon her death Anne left some twenty volumes of manuscript prose behind. In 1701 her expertise on religious subjects was recognized by the publication of two treatises. Her autobiography was published the same year. Anne seems to have composed her religious prose over a fifty-five-year period (1644–99); however, her autobiography – a candid record of personal and political events – seems to have been written in 1677–8.

2 Manner of life (converse = living).

3 Permission.

4 A pleasure garden frequented by the public, located near St James's Park.

8 Henry Fitzgeffrey, *Satyres*, etc., 1617

1 Henry Fitzgeffrey (fl. 1617) earned his reputation as a writer of satires and epigrams. His origins and education are not known; nor is his professional status.

In 1617 appeared *Certain Elegies, Done by Sundrie Excellent Wits. With Satyres and Epigrames.* A second edition appeared in 1618, and a third edition appeared in 1620.

A fourth, undated edition also appeared. The elegies contained therein were written by Francis Beaumont, Michael Drayton, and another author identified as 'N.H.', perhaps Nathaniel Hooke. The satires and epigrams that follow are divided into three books, in between which are verses by J. Stephens.

The third book, from which this excerpt is taken, consists of a short poem describing the gallants, dandies and loose women, as well as the refined ladies and gentlemen who come together in the audience at the Blackfriar Playhouse. The Blackfriars – a private theatre with higher admission fees than public playhouses such as the Globe – was supposed to attract an elite, selective audience. Fitzgeffrey's description, of course, undercuts this image.

2 A tittle is a whit, the least possible amount; hence, the Cheapside dame wears as little as possible on her head even though it should be covered more to meet the social expectations for modesty. Fitzgeffrey also implies that the dame has as little in, as on her head.

3 Surely.

4 A woman dressed in men's clothes who uses her disguise to sneak into the gallants' row undetected.

5 Truly.

6 This time 'by the hand' refers to the lady (cf. l. 16), meaning 'truly', but also with sexual innuendo.

7 Dandiprat, an insignificant, contemptible fellow.

8 Go-between, toy.

9 The word 'Egyptian' was used as an intensifier, as in the phrase 'Egyptian darkness', 'intense darkness'.

10 A ball of soap scented with musk, or a receptacle for musk (the odoriferous, glandular secretion used as the basis for many perfumes and thought to have aphrodisiac effects).

11 Spiritless man or youth.

12 Flatterer; the 1617 edition reads 'sincopace', which some editors have construed as 'syncopate', i.e., off-beat, displaced, but 'sycophant' makes better sense.

13 Courante, a seventeenth-century dance noted for its gliding steps.

14 Marzipan, probably with an emphasis on its pasty, bland quality.

15 Farthingale, a framework of hoops used by women to extend their skirts.

16 Galliards and jigs were both dances characterized by quick, lively steps.

17 Waste of time.

18 Entertainments to keep the mind going, idle occupations.

19 But despite this opinion.

9 John Chamberlain, from a letter to Sir Dudley Carleton

1 John Chamberlain (1554–1628) was born in London. His father was an alderman and master of the Ironmongers Company. John attended Trinity College, Cambridge, and Gray's Inn, but he never became a barrister. He lived as a bachelor, lodging with friends and relatives. Chamberlain described himself as a 'Paul's Walker', a person who spent much of his time around St Paul's Cathedral, a place for conducting business and exchanging news. Through this avocation he managed to catalogue many of the most important events of the time in letters sent to his friend Sir Dudley Carleton, ambassador to the Hague. Chamberlain's correspondence covers the years 1597–1626.

2 Thomas Middleton's *A Game at Chess.*

3 Diplomat and poet, Wotton was engaged in diplomatic duties in Venice for several terms covering nearly twenty years. At the time Chamberlain wrote this letter Wotton was lately returned to England after his third term of office.

4 Albertus Morton (knighted 1617) was son of Sir Henry Wotton's half-brother. He accompanied Wotton to Venice as secretary in 1604. At the time of this letter Morton was serving as ambassador to France, and was appointed Secretary of State a year later.

5 Sir Benjamin Rudyard, Surveyor of the Court of Wards and Liveries, married Elizabeth Harrington, cousin of Lucy, Countess of Bedford.

6 Courtier to James I, Lake had a chequered political career, having gained and lost the position of Secretary of State. His guilt in the affairs that led to his dismissal was extenuated by Lord Digby and Sir Francis Bacon. In 1625 he returned to public office through his election as MP for Wells.

7 Widow of Sir George Smith (b. Lytton, Lady Judith). The allusion to 'Sir G Peter' is unknown.

8 Toby Matthew, son of the Archbishop of

York, who, as recusant and exile, was an embarrassment to his father.

10 Thomas Cranley, *Amanda, or the Reformed Whore*, 1635

1 Little is known of Thomas Cranley. The first edition of *Amanda, or the Reformed Whore* (1635) is identified as 'composed, and made, by Thomas Cranley, gent., now a prisoner in the King's Bench'. In the introduction Cranley claims that he had been a prisoner in the Fleet Prison for many months prior to its writing. One day when he had been out walking on a high tower he saw a young woman 'of a comely feature and sweet grace, apparelled very richly, and attired according to the fashion then most in use'. She was standing in her chamber, looking out onto the street, and Cranley states that he began to wonder who she was. Upon further observation he was convinced that she was 'a woman apt to give entertainment to any that desired her company'. He also claimed to have noticed a pattern to the sorts of men who came and went from her chamber.

Cranley decided to write love letters to the young woman, which a friend delivered. These, he said, made her alternately angry and pleased. Writing yet another letter he managed – with the aid of a long pole – to place it just inside the casement, and then to shut the window so that the woman wouldn't know from whence it had come. Several days later Cranley claims that he observed the woman sitting near her window, embroidering a waistcoat with gold thread and coloured silk; and many times she 'cast her eye upon the tower . . . blushing exceedingly'.

The rest of the story concerns Cranley's attempt to 'use the best art and skill . . . to have her cast in a new mould, and to purge the dross out of her that she might be refined to purer metal'. In pursuit of her rehabilitation Cranley and the young woman share a series of conversations about poetry, and Cranley soon falls in love with her in earnest. However, one day he spies her among the crowd of spectators at a play, and she is behaving 'too familiarly' so Cranley returns home and writes the verses addressed to 'Amanda' in order to encourage his love to convert to a virtuous life. Whether Cranley's verses converted his love to chastity or not is open to speculation. They were, however, popular enough that a second edition followed four years after the initial printing, in 1639.

2 Hollows scratched out. Young birds need to learn to scratch, for a variety of reasons.

3 Woollen fabric, with the nuance of showing inferior quality.

4 Countess, i.e., earl's or count's wife or widow, or a woman with her own rank of earl or count.

11 Anon., *The Actor's Remonstrance*, 1643

1 Although this work is anonymous it is identified as the work of a player, its complete title being *The Actor's Remonstrance or Complaint: For the Silencing of their Profession, and Banishment from Several Playhouses*. The specificity of its publication date (24 January 1643) might well suggest that it was meant as an answer to a specific antitheatrical treatise, although the author doesn't identify exactly what its target was. In the conclusion, excerpted here, the author offers to guarantee that women will only come 'lawfully with their husbands' to the playhouses if the actors are again granted admittance to them.

2 Apollo, god of music, medicine and associated with higher moral and religious principles.

3 The Muses.

4 Apprentices.

5 Places diametrically opposite, especially Australasia as a region on the opposite side of the earth to Europe.

6 Be discontented with.

12 Henry Peacham, *The Art of Living in London*, 1642

1 Henry Peacham (?1576–?1643) was the son of the rector of North Mimms, Hertfordshire, and author of *A Garden of Eloquence* (1577). He was educated at Cambridge and, for a brief time, was master of Wymondham School, Norfolk. In 1606 Peacham published the first English instruction book for artists, *The Art of Drawing with the Pen and Limning in Water Colours*. His interests continued with his illustrations for James I's *Basilikon Doron*, rendered into Latin verse for presentation to James's son Henry, Prince of Wales (1610), and James's great work *Minerva Britanna* (1612), a survey of architecture and interior

decoration. Peacham travelled extensively on the Continent. He wrote elegies and satires. His most famous work was *The Compleat Gentleman*, a book of etiquette, manners and heraldry. The excerpt printed here is taken from his last work.

2 The area around the Royal Exchange, located in east London at the junction of Threadneedle and Cornhill.

3 Women's undergarment, frequently a loose-fitting, shirt-like garment hanging from the shoulders.

13 Sir John Harington, *Epigrams*, 1618

1 Sir John Harington (1561–1612), courtier and translator, was educated at Winchester and Christ's College, Cambridge. Queen Elizabeth I was his godmother and he remained one of her favourites throughout her life. It was at Elizabeth's suggestion that Harington translated Ariosto's long poem *Orlando Furioso*, which may have been one of Shakespeare's sources for *Much Ado About Nothing*. Harington invented the first water closet and was generally clever and witty; however, his bawdy satires (*Metamorphosis of Ajax*, 1596) caused him to be banished briefly from the queen's presence. Interestingly, in *Ajax* Harington writes: 'For the shrewd wife read the book of Taming a Shrew, which . . . made a number of us so perfect, that now every one can tame a shrew in our country, save he that hath her.' *The Taming of a Shrew* is one of the plays that Harington included in his personal library.

Harington served under the Earl of Essex in Ireland, and was knighted by him. Yet despite this association he managed to avoid involvement in the Essex conspiracy.

Harington's epigrams enjoyed three editions, the last one of which was printed in 1625 containing 346 poems. Topics for the epigrams ranged from 'Of Good Sauce' to 'Of a Painted Lady'. One (No. 76, 1618 edn) was dedicated to the Earl of Essex.

2 Edge of a garment, on the hem or collar.

3 Performance filling the interval between parts of a play, or at the end of a play.

4 Cheating, deceptive.

5 Trick, from the phrase 'cony-catching,' i.e., catching rabbits; here, with obscene overtones referring to the slang for female genitalia.

6 Unpleasant.

14 Sir John Finet, from his notebook, 1629

1 John Finet (b. 1571) served as a gentleman in Sir Robert Sydney's company in the 1590s, after which he entered the employment of Thomas Wilson, secretary to Robert Cecil, the principal adviser of Elizabeth I and her successor James I. During 1609–10 Finet was selected to accompany Cecil's son on his grand tour of the Continent. Upon Finet's return he replaced Wilson as Cecil's personal secretary. Upon Cecil's death in 1612 Finet was temporarily left without a position; however, he was soon appointed second 'officer of assistance' to Lewis Lewkenor, Master of Ceremonies. He had few duties and, for several years, served informally on various diplomatic missions. Finally, in 1618, he was awarded the reversion of the Master of Ceremonies position; but he didn't actually acquire the post until 1627.

The notebooks Finet kept from 1628 to 1641 provide a rich and detailed record of court life during the reign of Charles I. Finet was also known as a shrewd adviser and, like John Chamberlain, as a correspondent of Dudley Carleton, ambassador to the Hague (see Document 9). In addition, Finet was recognized as a composer of bawdy songs. His lyrics could be obscene, and Chamberlain reported that in January 1618 Finet sang a song 'of such scurrilous and base stuff that it put the king out of his good humour'.

2 Attendant at a meal who supervised the arrangement of the table, the seating of the guests, and the tasting and serving of food.

3 Several, various.

4 Large, flat dishes.

9 Women Performing

15 Anon., report of an incident in Oxford, 1598

1 The Thursday following Rogation Sunday (the fifth Sunday after Easter).

2 Traditional dance in fancy costume, frequently with bells.

16 From the Declared Accounts of the Office of the Works, 1607–9

1 The Office of the Works kept accounts for the King's or Queen's Exchequer relating to construction and repairs in various royal

palaces, castles, parks, etc., with files of receipts and other subsidiary accounts, containing information about wages of artificers and expenses of materials used in building and repair.

The following excerpt transcribes the account kept by Andrew Kerwyn, paymaster, for setting up various entertainments. The latter part (l. 30, 'fitting up . . . ') probably refers to Jonson's *Masque of Queens* and to Inigo Jones's designs for a House of Fame with the seats for the queen and her ladies above the great gates.

2 Part of a floor raised by a step; platform.
3 Stairs.
4 Corners or angles of a polygon, niches.
5 Ornamental carvings.

17 Vincent to Benson, *Calendar of State Papers*, 1605

1 This letter, preserved amongst the State Papers, is addressed simply 'A Monsieur Benson, Bruxelles'. Therefore the identities of the author and the recipient remain something of a mystery. The letter, written on three pages in a tiny crabbed hand, primarily discusses problems between the French and the Spanish ambassadors, along with Catholic issues. Consequently, one possibility is that the author and recipient were part of the English intelligence network.

The entertainment described in this excerpt is the *Masque of Blackness* performed in the old Elizabethan banqueting house at Whitehall. Scenery included a curtain painted like a landscape of woods and hunting scenes. The masquers, in azure and silver, were twelve nymphs, 'negroes and the daughters of Niger'; torchbearers, costumed in sea green, represented Oceaniae; the presenters acted Oceanus, Niger and Aethiopia the Moon. Musicians acted Tritons, Sea Maids and Echoes. Sir Thomas Edmondes stated that the masque cost the Exchequer £3,000. This was a Queen's masque, danced by the queen, the Countesses of Bedford, Derby and Suffolk, the Ladies Rich, Bevill, Howard of Effingham, Wroth and Walsingham, Lady Elizabeth Howard, Anne Lady Herbert and Susan Lady Herbert. (See E.K. Chambers, *The Elizabethan Stage*, vol. 3, pp. 375–8.)

2 Splendour.
3 6 January.
4 Show, display.
5 Hidden machines.
6 Lucy, Countess of Bedford, was appointed one of the Ladies of the Bedchamber to Queen Anne, and she eventually became the queen's closest friend. Lady Bedford assisted in arranging at least one masque, and she acted in a brilliant series of masques written by Ben Jonson. See the introduction to *Cupid's Banishment* in this volume.
7 Courtesan-like.
8 Masks.

18 Zuane Pesaro to the Doge and Senate, *Calendar of State Papers*, 1625/6

1 Zuane Pesaro served as ambassador in England to the Venetian Doge and Senate. In this letter he reports the court reaction to an unknown masque. Alessandro Antelminelli, also known as Amerigo Salvetti (for many years representative of the Grand Dukes of Tuscany at the English court) had more specific comments about the same masque:

> Her Majesty the Queen conducts herself with youthful grace. On the day of the carnival, for which Tueday was set aside, she acted in a beautiful pastoral of her own composition, asisted by twelve of her ladies whom she had trained since Christmas. The pastoral succeeded admirably; not only in the decorations and changes of scenery, but also in the acting and recitation of the ladies – Her Majesty surpassing all others. The performance was conducted as privately as possible, inasmuch as it is an unusual thing in this country to see the Queen upon a stage; the audience consequently was limited to a few of the nobility, expressly invited, no others being admitted.
>
> (Historical MSS. Commission, 11th Report, Appendix. Part I, 1887, p. 47)

2 See Document 9, note 1.
3 'Times change and [so must] we.'

19 Declared Accounts of the Office of the Works, 1631–2

1 For a description of the Office of the Works, see Document 16, note 1. The following excerpt details expenses for a masque and pastoral. The pastoral was Walter Montagu's *The Shepherd's Paradise*, performed at Denmark House on 9 January (and possibly repeated on 2 February). The masque has not been identified. Also, the monetary calculations

detailed throughout this account are sometimes in error.

2 Elm boards.
3 Stairs.
4 Machines.
5 Transportation costs.
6 Work paid for the job, piecework.
7 Payments made for individual jobs, over and above salary.
8 Abbreviation for *videlicet* ('that is to say', 'namely').
9 's' is the abbreviation for 'shilling'; 'd' for 'denarius', i.e., 'pence'.
10 Probably a type of spar or stout pole.
11 Probably a type of hinge or joint (from Greek καρπος, 'karpos,' 'joint').
12 Rope made up of such fibres as split rushes of straw.
13 In usual architectural terminology, a series of closely spaced, cylindrical objects used as ornaments.
14 Apparently the carpenters were paid different wages depending upon their level of experience, and whether they worked full- or part-time. (See labourers' wages below.)
15 Installing small, parallel beams for supporting floors, ceilings, etc.

20 William Prynne, *Histriomastix*, 1633

1 William Prynne (1600–69) was educated at Oriel College, Oxford, and later became a barrister at Lincoln's Inn. Although *Histriomastix* was printed in 1633, it is so lengthy that it was probably written written earlier, perhaps over several years. Prynne was sentenced by the Star Chamber in 1634 to be imprisoned for life, to lose both ears in the pillory, and to pay a fine of £5,000; the charge was slander against King Charles I and his queen. Prynne continued to write throughout his imprisonment in the Tower of London, and in 1637 was again fined £5,000; his cheeks were branded with 'S. L.' ('seditious libeller'), and he lost the remainder of his ears as well. Finally, in 1640 he was released by the Long Parliament and his sentences were declared illegal. The next twenty years were turbulent, with Prynne writing protests attacking various constituencies, including the government. However, by 1660 he was a staunch supporter of Charles II. Thereafter, Prynne was appointed Keeper of the Records in the Tower of London. Although *Histriomastix* is probably his best-known work altogether he published about two hundred pamphlets and books.

Sir Richard Baker's response to Prynne is excerpted as Document 21, following.

2 The *mima* ('mimics') and *scenicae mulieres* ('women of the stage') acted solo or in companies. Their performances ranged from extemporaneous pieces to more structured works. Most of the material was topical, farcical and indecent. One emperor ordered a real crucifixion to be inserted in a mime; another ordered mimic adulteries to be performed realistically; in the person of an emperor one *mima* reached the throne. They were favoured by the Roman emperors and beloved by the rabble.
3 The Floralia was a festival held on 28 April in honour of Flora, traditionally an occasion of great licentiousness.
4 An interlude is literally a dramatic piece, sometimes with music, performed between parts of a play; however, here it is used more generally to mean the festival, a holiday.
5 A private theatre built in part of the former convent owned by the Dominican order (the 'black' friars), and frequented by an elite audience.
6 Culpable.
7 Wearing a girdle or wide sash, as women would dress.
8 Root out, destroy utterly.

21 Sir Richard Baker, *Theatrum Redivivum*, 1662

1 The following excerpt – while printed much later than William Prynne's historic attack upon the theatre (1633, see Document 20 above) – is historically significant as a response to Prynne. Baker's full title is *Theatrum Redivivum, or the Theatre Vindicated by Sir Richard Baker in Answer to Mr Pryns 'Histriomastix'*.

Sir Richard Baker (*c*. 1568–1645) was the son of Sir John Baker, Chancellor of the Exchequer and Privy Councillor under Henry VIII. His uncle, also named Richard, entertained Queen Elizabeth I at the family home in Sissinghurst, Kent, in 1573.

Richard Baker became a commoner of Hart Hall (later Hertford College), Oxford, in 1584, but he left without graduating and went on to study law in London. Later he toured the Continent, following which he was elected to several positions in local government. After his marriage to Margaret, daughter of Sir George Mainwaring, he was plagued by a series of economic misfortunes. By 1625 he was reported to be a debtor to the crown, and by 1635 he was destitute. Baker was forced to take refuge in the Fleet Prison, which provided him with shelter for his literary work.

Baker was extremely prolific, making his reputation as a religious and historical writer. Among his publications are meditations on the Lord's Prayer and on the psalms of David, the latter book dedicated to Mary, Countess of Dorset. His major work was a *Chronicle of the Kings of England from the time of the Romans' Government unto the Death of King James* (1643). So popular was this book that eight editions were published during the next forty years. In 1649 it was translated into Dutch.

It is unclear as to when *Theatrum Redivivum* was written, although it was published posthumously in 1662. Interestingly, Baker includes references to three of the most important Elizabethan actors: Richard Tarlton (the most famous comedian of his time), Richard Burbage (the lead actor in Shakespeare's company), and Edward Alleyn (the actor who brought Christopher Marlowe's majestical protagonists to the stage). Given that Baker moved to London whilst a young man, he could well have seen all three actors perform in their prime.

2 Ideas, fanciful conceptions.
3 Native Americans.
4 The area opposite St Paul's Cathedral on the south bank, the entertainment district of this time.
5 Fabric of coarse wool woven on cotton warp.
6 Sausage made with blood.
7 Clement of Alexandria, a Christian convert who was ordained and served as head of the Catechetical School of Alexandria for a time. He wrote *The Tutor*, an exposition on the moral teaching of Christ and also the fine points of conduct: eating, drinking, dress and the use of wealth.
8 (A.D. 315?–386) Bishop of Jerusalem and Christian martyr.
9 Phillip Melancthon, German theologian and leader of the Lutheran Reformation. The reference to Macchabæus Alpinas is obscure.
10 'one out of many.'
11 (1483–1546), German theologian and originator of the Lutheran Reformation, translated the Old and New Testaments into German. The Latin statement is translated by Baker below.
12 In ll. 67–73 Baker is translating Luther (Latin, ll. 63–7 above).
13 Rather.
14 An obscure reference.
15 Baker translates the Latin immediately following.
16 In ll. 80–9 Baker quotes, then translates Lorinuse.

22 Consistory Court of London, Correction Book, 1612

1 The following excerpt concerns Mary Frith, a female transvestite who frequented the Swan Playhouse in early 1611. Popularly known as Moll Frith or Moll Cutpurse, Mary had underworld associations which, in addition to her sartorial habits, allowed her to cut a colourful image in Jacobean London. She was accused of stealing and slander, but most reports seem to suggest that her misdemeanours were pranks. In 1611 a play entitled *The Roaring Girl*, written by Thomas Middleton and Thomas Dekker, was published celebrating Moll's popular reputation. The play was performed at the Fortune Playhouse. In V.i, Moll states that she took a young gallant once to the twopenny gallery at the Fortune. (See *The Roaring Girl*, ed. Mulholland, pp. 13–17, and Rose, 'Women in Men's Clothing', *ELR*, 14 (1984), 367–91.)
2 Past.
3 A public playhouse built in 1600 and located just north of London Wall in the parish of St Giles without Cripplegate, near the modern Barbican Centre.
4 Ruffianly, violent, brutal.
5 Originally a lodging near St Bride's Well (a holy well), given by Edward VI for a hospital, but by the Renaissance converted into a house of correction for prisoners.
6 Officer in service by regular appointment.

10 Women in Theatrical Affairs

23 Edmund Howes, addition to John Stow's *Annales*, 1615

1 John Stow (1525–1605) was born and raised in London. He was admitted a freeman of the Merchant Taylors Company in 1547. Stow's enthusiasm for copying and transcribing was

brought to the attention of Archbishop Matthew Parker, who became Stow's patron. Stow edited the works of Chaucer (1561) and contributed to a second edition of Raphael Holinshed's *Chronicles of England, Scotland, and Ireland* (1585–7). His well-known *Survey of London* (1598, 1603) combined contemporary descriptions of the city with antiquarian knowledge and Stow's personal recollections. Howes added more material to the 1615 edition, in which the excerpt printed here appears. This is the first account of the formation of a playing company by a female patron.

2 Secretary of State, 1573–90.

3 Latin *videlicet*, 'that is to say, namely'.

4 Probably a mistake for Robert Wilson, a player in the Earl of Leicester's Men (1572, 1574, 1581), known for his cleverness. He is thought by some scholars to be the author of several plays.

5 Improvised, off-handed.

6 Richard Tarlton, perhaps the most famous clown of the period. He was an original member of the Queen's Men in 1583, and might well have been the second of the 'rare men' cited by Wilson.

24 Chancery Records, Draft Patent for Queen Anne's Men, 1603–4

1 In 1603 it was required that all playing companies have royal patronage. The reasons for this are still in dispute. Shakespeare's company (the Lord Chamberlain's Men) became the King's Men, while the Lord Admiral's Men (who were known for their lead actor Edward Alleyn, who performed the majestical roles in Christopher Marlowe's plays) became Prince Henry's Men. The document transcribed here is the patent to license Queen Anne's Men who seem to have been formed from two former companies, the Earl of Worcester's Men and the Earl of Oxford's Men. Queen Anne's Men performed at court and at the Red Bull Playhouse. Among the plays printed as theirs were: John Webster's *The White Devil* and Thomas Heywood's *Four Prentices of London*. The company also had some association with the Curtain Playhouse and the Boar's Head, as evidenced by the patent and by the claims made on the title pages of several plays printed during the period.

2 Christopher Beeston, Heywood, Perkins and Pallant were formerly associated with Worcester's Men.

3 A moothall was a council chamber or judgement hall, in which a 'moot' (assembly for judicature) was held.

4 Hindrances.

5 Literally 'given', i.e., 'drawn up'.

6 The last few lines of the patent are written according to a standard formula. Consequently, the scribe left blank spaces in which the day, date and regnal year could be inserted. Also, he employs abbreviations such as '&c', modern 'etc.'.

25 Last will and testament of William Browne, 1634

1 William Browne, an actor, was working as a hireling in 1616–17 for Queen Anne's Men (see Document 24). Little is known about his theatrical career. In the excerpt printed here Browne bequeathed his share in the Red Bull Company to his mother Susanna Baskervile, widow of Thomas Greene, also a player with Queen Anne's Men. When Greene died he left her his share of the Red Bull, which she had considerable trouble collecting. Finally, after several attempts to keep the company alive, it failed, some conjecture due to Mrs Baskervile's financial control.

Thomas Bond, Browne's brother-in-law (l. 26), was an actor associated with Queen Anne's Revels company which also performed at the Red Bull.

2 Literally 'given', i.e., 'drawn up'.

3 Latin, 'by me', i.e., 'signed'.

26 Indenture between Edward Alleyn and Marie Bryan, 1623

1 Edward Alleyn (1566–1626) was an actor, theatre owner, and Master of the Bears under King James I. By the time of this indenture he owned the Rose Playhouse, the First Fortune Playhouse (which burned down in 1621), and the Bear Garden (rebuilt as the Hope Playhouse, a combined bear-baiting arena and playhouse). He had also purchased the manor of Dulwich and endowed a school for poor scholars and pensioners called the College of God's Gift at Dulwich (now Dulwich College). Alleyn owned all of the First Fortune but when he rebuilt that playhouse – perhaps as he was nearing the end

of his life – he decided to sell shares to several people. Marie Bryan, here the lessee, purchased the lease to one whole share for 49½ years.

2 Lands, estates.

3 A dwelling-house with its adjacent buildings and lands.

Bibliography

PRIMARY SOURCES

Alciati. *Emblemata*, Paris: 1542, and Padua: 1621.

——*Imprese*, Lyons: 1551.

Anon. *Haec Vir*, London: 1620.

Anon. *Hic Mulier*, London: 1620.

Anon. *The Actor's Remonstrance*, London: 1643.

Aubrey, John. *Brief Lives*, ed. Oliver Lawson Dick, London: Secker & Warburg, 1949.

Baker, Richard. *Theatrum Redivivum*, London: 1622.

Brackley, Elizabeth. *The Concealed Fancies*, Bodleian Library, MS Rawlinson Poet 16.

——'The Concealed Fancies: A Play by Lady Jane Cavendish and Lady Elizabeth Brackley', ed. Nathan Comfort Starr, *Proceedings of the Modern Languages Association* 46 (1931), 802–38.

Carleton, Dudley. Boughton House, Winwood Papers III, Northamptonshire Record Office, Northampton.

——*Dudley Carleton to John Chamberlain, 1603–1624*, ed. Maurice Lee Jr, New Brunswick: Rutgers University Press, 1972.

Cary, Elizabeth. *Abraham Ortelius' 'Mirroir du Monde'* trans., MS at the Vicarage, Burford, Oxford.

——'An Epitaph Upon the Death of The Duke of Buckingham by the Countess of Falkland', BL Egerton MS 2725 fol. 60.

—— *The History of the Life, Reign, and Death of Edward II*, London: 1680.

—— *The Reply of the Most Illustrious Cardinal of Perron to the ... King of Great Britain*, Douay: M. Bogart, 1630.

—— *The Tragedie of Mariam, the Faire Queene of Jewry*, London: Thomas Creede, 1613.

—— *The Tragedy of Mariam, the Fair Queen of Jewry with The Lady Falkland: Her Life By One Of Her Daughters*, ed. Margaret Ferguson and Barry Weller, Berkeley: University of California Press, 1994.

Cavendish, Jane. *The Concealed Fancies*, Bodleian Library, MS Rawlinson Poet 16.

—— 'The Concealed Fancies: A Play by Lady Jane Cavendish and Lady Elizabeth Brackley', ed. Nathan Comfort Starr, *Proceedings of the Modern Languages Association* 46 (1931), 802–38.

Cavendish, Margaret. *Nature's Pictures Drawn by Fancy's Pencil*, London: 1667.

——*The Life of William Cavendish Duke of Newcastle*, London: Routledge, 1906.

Cecil Papers. Hatfield House, MS. 62/16, 9 June 1598.

Chamberlain, John. *Calendar of State Papers, Domestic Series*, 21 August 1624, PRO/SP14/171/66.

——*Letters*, ed. N. E. McClure, Philadelphia: American Philosophical Society, 1939.

——*The Chamberlain Letters*, ed. Elizabeth Thomson, New York: Capricorn Books, 1966.

Chancery Records, Court of. *Draft Patent*, PRO, SP14/2/100, 1603-4.

Chaucer, Geoffrey. *The Tales of the Clerk and the Wife of Bath*, ed. Marion Wynne-Davies, London: Routledge, 1992.

Consistory Court of London. Correction Book (27 January 1612).

Cranley, Thomas. *Amanda, or the Reformed Whore*, London: 1635.

Daniel, Samuel. *Certaine Small Poems Lately Printed With the Tragedie of Philotas*, London: 1605.

——*The Tragedie of Cleopatra*, ed. M. Lederer, London: David Nutt, 1911.

Dante (Alghieri). *The Divine Comedy*, trans. Charles S. Singleton, Princeton: Princeton University Press, 1970–5.

Davies, John of Hereford. *Muses Sacrifice or Divine Meditations*, London: T. S. for George Norton, 1612.

Declared Accounts of the Office of the Works. Exchequer Accounts, PRO, MS E351/3243, Whitehall, 1 October 1607 – 31 March 1609.

——PRO, MS E351/3266, Denmark House, 1 October 1631 – 30 September 1632.

——*Dramatic Records in the Declared Accounts of the Office of the Works, 1560–1640*, ed. F.P. Wilson, *Malone Society Collections* 10 (1977).

Dekker, Thomas. *Old Fortunatus*, London: 1600.

Dulwich College. MS Indenture between Edward Alleyn and Marie Bryan, Wodehouse Library, MSS. Second Series, Number 23, 24 March 1623.

Drayton, Michael. *Englands Heroicall Epistles*, London: 1597.

Elizabeth I. *Hercules Oetaeus*, Bodleian Library MS e Museo 55.

——*The Poems of Queen Elizabeth I*, ed. Leicester Bradner, Providence, RI: Brown University Press, 1964.

——*Queen Elizabeth's Englishings*, ed. Caroline Pemberton, London: EETS, 1899.

——Various translations in PRO Domestic Elizabeth 289.

Euripides. *The Complete Greek Tragedies*, ed. David Grene and Richard Lattimore, New York: Modern Library, 1956–9.

Finet, John. MS Notebook, Book 3, Rousham House, 19 November 1629.

——*Ceremonies of Charles I: The Note Books of John Finet, 1628–1641*, ed. Albert J. Loomie, New York: Fordham University Press, 1987.

Fitzgeffrey, Henry. *Satyres: and Satyricall Epigrams, with Certain Observations at Blackfriars*, London: 1617.

Fletcher, John. *The Faithful Shepherdess*, London: 1610.

Garnier, Robert. *Two Tragedies*, ed. C.M. Hill and M.G. Morrison, London: Athlone, 1975.

Gosson, Stephen. *Plays Confuted in Five Actions*, London: 1590.

Gosynhill, Edward. *The Schoolhouse of Women*, London: *c.* 1541.

Greville, Fulke. 'Mustapha' in *Certaine Learned and Elegant Workes by the Right Honourable Fulke, Lord Brooke*, London: 1633.

Grey, Elizabeth, Countess of Kent. *A Choice Manual of Rare and Select Secrets in Physick and Chyrurgery*, London: 1653.

Halkett, Lady Anne. *Autobiography*, British Library, Add. MS 32,376.

——*The Autobiography of Anne Lady Halkett*, ed. John Gough Nichols, London: Camden Society, 1875.

——*The Memoirs of Anne, Lady Halkett and Anne, Lady Fanshawe*, ed. John Loftis, Oxford: Oxford University Press, 1979.

Harington, John. *Epigrams*, London: 1618.

——*The Metamorphosis of Ajax*, London: 1596.

——*The Letters and Epigrams of Sir John Harington, together with The Prayse of Private Life*, ed. N.E. McClure, Philadelphia: University of Pennsylvania Press, 1930.

Henslowe, Philip. *The Henslowe Papers*, ed. W.W. Greg, London: A. H. Bullen, 1907.

Herbert, William. *Poems Written By the Right Honorable William Earl of Pembroke*, London: 1660.

Homer. *The Iliad of Homer*, trans. R. Lattimore, Chicago: University of Chicago Press, 1951.

Horace. *The Odes and Epodes*, trans. C.E. Bennett, London: Heinemann, 1968.

Howes, Edmund. *Addition to Stow's 'Annales'*, London: 1615.

Jonson, Ben. *Ben Jonson*, ed. C.H. Herford and Percy Simpson, Oxford: Clarendon Press, 1937.

Josephus, Flavius. 'Antiqities of the Jews' in *The Works of Flavius Josephus*, ed. W. Whiston, London: William Baynes & Son, 1825.

Juvenal. 'Satires' in *Juvenal and Persius*, trans. G.G. Ramsay, London: William Heinemann Ltd, 1918.

Lodge, Thomas. *The Famous and Memorable Workes of Josephus*, London: 1602.

Lyly, John. *Euphues, or the Anatomy of Wit*, London: 1578.

Marston, John. *The Works of Mr John Marston*, London: 1633.

Middleton, Thomas and Dekker, Thomas. *The Roaring Girl*, ed. Paul Mulholland, Manchester: Manchester University Press, 1987.

More, Richard. *Englands Helicon. Or, The Muses Harmony*, London: 1614.

North, Sir Thomas. *Lives*, London: 1579.

Northbrook, John. *A Treatise wherein Dicing, Dauncing, vaine Playes, or Enterluds, with other idle Pastimes . . .* , London: 1577.

Ovid. *Heroides and Amores*, trans. Grant Showerman, London: William Heinemann, 1947.

——*Metamorphoses*, trans. Rolfe Humphries, London: John Calder, 1957.

——*The Art of Love and Other Poems*, trans. J.H. Mozley, London: William Heinemann, 1985.

Peacham, Henry. *The Art of Living in London*, London: 1642.

——*The Compleat Gentleman*, London: 1622.

Pesaro, Zuane. MS Letter, *Calendar of State Papers, Venetian Series*, 6 March 1625/6 (24 February, English).

Petrarch, Francis. *Lord Morley's Tryumphes of Fraunces Petrarcke*, ed. D.D. Carnicelli, Cambridge, MA.: Harvard University Press, 1971.

——*Petrarch's Lyric Poems*, trans. Robert M. Durling, Cambridge, MA.: Harvard University Press, 1976.

Plutarch. *Plutarch's Lives*, trans. A. Steward and G. Long, London: George Bell & Sons, 1904.

Prerogative Court of Canterbury. MS Last Will and Testament of William Browne, PRO, PCC/PROB11/166, fols 317^{v}–^{r}.

Prynne, William. *Histriomastix*, London: 1633.

Rainolds, John. *Th'overthrow of Stage Playes*, London: 1599.

Rich, Mary. *Autobiography*, British Library, Add. MS 27,357.

Rowlands, Samuel. *The Bride*, London: 1617.

Seneca. *Tragedies*, trans. Frank Justus Miller, London: Heinemann, 1987.

Shakespeare, William. *The Riverside Shakespeare*, ed. G. Blakemore Evans, Boston: Houghton Mifflin Co., 1974.

Sidney, Mary. *The Countess of Pembroke's Translation of Philippe de Mornay's Discourse of Life and Death*, ed. Diane Bornstein, Detroit: Michigan Consortium for Medieval and Early Modern Studies, 1983.

——*The Psalms of Philip Sidney and The Countess of Pembroke*, ed. J.C.A. Rathmell, New York: New York Univerity Press, 1963.

——*The Tragedie of Antonie*, ed. A.A. Luce, Weimar: 1897.

——*The Tragedie of Antonie*, in Geoffrey Bullough (ed.), *Narrative and Dramatic Sources of Shakespeare*, London: Routledge, 1964.

——*The Triumph of Death and Other Unpublished and Uncollected Poems by Mary Sidney, Countess of Pembroke*, ed. Gary F. Waller, Salzburg: Salzburg University Press, 1977.

Sidney, Philip. *An Apology for Poetry*, ed. Geoffrey Shepherd, Manchester: Manchester University Press, 1973.

——*The Countess of Pembroke's Arcadia*, ed. Maurice Evans, New York: Penguin Books, 1977.

——*The Poems of Sir Philip Sidney*, ed. W.A. Ringler, Oxford: Clarendon Press, 1962.

Sidney, Robert. *The Poems of Robert Sidney*, ed. P.J. Croft, Oxford: Clarendon Press, 1984.

Swetnam, Joseph. 'The Arraignment of Lewde, idle, froward, and unconstant women' (1615) in K.U. Henderson and B.F. McManus (eds), *Half Humankind: Contexts and Texts of the Controversy about Women in England, 1540–1640*, Chicago: University of Illinois Press, 1985.

Tasso, Torquato. *Aminta*, Cremona: 1580.

Vincent, ——. MS Letter, *Calendar of State Papers, Domestic Series*, PRO, SP14/12/14, 10 January 1605.

Virgil. *The Aeneid of Virgil*, trans. Rolfe Humphries, New York: Charles Scribner, 1951.

White, Robert. 'Cupid's Banishment', Pierpont Morgan Library, MS MA 1296.

——*Cupid's Banishment* in John Nichols, *The Progresses, Processions and Magnificent Festivities of King James the First*, London: J.B. Nichols, 1828.

——'Cupid's Banishment: A Masque Presented to Her Majesty by Young Gentlewomen of the Ladies Hall, Deptford, May 4, 1617' ed. C.E. McGee, *Renaissance Drama*, 19 (1988), 227–64.

Wroth, Mary. *Loves Victory*, Huntington Library HM600.

——*Loves Victorie*, Penshurst Manuscript owned by Viscount De L'Isle.

——*Loves Victorie*, the Plymouth Manuscript in James O. Halliwell (ed.), *A Brief Description of the Ancient and Modern Manuscripts Preserved in the Public Library Plymouth*, London: 1853.

——*Loves Victorie*, ed. C.H.J. Maxwell, Master's Thesis, Stanford University, 1933.

——*Love's Victory*, ed. Michael G. Brennan, London: The Roxburghe Club, 1988.

——*The Poems of Lady Mary Wroth*, ed. Josephine A. Roberts, Baton Rouge: Louisiana State University Press, 1983.

——*Urania* I, London: 1621.

——*Urania* II, Newberry Library Case MS fy 1565 w 95.

SECONDARY MATERIAL

Bainton, Roland H. 'Learned Women in the Sixteenth Century' in Patricia Labalme (ed.), *Beyond Their Sex*, New York: New York University Press, 1980.

Bald, R.C. *John Donne*, Oxford: Oxford University Press, 1970.

Ballard, George. *Memoirs of Several Ladies of Great Britain* 1752, rpt. Detroit: Wayne State University Press, 1985.

Barish, Jonas. *The Antitheatrical Prejudice*, Berkeley: University of California Press, 1981.

Beauchamp, V. W. 'Sidney's Sister as Translator of

Garnier', *Renaissance Notes*, 10 (1957), 8–13.

Beilin, Elaine V. *Redeeming Eve: Women Writers of the English Renaissance*, Princeton: Princeton University Press, 1987.

Bell, Maureen, Parfitt, George and Shepherd, Simon (eds), *A Biographical Dictionary of English Women Writers 1580–1720*, Sussex: Harvester, 1990.

Belsey, Catherine. *The Subject of Tragedy*, London: Methuen, 1985.

Bentley, G. E. *The Jacobean and Caroline Stage*, Oxford: Clarendon Press, 1968.

Bergeron, David. *English Civic Pageantry*, Columbia, SC: University of South Carolina Press, 1971.

—— 'Women as Patrons of English Renaissance Drama' in G.F. Lytle and S. Orgel (eds), *Patronage in the Renaissance*, Princeton: Princeton University Press, 1981.

Bickley, Francis. *The Cavendish Family*, London: Constable, 1911.

Brennan, Michael. *Literary Patronage in the English Renaissance: The Pembroke Family*, London: Routledge, 1988.

Bullough, Geoffrey. *Narrative and Dramatic Sources of Shakespeare*, London: Routledge, 1964.

Burner, Sandra A. *James Shirley: A Study of Literary Coteries and Patronage*, London: University Presses of America, 1988.

Buxton, John. *Sir Philip Sidney and the English Renaissance*, New York: St. Martin's Press, 1954.

Callaghan, Dympna. 'Re-Reading Elizabeth Cary's *The Tragedie of Mariam, Faire Queene of Jewry*' in Margo Hendricks and Patricia Parker (eds), *Women, 'Race,' and Writing in the Early Modern Period*, New York: Routledge, 1994.

Camden, Carroll. *The Elizabethan Woman*, New York: Paul Appel Publications, 1975.

Cerasano, S.P. and Wynne-Davies, Marion (eds), *Gloriana's Face: Women, Public and Private, in the English Renaissance*, Hemel Hempstead: Harvester, 1992.

Chambers, E.K. *The Elizabethan Stage*, Oxford: Clarendon Press, 1923.

Cook, Ann Jennalie. *The Privileged Playgoers of Shakespeare's London, 1576–1642*, Princeton: Princeton University Press, 1981.

Cotton, Nancy. 'Elizabeth Cary, Renaissance Playwright', *Texas Studies in Literature and Language* 18 (1977), 601–8.

—— *Women Playwrights in England: c. 1363–1750*, London: Associated University Presses, 1980.

Dews, Nathan. *The History of Deptford*, London: Conway Maritime Press, 1971.

Edmond, Mary. 'Pembroke's Men', *Review of English Studies* 25 (1974), 129–36.

Eliot, T. S. 'Seneca in Elizabethan Translation' in *Selected Essays*, 1932, rpt. London: Faber & Faber, 1951.

Ezell, Margaret J.M. '"To Be Your Daughter in Your Pen": The Social Functions of Literature in the Writings of Lady Elizabeth Brackley and Lady Jane Cavendish', *Huntington Library Quarterly* 51 (1988), 281–96.

—— *The Patriarch's Wife: Literary Evidence and the History of the Family*, Chapel Hill: University of North Carolina Press, 1987.

Findley, Sandra and Hobby, Elaine. 'Seventeenth-Century Women's Biography' in F. Barker (ed.), *1642: Literature and Power in the Seventeenth Century*, Colchester: Essex University, 1981.

Fisher, Sheila and Halley, Janet E. (eds), *Seeking the Woman in Late Medieval and Renaissance Writings*, Knoxville: University of Tennessee Press, 1989.

Flügel, Ewald, 'Die Gedichte der Königin Elisabeth', *Anglia* 14 (1892), 346–52.

Foakes, R.A. and Rickert, R.T. (eds), *Henslowe's Diary*, Cambridge: Cambridge University Press, 1968.

Fullerton, Georgianna. *Life of Elizabeth Cary, Lady Falkland 1582–1639*, London: Burns & Oates, 1883.

Gossett, Suzanne, '"Man-maid, begone!": Women in Masques' in Kirby Farrell, Elizabeth H. Hageman and Arthur F. Kinney (eds), *Women in the Renaissance*, Amherst: University of Massachusetts Press, 1988.

Grant, Douglas. *Mary the First: A Biography of Margaret Cavendish, Duchess of Newcastle, 1623–1673*, London: Hart-Davis, 1957.

Greer, Germaine *et al.* (eds). *Kissing the Rod: An Anthology of Seventeenth-Century Women's Verse*, London: Virago, 1988.

Gurr, Andrew. *Playgoing in Shakespeare's London*, Cambridge: Cambridge University Press, 1987.

Hannay, Margaret P. *Silent but for the Word: Tudor Women as Patrons, Translators, and Writers of Religious Works*, Ohio: Kent State University Press, 1986.

—— *Philip's Phoenix: Mary Sidney, Countess of Pembroke*, Oxford: Oxford University Press, 1990.

Haselkorn, Anne M. and Travitsky, Betty S. (eds). *The Renaissance Englishwoman in Print*, Amherst: University of Massachusetts Press, 1990.

Hay, Millicent V. *The Life of Robert Sidney, Earl of Leicester (1563–1626)*, Washington: Folger Books, 1984.

Heinemann, Margot. *Puritanism and Theatre*, Cambridge: Cambridge University Press, 1980.

Hibbert, Christopher. *The Virgin Queen*, London: Viking, 1990.

Hopkins, Lisa. *John Ford's Political Theatre*, Manchester: Manchester University Press, 1994.

Howard, Jean E. 'Women as Spectators, Spectacles, and Paying Customers' in David Scott Kastan and Peter Stallybrass (eds), *Staging the Renaissance*, London: Routledge, 1991.

——'Sex and Social Conflict: The Erotics of *The Roaring Girl*' in Susan Zimmerman (ed.), *Erotic Politics: Desire on the Renaissance Stage*, London: Routledge, 1992.

——*The Stage and Social Struggle in Early Modern England*, London and New York: Routledge, 1994.

Jones, Ann Rosalind. *The Currency of Eros: Women's Love Lyric in Europe, 1540–1620*, Bloomington: Indiana University Press, 1990.

Krontiris, Tina. 'Breaking Barriers of Genre and Gender', *English Literary Renaissance* 18 (1988), 19–39.

—— 'Style and Gender in Elizabeth Cary's *Edward II*' in Anne M. Haselkorn and Betty Travitsky (eds), *The Renaissance Englishwoman in Print: Counterbalancing the Canon*, Amherst: University of Massachusetts Press, 1990.

——*Oppositional Voices. Women as Writers and Translators of Literature in the English Renaissance*, London: Routledge, 1992.

LaCapra, Dominick. *Rethinking Intellectual History: Texts, Contexts, Language*, 1983.

Lamb, Mary Ellen. 'The Myth of the Countess of Pembroke: The Dramatic Circle', *The Year's Work in English Studies* 11 (1981), 194–202.

—— 'The Countess of Pembroke's Patronage', *English Literary Renaissance* 12 (1982), 162–79.

—— 'The Cooke Sisters: Attitudes towards Learned Women in the Renaissance' in Margaret Hannay (ed.), *Silent But For the Word*, Ohio: Kent State University Press, 1986.

——'The Countess of Pembroke and the Art of Dying' in Mary Beth Rose (ed.), *Women in the Middle Ages and the Renaissance*, Syracuse: Syracuse University Press, 1986.

——*Gender and Authorship in the Sidney Circle*, Madison, WI.: University of Wisconsin Press, 1990.

Laroque, François. *Shakespeare's Festive World: Elizabethan Seasonal Entertainment and the Professional Stage*, Cambridge: Cambridge University Press, 1988.

Levine, L. 'Men in Women's Clothing: Antitheatricality and Effeminization from 1579 to 1642', *Criticism*, 28 (1986), 121–43.

Lewalski, Barbara. 'Lucy, Countess of Bedford' in Kevin Sharpe and Steven N. Zwicker (eds), *Politics of Discourse*, Los Angeles: University of California Press, 1987.

——*Writing Women in Jacobean England*, Cambridge, MA.: Harvard University Press, 1993.

Limon, Jerzy. *The Masque of Stuart Culture*, Newark: University of Delaware Press, 1990.

Lindley, David. *The Court Masque*, Manchester: Manchester University Press, 1984.

Luce, Alice. 'The Countess of Pembroke's *Antonie*' in *Literarhistorische Forschungen*, Weimar: Verlag von Emil Felber, 1897.

Lytle, Guy Fitch and Orgel, Stephen (eds). *Patronage in the Renaissance*, Princeton: Princeton University Press, 1981.

Mahl, Mary and Koon, Helene (eds). *The Female Spectator: English Women Writers before 1800*, Bloomington: Indiana University Press, 1977.

McLaren, Margaret Anne. 'An Unknown Continent: Lady Mary Wroth's Forgotten Pastoral Drama, "Loves Victorie"' in Anne M. Haselkorn and Betty Travitsky (eds), *The Renaissance Englishwoman in Print*, Amherst: University of Massachusetts Press, 1990.

Mendelson, Sarah Heller. *The Mental World of Stuart Women*, Brighton: Harvester, 1987.

Miller, Naomi J. and Waller, Gary (eds). *Reading Mary Wroth: Representing Alternatives in Early Modern England*, Knoxville: University of Tennessee Press, 1991.

Morrison, Mary, 'Some Aspects of the Treatment of the Theme of Antony and Cleopatra in Tragedies of the Sixteenth Century', *Journal of English Studies* 4 (1974), 113–25.

Murdoch, Kenneth B. *Sun at Noon: Three Biographical Sketches*, New York: Macmillan, 1939.

Nichols, John. *The Progresses and Public Processions of Queen Elizabeth*, London: J. Nichols & Son, 1823.

—— *The Progresses, Processions, and Magnificent Festivities of King James the First*, London: J.B. Nichols, 1828.

Orgel, Stephen. *The Jonsonian Masque*, New York: Columbia University Press, 1981.

Orgel, Stephen and Strong, Roy. *Inigo Jones: The Theatre of the Stuart Court*, London: Sotheby, 1973.

Patrick, J. Max. 'The Cleopatra Theme in World Literature up to 1700' in J.R. Conway Perkin (ed.), *The Undoing of Babel: Watson Kirkconnell, the Man and his Work*, Toronto: MacLelland & Stewart, 1975.

Prior, Mary (ed.). *Women in English Society, 1500–1800*, London: Methuen, 1985.

Quilligan, Maureen. 'Staging Gender: William Shakespeare and Elizabeth Cary' in James Grantham Turner (ed.), *Sexuality and Gender in Early Modern Europe: Institutions, Texts, Images*, Cambridge: Cambridge University Press, 1993.

Roberts, Josephine. 'The Huntington Manuscript of Lady Mary Wroth's Play, *Loves Victorie*', Huntington Library Quarterly 46 (1983), 156–74.

——*The Poems of Lady Mary Wroth*, Baton Rouge: Louisiana State University Press, 1983.

Rose, Mary Beth. 'Women in Men's Clothing: Apparel and Social Stability in *The Roaring Girl*', *English Literary Renaissance* 14 (1984), 367–91.

—— (ed). *Women in the Middle Ages and the Renaissance: Literary and Historical Perspectives*, Syracuse: Syracuse University Press, 1986.

Sabol, Andrew J. *Four Hundred Songs and Dances from the Stuart Masque*, Providence, RI: Brown University Press, 1978.

Scott, Otto J. *James I*, New York: Mason-Charter, 1976.

Shattock, Joanne. *The Oxford Guide to British Women Writers*, Oxford: Oxford University Press, 1993.

Shepherd, Simon. *Amazons and Warrior Women: Varieties of Feminism in Seventeenth Century Drama*, Brighton: Harvester, 1981.

Simpson, Richard (ed). *The Lady Falkland, Her Life From a MS in the Imperial Archives at Lisle*, London: Catholic Publishing and Bookselling Co. Ltd, 1861.

Smith, C. Fell. *Mary Rich: Countess of Warwick, 1625–1678*, London: Longmans, Green & Co., 1901.

Swift, Carolyn Ruth. 'Feminine Identity in Lady Mary Wroth's Romance *Urania*' in Kirby Farrell, Elizabeth Hageman and Arthur F. Kinney (eds), *Women in the Renaissance. Selections from 'English Literary Renaissance'*, Amherst: University of Massachusetts Press, 1988.

——'Feminine Self-Definition in Lady Mary Wroth's *Love's Victorie* (*c.* 1621)', *English Literary Renaissance* 19 (1989), 171–88.

Tomlinson, Sophie. '"My Brain the Stage": Margaret Cavendish and the Fantasy of Female Performance' in Clare Brant and Diane Purkiss (eds), *Women, Texts and Histories 1575–1760*, London: Routledge, 1992.

Travitsky, Betty. *The Paradise of Women: Writings by Englishwomen of the Renaissance*, London: Greenwood Press, 1981.

——'The *Feme Covert* in Elizabeth Cary's *Mariam*' in Carole Levin and Jeanie Watson (eds), *Ambiguous Realities: Women in the Middle Ages and Renaissance*, Detroit: Wayne State University Press, 1987.

Travitsky, Betty and Haselkorn, Anne M. *The Renaissance Englishwoman in Print: Counterbalancing the Canon*, Amherst: University of Massachusetts Press, 1990.

——'His Wife's Prayers and Meditations; MS Egerton 607' in Anne M. Haselkorn and Betty Travitsky, *The Renaissance Englishwoman in Print.*

Turberville, A. S. *A History of Welbeck Abbey and its Owners*, London: Faber & Faber, 1937.

Valency, Maurice. *The Tragedies of Herod and Mariamne*, New York: Columbia University Press, 1940.

Waller, Gary F. *Mary Sidney Countess of Pembroke, a Critical Study of her Writing and Literary Milieu*, Salzburg: Salzburg Studies in English Literature, 1979.

——*The Sidney Family Romance: Mary Wroth, William Herbert, and The Early Modern Construction of Gender*, Detroit: Wayne State University Press, 1993.

Waller, Gary F. and Miller, Naomi J. (eds), *Reading Mary Wroth: Representing Alternatives in Early Modern England*, Knoxville: University of Tennessee Press, 1991.

Walpole, Horatio. *A Catalogue of the Royal and Noble Authors of England, Scotland, and Ireland; with Lists of their Works*, London: John Scott, 1806.

Welsford, Enid. *The Court Masque*, New York: Russell & Russell, 1927.

White, Hayden. *Tropics of Discourse: Essays in Cultural Criticism*, 1978.

Wiesner, Merry. 'Women in the Sixteenth Century: A Bibliography', *Sixteenth-Century Bibliography* 23 (1983), 1–65.

Williamson, G.C. *Lady Anne Clifford*, London: Kendal, 1922.

Wilson, Jean. *Entertainments for Elizabeth I*, Woodbridge: D.S. Brewer, 1980.

Wilson, John Dover. *Life in Shakespeare's England: A Book of Elizabethan Prose*, Cambridge: Cambridge University Press, 1911.

Wilson, Katharina M. *Women Writers of the Renaissance and Reformation*, Athens, GA: University of Georgia Press, 1987.

Wiseman, Susan. 'Gender and Status in Dramatic Discourse: Margaret Cavendish, Duchess of Newcastle' in Isobel Grundy and Susan Wiseman (eds), *Women, Writing and History*, London: Batsford, 1992.

Witherspoon, Alexander. *The Influence of Robert Garnier on Elizabethan Drama*, New Haven: Archon Books, 1924.

Wynne-Davies, Marion. 'The Queen's Masque: Renaissance Women and the Seventeenth-Century Court Masque' in S.P. Cerasano and M. Wynne-Davies (eds), *Gloriana's Face: Women, Public and Private, in the English Renaissance*, Hemel Hempstead: Harvester, 1992.

Young, Frances B. *Mary Sidney, Countess of Pembroke*, London: David Nutt, 1912.

Index

The following index records surnames, titles and subjects. It does not include footnote references. Texts and documents reproduced in this collection are followed by dates.